50% OFF Online NCLEX-PN Prep Course!

Dear Customer,

We consider it an honor and a privilege that you chose our NCLEX-PN Study Guide. As a way of showing our appreciation and to help us better serve you, we have partnered with Mometrix Test Preparation to offer **50% off their online NCLEX-PN Prep Course.** Many NCLEX-PN courses are needlessly expensive and don't deliver enough value. With their course, you get access to the best NCLEX-PN prep material, and **you only pay half price.**

Mometrix has structured their online course to perfectly complement your printed study guide. The NCLEX-PN Prep Course contains **in-depth lessons** that cover all the most important topics, **80+ video reviews** that explain difficult concepts, **over 1,400 practice questions** to ensure you feel prepared, and **more than 600 digital flashcards,** so you can fit some studying in while you're on the go.

Online NCLEX-PN Prep Course

Topics Covered:	*Course Features:*
• Coordinated Care	• NCLEX-PN Study Guide
• Safety and Infection Control	○ Get content that complements our best-selling study guide.
• Health Promotion and Maintenance	• 9 Full-Length Practice Tests
• Psychosocial Integrity	○ With over 1,400 practice questions, you can test yourself again and again.
• Basic Care and Comfort	• Mobile Friendly
• Pharmacological Therapies	○ If you need to study on-the-go, the course is easily accessible from your mobile device.
• Reduction of Risk Potential	• NCLEX-PN Flashcards
• Physiological Adaptation	○ The course includes a flashcard mode consisting of over 600 content cards to help you study.

To receive this discount, simply head to their website: https://www.mometrix.com/university/nclex-pn/ or simply scan this QR code with your smartphone. At the checkout page, enter the discount code: **TPBNCLEX50**

If you have any questions or concerns, please don't hesitate to contact Mometrix at support@mometrix.com.

Sincerely,

 in partnership with

FREE Test Taking Tips Video/DVD Offer

To better serve you, we created videos covering test taking tips that we want to give you for FREE. **These videos cover world-class tips that will help you succeed on your test.**

We just ask that you send us feedback about this product. Please let us know what you thought about it—whether good, bad, or indifferent.

To get your **FREE videos**, you can use the QR code below or email freevideos@studyguideteam.com with "Free Videos" in the subject line and the following information in the body of the email:

   a. The title of your product

   b. Your product rating on a scale of 1-5, with 5 being the highest

   c. Your feedback about the product

If you have any questions or concerns, please don't hesitate to contact us at info@studyguideteam.com.

Thank you!

Next Generation NCLEX PN Study Guide 2024-2025

4 Practice Tests and NCLEX PN Review Prep Book
[7th Edition]

Lydia Morrison

Table of Contents

Welcome

Dear Reader,

Welcome to your new Test Prep Books study guide! We are pleased that you chose us to help you prepare for your exam. There are many study options to choose from, and we appreciate you choosing us. Studying can be a daunting task, but we have designed a smart, effective study guide to help prepare you for what lies ahead.

Whether you're a parent helping your child learn and grow, a high school student working hard to get into your dream college, or a nursing student studying for a complex exam, we want to help give you the tools you need to succeed. We hope this study guide gives you the skills and the confidence to thrive, and we can't thank you enough for allowing us to be part of your journey.

In an effort to continue to improve our products, we welcome feedback from our customers. We look forward to hearing from you. Suggestions, success stories, and criticisms can all be communicated by emailing us at info@studyguideteam.com.

Sincerely,
Test Prep Books Team

FREE Videos/DVD OFFER

Doing well on your exam requires both knowing the test content and understanding how to use that knowledge to do well on the test. We offer completely FREE test taking tip videos. **These videos cover world-class tips that you can use to succeed on your test.**

To get your **FREE videos**, you can use the QR code below or email freevideos@studyguideteam.com with "Free Videos" in the subject line and the following information in the body of the email:

  a. The title of your product
  b. Your product rating on a scale of 1-5, with 5 being the highest
  c. Your feedback about the product

If you have any questions or concerns, please don't hesitate to contact us at info@studyguideteam.com.

Quick Overview

As you draw closer to taking your exam, effective preparation becomes more and more important. Thankfully, you have this study guide to help you get ready. Use this guide to help keep your studying on track and refer to it often.

This study guide contains several key sections that will help you be successful on your exam. The guide contains tips for what you should do the night before and the day of the test. Also included are test-taking tips. Knowing the right information is not always enough. Many well-prepared test takers struggle with exams. These tips will help equip you to accurately read, assess, and answer test questions.

A large part of the guide is devoted to showing you what content to expect on the exam and to helping you better understand that content. In this guide are practice test questions so that you can see how well you have grasped the content. Then, answer explanations are provided so that you can understand why you missed certain questions.

Don't try to cram the night before you take your exam. This is not a wise strategy for a few reasons. First, your retention of the information will be low. Your time would be better used by reviewing information you already know rather than trying to learn a lot of new information. Second, you will likely become stressed as you try to gain a large amount of knowledge in a short amount of time. Third, you will be depriving yourself of sleep. So be sure to go to bed at a reasonable time the night before. Being well-rested helps you focus and remain calm.

Be sure to eat a substantial breakfast the morning of the exam. If you are taking the exam in the afternoon, be sure to have a good lunch as well. Being hungry is distracting and can make it difficult to focus. You have hopefully spent lots of time preparing for the exam. Don't let an empty stomach get in the way of success!

When travelling to the testing center, leave earlier than needed. That way, you have a buffer in case you experience any delays. This will help you remain calm and will keep you from missing your appointment time at the testing center.

Be sure to pace yourself during the exam. Don't try to rush through the exam. There is no need to risk performing poorly on the exam just so you can leave the testing center early. Allow yourself to use all of the allotted time if needed.

Remain positive while taking the exam even if you feel like you are performing poorly. Thinking about the content you should have mastered will not help you perform better on the exam.

Once the exam is complete, take some time to relax. Even if you feel that you need to take the exam again, you will be well served by some down time before you begin studying again. It's often easier to convince yourself to study if you know that it will come with a reward!

Test-Taking Strategies

1. Predicting the Answer

When you feel confident in your preparation for a multiple-choice test, try predicting the answer before reading the answer choices. This is especially useful on questions that test objective factual knowledge. By predicting the answer before reading the available choices, you eliminate the possibility that you will be distracted or led astray by an incorrect answer choice. You will feel more confident in your selection if you read the question, predict the answer, and then find your prediction among the answer choices. After using this strategy, be sure to still read all of the answer choices carefully and completely. If you feel unprepared, you should not attempt to predict the answers. This would be a waste of time and an opportunity for your mind to wander in the wrong direction.

2. Reading the Whole Question

Too often, test takers scan a multiple-choice question, recognize a few familiar words, and immediately jump to the answer choices. Test authors are aware of this common impatience, and they will sometimes prey upon it. For instance, a test author might subtly turn the question into a negative, or he or she might redirect the focus of the question right at the end. The only way to avoid falling into these traps is to read the entirety of the question carefully before reading the answer choices.

3. Looking for Wrong Answers

Long and complicated multiple-choice questions can be intimidating. One way to simplify a difficult multiple-choice question is to eliminate all of the answer choices that are clearly wrong. In most sets of answers, there will be at least one selection that can be dismissed right away. If the test is administered on paper, the test taker could draw a line through it to indicate that it may be ignored; otherwise, the test taker will have to perform this operation mentally or on scratch paper. In either case, once the obviously incorrect answers have been eliminated, the remaining choices may be considered. Sometimes identifying the clearly wrong answers will give the test taker some information about the correct answer. For instance, if one of the remaining answer choices is a direct opposite of one of the eliminated answer choices, it may well be the correct answer. The opposite of obviously wrong is obviously right! Of course, this is not always the case. Some answers are obviously incorrect simply because they are irrelevant to the question being asked. Still, identifying and eliminating some incorrect answer choices is a good way to simplify a multiple-choice question.

4. Don't Overanalyze

Anxious test takers often overanalyze questions. When you are nervous, your brain will often run wild, causing you to make associations and discover clues that don't actually exist. If you feel that this may be a problem for you, do whatever you can to slow down during the test. Try taking a deep breath or counting to ten. As you read and consider the question, restrict yourself to the particular words used by the author. Avoid thought tangents about what the author *really* meant, or what he or she was *trying* to say. The only things that matter on a multiple-choice test are the words that are actually in the question. You must avoid reading too much into a multiple-choice question, or supposing that the writer meant something other than what he or she wrote.

5. No Need for Panic

It is wise to learn as many strategies as possible before taking a multiple-choice test, but it is likely that you will come across a few questions for which you simply don't know the answer. In this situation, avoid panicking. Because

most multiple-choice tests include dozens of questions, the relative value of a single wrong answer is small. As much as possible, you should compartmentalize each question on a multiple-choice test. In other words, you should not allow your feelings about one question to affect your success on the others. When you find a question that you either don't understand or don't know how to answer, just take a deep breath and do your best. Read the entire question slowly and carefully. Try rephrasing the question a couple of different ways. Then, read all of the answer choices carefully. After eliminating obviously wrong answers, make a selection and move on to the next question.

6. Confusing Answer Choices

When working on a difficult multiple-choice question, there may be a tendency to focus on the answer choices that are the easiest to understand. Many people, whether consciously or not, gravitate to the answer choices that require the least concentration, knowledge, and memory. This is a mistake. When you come across an answer

choice that is confusing, you should give it extra attention. A question might be confusing because you do not know the subject matter to which it refers. If this is the case, don't eliminate the answer before you have affirmatively settled on another. When you come across an answer choice of this type, set it aside as you look at the remaining choices. If you can confidently assert that one of the other choices is correct, you can leave the confusing answer aside. Otherwise, you will need to take a moment to try to better understand the confusing answer choice. Rephrasing is one way to tease out the sense of a confusing answer choice.

7. Your First Instinct

Many people struggle with multiple-choice tests because they overthink the questions. If you have studied sufficiently for the test, you should be prepared to trust your first instinct once you have carefully and completely read the question and all of the answer choices. There is a great deal of research suggesting that the mind can come to the correct conclusion very quickly once it has obtained all of the relevant information. At times, it may seem to you as if your intuition is working faster even than your reasoning mind. This may in fact be true. The knowledge you obtain while studying may be retrieved from your subconscious before you have a chance to work out the associations that support it. Verify your instinct by working out the reasons that it should be trusted.

8. Key Words

Many test takers struggle with multiple-choice questions because they have poor reading comprehension skills. Quickly reading and understanding a multiple-choice question requires a mixture of skill and experience. To help with this, try jotting down a few key words and phrases on a piece of scrap paper. Doing this concentrates the process of reading and forces the mind to weigh the relative importance of the question's parts. In selecting words and phrases to write down, the test taker thinks about the question more deeply and carefully. This is especially true for multiple-choice questions that are preceded by a long prompt.

9. Subtle Negatives

One of the oldest tricks in the multiple-choice test writer's book is to subtly reverse the meaning of a question with a word like *not* or *except*. If you are not paying attention to each word in the question, you can easily be led astray by this trick. For instance, a common question format is, "Which of the following is...?" Obviously, if the question instead is, "Which of the following is not...?," then the answer will be quite different. Even worse, the test makers are aware of the potential for this mistake and will include one answer choice that would be correct if the question were not negated or reversed. A test taker who misses the reversal will find what he or she believes to be a correct answer and will be so confident that he or she will fail to reread the question and discover the original error. The only way to avoid this is to practice a wide variety of multiple-choice questions and to pay close attention to each and every word.

10. Reading Every Answer Choice.

It may seem obvious, but you should always read every one of the answer choices! Too many test takers fall into the habit of scanning the question and assuming that they understand the question because they recognize a few key words. From there, they pick the first answer choice that answers the question they believe they have read. Test takers who read all of the answer choices might discover that one of the latter answer choices is actually *more* correct. Moreover, reading all of the answer choices can remind you of facts related to the question that can help you arrive at the correct answer. Sometimes, a misstatement or incorrect detail in one of the latter answer choices will trigger your memory of the subject and will enable you to find the right answer. Failing to read all of the answer choices is like not reading all of the items on a restaurant menu: you might miss out on the perfect choice.

11. Spot the Hedges

One of the keys to success on multiple-choice tests is paying close attention to every word. This is never truer than with words like *almost*, *most*, *some*, and *sometimes*. These words are called "hedges" because they indicate that a statement is not totally true or not true in every place and time. An absolute statement will contain no hedges, but in many subjects, the answers are not always straightforward or absolute. There are always exceptions to the rules

in these subjects. For this reason, you should favor those multiple-choice questions that contain hedging language. The presence of qualifying words indicates that the author is taking special care with his or her words, which is certainly important when composing the right answer. After all, there are many ways to be wrong, but there is only one way to be right! For this reason, it is wise to avoid answers that are absolute when taking a multiple-choice test. An absolute answer is one that says things are either all one way or all another. They often include words like *every*, *always*, *best*, and *never*. If you are taking a multiple-choice test in a subject that doesn't lend itself to absolute answers, be on your guard if you see any of these words.

12. Long Answers

In many subject areas, the answers are not simple. As already mentioned, the right answer often requires hedges. Another common feature of the answers to a complex or subjective question are qualifying clauses, which are groups of words that subtly modify the meaning of the sentence. If the question or answer choice describes a rule to which there are exceptions or the subject matter is complicated, ambiguous, or confusing, the correct answer will require many words in order to be expressed clearly and accurately. In essence, you should not be deterred by answer choices that seem excessively long. Oftentimes, the author of the text will

not be able to write the correct answer without offering some qualifications and modifications. Your job is to read the answer choices thoroughly and completely and to select the one that most accurately and precisely answers the question.

13. Restating to Understand

Sometimes, a question on a multiple-choice test is difficult not because of what it asks but because of how it is written. If this is the case, restate the question or answer choice in different words. This process serves a couple of important purposes. First, it forces you to concentrate on the core of the question. In order to rephrase the question accurately, you have to understand it well. Rephrasing the question will concentrate your mind on the key words and ideas. Second, it will present the information to your mind in a fresh way. This process may trigger your memory and render some useful scrap of information picked up while studying.

14. True Statements

Sometimes an answer choice will be true in itself, but it does not answer the question. This is one of the main reasons why it is essential to read the question carefully and completely before proceeding to the answer choices. Too often, test takers skip ahead to the answer choices and look for true statements. Having found one of these, they are content to select it without reference to the question above. The savvy test taker will always read the entire question before turning to the answer choices. Then, having settled on a correct answer choice, he or she will refer to the original question and ensure that the selected answer is relevant. The mistake of choosing a correct-but-irrelevant answer choice is especially common on questions related to specific pieces of objective knowledge.

15. No Patterns

One of the more dangerous ideas that circulates about multiple-choice tests is that the correct answers tend to fall into patterns. These erroneous ideas range from a belief that B and C are the most common right answers, to the idea that an unprepared test-taker should answer "A-B-A-C-A-D-A-B-A." It cannot be emphasized enough that pattern-seeking of this type is exactly the WRONG way to approach a multiple-choice test. To begin with, it is highly unlikely that the test maker will plot the correct answers according to some predetermined pattern. The questions are scrambled and delivered in a random order. Furthermore, even if the test maker was following a pattern in the assignation of correct answers, there is no reason why the test taker would know which pattern he or she was using. Any attempt to discern a pattern in the answer choices is a waste of time and a distraction from the real work of taking the test. A test taker would be much better served by extra preparation before the test than by reliance on a pattern in the answers.

Bonus Content

We host multiple bonus items online, including all four practice tests in digital format. Scan the QR code or go to this link to access this content:

testprepbooks.com/bonus/nclexpn

The first time you access the page, you will need to register as a "new user" and verify your email address.

If you have any issues, please email support@testprepbooks.com.

Introduction to NCLEX-PN

Function of the Test

This guide outlines the National Council Licensure Examination for Practice Nurses (NCLEX-PN) along with practice questions and answer explanations so test takers can evaluate how well they might do on the actual exam. Those who wish to begin practicing and have received a diploma as an entry-level practical/vocational nurse should sign up to take the NCLEX-PN, as the test score is used as a step toward nursing licensure. In 2018, the total number of candidates who took the NCLEX-PN was 63,049. 46,307 passed the exam, with a pass rate of 73.4%.

Test Administration

The NCLEX-PN is offered via Pearson Centers throughout the United States, Canada, Australia, American Samoa, Guam, the Northern Mariana Islands, and the U.S. Virgin Islands. Note that you must have your Authorization to Test (ATT) before you schedule your exam appointment. Once you have your ATT, test takers must visit the Pearson website and sign up to take the exam there. The testing date must be within the validity date of the ATT.

Test takers are allowed to retake the exam up to eight times a year, providing they have applied for licensure or registration through an appropriate nursing regulatory body (NRB). Test takers must wait forty-five days before they retake an exam.

For test takers in need of accommodations during the test, they should contact their individual testing program. Test takers must do this well before the testing date, as documentation is required.

Test Format

Test takers should arrive at their testing center thirty minutes before the exam with a valid ID. A signature, photograph, and palm vein scan will be taken. Note that this exam is electronic, and an on-screen calculator and erasable note board and marker will be provided.

The PN exam is four hours long and includes a tutorial and two optional breaks. Once a test taker marks a question for submission, they are not allowed to return to that question. There is a computerized survey at the end of the exam. Once finished, test takers must raise their hands in order to be dismissed by a TA.

The NCLEX-PN is divided into four Client Needs sections: Safe and Effective Care Environment, Health Promotion and Maintenance, Psychosocial Integrity, and Physiological Integrity. A table below provides a more detailed view of what is on the exam.

Client Needs Categories	Percentage on Exam
Safe and Effective Care Environment	
ordinated Care	18–24%
ety and Infection Control	10–16%
Health Promotion and Maintenance	6–12%
Psychosocial Integrity	9–15%
Physiological Integrity	
sic Care and Comfort	7–13%
armacological Therapies	10–16%
duction of Risk Potential	9–15%
siological Adaptation	7–13%

Scoring

The NCLEX-PN uses Computerized Adaptive Testing (CAT) for scoring the exam. CAT works in a way that changes a subsequent question based on the way the test taker answered the previous question. Therefore, the exam is scored as the test taker submits their answers, and the test taker cannot go back to change any answers. The computer determines pass or fail based on three rules: 95% Confidence Interval Rule, Maximum-Length Exam Rule, and Run-out-of-time (R.O.O.T.) Rule. For the 95% Confidence Rule, the computer will stop giving questions once it is 95% sure you are above or below your ability to practice nursing. For the Maximum-Length Rule, the computer will disregard the 95% rule if it has not decided a pass/fail yet, and will take your final ability estimate into account. For the R.O.O.T. Rule, when you run out of time, the computer will use a set of alternate rules to determine a pass/fail grade. Scores are not released at the testing center but will be provided after the exam.

Recent/Future Developments

A Next Generation NCLEX (NGN) exam is coming soon with better questions for nurses to help them think critically and provide best outcomes for nurses, clients, and institutions.

Study Prep Plan for the NCLEX-PN

1 **Schedule** - Use one of our study schedules below or come up with one of your own.

2 **Relax** - Test anxiety can hurt even the best students. There are many ways to reduce stress. Find the one that works best for you.

3 **Execute** - Once you have a good plan in place, be sure to stick to it.

One Week Study Schedule		
Day 1	Safe and Effective Care Environment
Day 2	Health Promotion and Maintenance
Day 3	Physiological Integrity
Day 4	Physiological Adaptation
Day 5	NCLEX-PN Practice Tests #1 & #2
Day 6	NCLEX-PN Practice Tests #3 & #4
Day 7	Take Your Exam!

Two Week Study Schedule			
Day 1	Safe and Effective Care Environment	Day 8	Laboratory Values
Day 2	Safety and Infection Control	Day 9	Physiological Adaptation
Day 3	Health Promotion and Maintenance	Day 10	NCLEX-PN Practice Test #1
Day 4	Psychosocial Integrity	Day 11	NCLEX-PN Practice Test #2
Day 5	Physiological Integrity	Day 12	NCLEX-PN Practice Test #3
Day 6	Pharmacological Therapies	Day 13	NCLEX-PN Practice Test #4
Day 7	Reduction of Risk Potential	Day 14	Take Your Exam!

10

One Month Study Schedule

Day 1	Safe and Effective Care Environment	Day 11	Spiritual and Cultural Influences on Health	Day 21	Medical Emergencies
Day 2	Confidentiality/ Information Security	Day 12	Physiological Integrity	Day 22	NCLEX-PN Practice Test #1
Day 3	Legal Responsibilities	Day 13	Nonpharmacological Comfort Interventions	Day 23	NCLEX-PN Answer Explanations #1
Day 4	Safety and Infection Control	Day 14	Pharmacological Therapies	Day 24	NCLEX-PN Practice Test #2
Day 5	Emergency Response Plan	Day 15	Reduction of Risk Potential	Day 25	NCLEX-PN Answer Explanations #2
Day 6	Least Restrictive Restraints and Safety...	Day 16	Holter Monitor	Day 26	NCLEX-PN Practice Test #3
Day 7	Health Promotion and Maintenance	Day 17	Laboratory Values	Day 27	NCLEX-PN Answer Explanations #3
Day 8	Health Promotion/ Disease Prevention	Day 18	Potential for Complications of...	Day 28	NCLEX-PN Practice Test #4
Day 9	Psychosocial Integrity	Day 19	Physiological Adaptation	Day 29	NCLEX-PN Answer Explanations #4
Day 10	Cultural Awareness	Day 20	Basic Pathophysiology	Day 30	Take Your Exam!

Build your own prep plan by visiting:
testprepbooks.com/prep

As you study for your test, we'd like to take the opportunity to remind you that you are capable of great things! With the right tools and dedication, you truly can do anything you set your mind to. The fact that you are holding this book right now shows how committed you are. In case no one has told you lately, you've got this! Our intention behind including this coloring page is to give you the chance to take some time to engage your creative side when you need a little brain-break from studying. As a company, we want to encourage people like you to achieve their dreams by providing good quality study materials for the tests and certifications that improve careers and change lives. As individuals, many of us have taken such tests in our careers, and we know how challenging this process can be. While we can't come alongside you and cheer you on personally, we can offer you the space to recall your purpose, reconnect with your passion, and refresh your brain through an artistic practice. We wish you every success, and happy studying!

Safe and Effective Care Environment

Coordinated Care

Advance Directives

Advance directives, such as a **living will** or **durable power of attorney**, are forms that state a patient's choices for treatment, including refusal of treatments, life support, and stopping treatments when the patient chooses. **Do not resuscitate (DNR) status**, and its varying types, is also included in advance directives. The preoperative interview should include discussion of advance directives and DNR status. If the patient has advance directives, a copy should be placed in the medical record, and they should be reviewed by the nurse and physician. If the patient has a code status of anything other than full resuscitation, a conversation among the surgeon, anesthesiologist, and patient is necessary to discuss the patient's wishes in detail.

Older schools of thinking suggest all patients, regardless of preoperative DNR status, are considered full code while in the operating room; however, this is not true. A patient with DNR status of no intubation and no **cardiopulmonary resuscitation (CPR)** may proceed with the surgical procedure if the surgeon and anesthesiologist have a conversation with the patient and a plan is agreed upon among them. Consent must be obtained by the patient if there is a change in status or a suspension of the DNR order during surgery. However, if the patient wishes to keep DNR status of no intubation and no CPR during surgery, the surgeon and/or anesthesiologist may deem the patient a nonsurgical candidate. If a patient is entering surgery with a DNR order of anything other than full code, this must be communicated to the entire surgical team and documented in the medical record. **Healthcare power of attorney** is the legal term for the person appointed by the patient to make their healthcare decisions should they become incapacitated.

Reviewing Client Understanding of Advance Directives
The role of an LPN/VN in Coordinated Care is to work in tandem with the entire health care team to make sure that the needs and choices of each patient are effectively shared and communicated across the participating departments. This involves reviewing advance directives with the patient and ensuring they understand what these directives entail. These are guideline documents utilized for instituting or continuing medical care and are a U.S. healthcare facility requirement as per The Patient Self-Determination Act of 1990. Many of the subjects they cover are delicate in nature, such as death-related legal and/or ethical matters, euthanasia, DNR (do not resuscitate) orders, organ donation, the bill of rights of a dying person, the living will of the patient, and giving over the power of attorney to a trusted person (durable power of attorney). As a result, the utmost care and empathy should be followed.

Making a note of any questions the patient asks regarding the concept of advance directives is a good way to assess their understanding of the process. For example, if a patient asks whether they are allowed to alter their directive, this raises a red flag to the nurse that they don't fully understand the process. If the patient doesn't offer any feedback voluntarily, asking them what they know about the process is a good way to determine their level of knowledge.

Advocacy

The American Nurses Association (ANA) provides this definition of nursing practice:

> The protection, promotion, and optimization of health and abilities, prevention of illness and injury, alleviation of suffering through the diagnosis and treatment of human response, and advocacy in the care of individuals, families, communities, and populations.

The ANA also addresses the importance of advocacy in its Code of Ethics, specifically in Provision 3:

> The nurse promotes, advocates for, and protects the rights, health, and safety of the patient.

The ANA Code of Ethics further states that nurses must advocate:

> with compassion and respect for the inherent dignity, worth, and uniqueness of every individual, unrestricted by considerations of social or economic status, personal attributes, or the nature of health problems.

Advocacy is a key component of nursing practice. An **advocate** is one who pleads the cause of another; and the nurse is an advocate for patient rights. Preserving human dignity, patient equality, and freedom from suffering are the basis of nursing advocacy. Nurses hold a significant role that gives them the opportunity to care for patients in every way: caring for their needs, addressing any and all concerns, and ensuring that all outcomes are positive. More experienced nurses can aid in communicating with doctors and physicians while also serving as a guide through the complexities of the medical system. Nurses educate the patient about tests and procedures and are aware of how culture and ethnicity affect the patient's experience. Nurses strictly adhere to all privacy laws.

Advocacy is the promotion of the common good, especially as it applies to at-risk populations. It involves speaking out in support of policies and decisions that affect the lives of individuals who do not otherwise have a voice. Nurses meet this standard of practice by actively participating in the politics of healthcare accessibility and delivery because they are educationally and professionally prepared to evaluate and comment on the needs of patients at the local, state, and national level. This participation requires an understanding of the legislative process, the ability to negotiate with public officials, and a willingness to provide expert testimony in support of policy decisions. The advocacy role of nurses addresses the needs of the individual patient as well as the needs of all individuals in the society, and the members of the nursing profession.

In clinical practice, nurses represent the patient's interests by active participation in the development of the plan of care and subsequent care decisions. Advocacy, in this sense, is related to patient autonomy and the patient's right to informed consent and self-determination. Nurses provide the appropriate information, assess the patient's comprehension of the implications of the care decisions, and act as patient advocates by supporting the patient's decisions. In the critical care environment, patient advocacy requires the nurse to represent the patient's decisions even though those decisions may be opposed to those of the healthcare providers and family members.

Professionally, nurses advocate for policies that support and promote the practice of all nurses with regard to access to education, role identity, workplace conditions, and compensation. The responsibility for professional advocacy requires nurses to provide leadership in the development of the professional nursing role in all practice settings that may include acute care facilities, colleges and universities, or community agencies. Leadership roles in acute care settings involve participation in professional practice and shared governance committees, providing support for basic nursing education by facilitating clinical and preceptorship experiences, and mentoring novice graduate nurses to the professional nursing role. In the academic setting, nurses work to ensure the diversity of the student population by participating in the governance structure of the institution, conducting and publishing research that supports the positive impact of professional nursing care on patient outcomes, and serving as an advocate to individual nursing students to promote their academic success. In the community, nurses assist other nurse-providers to collaborate with government officials to meet the needs that are specific to that location.

The nurse must function as a moral agent. This means that the nurse must be morally accountable and responsible for personal judgment and actions. **Moral agency** is defined as the ability to identify right and wrong actions based on widely accepted moral criteria. The performance of nurses as moral agents is dependent on life experiences, advanced education, and clinical experience in healthcare agencies.

The role of moral agent requires nurses to have a strong sense of self and a clear understanding of the definition of right and wrong; however, nurses must also be aware that these perceptions of right and wrong will be challenged every day. In reality, nurses who act as the moral agents and are accountable for right and wrong decisions commonly encounter situations where the correct and moral action related to the patient's right to self-determination is opposed to the right and moral action with respect to competent patient care.

Client Care Assignments

Every day when the nurse reports to duty, a team of patients will be assigned to them. A caseload of patients will vary in size based on the acuity of the patients' illnesses and the unit policies that the nurse belongs to.

Acuity refers to the severity of the patient's illness. Some patients are high acuity, meaning a lot of time and resources are put into their daily routine due to the severity of their illness. Others are low acuity and do not require much oversight from the nurse to get through the day. High-acuity patients might be more difficult for many nurses because their care can often take away from the care of others. A team full of high-acuity patients, then, can be a great burden for a nurse to bear.

When patient assignments become too burdensome for nurses, those nursing-sensitive indicators are the first signs that there is a problem. When the nurse is busy with a team of high-acuity patients, it is difficult to perform all the tasks of the day, let alone perform them carefully and thoughtfully. It is then in the best interest of those making team assignments for nurses to weigh carefully the patient load and ensure equitable and fair decisions are made.

Dividing up teams of patients is often the task of the charge nurse. To fairly assign patient teams to nurses, the charge nurse must bear in mind each patient's acuity. Conflict arises when nurses feel that there is inequity in the assignment of patients and they are unduly burdened with an unfair patient load compared to other teams or units.

Nurse satisfaction directly correlates with patient care. If nurses do not feel their patient assignments are fair and the burden is too great, their performance suffers as well as their job satisfaction. Nursing performance can be linked to the following nurse-sensitive indicators: how well patient pain is managed; the presence and treatment of pressure ulcers, patient falls, and medication errors; patient satisfaction; and nosocomial or hospital-acquired infections.

Client Rights

Each patient has certain rights that must be respected. When patients are admitted to a facility, they are put in a position of vulnerability. This special position of power held by the health care provider should never be abused to violate the rights of the patient. Caring for a patient is an honor, and certain rules of conduct should be followed.

The patient has the right to have health information kept private and only shared with those who are given permission to view it. The **Health Insurance Portability and Accountability Act (HIPAA)** was passed by Congress in 1996 to protect health information. The term HIPAA is often used to reference patient privacy. There are many different ways a patient's personal health information can be shared: verbally, digitally, over the phone or fax, or through written messages.

Along with protecting the patient's health information, the nurse must be respectful of the patient's privacy in general. Knocking on the patient's door before entering the room, keeping the door shut to the busy corridor outside the room, and not asking unnecessary personal questions are all ways the nurse can extend common courtesy to the patient. The nature of the nurse's relationship with the patient is already quite personal in nature, so there is no need to exploit that relationship.

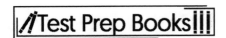

Each patient has the right to fair treatment. This means that no patient should be treated any better or worse than another patient for any reason, such as a racial bias or unfair prejudice based on the nurse's personal opinions and beliefs. Giving one patient preferential treatment over another is a violation of the patient's rights, and the nurse will be subject to disciplinary action if they are discovered to be treating patients poorly.

No patient should ever be abused or neglected. This should go without saying, but it is a patient right that is perhaps the most important. Abuse can be physical, emotional, sexual, mental, or financial. Neglect is when the patient's needs are being ignored, usually resulting in patient harm.

The patient has the **right of self-determination**, which means that they have the right to make decisions regarding their own health care. Patients are members of the healthcare team along with the doctors and nurses. What the nurse may think is the right course of action for a patient may not align with what the patient thinks is right, and that is to be respected. The healthcare team forms the plan of care and educates the patient as to what a plan entails, but it is the patient who makes the final decision to accept or reject a plan. If the patient is not capable of making their own decisions, the **power of attorney**—usually a close family member such as a wife, husband, or adult child—has the power to make healthcare decisions for the patient.

Along with self-determination, the patients also have the freedom to express themselves and their opinions. Simply being admitted to a facility does not take away their freedom of speech. Patients may have opinions about all aspects of their care, and they have every right to express these feelings. The nurse needs to be respectful, listen, and try to help when there is a problem that can be solved. Issues voiced by patients can always be escalated by the nurse, using the appropriate chain of command.

If the nurse suspects abuse or neglect, they are mandatorily required to report it to the appropriate entity. The charge nurse and/or nurse manager should be notified, so the appropriate action can be taken to right the situation. There are also hotlines that can be called, such as the National Center on Elder Abuse (1-800-677-1116).

There are different types of abuse. **Physical abuse** involves injuries to the body from punching, kicking, etc. If the nurse notes various bruises or cuts in various stages of healing without explanation, it may be a sign of physical abuse.

Sexual abuse is when sexual contact is made without the consent of one party, including rape, coercion into doing sexual acts, and fondling of genitalia. The nurse should look for unexplained bruising of or bleeding around the perineal area, new difficulty sitting or walking, or increased agitation/aggression as potential signs of sexual abuse.

Emotional abuse and **mental abuse** are not quite as obvious as physical abuse, as the damage inflicted is internal or hidden. Emotional and mental abuses are usually caused by verbal assaults. The abuser may belittle and criticize the victim to the point that the victim feels worthless, insecure, and afraid. If the nurse senses an uncomfortable relationship between an informal caregiver or family member and the patient, this should be monitored, investigated, and reported if abuse is suspected.

Financial abuse is a type of abuse in which the abuser limits the victim's access to money and financial information, sometimes stealing directly from the victim without the victim's knowledge. Being the caregiver of an older person grants a person special access to personal documents and financial resources; this privilege can be abused. If the nurse suspects that checks and other financial means meant for the patient are being rerouted and misused by a caregiver, this abuse should be reported right away.

It is the patient's right to deny treatment. Patients can deny treatment if fully informed of their medical condition and the likely outcomes resulting from the refusal. This is known as the right to informed consent. They may decide to refuse treatment because of a number of reasons, including religious or cultural beliefs, fear of the procedure or its side effects, they feel it is not necessary, or they simply do not want to do it. This right can be legally challenged if

overwhelming reasons are determined to necessitate overriding the wishes of the patient, such as the endangerment of another person's life, a situation where a parent's decision threatens the life of a child, a patient stating whether they want to live, and the best interest of the public takes precedence over the patient's right. The LPN/VN needs to be able to contribute to a modified plan of care that includes these possibilities.

Collaboration with Interdisciplinary Team

Interdisciplinary rounding can provide an opportunity for team collaboration after a patient's surgery. Much like a clear hand-off process, interdisciplinary rounds reduce patient care errors, decrease mortality rates, and improve patient outcomes. Interdisciplinary rounds are an excellent place to discuss social service needs, nutritional care services, and transportation needs with all teams coordinating care for the patient in a single setting.

The patient's service needs may vary in depth for the inpatient stay and at the time of discharge; however, there should be an evaluation of these needs and a coordination of care for those services in which there is a need. Nurses document the action plan as it relates to services and requirements for the patient and collaborate with members of the interdisciplinary team to see that next steps are executed in a timely fashion. In many instances, rounding may not be possible due to the rapid pace and turnover of the medical environment, and thus, clear documentation will be an absolute must to allow for synchronous care coordination.

Nurses, physicians, surgeons, nurse aids, physical and occupational therapists, mental health professionals, and medical assistants are just some of the members who may be collaborating on the care of one patient. Perception of power between these professionals can sometimes create a stressful environment that can also affect patient outcomes. The ability of each one to collaborate with the other is imperative so that patient safety does not become an issue. Collaboration involves joint decision-making activities between both disciplines rather than nurses only following physician orders. Although each role may have a particular focus throughout the assessment and plan of care activities, they must jointly come together to formulate the best possible treatment plan throughout the treatment period. Studies show that an attentive communication style between nurses and physicians has the most positive impact on patients.

Ongoing education of physicians and nurses may be a necessity to support a collaborative environment. In addition to continuing education and in-services, job shadowing, which exposes both the nurse and physician to each one's role, can assist in promoting understanding and teamwork.

Concepts of Management and Supervision

Delegation

Nursing staff take on many responsibilities that can be delegated to other clinical and non-clinical colleagues. However, learning how to **safely delegate tasks**, while still making patients feel cared for, is a skill that can take time to develop. It requires knowing not only what the needs of the patient are, but also the strengths and weaknesses of assistive personnel and how to best communicate professional needs with them. It also requires personal development in becoming comfortable with outsourcing responsibilities, as the nurse who delegates still remains accountable for the patient.

Assistive personnel may be supervised by nurses, but clinical assistive staff can provide basic medical assistance such as monitoring patients' vital signs, assisting with caretaking duties, monitoring any abnormalities or changes in the patient, maintaining a sterile and safe environment, and any other request made directly by nursing staff. Non-clinical assistive personnel, such as front desk staff, can assist with patient communication (such as wait times), managing paperwork and ensuring it is complete, and performing any other administrative task that may support the nursing staff's cases.

When nursing staff choose to delegate tasks, they may feel worried about risking their own accountability or work ethic. However, relating with assistive personnel, understanding their strengths and weaknesses, understanding their interests, and remaining transparent about the needs that are present in the department can ensure that delegated tasks are a good fit for the person who is taking the responsibility. In this regard, nursing staff take on a leadership and managerial role that requires developing their problem-solving, time management, and interpersonal skills. Some effective tools for delegation can include standardized checklists that cover the procedure that is being delegated, formal and informal meetings about assistive personnel's comfort levels and interests in performing certain tasks, and matching professional needs with individual qualifications. When delegation is effective, it can help the entire department work in a more efficient manner. Additionally, both nursing staff and assistive personnel are more likely to feel like part of a cohesive team and less likely to feel overworked or undervalued.

Supervision

After the nurse has successfully and effectively delegated a task, the nurse then takes on the role of supervisor of the person to whom they delegated the task. Delegation requires **supervision**, to ensure the task is done appropriately and to protect the nurse's own licensure.

The key to supervision is the **follow-up**. After the task is delegated, the nurse must then make a note to investigate whether the task was done, whether it was done in a timely manner, and whether it was done correctly. Asking the person who was supposed to perform the task to report back is appropriate. All conversations and interactions must be performed professionally and with respect for both the inferior and superior party.

Many nurses were once **certified nursing assistants (CNAs)** and understand the role and responsibility of the person they now delegate to. If the two nurses were former co-workers and one has risen to the role of nurse from CNA, tensions may arise. Tensions that arise between nursing staff and those they delegate to may be resolved through careful interactions in which each party is respected and an effort is made by both parties that shows they are both working hard together with the best interest of the patient at the forefront of their minds.

At times, it may be necessary for the nurse to coach and support the staff member, giving tips for better performance where appropriate. Again, this interaction must be done with professionalism and respect. It is important as an employee in any field to be receptive to constructive criticism, as well as being able to offer it when appropriate and allowing plenty of discussion on the point.

The nurse must ensure that the task delegated, such as taking vital signs or cleaning up an incontinent patient, has been appropriately documented. Documentation is necessary for legal reasons, to show that proper care was given to the patient. If the person to whom the task was delegated did not document the task, it is necessary for the nurse to confront them directly and confirm that it was done.

Recognizing and Reporting Staff Conflict

Staff conflict occurs when people have differing views or thoughts on something. Conflict on the job can be disturbing and anxiety-provoking. However, it is an inevitable part of working as a team. Recognizing and reporting it involves the following steps:

- Defining the conflict: Conflicts occur when two or more people have differing attitudes or viewpoints. Conflict can actually be helpful when it is resolved in a healthy manner, equally fulfilling to both parties, so that they both get closure.

- Evaluating the various factors that can provoke conflict: Arguments, a lack of trust, workflow disruptions, impaired interpersonal relationships, criticism of others, and frustration are examples of issues that can incite conflict.

- Recognizing the variations of personality types: It is imperative to embrace the various ways team members think and feel and how these diverse factors will affect the outcome of the conflict.

- Distinguishing types of communication: Team members can display a wide range of communicative techniques/methods during any type of interaction, but conflict can cause people to behave in varying ways, such as becoming guarded or aggressive. It is important for team members to be aware of this possibility.

- Here are a few ways to resolve team conflict:

  - Collaboration and Open Communication: Working together and maintaining an open exchange between team members helps to cultivate relationships among group members and encourages the conflicting parties to actively participate in the resolution, thus fostering a more in-depth understanding of the dispute.

  - Compromise and Negotiation: Maintaining a level playing field encourages both parties to remain confident but not belligerent, promoting equality between team members. Discussing the issue rationally allows team members to focus on common goals and interests rather than individual parties and their diverse opinions, allowing the conflicting parties to separate themselves from the conflict and the issue at hand.

  - Mediation: Sometimes one-on-one communication with each team member is required in order to discern each person's concerns, beliefs, and opinions. Once this occurs, the team can investigate resolving the conflict via methods that are satisfactory to all involved.

- Here is a 6-stage list of team conflict resolution:

  1. Clarifying the disagreement and making sure both sides agree on the topic of the issue.

  2. Establishing a common goal agreed upon by those involved in the conflict.

  3. Discussing the various techniques the team can use to gain a common understanding.

  4. Defining the issues that are in the way of reaching the common goal.

  5. Coming to an agreement regarding the best way(s) to resolve the conflict.

  6. Agreeing upon a solution and deciding the responsibilities of each member.

- Acknowledging personal reactions of team members: Every team member may have a totally different response to conflict and how it is being handled by the team. These include being evasive, dominating, accommodating, collaborative, or cooperative.

- Choosing useful conflict resolution techniques: When a conflict arises, it is important to be aware of the fact that team members will have varying principles and priorities on how to settle it. Therefore, selecting the best technique for resolving conflict will depend on each situation and those involved.

- Recognize the benefits and drawbacks of team conflict-resolution strategies: This includes dealing with the issue, thinking it through, discussing it in person, using a mediator, apologizing when needed, and communicating clearly and effectively.

- Be aware of situations that typically require employee disciplinary action: Since conflict can disrupt the workflow of the whole team and covers a wide range of behaviors, sometimes disciplinary action is required.

Confidentiality/Information Security

Patient privacy and confidentiality is a constant for all healthcare providers. Given the sensitivity of medical procedures, the healthcare team must maintain strict patient confidentiality. Under the **Health Insurance Portability and Accountability Act (HIPAA)**, a patient's information is required to be protected and kept confidential regardless of the form, including electronic, written, and spoken communication. **Protected health information (PHI)** should be shared only on an as-needed and minimum necessary basis. When discussing patients or cases in settings where other personnel may overhear the conversation, the medical team should be careful not to include any PHI that may violate the patient's confidentiality. Additionally, when information is displayed electronically to families and visitors in waiting rooms, patient names should be avoided. HIPAA violations can have negative consequences for the providers and/or the facility.

The nurse plays an important role in keeping a patient's health information private. Sharing personal details—such as a patient's name, condition, and medical history—in an inappropriate way violates the person's right to privacy. For example, a nurse telling a friend who does not work in the facility that the nurse took care of the friend's aunt, without the aunt's consent or knowledge, is considered a violation of privacy. Another way a nurse could violate a resident's privacy is to access the medical record when they are not actually caring for that particular patient. For example, if a celebrity has been admitted to a different unit, and the nursing assistant accesses the celebrity's electronic health record, then they are in violation of HIPAA. Those who violate HIPAA and are caught could lose their jobs, among other punitive actions. Nurses should also ensure that other staff members—such as nursing assistants—as well as patients understand the confidentiality requirements of the facility, state, and country.

Continuity of Care

If one imagines a patient's illness as a road, what would the ideal road look like? Smooth, no potholes, appropriate signage to guide and direct the patient from illness to wellness, right? In the real world of health care, the road the patient travels from illness to wellness often has bumps and miscommunications. Things do not go as planned, missteps are taken, unexpected events and miscalculations can and unfortunately do occur.

All members of the healthcare team should be striving to provide patients with a high quality of care over time, or **continuity of care**. The patient begins their journey with an illness, at a doctor's office, convenient care clinic, or an emergency room. From there, the road proceeds through various tests and procedures to diagnose and treat the illness. Management teams that include doctors and nurses provide input into this process, and resources also contribute. The patient is at the center of the continuity of care model. In continuity of care, the whole patient is treated, not just an organ or an illness. Ideally, the community surrounding the patient is also involved in promoting good health and high quality of life.

The roots of continuity of care lie in a meaningful, long-term relationship between the patient and the healthcare provider. This relationship ensures that the patient is known. Their needs are anticipated through regular check-ups and follow-ups after the illness has run its course. The ideal is to form a firm bond of trust between the healthcare provider and the patient. This trusting relationship and deep knowledge of the case allow the provider to better advocate for the patient.

The physician or nurse practitioner coordinating care for the patient will look for ways to make the plan of care cost-effective for the patient. Tests and procedures are carefully weighed for their usefulness in the patient's case, looking for ways to eliminate wasteful healthcare spending.

The main idea behind continuity of care is to avoid what happens all too often in healthcare: fragmentation of care. The responsibility of the patient's case is often shifted from one entity to another over the course of an illness. Initially, the patient's case is handled in a primary care setting or perhaps an emergent care setting, depending on

the illness. Then the patient may become hospitalized, at which point the hospitalist and various specialists step in and take over. At discharge, the patient's case is then handed over to their primary care physician and community centers. Due to this shifting of care, it becomes ambiguous just who is overseeing the patient's care. The patient has a fragmented experience rather than continuity of care.

One issue faced by healthcare providers is not having the infrastructure to effectively coordinate patient care and avoid the problems associated with fragmented care. A case manager comes into play here because their role is perfect for coordinating the patients' care as they move through the system.

Primary care physicians face a hurdle when coordinating patient care because they have limited communication with the hospital team when their patient is admitted. Nowadays, there is a team of healthcare providers called **hospitalists**, whose job it is to care for patients while they are in the hospital, but not pre- or post-admission. This is helpful because they know the ins and outs of the facility and have good communication with the hospital's specialists and surgeons. They can all work together to get the patient in and out of the hospital relatively quickly.

A **patient-centered medical home (PCMH)** comes into play pre-admission to prevent a costly hospital visit. The idea of a PCMH is to combat fragmentation of care and promote better continuity of care for the patient on their road to wellness. The PCMH is a model of care that is well-coordinated, proactive, and centered on the patient. In this model, a patient is paired with a personal physician to oversee their care. Their family and loved ones are recruited to assist in promoting a whole patient-focused wellness plan. The PCMH moves away from fee for service; instead, it focuses on fee for value, meaning the level of success in keeping the patient healthy determines how the healthcare team is reimbursed. The patient must regularly keep in touch with their primary care physician, a factor that has been associated with better patient outcomes.

Many communities are adopting the PCMH model of healthcare, attempting to promote a better continuity of care for patients on their road from illness to wellness.

Nurses are aware that the patient often requires continued reinforcement of the educational plan after discharge, which necessitates coordination with home care services. As facilitators of learning, nurses may be involved in a large-scale effort to educate all patients. The first step of any teaching-learning initiative is the assessment of the learning needs of the participants. Specific needs that influence the design and content of the educational offering include the language preference and reading level of the participants. Nurses must also consider the effect of certain patient characteristics identified in the Synergy Model on the patient's capacity to process information. Diminished resiliency or stability, and extreme complexity, must be considered in the development of the educational plan. Nurses are also responsible for creating a bridge between teaching-learning in the acute care setting and the home environment. A detailed discharge plan, close coordination with outpatient providers, and follow-up phone calls to the patient may be used to reinforce the patient's knowledge of the plan of care.

Establishing Priorities

The ability to **establish priorities** is one of the nurse's most important skills. The nurse must be able to look at their patient load for the day, assess the needs of each patient, organize tasks in chronological order, and prioritize each task based on its importance and necessity.

When prioritizing the tasks for the day, the nurse must first employ their knowledge of the body, how it works, and what it needs to function. The nurse starts with ABC: airway, breathing, and circulation. Are any patients compromised in these respects? If so, they are immediately placed at the top of the list of priorities. If the patient cannot breathe, is hemorrhaging, or their heart has stopped beating, they require the nurse's immediate assistance. The **ABCs** are considered the first priority of patient needs.

Emergency Trauma Assessment

- A: Airway
- B: Breathing
- C: Circulation
- D: Disability
- E: Examine
- F: Fahrenheit
- G: Get Vitals
- H: Head to Toe Assessment
- I: Intervention

After the ABC patient needs are taken care of, the nurse can move down the scale to the next priority. A helpful acronym to remember is **M-A-A-U-A-R**. These are considered second-priority needs.

- M is for mental status changes and alterations
- A is for acute pain
- A is for acute urinary elimination concerns
- U is for unaddressed and untreated problems requiring immediate attention
- A is for abnormal laboratory/diagnostic data outside of normal limits
- R is for risks that include those involving a healthcare problem such as safety, skin integrity, infection, and other medical conditions

Along with the ABC-MAAUAR methods of prioritization, the nurse may also utilize **Maslow's hierarchy of needs**. Maslow argues that physiological needs such as hunger, thirst, and breathing are among the first that have to be met. The same goes for patients. For example, a patient in pain needs to be addressed before a patient who needs education on a procedure that is to happen tomorrow.

After the basic physiological needs have been met, the nurse knows that on the next level of the pyramid are safety and psychological needs. Mental health fits on this tier of the hierarchy and is a crucial step toward wellness. Love and belonging follow; for this part of care the nurse can enlist the help of social services and family members. The next level of Maslow's hierarchy is "self-esteem and esteem by others." In nursing terms, this level represents the patient's need to feel they are a respected and esteemed member of the care team. The final level of Maslow's hierarchy is self-actualization, in which a person reaches their fullest potential and highest level of ability. The nurse

does everything they can to help the client reach this level, pushing them to do their best and be their best at all points in the care journey.

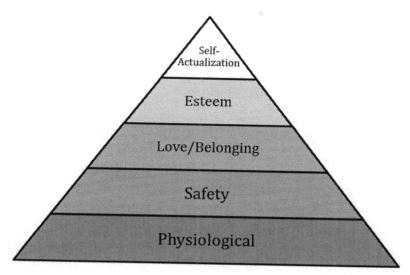

Recognizing the patient's needs and establishing priorities based on Maslow's hierarchy, the nurse can then move on to the next step of the process. After goal-setting and client care delivery comes the evaluation stage. The nurse must be continually evaluating the plan of care for each patient. The plan may need tweaking and revision throughout the day, based on how the patient responds to interventions. Quality evaluation of interventions ensures needs are being met and proper care is being delivered.

Sound nursing judgment will guide the nurse as they endeavor to prioritize and adequately meet the needs of their patients in a timely manner.

Time Management and Work Prioritization

One of the most important skills a nurse must master in the busy healthcare environment is that of time management and prioritization of tasks. The work day is filled with tasks, scheduled activities, unexpected time conflicts, and constant interruptions.

As best as the nurse can, they should have a way of planning the day. Some find it best to have some sort of written system to take notes and jot down vitals in between charting periods. Meal times can be the busiest times of day, so it should be accounted for in planning.

Countless interruptions will occur throughout the day, such as a call light going off when the nurse was planning to start a bath or a patient needing assistance to the bathroom when the nurse was planning on taking a break. It is vital that the nurse prioritizes tasks and makes sure the most important tasks get done in a timely manner. It is easy to put off tasks for later that really should be done immediately, but that sort of procrastination can have adverse results. The day will be busy; that is a given. Developing one's time management and prioritization skills will help the day go a lot more smoothly.

Ethical Practice

Healthcare providers routinely face situations with patients where they must analyze various moral and ethical considerations. In the emergency department, where quick judgment and action is necessary to care and where patients are often not fully sound in body or mind, ethical dilemmas can arise without much time to process resolutions.

Nurses are held to the American Nurses Association's Code of Ethics, which states moral and ethical guidelines that nurses should incorporate into their practice. Above all else, nurses have the responsibility to do no harm while advocating for, promoting good health outcomes for, minimizing injury to, and protecting the overall health and functioning of their patients. It is important to consider the patient holistically when applying these values, such as considering what the patient may view as a good quality of life, what family values the patient holds, other family members that may be affected, legal considerations, and logistical considerations, such as how much time and medical resources are available. When patients are unable to make decisions autonomously, or even to indicate consent to treatment, nurses should act from these responsibilities to make wise and compassionate decisions on the patients' behalf.

Dilemmas that can arise for nursing staff include situations where the patient may have cultural or personal beliefs that prevent lifesaving treatment. For example, a female emergency patient may not want to be treated by any male staff, or a patient that needs a blood transfusion may not accept this procedure due to religious beliefs. In cases where the patient is able to directly communicate their wishes, the nurse may need to defer to the patient's wishes in order to preserve the patient's autonomy.

This may mean providing alternative means of care, such as finding available female medical providers to assist with the female patient who does not want to be treated by male staff. It may mean withholding treatment that the patient refuses. If the patient's life is in question and rapid medical action is necessary to save the patient's life, nursing staff may need to intervene even if it is against the patient's wishes. Ethical considerations like these will vary by case and patient, and will depend on the severity of the case, the medical and personal history of the patient, and the judgment of the nurse in question. In all cases, it is ideal if the nurse and patient are able to communicate openly with each other about the case and potential medical options.

Informed Consent

Before a major medical procedure can be performed, the patient's consent must be obtained. Obtaining this consent requires educating the patient on what the procedure is, how it is performed, what types of outcomes are to be expected, and most importantly, why the procedure will be done. This process of educating the patient and getting their permission is called **informed consent**.

There are two key aspects of the term informed consent. The term "informed" implies that the patient has been given information pertaining to the procedure. This requires a conversation between the patient and their health care provider. Education must be provided to ensure that the patient has been given information about the procedure to be done as well as time to consider their options. If a patient signs a consent without having a proper understanding and comprehension of what's to be done, it is not a true informed consent.

The second part of the term is "consent." This means that the patient agrees with the plan and gives their permission for what is going to be done. Without consent, it is illegal or improper to perform certain healthcare procedures.

Consent can be given through three different avenues: implied, verbal, and written. **Implied consent** does not involve the patient signing a document or even verbally granting permission, but rather it is assumed that any reasonable person would consent to the health care interventions being performed. This can get into a gray area on some issues. For example, let's say a patient drops to the floor in full cardiac arrest. They are unresponsive. A nurse witnesses the fall and begins cardiopulmonary resuscitation (CPR) and activates the emergency response system. The patient did not say they agreed to have CPR done on them nor did they sign a document agreeing to the procedure, but it is assumed that the patient is complicit. This is due to the patient's being in danger of death and in need of swift action. On a much smaller scale, a patient coming into a doctor's office does not sign a document of

26

consent to have their vital signs taken, yet they willingly comply with having their blood pressure taken. All parties present assume and agree upon certain procedures and thus no formal consent is required.

Verbal consent is obtained by having the patient saying something along the lines of "Yes, it is okay to do this." This is the in-between consent, slightly more formal than implied consent and less formal than the signed legal document that is informed consent.

Written consent involves a formal conversation between the health care provider, the physician performing the procedure, and the patient. It is vital that the patient is adequately educated on the procedure and has a full understanding before consenting. Obtaining consent without proper patient education is fraudulent and poor practice. Not properly informing the patient may lead to legal trouble down the road for both the nurse and the physician, not to mention potential complications following the procedure. Above all, it is a violation of a patient's rights to not be properly informed before giving consent.

While the physician is legally responsible for satisfying all elements of informed consent, nurses are ethically responsible for assessing the patient's ability to process and understand the implications of informed consent. Nurses should ensure that the patient understands the purpose of a procedure and any possible risks, whether the physician or the nurse themselves explained the information to the patient. The nurse should also be sure the appropriate person to provide informed consent for the patient has been identified and understands the procedure. This may be the patient, their legal guardian, parent, etc. Nurses protect the patient's autonomy by raising these questions and concerns.

Information Technology

Information technology (IT) is a field of nursing that continues to evolve with the rest of healthcare. Nurses must not only understand the science that is associated with nursing, but they must also be able to navigate various forms of technology. While there are nurses still in the workplace who can recall what it was like to physically fill out forms and track vitals on paper, there are also nurses who have no concept of having documented their activities in these systems. All nurses must be able to function within today's technologically advanced world.

IT is important for many reasons including:

- Cost savings
- Need to decrease or eliminate medication errors
- Improving documentation efficiency by removing paper charting
- Enhancing accessibility to quality health care

Medical technology needs to be fully integrated with a larger system within an institution to support the continuum of patient care. This connection provides information sharing throughout each stage of the treatment period and eventually allows for the collection of statistical data at a later date.

Next, medical technology has to support the user's ability to navigate without difficulty. The goal here is to not slow down the pace of the medical environment but allow for increasing efficiency so that technology is seamless. These qualities then allow for real-time data and real-time decision-making capabilities while reducing the risk of errors or redundancy.

There are a few gaps that remain on the IT front of the medical environment that have their roots in the **computerized physician order entry (CPOE)** arena. In some instances, CPOE software is not able to meet the needs of various interdisciplinary roles in the OR. The reason for this is that it tends to favor the inpatient setting.

Health Care Information Technology

Health care IT (HIT) has characteristics that are steeped in supporting broad processes or functions.

HIT is software that can perform operations associated with:

- Admissions
- Scheduling
- Clinical documentation
- Pharmacy
- Laboratory
- Clinical Information Technology

Clinical IT (CIT) concentrates on a particular set of clinical tasks, instruments, equipment, and imaging.

Radio Frequency Identification

Radio frequency identification (RFID) provides support for real-time surgery scheduling. This technology has been shown to drastically enhance the structure and functions within medical software. RFID functions on wireless networks and helps to "tag" items and track the movement of the items as they remain on or leave a particular unit. This may be especially important when tracking equipment or supplies that are used to care for the patient or during a surgical procedure.

Nurses will need to stay current with IT trends and engage in ongoing education and exposure to technology. Continuing education and training can be accomplished through independent reading, e-learning, and live classroom instruction.

Finally, nurses may encounter a broad range of technologies including:

- Robots
- Medication delivery devices
- Instruments
- Biotechnology and nanotechnology
- Digital tracking
- Mobile and wireless devices
- Nurses and Informatics

Nurses may assist in the development of standards for EHR (electronic health record) or other clinically based IT systems that nurses utilize for their sphere of health care. In today's landscape, many nursing applications fall into a variety of categories including:

- Internet-based patient education systems
- EHR
- Telemedicine and telenursing

These systems have the capacity to exchange information and enable the decision-making process to progress along the continuum.

Some nurses possess a master's degree in informatics and also work in a variety of roles to assist with development of clinical systems designed to support nurse activities including:

- Business or clinical analyst
- Project management
- Software developer

These systems are designed to accommodate patient education resources, nursing procedures, and critical pathways, to name a few.

Nurses may also serve in the role of perioperative robotics nurse specialist. As robotic surgery utilization continues to evolve into standard practice, the robotics nurse specialist supports a variety of tasks ranging from scheduling maintenance to assisting during surgery.

Legal Responsibilities

The nurse must uphold and answer to certain legal rights and responsibilities within their profession. From simple things like managing a patient's property to more complicated issues such as reporting abuse and neglect, the nurse has a legal responsibility to act, or their license could be in danger.

Nurses need a knowledge of the common legal terminology in their practice. The following is a list of terms the nurse should know:

- **Common law**: Common law is based on legal precedents or previously decided cases in courts of law.

- **Statutory law**: These are laws based on a state's legislative actions or any other legislative body's actions.

- **Constitutional law**: Laws based on the content of the Constitution of the United States of America are referred to as constitutional law.

- **Administrative law**: For a nurse, this is a type of law passed down from a ruling body such as a state nursing association. For example, each state's nursing board passes down regulations on continuing education requirements for licensed nurses.

- **Criminal law**: This type of law involves the arrest, prosecution, and incarceration of those who have broken the law. Such offenses as felonies and misdemeanors are covered under criminal law.

- **Liability**: Nurses are liable for their actions while practicing. Thorough documentation and patient charting are important. If an act is not charted, it was not done, so to speak. Nurses must protect themselves legally to maintain their practice.

- **Tort**: In a nursing context, this legal term refers to nursing practice violations such as malpractice, negligence, and patient confidentiality violations.

- **Unintentional tort**: Negligence and malpractice may be unintentional forms of tort.

- **Intentional tort**: On the other hand, torts may be proven to be intentional, including such violations as false imprisonment, privacy breaches, slander, libel, battery, and assault. A nurse using a physical restraint without meeting protocol or getting a physician's order is guilty of false imprisonment. Slander is a form of defamation in which the person makes false statements that are verbal, and libel is written defamation.

A nurse is legally responsible for maintaining an active licensure according to their state's regulatory board's laws. Failure to maintain licensure requirements such as continuing education credits will result in disciplinary action. Nursing licenses may be revoked or suspended because of disciplinary actions.

Nurses must report abuse, neglect, gunshot wounds, dog bites, and communicable diseases. Nurses are also legally mandated to report other healthcare providers whom they suspect may be abusing drugs or alcohol while practicing, because they are putting patients and themselves at risk.

Nurses have a legal obligation to accept the patient assignments given to them, if they believe they are appropriate and it is within their scope of practice to perform duties related to these patients. However, if they are assigned tasks that they are not prepared to perform, they must notify their supervisors and seek assistance

Laws at the national, state, and local level must be complied with by practicing nurses. Such laws include those in relation to the Centers for Medicare and Medicaid services. Another example would be adhering to local laws regarding the disposal of biohazardous waste.

Legal Reporting Obligations

Reporting patient information and work issues in a timely manner and using the correct route on the chain of command are a legal obligation of nurses. Not reporting important information could result in serious ramifications and punitive action for the nurse, up to loss of employment and/or revocation of certification. When important information goes unreported, it can result in patient harm or unresolved conflicts that turn into bigger problems to deal with later on. Addressing patient issues and resolving conflicts all start with accurate and timely reporting.

A basic definition of a **report** is the relaying of information that one has observed or heard. When this report is given to an authority figure who can intervene, it will contain different elements, such as patient name, situation, time of event, and circumstances surrounding the event.

As one shift ends and another begins, there is a **handoff report** that is given from the off-going team to the oncoming team. The nurse who has completed the shift will tell the nurse beginning the next shift all pertinent information related to each individual patient. Another type of reporting is the exchange of smaller pieces of information between members of the healthcare team that occurs throughout a shift.

In the handoff report, the nurse should strategically relay information in a simple, concise manner that is easily understood by the oncoming nurse. It can be easy to get carried away with reporting and include every little detail of the day, opinions about patients or other coworkers, and stories of particular conversations or interactions that occurred during the shift. These superfluous details should be limited, and the report should be kept to the essential items only.

Some organizations employ the **SBAR method** to help guide communication. SBAR is an acronym for situation, background, assessment, and recommendation. An SBAR report starts with the situation: why is this communication necessary? The background is a brief explanation of the circumstances leading up to the situation. The assessment is what the reporter thinks the issue is, and the recommendation is what the reporter needs in order to correct the situation.

In addition to reporting patient information, the documenting of patient information and interventions performed is also important. A patient's chart is a legal record of observations about the patient and any care given for the patient. Most facilities use an electronic health record, which the nurse will generally be trained to use as a part of new employee orientation. Documentation may include time of observation, time task was performed, what was done, how it was done, and reaction to intervention.

There are various charting systems used to document patient data by patient care facilities. Documentation requirements will be dictated by facility policy and regulatory guidelines. Two methods are used: charting by exception and comprehensive charting.

Charting by Exception

Charting by exception means that besides recording of vital signs, only abnormal findings are documented. This charting method is somewhat controversial as so much information about the patient is usually left out. It is sometimes argued that this is the safer way to chart, as only what is deviant from normal is noted, and thus, there is less room for documentation errors. The normal is assumed, unless otherwise noted. This method also saves time, as less information needs to be documented, leaving more time for patient care.

Comprehensive Charting

Some facilities prefer a **comprehensive method** of documentation, charting everything about the patient—normal and abnormal—in a very thorough manner. This way, when the patient's chart must be reviewed, especially in the case of a safety incident (e.g., a pressure sore develops or a patient falls), all details surrounding the event should be present in the medical record. This method works as long as everything is actually documented, although it can be quite time-consuming and take away from patient care time.

Documentation provides a defense for healthcare workers and patients in the case of patient incidents to show what was done for the patient. There is an adage that says, "If it wasn't charted, it didn't happen." The nurse needs to be mindful that the medical record is a legal document—a complete, thorough, and accurate documentation of care, according to facility policy.

Performance Improvement

Performance improvement is a mechanism to continuously review and improve processes in a system to ensure that work is completed in the most cost-effective manner while producing the best possible outcomes. Healthcare facilities are constantly hoping to drive down cost and increase reimbursements while delivering the highest quality of healthcare and utilizing analytical methods to achieve this. These analyses and implementations may be done by top administrative employees at the organization and be executed across the healthcare system, or within a particular department. Leadership support is always crucial for positive change to occur and sustain itself.

All processes should be regularly monitored for opportunities for improvement. Common opportunities include areas of reported patient dissatisfaction; federal, state, or internal benchmarks that are not being met; areas of financial loss; and common complaints among staff. While multiple opportunities for improvement may exist, focusing on one at a time usually produces the greatest outcome. When choosing a process to improve, it is important to select a process that can actually be changed by the members involved (i.e., medical staff often do not have control over external funding sources). Processes where minimal resources are required for change, but that can produce positive end results, are also preferable to costlier improvements. Once the process has been selected, a group of stakeholders that are regularly involved in the process should map out each step of the process while noting areas of wasted resource or process variation. From here, stakeholders can develop a change to test.

The **PDCA cycle** provides a framework for implementing tests of change. Plan, the first step, involves planning the change. This will include accounting for all workflow changes, the staff members involved, and logistics of implementation. It should also include baseline data relating to the problem. Do, the second step, involves implementing the change. During this step, data collection is crucial. For example, if a department believes that implementing mobile work stations will decrease nurses' wait time between patients, the department should keep a detailed record of the time spent with and between each patient. Check, the third step, involves checking data relating to the change with the baseline data and determining if the change improved the process. Act, the final step, involves making the change permanent and monitoring it for sustainability.

Evidence-Based Practice

Evidence-based practice (EBP) is a research-driven and facts-based methodology that allows healthcare providers to make scientifically supported, reliable, and validated decisions in delivering care. EBP takes into account

31

rigorously tested, peer-reviewed, and published research relating to the case; the knowledge and experience of the healthcare provider; and clinical guidelines established by reputable governing bodies. This framework allows healthcare providers to reach case resolutions that result in positive patient outcomes in the most efficient manner. This, in turn, allows the organization to provide the best care using the least resources.

There are seven steps to successfully utilizing EBP as a methodology in the nursing field. First, the work culture should be one of a "spirit of inquiry." This culture allows staff to ask questions to promote continuous improvement and positive process change to workflow, clinical routines, and non-clinical duties. Second, the PICOT framework should be utilized when searching for an effective intervention, or working with a specific interest, in a case. The **PICOT framework** encourages nurses to develop a specific, measurable, goal-oriented research question that accounts for the patient population and demographics (P) involved in the case, the proposed intervention or issue of interest (I), a relevant comparison (C) group in which a defined outcome (O) has been positive, and the amount of time (T) needed to implement the intervention or address the issue. Once this question has been developed, staff can move onto the third step, which is to research. In this step, staff will explore reputable sources of literature to find studies and narratives with evidence that supports a resolution for their question.

Once all research has been compiled, it must be thoroughly analyzed. This is the fourth step. This step ensures that the staff is using unbiased research with stringent methodology, statistically significant outcomes, reliable and valid research designs, and that all information collected is actually applicable to their patient. For example, if a certain treatment worked with statistical significance in a longitudinal study of pediatric patients with a large sample size, and all other influencing variables were controlled for, this treatment may not necessarily work in a middle-aged adult. Therefore, though the research collected is scientifically backed and evidence-based for a pediatric population, it does not support EBP for an older population. The fifth step is to integrate the evidence to create a treatment or intervention plan for the patient. The sixth step is to monitor the implementation of the treatment or intervention and evaluate whether it was associated with positive health outcomes in the patient. Finally, practitioners have a moral obligation to share the results with colleagues at the organization and across the field, so that it may be best utilized (or not) for other patients.

Evidence-Based Practice Flowchart

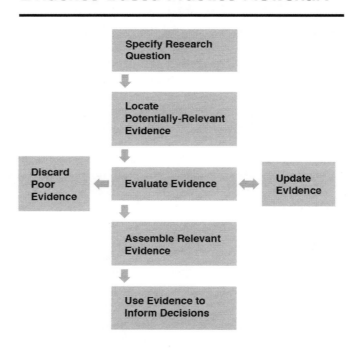

Referral Process

As patient advocates, nurses should be knowledgeable about referring clients when a need arises. The nurse is aware of many branches of the healthcare tree that are designed to assist with each patient's specific needs. A referral is a method by which the nurse contacts another member of the healthcare team to meet the patient's care needs in the most appropriate setting. This is part of care coordination and must happen throughout all stages of the client's continuum of care. Case managers play a key role in making appropriate referrals.

Referral occurs during the first stage of the nursing process: assessment. The nurse assesses the patient and identifies a need. For example, a school nurse may become aware of students who have learning or developmental disabilities. In these cases, the nurse may refer the child and their parents to a speech therapist, a language therapist, or a developmental therapist, depending on the case.

In the hospital environment, the nurse may recognize the need for an auxiliary team and refer the client to them. Such **auxiliary teams** include the palliative care and hospice team, respiratory therapy, physical and occupational therapy, and speech/language therapy. Community resources should be used when appropriate, such as extended-care therapy, social service support, and shelters for the homeless and disadvantaged. Patients may also need spiritual care, in which case clergy can be requested to make a bedside visit.

With any referral, the nurse must follow the appropriate protocols and remain within their scope of practice. Other members of the health care team such as physicians and nursing management should be consulted. Doctor's orders must be obtained where necessary.

After the referral has been made, it is vital that the nurse or case manager evaluates the patient for their response to care. Evaluation is a key component of the nursing process. Without evaluating for effectiveness, the process is incomplete. Only after evaluation has shown effectiveness and the patient is on their way to recovery can the plan of care be deemed successful.

Resource Management

As managers of client care, nurses must decide which supplies, materials, and equipment are necessary to fulfill the patient's needs as part of the preliminary and ongoing client evaluation. They do this by assessing and determining the patient's condition, at time of primary contact. This involves measuring and recording a patient's vital signs using healthcare tools such as stethoscopes, blood pressure cuffs and thermometers, as well as other patient care equipment, medical technology, and devices. After this initial determination, the next step is ensuring that the patient is supplied with the proper resources, such as patient lifts, ventilators, compression devices, or catheters.

Each nursing team member has varying skills and duties according to the training and degrees he or she received. These skill sets are matched with the client care requirements in the healthcare setting. Depending on the training received, a nurse will be licensed to handle a specific range of materials and supplies. **Nursing assistive personnel (NAPs)** are responsible for providing support services such as assistance with daily living activities, basic hygiene, and comfort care. It is important for all team members to understand how to utilize these associated materials efficiently and effectively.

Nurses should go over all the functions of the patient care materials with the NAPs. A good knowledge check is to quiz or question staff members on the various medical devices under their care. This provides an extra level of patient safety, ensuring that all team members are aware of the required equipment and how to utilize it correctly.

The term **cost-effective** means that the cost of a product or service is not too high for what is being purchased. Therefore, a **cost-benefit ratio** refers to weighing the value or likely costs of a project or plan with its desired benefit. Contrary to what might seem logical, effective patient care with a good cost-benefit ratio is not necessarily

always least expensive. For example, it has been shown that the length of time between some routine tests could be altered, such as a Pap smear screening, which has been determined to be just as effective to get checked once every two years instead of annually for most women. Regardless, patient care and services must be as cost-efficient as possible while still maintaining high quality standards and client needs requirements.

As a result, providing cost-effective healthcare is often a balancing act performed by all involved. Client care planning by nurses and other members of the healthcare team is determined according to what they deem suitable, economical, and cost beneficial while still maintaining optimal care quality and results. Therefore, the nursing team must carefully select therapies, interventions, and resources that are not only cost-effective, but also the most useful and applicable based on the patient's needs.

For instance, nurses could determine the costs of patient falls within their facility and show how nursing assistance could help prevent them. Another example would be to use cost-analysis data to determine the cost benefit and birth outcome (premature vs normal births) for pregnant teens who received prenatal care in a school setting compared those who received routine care. A third example would be assessing the rate of various health issues in their communities such as smoking, car accidents, elderly injuries, teen drinking, and drug usage and determining how nursing intervention could help improve these outcomes, ultimately decreasing the rate of admissions at their facility.

Safety and Infection Control

Accident/Error/Injury Prevention

The safety of both patients and team members is a major concern for healthcare organizations. Nurses must have an understanding and the necessary skills to prevent accidents, errors, and injuries.

The majority of accidents that occur in the older population happen in their homes, with falls being the most common accident. **Accident prevention** involves maintaining a clean home and living area and recognizing potential hazards. In addition, individuals should be knowledgeable and aware of their level of health and their own body's capabilities and weaknesses. Keeping regular appointments at the physician's office and following any medication regime correctly will keep one's health in check. It is important for people to understand and be aware of potential side effects of any medications that they may be taking. Recognizing a side effect could be a way to prevent an accident, especially if it relates to mental status or mobility. For example, blood-pressure medications have the potential to lower blood pressure to the point of the person passing out, ultimately causing a fall. Informal caregivers such as family members should check on elderly family to ensure they are able to continue taking care of themselves and to survey the home for safety hazards.

If an older adult is still living in their home, the following measures should be addressed to avoid accidents related to poisoning, burns, hypothermia, and falls. The main causes of poisoning in adults aged sixty-five and older are medicines and gases. Gases would include carbon monoxide and pipeline gases, such as propane or natural gas for heating the home. Fuel-burning devices should be checked regularly for proper functioning. Chimneys and flues should be cleaned once a year.

Older adults are often on a complicated medication regime involving multiple pills, various dosages, and the different times of the day and week that they should be taken. Medicines should be taken exactly as prescribed, and an organized schedule should be in place to prevent mistakes. One example for organizing medications is a pillbox that has individual compartments for each day of the week.

Burns and scalding in the home can be prevented if water heaters are not set too high, and if the cold water is turned on first. Kettles should be avoided if possible. If necessary, spout-filling kettles, cordless kettles, or wall-

mounted heaters can be used instead. Items in the kitchen and the flow of the kitchen should allow for the least amount of distance for carrying hot food or beverages. On the stove, rear burners should be used and handles should be kept away from the edges in order to avoid accidentally knocking a pan off the stove.

An additional accident not often thought of in the older population is hypothermia, which means the body's temperature drops below 95 °F. Strategies to prevent hypothermia in the elderly include making sure the home is heated properly in colder weather, providing several layers of clothing, encouraging movement and exercise around the home to increase body heat, and making sure there's enough food and drink available.

As previously discussed, falls are the most common accident in the older adult population. Whether the person lives in their home or in a care facility, there are preventative measures that should be put into place.

Fall-prevention interventions include:

- Identification of patients at high risk for falls
- Assessment of the patient's room or environment for hazards that can be removed, such as:
  - Rugs
  - Slippery floors
  - Clutter
  - Poor lighting
- Use of assistive devices, such as:
  - Canes, used for stability
  - Walkers, used for balance because of their wide base
  - Reachers or grabbers, used to pick up items off of the floor or reach items on a shelf
  - Gait belts, used with an aide or caregiver, placed around the patient's waist to assist in walking or when standing up from a sitting position
  - Railings in bathrooms, hallways, and tubs
- Proper footwear is worn, such as rubber-soled shoes
- Staff, family-member, and patient education on fall-prevention strategies
- Assistance for patients with daily activities and routines if necessary
- Stairways that are well lit, have railings, and are lined with nonslip flooring

Fall prevention for bed-ridden patients includes:

- Keep two side rails up at all times when a patient is in bed.
- Keep the call light and personal items on a table within reach of the patient's bed.
- Place bed alarms on the patient's bed to alert the staff of any attempt to get out of bed.
- Offer toileting at least every two hours to prevent patients from getting up without assistance.

Falling with a Patient

Sometimes it becomes necessary to assist a person to the ground safely if it becomes clear that they are about to fall. When standing in front or behind the falling person, spreading one's legs shoulder width apart allows for a wide base of support. Try to keep an arm under their shoulders or under their arms and ease them to the floor. Always attempt to protect their head first, and try to direct them away from hard objects, such as furniture.

Healthcare facilities should identify which patients are at a higher risk for falls, as these patients will require special fall precautions. Some facilities have signs on patients' doors that say "Fall Risk," or a patient may wear a certain color bracelet as a reminder to staff and/or family. Keep in mind that all patients are at risk for a fall, especially if they are elderly. Staff will be educated regarding how much assistance is needed for each patient. For example, patient A may be able to walk with assistance or walk with stand-by assistance. Patient B may need assistance x 2, or two staff persons, to help transfer.

Assistance for Ambulation

The types of assistance needed for ambulation are as follows:

- **Standby assistance (SBA)**: This patient does not require any assistance to move and can walk independently, though someone should be standing by to monitor. A gait belt is not required.

- **Contact-guard assistance (CGA)**: This patient requires an assistant to be within reach in case of a fall. These patients can walk independently but have a high risk for falls.

- **Minimum assistance (MIN)**: This patient needs a little support when moving about, and an example would be the use of a gait belt.

- **Maximum assistance (MAX)**: This patient is unstable and may not be able to walk or stand without help. At least two staff persons are needed for assistance.

Patients who use assistive devices for ambulation need instruction on how to use them and may need reminders to ensure they are still using the device properly. It is important to stay with a patient who is learning to use an assistive device. A gait belt should be used while the patient is learning to use a walker.

Canes

The purpose of the cane is to help stabilize a leg that is weak. Steps for using a cane are listed below:

- Have the patient place the cane in their strong hand and move the cane out one step while stepping the weak leg out with the cane.
- With their weight on the cane, have them step out with their stronger leg.
- After each step, the patient can rest to ensure they feel balanced.

A Walker Without Wheels

A walker is used to give the patient extra stability when a patient is weak in both legs or has trouble with balance when walking. Steps for use are listed below:

- Instruct the patient to stand inside the walker while holding onto the walker with both hands.

- Have the patient lift and move the walker forward so that the back legs of the walker line up with their toes.

- With their weight on their stronger leg, have the patient take a step with their weaker leg while gripping the handrails of the walker. They should step into the center of the walker.

- Finally, their stronger leg steps up to evenly meet their other leg. They may rest in between steps if necessary.

Care must be taken to ensure that the flooring surface is flat when using a walker or a cane. Trips or falls can occur if rugs or thick carpet get caught in the walker or cane. Some walkers have wheels on the bottoms of the legs so that a patient can push the walker while walking. The wheels may be on all four legs or just the front two legs. The patient's weight is placed on the walker with their hands, and this helps with extra support as they lean forward. These types of walkers are not lifted during walking and allow for a bit faster pace. Make sure while walking that the walker does not move too far ahead of the patient.

Here are steps for moving from a chair to standing with a walker:

- Place the walker in front of the patient and have the patient place their hands on the arms of the chair.
- Assist the patient with standing up.
- Encourage the patient to place one hand at a time onto the handgrips of the walker.

- Ensure the patient feels steady and is not dizzy before walking.

Use of Crutches

Crutches can be used on a short-term basis when a patient has limitations for weight bearing on a leg. An example would be a patient that has a cast or a splint on their ankle, foot, or leg. Putting weight on an injured leg may interfere with healing and may be painful. A physical therapist will be responsible for fitting the crutches. Ensure the crutches are the appropriate length for the patient. The armpit, or axilla, rests should fit into the patient's armpit without lifting the shoulders and without causing stooping. The pads should be one to one-and-a-half inches below the axilla. If the crutches are too tall, the patient could trip over the crutches and too much pressure will be placed in their armpits. If the crutches are too short, leaning over will put unnecessary strain on the patient's back. The handgrips should also be adjusted so that the arms are slightly bent at the elbow. The grip should be comfortable.

Crutch Gaits

The **three-point crutch gait** helps with an inability to bear weight on one leg, such as with fractures, pain, or amputation.

- Move both crutches and the weaker leg forward. Then place all weight down on the crutches and move the stronger or unaffected leg forward. Repeat this pattern.
- Good balance is required for this type of gait.

The **two-point crutch gait** is used for weakness in both legs and poor coordination.

- Move the left crutch and right foot together.
- Then move the right crutch and left foot together.
- Repeat the pattern.
- This is a faster gait but difficult to learn.

The **swing-through crutch gait** helps with an inability to bear full weight on both legs.

- Move both crutches forward then swing both legs forward at the same time. The legs must swing past the crutches.
- This is the fastest gait but requires a lot of arm strength and energy.
- It will not be used in the elderly.

The **swing-to crutch gait** is used for patients who have weakness in both legs.

- Move both crutches forward.
- Put weight on both crutches and swing both legs forward together to the crutches. The legs must not swing past the crutches.
- This requires good arm strength, so it most likely will not be used for the elderly.

Standing up with crutches:

- Have the patient hold both crutches on their injured side, and then lean forward off of the chair while pushing off with their arm from the chair.
- Once standing, place the crutches under the arms.

Sitting down with crutches:

- Have the patient place both crutches on their injured side.
- Holding the handgrips in one hand, they can use their other hand to brace on the chair as they sit.

Using crutches on stairs should not be attempted until the patient is confident on level ground. Until then, or at any time, the patient can also slide up or down the stairs on their bottom. Also, the railing of the stairs can be used with one hand while holding the crutches in the other arm.

- The crutches should stay on the step the patient is standing on.
- The good leg is brought up to the next step while letting the injured leg lag behind.
- As the patient straightens up to their good leg, they should bring the crutches and their injured leg up onto the step.

Going down steps:

- Have the patient place the crutches on the next step lower and bring their injured foot forward.

- Next, the good foot is moved down to meet the crutches on the lower step. The weight is on the crutches at this time.

Transfer Devices

Nurses will be educated on the lift and transfer equipment available in their facility, and this equipment will be used every day to ensure the safety of patients and staff. Using **transfer devices** will greatly reduce the risk of lower-back stress and injury. Transfer devices eliminate manual lifting and transfers, as well as manual transfers in confined spaces, and they reduce the number of transfers needed per task. For example, it may normally take three steps to move a patient without a transfer device. With a transfer device, however, the task can be completed in only one step. Types of **protective transfer devices** include hoists, walking belts with handles (called gait belts), shower chairs, repositioning devices, and weighing devices that use slings. Examples of **repositioning devices** may be a draw sheet, a roller board, or a sliding sheet. Beds can have scales built in so that a patient can be weighed while staying in their bed. Also, there are scales that are large and wide, which will accommodate a wheelchair-bound or morbidly obese patient.

Fire Hazards

Recognizing fire hazards in the workplace is important in the prevention of fires and the promotion of safety for patients and employees. Staff will be trained on the fire policy and regular drills should be performed so that each staff person's role is known and practiced. Below are some potential workplace fire hazards:

- Candles may not be allowed in certain facilities. If they are allowed, make sure they are never left unattended, are not within reach of children or pets, and are not placed near windows or material that could burn.

- To mitigate electrical hazards, unplug appliances when not in use and keep them clean and in good working order. If there is concern about a piece of electrical equipment that is not working properly, report it and stop using it. Keep three feet of space around heaters. Do not overload outlets with too many cords, and do not pinch cords behind devices or furniture. Do not use cords that are cracked or broken.

- Use of a stove and cooking appliances may not be allowed in certain facilities, but these guidelines are useful for anyone that may be cooking:

- Never leave cooking unattended.

- Don't cook if too sleepy or if taking medication that causes drowsiness.

- Use back burners on the stove to prevent spills and burns.

- Turn handles away from the front of the stove.

- Don't leave towels or potholders laying on the stovetop.

- Keep the oven and stove clean and wipe up spills.

- In case of a grease fire, do not use a fire extinguisher. Smother the fire in the pot or pan with a lid and turn off the burner.

- For an oven fire, turn off the oven and leave the door closed.

- For a microwave fire, leave the door closed, turn off the microwave, and unplug it.

- Healthcare facilities are smoke-free, but there may be designated smoking areas outside. Ensure that guests or employees use the appropriate area and extinguish the cigarette completely.

- Do not allow smoking near someone who is using oxygen, because oxygen can increase the strength of a fire.

Each year, there are many structure fires in health care facilities. These fires happen in nursing homes, hospitals or hospice houses, mental health facilities, and doctors' offices or clinics. Cooking equipment is the primary cause of fires. Other causes of fires include clothes dryers or washers, intentional fires, smoking materials, heating equipment, electrical distribution or lighting equipment, and playing with a heat source.

Employees will be educated on the location of fire alarms, any alarm systems that are in place, sprinklers, and fire extinguishers. The danger of a fire is mainly from the smoke it creates. Smoke can travel quickly in a fire and can affect areas in a building that are not close to the fire itself. With elderly and sick patients, lack of mobility inhibits a quick escape; therefore, proper evacuation and rescue planning is essential. When responding to a fire or an alarm, always treat it as a true emergency. Call 911 even if an alarm system is monitored and activated, to ensure that help is on the way. If it is a false alarm, the fire department may still search to make sure everything is safe.

Facilitating Correct Use of Infant and Child Car Seats

As per the National Highway Traffic Safety Administration (NHTSA), car seats that are used and fitted appropriately can considerably lower infant and child death and injury in motor vehicle accidents. Estimates state that the proper use of infant and child car seats can prevent infant death by 71 percent and the death of toddlers and young children under 3 years of age by 54 percent.

It is imperative that infant seats and car seats are not only properly installed, but also that they are the correct size for the infant/child using them in order to be effective against injures and death. For instance, rear-facing infant seats should be mounted in the back seat facing the rear of the automobile until the child is about 2 years of age and around 20 to 30 pounds. Convertible safety seats can be installed as either rear or forward facing. In most cases, regular car seat belts can be used when the child reaches at least 40 pounds and about 4 years of age. Nurses should go over these various safety regulations with patients who are parents-to-be or caring for infants or young children to make sure they are aware of the correct ways to install and use car seats.

Factors Related to Mental Status That May Contribute to the Potential for Accident or Injury

A variety of issues related to a patient's mental status can influence the potential for injury. The American Psychiatric Association's (APA) *Diagnostic and Statistical Manual of Mental Disorders (DSM) V* recognizes four main mental illness categories: thought disorders, mood disorders, behavioral disorders and mixed mental health disorders. Agitated and altered thought processes can result from a variety of factors and causes, including hallucinations, dementia, concussions and other issues that affect the brain such as a tumor or trauma.

It is important for nursing team members to recognize the signs and symptoms of impaired cognition such as memory loss and poor hygiene, as well as signs and symptoms of acute and chronic mental illness, which could

indicate conditions such as schizophrenia, depression, and bipolar disorder. Impaired cognition, also known as a disturbed thought process, interrupts and distracts a patient's mental and thought abilities, processes and activities. Attributes that could impact safety include short and/or long-term memory loss, mental conflict, a lack of understanding regarding speech and writing, confusion, disorientation, a lack of good judgment and insight, and the inability to perform the basic and vital life skills and activities.

For patients with acute and chronic mental illness, it is important to oversee and gauge their safety needs and changes in terms of their mental status and behaviors at all times. This is done by evaluating the patient's mental capacity through an assessment of the way they look and behave, checking for odd thoughts or viewpoints such as delirium or delusions, their mood, and cognitive functions like alertness and memory. Checking up should be done as often as the nurse deems necessary based on the patient's past and present mental condition. This includes situations such as protecting their safety when experiencing hallucinations or delusions or during the manic phase of bipolar disorder.

Utilizing Facility Client Identification Procedures

Failing to identify patients correctly can cause mistakes and miscalculations regarding medication, transfusions, test procedures and results, procedures involving the wrong person, and discharging infants to the wrong families. It is essential for the patient to be involved in the identification process and utilizing "two patient identifiers" to improve and ensure identification dependability and consistency. Using two identifiers also helps guarantee an accurate match between the service or treatment and the patient, helping to prevent mistakes and improve patient care.

There are a number of patient identifiers depending on the healthcare facility. Some examples include: patient name, birthdate, address, phone number, Social Security Number (SSN), photograph, or their medical record number.

The nursing team must make sure that two of these above identifiers are assigned to each patient according to the facility's policy and that these same two identifiers are linked to the patient's medication, blood product, treatment, procedure, or specimen container via an attached label. It is imperative to always check a client's ID band and make sure it matches the name on the chart and the orders you are carrying out. These identifiers must be used to verify a patient's identity when admitted or transferred to another hospital or care location and prior to caring for the patient. It is important that neither identifier is the patient's room number, which could result in a patient mix-up. The nursing team also needs to be aware of how to integrate automated systems into the patient identification process if used in their facility. These are utilized in order to decrease the likelihood of identification inaccuracies and reduce medication errors. Some examples include the following:

- **Computerized provider order entry (CPOE)**: A system that allows healthcare personnel to enter and send treatment orders electronically.

- **Bar coding**: Computerized reference numbers that contain descriptive and other essential data.

- **Radio Frequency Identification (RFID)**: Wireless technology utilizing radio waves and signals to communicate data.

- **Biometric identification**: The measurement and statistical analysis of a patient's individual features for the purpose of identification.

Identifiers should be listed on an identification band (ID) applied to the patient's wrist. A separate band must also be worn to indicate any known allergies; if the patient does not have any known allergies, a band still must be worn affirming this information. If the patient is predisposed towards falling, a fall risk name band also needs to be worn. Facilities typically assign a specific color for each type of ID band. Often, name bands are white, allergy bands are red and fall risk bands are yellow. Some facilities may also stipulate the exact arm on which each band must be worn. In some facilities, a do not resuscitate (DNR) order is also noted on a specific ID band. Since these ID bands

are so important and imperative to patient safety, they are designed to be waterproof and difficult for the patient to remove.

Protecting Clients from Accident/Error/Injury

Healthcare providers and facilities must ensure that patients, visitors, and employees are safeguarded from injury. Examples of injuries that happen most frequently include burns, falls, electrical shock, accidental poisoning and disaster incidents.

Injuries involving heat can result from defective heating and cooling devices, as well as when these devices are incorrectly applied to the patient, especially when they are affected by a sensory and/or neurological issue that impedes their capacity to recognize and feel bodily harm resulting from the hot or cold therapy. Falls, both with or without injury, are a frequent and expensive accident that affect nearly every healthcare facility. As a result, all patients should undergo fall risk screening when they are admitted, as well as when their condition is flagged to indicate substantial changes in physical, psychological and/or cognitive attributes.

After undergoing the screening process, any patients deemed to be at risk for falling need to be immediately marked and documented to receive special instructions and procedures to prevent them from falling. There are a number of risk factors related to falls that are often included in a falls risk screening and assessment. These include:

- Incontinence: Patients with incontinence issues are more likely to fall than those not affected with these types of bathroom problems. This is usually a result of slipping and rushing to get to a toilet.

- Confusion: Patients who are confused may experience judgment issues and be unaware of environmental hazards that could cause them to fall.

- Poor vision: Those patients with vision issues are more likely to trip over items, especially when in an environment that is new or different. It is important that clients have their eyeglasses nearby and are urged to utilize them.

- Reaction time: Patients who experience reaction times that are slow or delayed are more likely to fall. This occurs more often with elderly patients, who may not react in time to steer clear of something that could cause them to slide or fall, such as a floor that is wet or slippery.

- Age: Patients that are at the greatest risk of falling include the elderly and young children.

- Medications: Patients taking painkillers or other tranquilizing drugs may have side effects causing them to feel disoriented due to sleepiness, dizziness, muscular weakness or orthostatic hypotension, therefore increasing the chance of falling.

- Poor muscular strength, balance, coordination, gait, and range of motion (ROM): Patients with compromised balance, coordination, ability to walk, and range of motion are more likely to fall. One effective strategy is to have them work with a physical therapist to strengthen these functions in order to prevent falls.

- Environmental hazards: The room or area occupied by the patient should be free of clutter and glare, the floor should be kept dry and clean and have adequate lighting and a working nurse call bell. These are all dangers that could exacerbate the chance of a fall. It is considered the nurse's responsibility to make sure the patient's environment is kept free of these types of environmental hazards.

- Past incidence of falls: Patients who have exhibited a prior history of falls, especially those who have fallen more often and in the recent past, are more likely to fall again.

- A fear of falling: It has been found that patients who have indicated they are afraid of falling are at a greater risk of a fall occurrence.

- Certain diseases and disorders: There are a number of diseases and health ailments that can increase the likelihood of a fall, especially those involving the musculoskeletal and/or neurological systems. These include conditions such as muscular dystrophy, Parkinson's disease and seizure disorders.

In addition to these fundamental patient-related factors, there are a number of external and environmental influences that should be considered as risk factors and need to be corrected as soon as possible:

- Insufficient patient footwear: Shoes, slippers and other footgear that do not fit properly, are slippery and/or unsafe in any other way increase the chance of a fall occurring. The items worn by patients on their feet should be skid proof, durable, safe, and the correct size. Skid proof socks are highly recommended to help prevent falls.

- Nonworking and/or incorrect usage of patient equipment: Medical equipment that is not working correctly such as a broken wheelchair or cane can lead to falls. These types of items should be reported at once and taken away for repair until they are authorized as safe to use again. Nurses also need to make sure they are aware of the correct usage of all patient equipment. A patient can fall as a result of a device, such as a mechanical lift being used improperly.

- Not receiving a response to calls for help: Nurses must answer patient calls quickly in order to avert the chance of a patient falling or suffering from some other type of accident or injury.

Besides patient risk assessment, other procedures that nurses can follow to avoid falls and decrease the level of harm caused by a fall include:

- Using supportive equipment such as walkers and canes

- Wearing padded clothing and/or placing padded gym mats next to a patient's bed

- Making sure a patient's bed is not raised too high

- Equipping a bed or chair with an alarm to signal staff when a patient is getting up

- Stepping up the level of patient monitoring and observation so that the patient is checked more often

- Making sure the patient has high toilet seats and grab bars in the bathroom

Providing Patients with Appropriate Methods to Signal Staff Members

It is important that patients have some kind of device nearby to alert nurses that they need something. This is a big step towards preventing accidents and injuries. At the same time, it is the responsibility of the nurse to answer calls for assistance right away so that the patient's needs are quickly addressed and safeguarded against some kind of mishap. The types of signal methods vary by facility and according to each patient and their situation. Nurses need to be aware of the various types and circumstances of clients under their care.

For example, although most of the time patients have the ability to contact a nurse with a call bell and light, there might be some patients who can only vocalize their calls. These types of patients should be positioned near the nurses' station or another high traffic area so they are heard and their needs addressed. Other patients may not be able to alert the nurse on their own at all. Those who are unable to alert the nurse by pressing a call signal or shouting out for help need to be located near the nurses' station or another busy place so that they can be checked frequently. In the case of a power or other failure or system breakdown that renders call bells unusable, patients should be equipped with handheld bells or buzzers to converse with the nursing staff.

Evaluating the Appropriateness of Healthcare Provider's Orders for a Patient

Nurses are responsible for executing two types of tasks: independent and dependent. Those considered independent are patient duties that do not require a doctor's order; those that are dependent are patient duties that can only be administered as per instruction from a doctor or other independent licensed practitioner.

When receiving an order, the nurse is required to make sure it is thorough, appropriate and executed quickly. Nurses should never act on any orders from a healthcare provider that are unclear or inappropriate. Instead, the nurse should follow up on any order that seems uncertain by contacting the HCP right away for an explanation.

For an order of restraints to be considered complete, it must at least include why the order is needed, the kind of restraint required, the length of time it should be used, patient actions that necessitate its usage, and the signature of the person who ordered it. An order for medication must also designate the name of the patient, the dosage, type, how it is administered and how often as well as stating why it was ordered and a signed confirmation of the person who ordered it. Any part of this process that deviates from these requirements or seems incorrect requires intervention from the nurse.

Emergency Response Plan

In the case of an emergency, a nurse must be prepared to recommend certain clients for an immediate discharge, activate the emergency response plan, and participate in disaster drills. Each facility must have plans for emergency situations, and the nurse may be a part of such planning.

Disasters can be internal or external. Examples of internal disasters include fires; violence in the workplace; failure of utilities such as water or electricity; or electrical outage or flooding in the building caused by weather disasters such as tornadoes, hurricanes, or earthquakes. An external disaster can include a serious community event in which a population sustains many injuries. Such events can include mass shootings, train wrecks, and airplane crashes. Acts of terrorism or bioterrorism can affect a facility both internally and externally. Weather events can affect a healthcare facility both internally and externally, depending on the extent of damage that occurs.

An example of an act of terrorism that caused a massive influx of patients to local hospitals was the Route 91 shooting in Las Vegas. This was an external event that caused the activation of certain emergency response plans to deal with the influx of incoming patients. Such events must be discussed as a potential occurrence in each facility. Healthcare facilities must put plans in place to deal with such catastrophes in a smooth, coordinated manner to effectively care for the maximum number of patients.

The hurricanes Irma and Harvey that recently struck the Gulf states are an example of an external weather situation that directly affected those communities with electrical power losses, flooding, destruction of property, and injuries and illness related to the flooding and high winds. The healthcare system must be ready for these situations with an effective emergency response plan.

One of the first steps when activating an emergency response plan is to discharge patients who are medically stable enough, in order to clear beds for incoming patients. Facilities only have a set number of beds available for patients. When the influx of patients is greater than the number of beds available, a crisis arises. When a catastrophic event occurs, the nurse is part of a triaging process that determines whether certain patients can be relocated to open beds for incoming patients. Unstable clients will stay put; they are at the top of the rung of patients to stay. Stable patients may be discharged only if it is likely they will remain stable without ongoing nursing and medical care. On the bottom rung below unstable and stable clients are ambulatory and self-care clients. These are patients who are walking around and able to independently care for themselves outside a hospital facility. Ambulatory and self-care patients will be discharged to clear beds for incoming disaster patients.

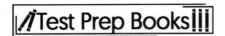
The nurse plays a key role in disaster preparedness and knowing that role is key to a successful execution of each emergency response plan. During a fire, for example, the nurse must competently implement all four elements of the **RACE** acronym, as follows:

- **R** is for rescuing all those in danger, including patients, visitors, and staff.

- **A** is for activating the alarm after those in danger have been cleared.

- **C** is for containing the fire in the smallest possible area. This is accomplished by closing all windows and doors, preventing the fire from spreading.

- **E** is for extinguishing the fire if it is small enough and the nurse can do so safely.

Concurrent with knowledge of the RACE acronym during a fire is knowledge of how to use a fire extinguisher. There are five main types of fire extinguishers: Type A, Type B, Type C, Type AB, and Type ABC. **Type A extinguishers** are used for common solids such as paper, mattresses, and clothing. **Type B extinguishers** target oil, gasoline, and grease fires, common in kitchens. **Type C extinguishers** fight electrical fires. **Type AB extinguishers** combines the roles of Type A and Type B, while **Type ABC extinguishers** combines all three. Type ABC is the most commonly seen due to its ability to extinguish all types of fire sources. This is likely the type of extinguisher located within a hospital facility for that reason.

When attempting to use a fire extinguisher, the nurse must remember the acronym **PASS**, which describes the following steps for effective use:

- **P** is for pull, pulling the pin to begin using the fire extinguisher.

- **A** is for aim, aiming directly at the bottom of the fire.

- **S** is for squeeze, squeezing the trigger to release the spray.

- **S** is for sweep, moving from side to side across the base of the fire. This will effectively extinguish the fire.

Along with knowing their role when fire threatens the safety of patients, the nurse must also know what to do when the hospital's utilities fail. Electricity powers many life-supporting machines for patients, such as oxygen delivery systems and mechanical ventilation machines. Most hospitals have back-up generators to keep these machines going when the power goes down. The nurse must alert maintenance and management immediately if the power goes off. Many hospitals have special red outlets into which important patient machinery should be plugged for just that reason.

There are times in the workplace when the nurse may encounter violence, harassment, or aggression. The source of these behavioral conflicts may be a visitor, fellow staff member, or patient. Causes of workplace violence may include delirium and disorientation, especially in hospitalized patients with illness and medication side effects in play. Visitors and family members may become disruptive for any number of reasons, including misunderstandings about care during high-stress and emotionally charged healthcare situations involving a loved one. Whatever the cause, the nurse must work to deescalate the situation verbally as well as enlisting help from team members and hospital security staff.

Each healthcare facility will have explicit guidelines that must be followed in the case of a weather emergency, such as a hurricane, tornado, or earthquake. Closing windows, doors, and curtains as well as moving patients to the appropriate predetermined safe place are all part of the nurse's role during these situations.

For all these emergencies, a chain of command needs to be established long before a catastrophic event occurs. This lays out in clear terms who is in charge during the disaster, who needs to know what, who takes on leadership

roles, and so on. Clearly defining the roles of each team member and rehearsing what will happen by using emergency drills ensures that things are run smoothly and efficiently in the event of a disaster.

Ergonomic Principles

Ergonomics is the science of matching the physical requirements of a job to the physical abilities of the worker. Musculoskeletal injuries can occur if physical demands are greater than the employee's physical capabilities. Body mechanics refers to how the body moves during activities of daily living. Understanding and practicing the use of proper body mechanics is imperative to preventing associate injury. The physical requirements of a job are explained during the interview process, and the physical capabilities of the associate are assessed during the pre-employment physical examination. Education on the use of proper body mechanics begins in nursing school and continues during employment. New associate orientation should include validation of proper body mechanics.

Principles of Body Mechanics

One way the nurse can take care of themselves is to employ proper body mechanics. The job of the nurse is often highly physical in nature, with much time being spent on turning patients in bed, transferring them from the bed to the chair or bedside commode, and assisting with **ambulating** (walking) patients to the bathroom or around the unit. Moving another person, especially one with limited ability to assist, can be extremely difficult and taxing on the body.

Depending on the facility in which the nurse works, different equipment will be available to assist with moving patients. Becoming acquainted with how and when to use this equipment will be part of the nurse's training in that facility. The nurse should use this equipment whenever possible, even if it takes a little more time to do so.

Basic **safe lifting techniques** include lifting with one's legs, not one's back, avoiding twisting and awkward positions when lifting and moving the patient, and keeping the back upright as much as possible to avoid straining. The individual should make sure to keep their feet as balanced as possible and not rush lifting or moving a patient. The nurse should ask for help from other nurses whenever needed to avoid injury.

The medical environment can present potential hazards that increase risk of injury to the nurse. Examples of these are transferring the patient from the cart to the operating room bed, positioning the patient, and standing for prolonged periods. Repetitive motions, such as turning the head to one side for visualization of monitoring equipment and holding a retractor for an extended time period, can also present ergonomic hazards. Proper body mechanics should be consistently followed to prevent injury. There are three foundational principles of proper body mechanics that should be followed by nurses. First, bending at the hips and knees instead of at the waist uses the large muscle groups of the legs instead of the back muscles, and helps to prevent back injury. Second, standing with feet at about shoulder-width apart helps to reduce risk of injury by providing foundational support. Finally, the nurse should keep the back, neck, pelvis, and feet aligned when turning or moving. Twisting and bending at the neck and waist can increase risk of associate injury.

As a standard of care, many healthcare institutions have mandated use of **safe patient mobilization (SPM) equipment** in an effort to reduce associate injuries, as well as to promote patient safety. SPM equipment in the medical environment can be used during patient transfers and positioning. Slide sheets are often used in patient transfers. These sheets are placed underneath the patient prior to lateral or vertical transfer. They decrease the surface tension, making transfers easier for the associates. However, since the slide sheets do decrease surface tension, they must be removed after use, so that the patient is not at risk of sliding off the operating room bed.

Inflatable blankets can be placed under the patient to assist in lateral transfers, as well. When engaged, the forced air blanket helps to support the weight of the patient, making lateral transfers easier. The mattress should be deflated after completion of transfer. Another type of SPM equipment is lift equipment. **Lift equipment** works by

placing a sling under the patient's limb or underneath the entire patient, connecting the sling to the lift machine, and programming the machine to lift the body to the desired height. The weight limits of these machines vary, so the nurse must ensure the patient's weight does not exceed the weight limit set by the manufacturer.

Injury Prevention

A member of the healthcare team who is not careful could easily become injured, potentially resulting in physical harm, missed days of work, lost wages, and medical bills. Nurses are at high risk for injury due to the amount of lifting they do during a shift. Using the appropriate lifting techniques can help prevent an injury to the back and strains or sprains to the joints of the body. The nurse should employ assistive devices such as gait belts and mechanical lifting devices whenever possible. It is important to ask for help whenever necessary to prevent injury. The following depicts eight steps to use when lifting a heavy object:

1. Plan for lift and test the load
2. Ask someone for help
3. Get a firm footing
4. Bend your knees
5. Tighten stomach muscles
6. Lift with legs
7. Keep the load close to you
8. Keep your back straight

Handling Hazardous and Infectious Materials

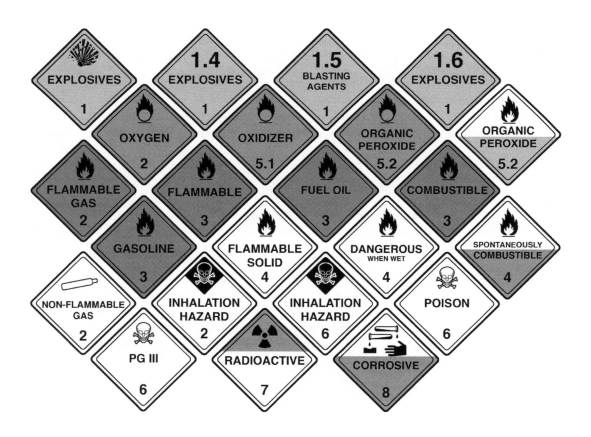

46

According to the Institute of **Hazardous Materials Management (IHMM)**, a hazardous material is defined as "any item that has the potential to cause harm to humans, animals, or the environment, either by itself or through interaction with other factors." A hazardous item may be biological, chemical, radiological, and/or physical in nature. Agencies such as the United States Environmental Protection Agency (EPA) and the Occupational Safety and Health Administration (OSHA) provide regulation and guidelines as to how hazardous materials are handled.

Hazardous materials in the medical environment can include biological, chemical, radiological, and physical hazards. Biological hazardous materials are commonly referred to as **biohazards**. These are materials that present a threat to the health of living things, primarily humans. Biohazards are typically introduced into the medical environment in the form of patient body fluids and excreta. Examples of biohazardous materials are blood, body fluids, viruses, and bacteria. Items in the medical environment that have been exposed to biohazardous materials are considered to be biohazardous as well, until the decontamination process is completed. For example, used surgical instruments are considered biohazardous until they have been cleaned of bioburden and sterilized.

Chemical hazardous materials in the medical environment include solid, liquid, or gas materials that pose a threat to health. Primarily, solid and liquid chemical hazards include materials used to clean, disinfect, and sanitize the medical environment. They may also include cytotoxic and chemotherapy medications. Gas chemicals are primarily anesthetic gases. Containers for chemical hazards are labeled with symbols representing the type of potential hazard, along with instructions for steps to take in the event of exposure.

Radiological hazards found in the medical environment are seen in the forms of thermal, radioactive isotopes, and electromagnetic radiation. The most common thermal radiological hazard is in the form of lasers. The use of lasers exposes the patient and the healthcare team to risk of eye damage, as well as increasing the risk of fire in the operating room. Laser operators must be trained on the correct usage of the laser, along with indicated safety precautions. Radioactive isotopes are used in brachytherapy. **Brachytherapy** is a form of cancer treatment where radioactive beads are inserted near or inside a cancerous tumor in order to deliver a high dose of radiation to the tumor while sparing the surrounding healthy tissue. **Electromagnetic radiation** is seen in the form of X-ray and ultraviolet radiation. During a procedure where electromagnetic radiation is used, the patient is protected by shields and/or drapes specifically designed to minimize exposure to the radiation. The perioperative team utilizes shields, gowns, and eyewear to minimize radiation exposure.

Physical hazards also exist in the medical area. Autoclaves are used to steam sterilize surgical instruments, and this steam can potentially cause burns. Removing surgical instruments straight from the autoclave can cause burns to the hands if the proper gloves are not used. Liquid on the floor can cause someone to slip or fall, causing injury. Handling carbon dioxide tanks or cryogenic material can cause severe burns to the hands if gloves are not worn.

The types of hazards should be discussed at the beginning of employment in the medical environment. This should include identifying the potential hazards and known hazards, steps to minimize exposure to them, and discussing the necessary steps to take in case of exposure. Healthcare facilities are required to provide **material safety data sheets (MSDS)** and keep them in a central area. For most healthcare facilities, education on hazardous materials management is done on an annual basis.

Home Safety

The nurse works to promote patient safety by ensuring their home environment is safe. The nurse will begin this process by first assessing the client's home for safety opportunities. This can be done by walking through the client's home taking mental and written notes as well as interviewing the patient and their caregiver.

The patient themselves must be assessed for their ability to live safely in their own home. Patients with dementia, Alzheimer's, and other cognitive dysfunctions present more of a risk to themselves than a patient whose cognitive

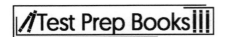

faculties are well intact. The nurse may assess whether the patient is able to live independently, need constant supervision, or need assistance with only a few daily activities. An important consideration is how well the patient can follow their own medication regime. The nurse should consider whether the use of divided days-of-the-week pill boxes would be appropriate, for example. Once the client's cognitive function is assessed and addressed, the nurse can then move on to ensuring the external environment is safe.

The external environment of the patient's home poses many potential safety hazards. The patient may live in a multiple-story house, in which case the stairs present a fall risk for elderly and deconditioned patients. A hand rail may be helpful if it is not already present, as well as safety treads on the staircase. Some patients with chronic conditions that restrict them from climbing up and down stairs may require a chair elevator. The nurse can connect the patient and their family to community resources for such items.

The lighting in the home is as important as the lighting in a hospital room. One of the classic fall prevention tips in the hospital is to ensure the patient's room is adequately lit both in the daytime and at night. The same goes for the client's home. The nurse needs to ensure nightlights are available in rooms that the client may need to ambulate across during the night, such as the bedroom. Visits to the bathroom should be unencumbered and easily navigated, without fall risks in the way. Due to medication and chronic illnesses such as heart failure, visits to the bathroom often increase in the elderly patient, thus increasing fall risk.

The nurse should discourage the use of throw rugs in the homes of patients at risk for a fall. This type of rug can easily catch the client's foot, throwing them off balance and potentially causing a fall.

The house should be well kept, clean, and sanitary. If the client is not able to keep up with their normal housekeeping duties, assistance should be sought. The nurse can, again, connect the client to community resources in this case. Perhaps a church friend, community volunteer, or local housekeeping service may be used if affordable for the client. A cluttered home may present a fall risk, and it also negatively affects the mental health of the client, causing anxiety and depressive symptoms.

Some clients, such as those with diabetes, may have syringes to administer insulin that will need proper disposal. The nurse may provide the client with a sharps container for syringe disposal as well as educating the patient on proper syringe hygiene and disposal. The nurse should ensure that the client understands these concepts to prevent at-home injuries.

Food hygiene is an important topic to address with the client if they are still preparing their own food. Hand hygiene before, after, and during food preparation is vital to preventing the spread of food-borne illnesses. The client should be educated on the proper handling of meats, ensuring that they not only perform frequent hand hygiene, but that they properly sanitize surfaces that raw meat touches, such as cutting boards.

The nurse needs to assess household alarms such as fire, smoke, and carbon monoxide alarms and ensure that they have fresh batteries and are in working order. The client should be educated to monitor these alarms as needed so they are ready to go in the case of a fire or carbon monoxide leak.

Patients receiving oxygen therapy should be educated on proper oxygen use and maintenance of their oxygen tank. They will be taught not to smoke while receiving oxygen, because this is a fire hazard. They will also need to monitor the tank's gauges to make sure they know when they are running low on oxygen and need a replacement tank.

Least Restrictive Restraints and Safety Devices

Restraints can be defined as anything that is used, done, or said to intentionally limits a person's ability to move freely. Restraints, when applied properly, cannot be easily removed or controlled by the person. In addition to physical form, restraints can also be emotional, chemical, or environmental. Use of restraints is very controversial

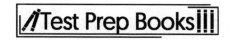

due to the ethical issue of personal freedom. These are a temporary solution to a problem and must always be used as a last resort. Restraints are used to limit a patient's movement to prevent injury to themselves or others, and they always require a physician's order.

Types of restraints include:

- Physical: vests, wrist restraints, straps, or anything that confines the body
- Emotional: verbal cues or emotions used to coerce the patient to act a certain way
- Environmental: side rails, locked doors, closed windows, locked beds
- Chemical: any medication used to restrict a patient's movement

The medical doctor or practitioner is responsible for ordering the use of restraints. Nurses and caregivers are responsible for applying restraints safely and for the management of a patient with a restraint. After an order is given, the physician must visit the patient within twenty-four hours of placing the order to assess its further necessity.

Alternatives to Restraints
Other methods must be tried before restraints. They include:

- Talking with the patient about being cooperative
- Using distractions such as television, music, knitting, and folding towels or cloths
- Placing the patient within view of a caregiver, such as near the main desk
- Having someone sit with the patient
- Moving the patient to a quiet area
- Ensuring that the patient's bathroom needs are being met
- Ensuring personal items are within reach

When to Use Restraints
Each facility will have a specific protocol that must be followed for restraint use. Circumstances under which restraints are used include:

- Signs of patient aggression toward self, staff, or other patients
- Interference with important medical devices, such as an IV or a catheter
- Patient movements that are potentially harmful to their health, or may cause further injury
- Potential for a patient to interfere with a procedure

Applying Restraints

- Always follow the facility's restraint policy.

- Obtain an order from a physician or medical practitioner unless it is an emergency situation.

- Obtain consent from the patient or from next of kin if the patient is not capable of understanding.

- Explain to the patient what is going to happen, even if the patient is unable to understand due to confusion or dementia.

- Always monitor the patient per facility policy—check the positioning of the restraint every thirty minutes and remove every two hours for range of motion. Remember to reposition the patient and offer toileting every two hours.

- Explain the need for restraints and how long the restraints will be used.

Applying Physical Restraints

Vests have holes for the arms and the opening crosses in the back. The straps will be secured on either side of the bed or chair, depending on the patient's location. Tie it in a quick-release knot to a lower part of the bed that does not move. Make sure that two fingers fit underneath the vest on the patient's chest so that it is not too tight.

Wrist or ankle restraints are cloths that wrap around each wrist or ankle. They have a strap that is tied to a lower, immovable part of the bed or chair. Tie it in a quick-release knot. Ensure the restraints aren't too tight and that the patient's arms or legs aren't in an awkward position. Usually, a pillow will be placed under the arms and/or the knees and heels.

Legal Implications in the Use of Restraints

If restraints aren't used correctly or are used for the wrong reasons, the patient's family can take legal action against the facility. A patient in restraints becomes completely vulnerable and may feel helpless. They are at a greater risk of sexual abuse, elder abuse, psychological abuse, or violence from other patients.

Possible injuries from restraints can include:

- Broken bones
- Bruises
- Falls
- Skin tears or pressure sores
- Depression or fear due to lack of freedom
- Death from strangulation

Reporting of Incident (Event, Irregular, Occurrence, or Variance)

If there is an unanticipated or adverse event, the nurse should follow the facility's policies and procedure for reporting and documentation. One of the first activities, after the patient is stable, should be to inform the respective manager or charge nurse of the event. The facility may have internal processes to follow as well to ensure they are protected as best as possible from medicolegal action.

One of the more common reportable events that the nurse will be involved in is an incorrect count. In the event of an incorrect count, the circulator should make attempts to recover the missing item. The circulator should also follow the facility's policies and procedures; at some facilities, X-ray may not be required for needles smaller than a certain size because they are typically not visible on X-ray. If an intraoperative X-ray is required for a potentially retained object, the team should ensure that the integrity of the sterile field is maintained because the X-ray may be performed prior to full closure of the incision.

Following reasonable attempts to recover the potentially retained object, the circulator should complete the necessary documentation in the patient's chart, such as which count is incorrect, what actions were taken to recover the object, and who was notified. In addition to the documentation in the patient record, the facility's policies may require reporting of the incident in an internal system. This allows the facility to gather additional data that may not be appropriate for the patient record. In the event of a retained foreign object, the facility can use this information to determine if all appropriate actions were taken.

Safe Use of Equipment

Nurses should assure that all equipment that is to be used is safe and functioning properly. The use of medical devices, including equipment used in the operating room, is regulated by the United States Food and Drug Administration (FDA). The Joint Commission (TJC) and the Centers for Medicare and Medicaid Services (CMS) also

50

provide oversight on the proper use of surgical equipment. Both TJC and CMS require the presence of manufacturer's instructions for use (IFU) to be present in areas where the equipment is used. Prior to surgical equipment being used on patients, the IFU are established by the device manufacturer. It is important for care providers to use the equipment only per manufacturer guidelines, since these guidelines are the ones tested and approved as safe for patient use by the FDA. If a safety concern regarding the equipment arises, the FDA recalls the product until the safety issue is resolved. For example, if a specific type of surgical guidewire breaks off at the tip and causes patient harm, the product may be recalled and pulled from circulation until further investigation.

The product manufacturer's IFU indicates if the equipment poses a fire, electrical, laser, or radiation hazard. If the product does pose one of these hazards, the IFU indicates the type(s) of hazard and the recommendations for protecting the patient and equipment users from the hazard. For instance, if the product poses a fire hazard, the IFU contains information stating which type of fire extinguisher should be available. Also, the IFU states whether to have liquid (sterile water or sterile saline) on the surgical field as a precautionary measure.

TJC and CMS observe infection control practices such as chemical disinfection and sterilization of surgical instruments during site visits to ensure healthcare facility compliance. If disinfection and sterilization are not performed according to manufacturer guidelines, the cleanliness/sterility of the surgical equipment cannot be verified. Manufacturer instructions for use should be available in each area where surgical equipment is used. Many healthcare facilities utilize OneSOURCE, an online database of manufacturer instructions for use. Since OneSOURCE is an electronic database, the contents are updated automatically, eliminating the need to update unit-based binders.

Security Plan

Within the healthcare facility, maintaining a strong **security system** is vital for patient and staff safety. The nurse will likely be trained in and involved with the hospital's security team, playing an active role in promoting a safe environment.

There are many ways a hospital can be threatened. A baby may be abducted from the hospital nursery, a hacker may breach the hospital's firewall and access private patient data, a violent person may enter the hospital and begin shooting people, a patient may run away, or a person may make a bomb threat. Whatever the threat, the facility will likely have a plan in place to quickly deal with the threat and neutralize it.

The nurse may be involved with a hospital security planning team. These types of teams meet to discuss potential threats and draw up a plan. The nurse can voice their opinion and contribute helpful ideas to effectively deal with the situation. The security team can share key tips with the rest of the staff based on their training and experience. These tips benefit the overall security of the facility. Planning, training, and drills all ensure that if a threat were to happen, the team is ready to respond.

Within the hospital, there are various methods of alerting the staff to a security breach. There may be alarm systems, announcements made over a PA system, or a text alert system on the staff's phones that notifies everyone of the situation. Many hospitals have closed circuit television security monitoring systems that employ cameras and video screens to monitor high-risk areas such as entrances and isolation rooms for violent patients. Certain security doors may be used to keep areas of the hospital off-limits to visitors or can close off areas of the hospital as needed.

Many hospitals use identification badges and bands to identify who is who and ensure only authorized persons and personnel are in certain areas. For example, the mother and father of a baby often get a special ID band identifying them as such, ensuring that no one else is permitted access to a baby, in case they might attempt an abduction.

If the nurse receives a bomb threat over the phone, they should attempt to stay on the line with the person making the threat as long as possible. The nurse may alert other staff of the bomb threat to get the security team in action,

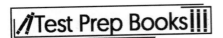

while trying to collect as much data on the perpetrator as possible. This information can include sound of their voice, whether they are male or female, and any other information the nurse can get out of them such as their location, the bomb location, and their motive. The nurse may even be able to deescalate the situation over the phone if they remain calm and collected, but the situation should be handed over to the experts on the security team as soon as possible.

Standard Precautions/Transmission-Based Precautions/Surgical Asepsis

Infection prevention is an important theme in healthcare, particularly in the surgical patient population. A main focus of nurses is protecting patients and healthcare associates from transmission of infectious organisms. Standard precautions are applied during direct patient contact and the patient's environmental contact. Standard precautions are followed universally by healthcare providers, and they are the foundation for preventing disease transmission in all healthcare settings. Included in standard precautions are hand hygiene, **personal protective equipment (PPE)**, environmental control, and sharps safety. Hand hygiene is the gold standard for preventing disease transmission. In compliance with standard precautions, the nurse performs hand hygiene before and after patient contact, before and after applying exam gloves, after touching anything in the patient's environment, before eating, and after using the restroom. PPE protects the nurse from coming into contact with the patient's bodily fluids and other potentially infectious material.

Examples of PPE are gloves, masks, gowns, shoe covers, and eye shields. Surfaces in the patient environment are laden with bacteria and other infectious agents. Environmental contamination is directly linked to pathogen transmission and **hospital-acquired infections (HAIs)**. Reusable laundry and textiles should be changed and laundered between each patient and in a healthcare-accredited laundry facility. Syringes and needles should be limited to single-patient use in compliance with evidence-based care related to infection control. Sharps should include safety devices, when possible. Angiocaths (IV needles) and surgical blades are available with built-in safety features that cover the sharp when not in use, decreasing the change of needle-stick exposure to patient body fluids. Transmission-based precautions are to be used with patients with known or suspected infection with highly transmissible pathogens. These are to be used along with standard precautions.

Transmission-based precautions are classified in three ways: contact, droplet, and airborne. **Contact precautions** are used with patients infected or colonized with microorganisms transmitted by direct or indirect contact. These include *Clostridium difficile (C. diff)*, methicillin-resistant *Staphylococcus aureus* (MRSA), and vancomycin-resistant *Enterococcus* (VRE). When caring for these patients, the nurse dons a gown and gloves prior to entering the patient room. The PPE is discarded immediately prior to leaving the patient room, and hand hygiene is performed immediately. Droplet precautions, in addition to standard precautions, are used if a patient has a confirmed or suspected infection transmissible through respiratory droplets. PPE associated with droplet precautions are gloves, gown, and mask. The patient is also placed in a single-patient room. Influenza and respiratory syncytial virus (RSV) are indications for droplet precautions. Airborne precautions are taken when providing care to a patient with known or suspected infection transmissible via airborne route. The patient's respiratory particles are airborne for prolonged time periods and are carried by normal air currents. PPE for these patients includes gloves, gown, and surgical mask with respirator level of N95 or higher. The most common airborne-transmissible infections are tuberculosis, measles, and varicella.

Spread of Disease-Causing Organisms

Microorganisms that cause infection can be spread by touching surfaces, equipment, people, and bodily fluids, as well as by breathing in **airborne droplets**, such as those that exit the nostril when a person sneezes. Touching infectious microorganisms followed by contact on the hands, face, mouth, eyes, or with food can spread the germs. A clean environment and good handwashing not only protect healthcare workers from infectious germs, but protect the patients as well. Infections can spread from patient to patient, from caregiver to patient, and vice versa.

There are three types of infections: viral, bacterial and fungal. **Fungal infections** are caused by spores of fungus that usually affect the skin but also can be inhaled and cause respiratory infections. Examples of fungal skin infections include Athlete's foot, ringworm, and yeast infections. Fungal infections can be spread by touching the lesion or skin area that is infected.

Bacterial infections and **viral infections** are caused by microbes, or microscopic organisms. Both of these types of infection can produce similar symptoms, including:

- Coughing and/or sneezing
- Inflammation (swelling)
- Fever
- Vomiting
- Diarrhea
- Fatigue

Even though bacteria and viruses both must be viewed through a microscope, they differ tremendously in how they infect the body. Bacteria are complex and can reproduce or multiply on their own. They can live in extreme environments, such as heat and cold, and can infect both the bodies of animals and humans. Bacterial infections are usually localized or found in contained areas of the body, such as the sinuses (sinus infection). Most bacteria are harmless and actually necessary to the body. One example is the bacteria in our gut, which is important for digesting food. Bacterial infections are treated with antibiotics, which will either kill the bacteria or stop the growth of the bacteria that has entered the body.

There are many different types of bacterial infections. Some common bacterial skin infections include cellulitis, folliculitis, impetigo, and boils. Foodborne bacterial infections usually cause vomiting, diarrhea, fever, chills, and abdominal pain. Harmful bacteria may be in raw meat, fish, eggs, and poultry, and in unpasteurized dairy products. The bacterial growth can be caused by unsanitary food preparation and handling.

Sexually-transmitted bacterial infections include chlamydia, gonorrhea, syphilis, and bacterial vaginosis. There are many additional types of infections, such as otitis media (ear infection), urinary tract infections, and respiratory tract infections. Infections in the respiratory tract can be from bacteria or a virus, and they can cause a sore throat, bronchitis, sinus infections, tuberculosis, or pneumonia.

Viruses are different from bacteria in that they need another cell in order to reproduce, or multiply. They attach to a cell in the body and change the cell to make more of the virus. Eventually, the original body cell dies. Viral infections do not respond to antibiotics and are more difficult to treat. Unlike bacteria, most viruses cause infection. The common cold is most often caused by a virus in the rhinovirus family and is an example of a mild virus. An example of life-threatening viruses is the human immunodeficiency virus (HIV). Vaccines do a good job of protecting against viruses such as polio, chicken pox, influenza, and measles. There are antiviral drugs available to treat certain viruses.

Common types of respiratory viruses include influenza-causing viruses, respiratory syncytial virus, and rhinoviruses, which are most often the cause of the common cold. Viral skin infections can include Molluscum contagiosum (small, harmless bumps on the skin), herpes simplex virus-1 (cold sores), and varicella zoster virus, which is similar to the chickenpox. Foodborne viral infections are the most common cause of food poisoning and can include the hepatitis A virus, norovirus, and rotavirus. Viruses that are transmitted sexually include human papilloma virus, hepatitis B, genital herpes (herpes simplex-2), and HIV. Other types of viruses include Epstein-Barr, West Nile, and viral meningitis.

Bacteria and viruses can be spread by:

- Droplet contact from coughing and sneezing
- Contact with infected people
- Contact with infected animals, like livestock, pets, fleas, and ticks
- Contact with infected surfaces, like tabletops or railings
- Contact with contaminated food or water

Microbes can cause acute infections, chronic infections, or latent infections. **Acute infections** last for a short period of time and **chronic infections** can last for weeks, months, or years. **Latent infections** may not show any symptoms at first and then may reappear, or show up after months or years.

Handwashing with soap and water is the number one way to prevent the spread of germs. The soap removes the visible dirt and invisible germs from the hands, and the water rinses them off.

Handwashing steps:

- Remove any jewelry or watches and pull long sleeves up past the wrists.
- Turn on the water and use warm water.
- Place soap in one hand and rub for at least twenty seconds.
- Make sure to rub the top and palms of the hands. Rub between the fingers and around the nails.
- Wash above the wrists.
- If there was contact with bodily fluids, wash for at least one minute.
- Be sure not to touch the sides of the sink during the process (the washing process would then need to be repeated).
- Rinse hands with fingers facing down so that the soap and germs run off rather than back up the arms.
- Dry hands with a paper towel or clean hand towel.
- Use the towel to turn off the faucet.

When to perform handwashing:

- After using the bathroom
- After sneezing or handling tissues
- Before and after eating
- Before entering and after leaving a patient's room
- Before and after feeding a patient
- Before and after performing a procedure on a patient
- Before and after coming in contact with a wound
- After coming in contact with dirty linens or clothes
- After coming in contact with bodily fluids of any kind (blood, urine, vomit, mucus, or stool)
- After leaving a patient's room

Cleansing the hands with an alcohol-based hand sanitizer is also available in healthcare facilities, but it is best to wash with soap and water. Hand sanitizers can get rid of many, but not all, microbes. For example, clostridium difficile, commonly referred to as **c-diff**, is a microbe that is not killed by alcohol-based sanitizers. A c-diff infection causes a patient to have copious amounts of watery diarrhea. In addition to standard infection-prevention precautions, the nurse must wash hands with soap and water before and after caring for a patient with c-diff.

Hand sanitizer should not be used when the hands are visibly soiled, or if bodily fluids have been touched. After several uses of hand sanitizer, oils build up on the hands and should be removed by washing with soap.

Educating patients about cleanliness and proper handwashing will also help prevent the spread of disease. Make sure to assist patients with washing their hands, or use a soapy washcloth on their hands throughout the day, especially after toileting and prior to eating. Proper handwashing in the community reduces the number of people who get sick with diarrheic illnesses and respiratory illnesses, such as colds.

Isolation Techniques

One unfortunate downside of staying in a healthcare facility is the chance of contracting a healthcare-related infection. According to the World Health Organization (WHO), many of these can be prevented through the use of appropriate isolation techniques.

The types of infections that necessitate isolation are those that are easily transmitted and accessible to those with compromised immune systems, making it difficult for them to fend off the infection. C. diff and influenzas are the most common illnesses that are transmitted in healthcare settings. Therefore, nurses should be especially aware of these types of patients and conditions, for example, patients with an existing bloodborne disorder, such as HIV, hepatitis B or TB. In these cases, isolation safeguards may be necessary so that the person is not exposed to common pathogens, such as a cold.

Isolation techniques are categorized into one of five types:

- **Contact precautions**: Conditions with a high risk of contract transmission that often warrant isolation include C. diff, the Herpes simplex virus, scabies, MRSA, and fungal infections. This technique includes wearing gloves, using a face shield, wearing a mask, covering your shoes, washing your hands, and immediately reporting any exposure.

- **Droplet precautions**: These involve diseases spread by coughing or sneezing such as influenza, rhinovirus, pertussis, and group A streptococcus. Precautions include wearing a mask, wearing goggles, and removing protective gear and washing your hands after leaving the patient's room.

- **Airborne precautions**: Airborne infections are those that incorporate pathogen spores or dehydrated nuclei, such as Aspergillus or tuberculosis, and have a range distance of more than 10 feet. Patient isolation involves keeping them in a negative-pressure room with a lower pressure ventilation system that prevents airborne pathogens from escaping, wearing an appropriate respirator, and disposing of protective gear in an adjacent room.

- **Neutropenic precautions**: These are used in patients who have a comprised immune system resulting from a low number of neutrophils in their immune system, such as AIDS patients or those taking immunosuppressants. It is important to keep contaminants out of these patient's rooms, which may involve donning protective gear, washing hands prior to entering, and screening any items such as food or gifts.

- **Radiation precautions**: Radiation safeguards are comparable to neutropenic precautions because they also involve the possibility of a comprised immune system. When a patient is undergoing radiation therapy, time limits may be enforced for both visitors and healthcare staff to limit their exposure. The use of gowns, shoe covers, or other protective gear may be required. An exposure-guideline chart should be placed on or near the patient's door.

Practice Quiz

1. Which of the following is the best way to prevent the spread of infection?
   a. Keeping the mouth covered when coughing or sneezing
   b. Disinfecting shared patient equipment
   c. Practicing proper hand hygiene
   d. Avoiding contact with infectious patients

2. What are the correct steps to follow when using a fire extinguisher?
   a. Pull the pin, Squeeze the handle, Aim the nozzle, Swirl around the fire
   b. Pull the pin, Aim at the base of the fire, Squeeze the handle, Sweep from side to side
   c. Squeeze the handle, Aim at the base of the fire, Pull the pin, Sweep from side to side
   d. Stand back, Pull the pin, Squeeze the handle, Sweep from side to side

3. When preparing to transfer a patient from their bed to a wheelchair, what is the first step to take?
   a. Ensure that the bed is locked.
   b. Inform the patient about what is going to happen.
   c. Get another staff member to help.
   d. Have the patient sit up in bed.

4. When attempting to lift something heavy, which of the following should not be done?
   a. Keep the legs straight and bend over to use back muscles.
   b. Spread legs apart and bend at the knees.
   c. Stand close to the object.
   d. Use only feet and legs to turn.

5. An aide is caring for a patient in their home. Which of the following items should the aide recognize as a fire hazard?
   a. Multiple electrical cords plugged into a power strip
   b. A pack of matches on a coffee table
   c. A potholder lying on the stove
   d. A toaster left out on the counter

See answers on the next page.

Answer Explanations

1. C: All of the answer choices are types of standard precautions, but research has shown that proper hand hygiene using soap and water or alcohol-based hand rub (if appropriate) is the best way to prevent the spread of germs.

2. B: Use the acronym PASS to answer this question. The pin should always be pulled first. Choices *A, C,* and *D* are not listed in the correct order or with the correct wording. The correct directions and order are: Pull the pin, Aim at the base of the fire, Squeeze the handle, and Sweep from side to side.

3. B: Anytime a task or procedure is about to occur, the patient should be informed first. All of the other options are part of the procedure, but the first step is to explain the task to the patient. Another staff person may not be needed, the patient may not be able to sit up in bed on their own, or they may wonder why they are being asked to sit up.

4. A: When lifting a heavy object, the lower back should not be strained; therefore, bending over and using the back muscles should be avoided. Choices *B, C,* and *D* should be done when lifting. Stand close to the object, bend at the knees with legs apart, and use feet and legs to turn if needed.

5. C: Anything flammable that is on top of a stove should be moved off of the stove surface to avoid a fire if the burners are turned on. Keep in mind that this patient is in their own home. All of the other choices are acceptable and pose no immediate fire hazard. Multiple cords should be plugged into a power strip, and a toaster left on the counter is not a hazard. The pack of matches on the table could be a hazard, but the patient is still living independently and may still be capable of using matches correctly. If there are no children in the home, the matches are not of immediate concern.

Health Promotion and Maintenance

Aging Process

Across the lifespan, from conception to birth, infancy to school-age, adolescence to adulthood, and middle age to death, the human experience is not unique. Like most other mammals, humans are said to be sentient beings, in possession of all of the five senses and self-awareness. With self-awareness comes the realization of one's own mortality. The aging process is linear, beginning at the moment of birth. Distinctly, the aged population is generally said to include those over the age of sixty-five. Although many expect to see a marked decline in physiological and neurological functioning, this is not necessarily the case. Depending on individual lifestyle choices, high-risk behaviors, and adherence to annually recommended health screenings, the aging process can be uneventful.

For all patient populations, one of the most important topics to discuss is their diet. Especially for older adults, proper nutrition is critical. Income fluctuations due to retirement or lost income from a deceased or divorced spouse may affect the grocery budget. Vitamin deficiencies can quickly become problematic, resulting in a brief or prolonged hospitalization. Neurological concerns may also affect memory, and patients may simply forget to eat. Simple questions regarding favorite meals, restaurants, or eating preferences can yield answers. It is important to note that missing meals can also become commonplace if a depression diagnosis exists. Inserting a brief depression inventory early in the visit may reveal the major reason for the patient's current health status and uncover areas of concern regarding daily nutrition.

Exercise is also a crucial piece of the assessment puzzle when discussing healthy lifestyle choices. Chronological age is not synonymous with physical decline, and patients should be encouraged to continue with exercise as tolerated. Simply walking daily for 30 minutes, broken into segments, if necessary, is a great starting point. Weight-bearing exercise, isometrics, swimming, yoga, Pilates, or Tai-Chi all provide patients with the opportunity for gentle movement if some mobility issues exist. If needed, physical or occupational therapies can aid in the restoration of mobility and should be suggested after injury or with sedentary patients. Older patients must be reminded that retirement is not a signal to simply age, but the opportunity to age well.

Apart from the maintenance of diet and exercise is the importance of socialization and hobbies. Aging can be an isolating experience; especially as adult children move away and manage separate families. Less time may be spent with extended family and, once retired, the older adult may see less need for meeting new people in general. It is important for the nurse to assess the patient's perceived need for companionship. What do they do for fun? How do they unwind? Do they have a bucket list and what's on it? These types of open-ended questions not only create dialogue but can quickly become a goal-setting session.

When discussing high-risk behaviors with members of the aged population, it is imperative that the nurse include sexual activity. Although thought to be less sexually active than younger patients, this age group has seen a dramatic increase in sexually transmitted disease (STD) in recent years. Many have lost a spouse or life partner to death or divorce, and experience bouts of profound loneliness and sexual frustration. Although some may be seeking to remarry, most are interested in companionship and may not consider STDs to be a major concern. It is not as necessary to discuss birth control with a postmenopausal woman or elderly man as it is to discuss chlamydia, gonorrhea, herpes, and HIV. A simple question regarding intimate partners or social life will likely yield more information that the nurse can use to gently introduce the subject.

Nurses must carefully assess the likelihood of the progression of both medical and mental health concerns. Historically, the longer an individual manages chronic disease, the more complicated the illness becomes. More biological systems are impacted, leading to further physiological compromise. For example, diabetes mellitus, if managed well over a number of years, may still result in renal, visual, and cardiovascular complications in later

58

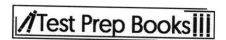

years. The nurse must discuss basic diabetic care with the patient at every encounter. Annual eye exams, podiatric care, consultation with a diabetic nutritionist or dietician, and adhering closely to the diet plan, are all essential.

An additional, distinctive aspect of the aged population is neurological decline. Alzheimer's disease and dementia are said to contribute to a majority of hospitalizations and nursing home placements. Nurses must be familiar with a brief neurological assessment, also referred to as a **mental status exam**, in order to provide appropriate care. It is also necessary to assess the patient frequently for abrupt decline in functioning. Patients have a tendency to be forgetful, combative, and/or behave in a childlike manner. Neurological compromise can affect balance and gait, often resulting in falls and injury. Careful consideration of the safety of the patient's home environment is critical. Caregivers must be educated, trained, and prepared regarding the signs and symptoms of neurological impairment, along with appropriate interventions. It will also be necessary to discuss or review end-of-life care plans.

One final integral piece to the assessment of the older adult is preparation for the treatment and care of the patient and the family at the end of life. Some patients may have previously determined their preferences for end-of-life and palliative care. Obtain a copy of all advance directives and review for accuracy with the patient or caregiver. Does the patient possess the ability or desire to make changes to the documents? Are the primary and secondary proxy agents present or readily available if needed for consultation? The nurse must approach the discussion of comfort care with an awareness of the appropriate parties to include from the patient's preferred circle of confidants. If the nurse is unfamiliar with these topics, enlisting the assistance of a chaplain, social worker, or hospice care professional is vital. Respite care, bereavement counseling, and support-group referrals also are essential for the patient and family to ease their transition through the dying process.

Antepartum, Intrapartum, Postpartum, and Newborn Care

Excellent nursing care prior to, during, and immediately following childbirth is essential. Pregnancy as a medical state comprises several distinct stages: antepartum, intrapartum, postpartum, and newborn care. **Antepartum care** can be defined as care during pregnancy. During this period, the pregnant patient must be assessed periodically for appropriate fetal growth, responsiveness in-utero, and the mother's overall health status. Any fluctuations in these areas signal the potential for maternal or fetal distress. It is necessary to obtain a complete medical, gynecological, and obstetrical history. The nurse must be aware of any sexually transmitted diseases, previous abortions or full-term pregnancies (gravida), any complications, and the number of vaginal and cesarean births (para), as well as estimated date of delivery (EDD) and current birth plan.

The term **intrapartum care** refers to care provided during childbirth. Pregnancy is a progressive medical state; nursing care during the intrapartum period is based on all information gathered during the antepartum period. The mother and fetus are monitored simultaneously for signs of distress. Although continuous fetal monitoring is the standard of care, intermittent auscultation is acceptable if performed hourly. On average, fetal heart tones range from 120 to 160 beats per minute (bpm), with periodic accelerations over 160 bpm denoting a positively responding fetus. The nurse must be equipped to discuss preferred treatment for uterine contractions and provide emotional support during delivery. Once cervical dilation reaches 10cm, the nurse must contact the provider and begin preparations for delivery of the infant. Once delivered, the mother and infant enter the postpartum stage.

The **postpartum phase** is considered to begin immediately after childbirth and ends after six weeks. Once the infant is delivered, it becomes a second patient and must be cared for separately from the mother. The nurse must assess both patients every 15 minutes for 2 hours to confirm that both mother and infant are adjusting well. Continued hospitalization is generally no longer than one day for a vaginal birth and two to three days for a cesarean section. Upon discharge—with infant care manual, feeding plan, and patient education completed—the couplet and other caregivers return to the home environment. Within weeks, the couplet will visit the physician, for well checks. This nursing assessment includes a depression inventory and discussions of progress with infant feeding.

Infants born prior to 37 weeks' gestation are considered to be preterm and at a high risk for complications at birth and throughout infancy. Specialized care of preterm infants and those born with twice-repeated Apgar scores below 7 must occur in the neonatal intensive care unit. Well infants are roomed in with their mothers, as a couplet. The postpartum nurse must be prepared to teach the parent(s) on feeding, changing, and general care of the infant. Umbilical cord care, as well as proper cleaning of a circumcised penis, is also vital in preparation for the discharge home. Within the first 24-to-48 hours after birth, careful assessment must be performed to ascertain if the infant is not adjusting to their new environment.

Identifying Emotional Preparedness for Pregnancy

Pregnancies can result in a wide range of emotions and sensitivities, including happiness, dread, mood fluctuations, worry, financial uncertainties, despair, and uncharacteristic responses. These can be experienced by either parent and vary significantly among patients depending on any number of factors.

It is important for nurses to check for any warning signs such as any of the above-listed emotional cues, physical appearance, or financial situation that might signal the degree of emotional readiness of the parents-to-be and their support systems, including family and community members and systems. These types of social support systems are invaluable to patients dealing with a pregnancy. It is estimated that around half of all pregnancies are unplanned, which may involve single and/or teen mothers.

Some women may have a great deal of support and others may have little or none, especially when the father is not around and/or unwelcoming of an unwanted pregnancy. When those involved in these situations are not emotionally prepared, it is important for the nurse to support any decisions related to abortion and/or adoption that might arise.

Performing Nonstress Test

A **nonstress test** is performed in the third trimester to check the wellbeing of the baby by gauging the fetal heart rate and movements of the baby in a noninvasive way. The procedure involves placing a stretchy belt monitor around the pregnant mother's stomach and asking her to track each of the baby's movements. Sometimes this is done with a handheld clicker which the mother is asked to press each time she feels a movement. The process typically takes 20 to 40 minutes. Normal results occur when the heart rate of the fetus increases by at least 15 beats per minute over a period of 15 seconds during fetal movement. An abnormal and nonreactive test result should be noted when the heart rate of the fetus does NOT increase by at least 15 beats per minute over 15 during fetal movement.

Fetal Heart Monitoring for the Antepartum Client

Antepartum monitoring (the time just before childbirth) is key to preventing fetal death and is a widely accepted tool in dealing with high-risk pregnancies or problems such as fetal distress, atypical uterine contractions, hypertension, diabetes, post-term births, and multiple birth situations.

Fetal heart rate monitoring can be external or internal. In **external heart rate monitoring**, a device such as a Doppler ultrasound is placed on the mother's abdomen to record the heartbeat of the baby. During the antepartum period, an ultrasound probe (also known as a transducer) strapped to the abdomen can be used to transmit the baby's heartbeat to a computer where the heart rate and pattern are displayed on the screen and a physical printout. **Internal heart rate monitoring** utilizes a thin electrode that is attached to the baby's scalp via the cervix to connect to a monitor to give a more accurate reading. This method is only possible if the mother's water (amniotic sac) surrounding the baby has ruptured and the cervix has opened. It is typically used when the external method of fetal heart monitoring is not giving a good reading.

Monitoring a Patient in Labor

There are two ways to monitor fetal heart rate during labor: **auscultation** is intermittently checking the fetal heartbeat, and **electronic fetal monitoring** is using electronic instruments to regularly log the fetus's heartbeat and

contractions of the mother's uterus during labor. The type of monitoring typically depends on the policies of the healthcare provider and medical facility, whether the pregnancy/birth is deemed to be high-risk, and how the labor is progressing. Either method is fine as long as there are no predetermined complications or risk factors, and none arise during labor.

The mother's condition and vital signs should be assessed during the various stages of labor. These assessments should include the following:

- An evaluation of the mother's status
- An account of the mother's uterine activity
- Fetal status
- Vaginal examination and description
- Position of the baby
- Change in fetal membranes and progression of the pregnancy
- A summary of the baby and mother and the pregnancy plan, including plans for medical intervention and managing pain.

Care of Postpartum Patients

Caring for the mother after the baby is born involves checking for signs of postpartum complications such as infections and hemorrhage and making sure the baby is getting the proper nourishment from the mother, either through breast or bottle feeding. The mother's vital statistics such as temperature, blood pressure, etc. should normalize within 24 hours of the baby's birth. Atypical readings as well as symptoms such as location-specific pain, a flushed appearance, feeling hot or swollen, feeling tired, chilled or confused, exhibiting an irregular heartbeat, the malfunction of a body part or organ, unable to go to the bathroom, or gastrointestinal distress are all signals to the nurse to perform additional health checks on the mother.

Newborn Plan of Care

After the baby is born, it is important for the nurse to help a new mother and others who will be caring for the baby to understand what is involved in feeding and tending to the needs of a newborn so they feel ready to care for the newborn once they leave the medical facility. Essential points to go over with the patient and others involved in the care include the baby's dietary needs, the basics of breast and/or bottle feeding, how to care for the umbilical cord and circumcision site, how to change and secure a diaper, how to prevent life-threatening accidents, how best to answer and cope with a crying baby, as well as emotional components such as bonding and attachment.

Community Resources

Community Resources for Patients

Sometimes it is deemed necessary or at least helpful to refer a patient to a health care or other support contact following discharge from the facility. The healthcare team, including nurses, evaluate each patient accordingly and establish their needs in relation to present and possible issues.

Community resources include groups providing support for topics such as:

- Psychological care for those in a crisis situation (abuse, trauma, etc.)
- Managing anger (especially for those causing abuse)
- Social service organizations for patients without insurance and those requiring welfare aid
- Relief for caregivers who feel overburdened
- Self-help counseling support groups
- Housing assistance, including shelters for victims and children of abusive situations
- Providing transport to and from medical appointments

- Elder day care, home healthcare aid and recreational activities geared for senior citizens
- Childrearing support, including resources offering childcare and education assistance for infants, children, and teens
- Nutritional guidance to help individuals, families, and specific groups within a community attain a better dietary understanding and cope with issues such as obesity, diabetes and heart disease
- Exercise classes or programs to help promote health and fitness within a community
- Group and individual guidance for smoking cessation and substance abuse

Community Health Education

Sometimes it is the responsibility of the nurse to help devise and/or join in health educational programs in the community. These settings can vary significantly depending on the type of service offered, their degree of formality and the number of participants.

In order to correctly design a community health program, a nurse must evaluate the educational needs of those involved and come up with a plan that fulfills these requirements. Depending on the proposed strategy, the role of the nurse can range from providing in-person talks to a large community group, informing a small group of members about a specific health topic or issue, or providing personal assistance and informational sessions. It is important for the nurse to remain organized and proficient at all times no matter what the duties necessitate.

Reinforcing Teaching About Health Risks

Patients are often at risk for healthcare issues that radiate wider than their individual needs. Nurses must evaluate the awareness level of the patients under their care regarding their health risks based on their individual families, populations and communities. Each of these groups has varying facets and risk factors that could impact the patient. For example, there are many developmental transformations and milestones that affect children in a family; patients should be advised of these stages and any suitable actions the patient can do to avoid the risk of developmental delays. The population could be impacted by the advent of an influenza outbreak, and so should be informed about the benefits of getting a flu vaccination. Communities often contain various parks and other recreational resources; these should be communicated to the patient and made aware of the benefits of exercise.

Data Collection Techniques

Collecting Data for a Health History

Nurses must perform a **health history** in order to gather essential statistics and information about present and prior health conditions, and health risks and requirements of the patient and their family. The information collected can consist of the following:

- **Primary data**: Information given directly by the patient
- **Secondary data**: Information taken from sources other than the patient
- **Subjective data**: Information that is inferred by the nurse but cannot be demonstrably observed
- **Objective data**: Data that is observed based on senses such as sight, smell or touch
- **Quantitative data**: Statistical data such as vital signs readings and lab results
- **Qualitative data**: Descriptive information such as the patient's pain level explanation

Collecting Baseline Physical Data

The nurse makes a note of a patient's baseline data following their health history but prior to their full head to toe analysis. This general survey provides a comparative starting point for the healthcare team to help evaluate condition and make care decisions. It consists of the patient's height, weight, body type, posture, walking ability,

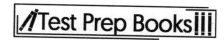

signs of pain, personal hygiene and grooming conditions, skin pallor, vital signs, oxygen levels, and the true age of the patient versus the age in appearance.

Preparing a Patient for Physical Examinations

It is important for nurses to effectively and efficiently get patients properly situated and ready for their physical examination. This includes ensuring a private setting, clarifying and emphasizing procedures, and making sure the patient is as comfortable as possible during the exam.

Documenting Findings

As is typical with all facets of nursing care, the information gathered during the patient's health history and physical examination are noted and recorded as per the guidelines and standard practices of the healthcare facility. Some facilities employ special forms to document this type of data.

Reporting Physical Examination Results

It is the responsibility of the LPN to evaluate the patient's past medical record and the results of their baseline physical exam and continually compare it to their present health situation while under their care. They should also record and convey all noteworthy results of the physical exam to the head registered nurse and/or patient's health care provider.

Developmental Stages and Transitions

Nurses must be able to recognize and document any patient data that differs from what is considered normal regarding physical and mental growth and maturity. In addition, they need to adjust the level and way they will care for the patient based on their findings. Changes that are to be expected include those associated with standard developmental stages such as puberty, menopause, pregnancy and aging. Abrupt weight gain or loss or stunted growth are not normal. Examples of atypical situations that would signal a problem and should be reported by the nurse include when a girl menstruates early (10 years or younger), a woman entering menopause at a young age (early 40s), teenage pregnancy, or severe weight loss, the latter of which could be a sign of anorexia, bulimia, or other malnutrition reasons.

Nurses should evaluate how anticipated changes in body image may influence the patient's quality of life and daily activities. These can include feelings and thoughts that strike during puberty, menopause, pregnancy, and as part of aging. If the nurse has any reason to believe that the patient cannot adapt or cope properly, this evidence should be established, noted, and reported so that the healthcare team can alter the patient's care strategy in order to manage these issues. Nurses can ask the patient how they perceive themselves in terms of body image, how they think they look to others, how the changes in their body make them feel, and how long they have felt this way. Signs that a patient may be having body image issues can include the following:

- Trying to cover the body or specific area in question
- Refusal to acknowledge the change
- A decline in personal hygiene
- Social withdrawal
- Obsession with the body or body part
- Poor self-esteem

Erikson's Psychosocial Stages of Development

Erikson's Psychosocial Stages of Development is an alternative to Freud's psychosexual stages. According to Erikson's epigenetic principle of maturation, human beings pass through eight developmental stages, each of which build upon the preceding stages and set the groundwork for the stages that follow.

All eight stages are present at birth but remain latent until both an innate schedule and an individual's cultural upbringing cause a stage to begin to unfold.

An individual does not have to "master" a stage in order to proceed to the next stage, and the outcome of a particular stage may later be changed by an individual's life experiences.

As with Freud's theory, Erikson proposed that each stage of development is characterized by a crisis; however, for Erikson, the crisis involves a conflict between the needs of the developing individual and the needs of society.

Successfully mastering a stage and its psychosocial crisis leads to the development of a healthy personality and possession of basic virtues.

Erikson's theory centers on the development of ego, or a sense of self that is acquired by interacting with the social environment.

Self-Image Throughout the Life Cycle

Self-image has to do with how people view themselves. This concept includes **self-esteem**, whether a person has feelings of high or low worth. The concept of self evolves throughout the lifespan, but it always plays a significant role in how a person functions in life.

Infancy: The ego is in charge. The baby thinks primarily of basic needs, such as food or warmth.

Childhood: In early to middle childhood, children tend to rate themselves higher than peers in terms of talents and intellect. As middle school approaches, there is a decline in self-evaluations. This could be related to feeling unattractive due to physical changes or being teased or bullied by peers in that age group.

Adolescence: In the early stage of adolescence (ages nine to thirteen), another drop in self-esteem occurs. This is thought to be related to the need to let go of childish pleasures, such as a beloved toy or previous interests, and step up to the plate of becoming a more responsible person. This can be a painful sacrifice for some youth. The next drop in self-worth occurs at the end of adolescence and beginning of young adulthood (ages eighteen to twenty-three). It is during this period that young adults realize that they truly are responsible for their own lives, yet they have not yet achieved a sense of mastery in the academic or vocational world. They are fearful and full of doubt about the ability to be successful as an independent adult.

Adulthood: Studies indicate a small but steady increase in self-image by mid-twenties. In general, during this period, men tend to have higher self-esteem than women. Persons who live in poor socioeconomic conditions tend to have lower self-esteem than their more financially stable peers. As later adulthood nears (the seventies), women tend to catch up with men in terms of how they evaluate themselves. Women in their eighties tend to have a more positive self-image than male counterparts. As a general rule, for both genders, there is a gradual increase in one's sense of self-worth throughout the life span until late middle age. Research shows that most adults' self-image peaks at around age sixty.

Influence of Age on Behaviors and Attitudes

There are various, and sometimes conflicting, hypotheses with regard to how and whether attitudes change with age.

- **Impressionable-years hypothesis**: The environment and socialization that people experience when they are young shape their worldviews and have a profound effect on their attitudes for the remainder of the lifespan.

- **Increasing persistence hypothesis**: People exhibit flexible and impressionable thinking when they are younger but become increasingly inflexible with age.

- **Life-long openness hypothesis**: People exhibit flexible and impressionable thinking throughout the lifespan, and their attitudes are dependent upon evolving life circumstances.

Some changes in behavior and thinking may be related to the changes that older adults often experience as they navigate their later years. For example, they may experience a loss of independence due to impaired health or a loss of identity and confidence as they cope with retirement. People who have always had difficulty with change are particularly likely to experience negative effects of change during older adulthood.

Examples may include somatic complaints, denial that change has occurred, feelings of powerlessness, rigid thinking, isolation, anger, depression, grief, or regression to earlier behavior.

Barriers to Communication

There are several different types of communication, including verbal, written, and nonverbal. **Verbal communication** occurs when two parties are speaking out loud; this can be in person, through video technology, or over the phone. **Written communication** can be through physical or digital writing or printing, such as e-mails, faxes, and instant messages. **Nonverbal communication** is transferred through one party's observations of the other party's body language and facial expressions.

Good communication depends on a number of factors. Do the speakers speak the same language? Language can be a barrier to communication and can be overcome with a translator. Sometimes, a family member can help with communication. Cultural barriers exist in communication as some cultures have certain beliefs about how one should talk, who should do the speaking, and how much one should speak.

The nurse should be careful not to create **nonverbal barriers** to communication with patients and coworkers. An example of a nonverbal barrier is the nurse having a personal smartphone in hand and scrolling through social media while a patient or coworker is trying to talk to them. This action suggests the nurse is not paying attention and does not care about what is being said, which inhibits good communication.

Physical barriers to communication may exist, such as a patient having a speech, hearing, visual, or other sensory impairment. The patient may have cognitive difficulties understanding basic communication, brought on by illness, change in level of consciousness, or dementia.

Barriers to Learning

Facilitation of learning refers to the process of assessing the learning needs of the patient and family, the nursing staff, and caregivers in the community, and creating, implementing, and evaluating formal and informal educational programs to address those needs. Novice nurses often view patient care and patient education as separate entities; however, experienced nurses are able to integrate the patient's educational needs into the plan of care. Nurses are aware that the patient often requires continued reinforcement of the educational plan after discharge, which necessitates coordination with home care services.

As facilitators of learning, nurses may be involved in a large-scale effort to educate all patients over 65 admitted to the nursing unit about the need for both Prevnar 13 and Pneumovax 23 to prevent pneumonia. In contrast, nurses may provide one-on-one instruction for a patient recently diagnosed with diabetes. The first step of any teaching-learning initiative is the assessment of the learning needs of the participants. Specific needs that influence the design and content of the educational offering include the language preference and reading level of the participants. Nurses must also consider the effect of certain patient characteristics identified in the Synergy Model on the patient's capacity to process information. Diminished resiliency or stability, and extreme complexity, must be considered in the development of the educational plan. Nurses are also responsible for creating a bridge between teaching-learning in the acute care setting and the home environment. A detailed discharge plan, close coordination with outpatient providers, and follow-up phone calls to the patient may be used to reinforce the patient's knowledge of the plan of care.

Successful learning plans for staff members and colleagues also consider the motivation of the participants to engage in the process. Successful facilitators include a variety of teaching strategies to develop the content and evaluate learning, in order to address adult learning needs and preferences, such as preferred language and reading level. Research indicates that when adults do not have a vested interest in the outcomes of the teaching/learning process, they may not participate as active learners.

The remaining element of successful facilitation of learning is the availability and quality of learning resources. There is evidence that individuals with different learning styles respond differently to various learning devices. The minimum requirements for successful facilitation of learning include the skilled staff to develop the educational materials, paper, a copy machine, and staff to interact with the patient in the learning session.

Barriers to the facilitation of learning must be anticipated and accommodated. Changes in the patient's condition commonly require reduction in the time spent in each learning session due to fatigue. Cognitive impairment can impede comprehension and retention of the information and will require appropriate teaching aids. The learning abilities of the patient's family members must also be assessed. Adequate instruction time might be the greatest barrier. Learning needs are assessed and discharge planning is begun on the day of admission; however, shortened inpatient stays require evaluation of the patient's comprehension of the plan of care.

Health Promotion/Disease Prevention

Two of the most important aspects of providing exceptional nursing care are health promotion and disease prevention. Both are integral to ensuring the physical and psychological wellbeing of individuals, groups, and the community at large.

Health promotion can be loosely defined as the direct or indirect presentation of information, specifically designed to influence behaviors that are expected to result in positive health outcomes. When presented directly, the instruction may be in written form such as brochures, books, or articles in magazines or newspapers. Historically, these publications were typically available in physician's offices, clinics, and hospitals. For nurses, health promotion is no longer relegated to easily discarded brochures or pamphlets. With the introduction of the Internet, information targeting healthy activities can be found instantly after several keystrokes. Nursing interventions can be provided via webinars, face-to-face coaching sessions, telephonic care, and social media sites. These mediums allow the nurse to contact thousands of individuals at once and increase exposure.

Indirect presentation of healthy lifestyle choices often occurs through billboards, signage, or posters in physicians' offices, as well as strategic mention or product placement in movies and television shows. Increasing numbers of "reality TV" stars can be seen holding bottles of a specific brand of vitamins or diet pills, or leaving a restaurant noted for healthy dishes. Albeit not as successful as the direct-to-consumer approach, this allows for health promotion to sneak in the back doors of viewers' minds, slowly affecting their daily habits. Traditionally, nurses are

not involved in this type of health promotion, but nurses can use this type of behavior when interacting with patients. Ensuring that hand washing posters are present in restrooms, display cases of vitamins and supplements in the office waiting area, and sponsorship or participation in local health fairs all support higher awareness.

In an effort to actively guide the **prevention of disease**, community health nurses employ numerous tactics. Each strategy is specific to a particular population to intervene at several stages of the disease process.

Primary prevention consists of the nursing strategies implemented to prevent the onset of a particular disease process. One well-known example of primary disease prevention is the "say no to drugs" movement. Nurses in this campaign can specifically target young children and teens to prevent their initial use of drugs with the use of buttons, posters, commercials, and rallies. **Secondary prevention** focuses on the early detection of disease and prevention of considerable damage from the disease process. Finally, **tertiary prevention** efforts with this same patient population would be nursing interventions implemented in drug treatment centers, clinics, and detox units in the hospital. These nurses work with the patients actively addicted to substances and collaborate to manage their disease.

Risk Factors for Disease

The nurse gathers information and evidence regarding a patient's **risk factors** for disease from their health history upon admission to the facility, during their physical exam, and through the duration of their care. Risk factors are influences that could trigger a health-related issue such as sickness, infection, disease or some other ailment. They can be inherent, such as high blood pressure, which increases the likelihood of other disorders; or external, such as smoking, which increases the risk of lung cancer. Certain risk factors can be diminished or eradicated, especially those related to lifestyle habits such as poor diet, smoking or drinking.

Immunizations

Some types of vaccinations are obligatory as per the CDC (Centers for Disease Control and Prevention) and state regulations, such as childhood inoculations to prevent communicable diseases; others are voluntary but CDC-recommended, such as adult vaccinations for pneumonia.

Nurses need to have a working knowledge of the various immunization laws and endorsements for the age group under their care. For example, when working with young patients, nurses must know the CDC's schedule for childhood immunizations. They also need to be aware of CDC-recommendation vaccinations for adult patients who are considered at-risk for various illnesses when under their care. For instance, elderly patients with a risk respiratory disease should get the pneumonia vaccine and an annual flu shot.

The CDC has some contraindications and safeguards for certain vaccines that nurses need to be aware of. For instance, second doses of the hepatitis and DTaP vaccines should not be given when the person has had an anaphylactic episode after the first dose. They should also be used with caution on patients who have a serious illness with or without a fever. It is important for nurses to be aware that there are many myths and rumors constantly circulating about vaccines and to address any patient concerns empathically in order to reassure any apprehensive patients.

Hearing Aids, Dentures, and Eyeglasses

Patients who have difficulty hearing may require a referral to an audiologist who may then fit them with a hearing aid. Hearing aids, along with glasses, should be kept in a safe place when not in use. Small assistive devices such as hearing aids, dentures, and eyeglasses can easily be lost in the linens when they are changed or carried away with the food tray if they are left on top. The nurse and nurse's aid should work with the patient and family to ensure that these items are stored properly to avoid losing them. These items can be very difficult to track down if lost in the linens, in a bedside waste basket, or on the food tray. They are often very expensive to replace for the patient.

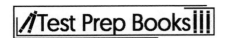

Health Screening

Historically, nurses have been primarily responsible for conducting **health screenings**. Every biological system within the human body should be screened periodically to ensure that it is operating at optimal levels. At the start of every developmental stage, it is recommended that patients be screened and, if found deficient, treated and monitored for progress. Health screenings are suggested based on chronological age to guide both individual treatment and trends for developing community outreach. Armed with the data, nurses collaborate with patients, providers, and caregivers to formulate an effective treatment plan.

Nurses working within the community health sector also utilize health screenings to guide disease-prevention efforts on a larger scale. Nurse researchers can use the data to aid in the creation of medications and advertisement campaigns to target those individuals on the borderlines of a particular disease process. Further, community-health nurses can conduct health screenings to identify gaps in access to healthcare, barriers to care, and disease maintenance. Once the information is disseminated to surrounding healthcare providers, clinics, and local government officials, the community-health nurse can begin the dialogue to effect policy changes. More engagement with health fairs, educational seminars, and print and social media campaigns may also result from health screenings.

Overall, health screenings are an integral piece of the healthcare puzzle. As nurses, it is often necessary to discuss the importance of annual health-screening recommendations upon each patient encounter. If patients reject or accept the recommended testing, they become aware of any present risk factors. Nurses can probe for information as to their ambivalence. For example, while completing a depression screening, a nurse can determine if an individual is at risk for depression. A patient who scores higher on the questionnaire can reveal if the answers are an accurate representation of daily high-risk behavior, or situational in nature.

Nurses are required to educate, prep, and help clients when undergoing a screening exam. These preventative procedures are designed to detect diseases, infections, and other health ailments in their initial stages. Examples include colonoscopy screenings, Pap smears, mammograms, and ultrasounds. Nurse responsibilities include evaluating the results of the screening test and then following up with the patient. They also communicate results to the patient's doctor and make sure they are documented on the patient's medical record as per the facility's specific guidelines and practices.

A **mammogram** involves compressing the patient's breasts between two plate-like surfaces to expand the breast tissue area. An X-ray then displays images of the breasts via a computer screen so they can be checked by a doctor for signs of cancer. Nurses can help patients prep for this exam by advising them to schedule it during a time their breasts are likely to be less tender (e.g. not right before their period), not to use deodorant before the screening as it can obscure the image, and making them feel comfortable the day of the exam.

During a **colonoscopy**, a doctor uses a long, flexible tube to look inside a patient's colon for abnormalities. This screening procedure requires the patient to be sedated and follow a liquid diet and take a preparatory course of drinkable laxatives starting the day before. Nurses can help advise patients regarding the specific prep involved and also about any discomfort they might feel during and after the procedure.

Pap smear screenings scrape cells from the cervix to check for precancerous or cancerous cell abnormalities. For this test, the doctor inserts a speculum into the patient's vagina to widen the vaginal walls and provide easier access to the cervix. Nurses can help prep patients by advising not to schedule the exam during menstruation since it can skew results, to avoid sexual activity, to avoid using a douche or spermicidal products the day before the test, and help keep the patient relaxed the day of the test.

Cancer Screening

Cancer screening tests relevant to several organ systems have effectively decreased the incidence and mortality of cancer in those systems. Common screening tests include the Papanicolaou (PAP) test for cervical cancer, colonoscopy for colon cancer, and mammography for breast cancer. Recently, screening for lung cancer with advanced computed tomography (CT) technology in patients with a history of smoking has been proposed, in an effort to identify lung cancers at an earlier stage that may be treated more successfully. Conversely, the research indicates that there is insufficient evidence to support any relationship between decreased disease incidence and morbidity and the prostate-specific antigen test (PSA) measurements for prostate cancer, or the annual full-body skin assessments by a dermatologist. In addition, there are no screening tests available for ovarian cancer.

Osteoporosis Screening/Bone-Density Scan

Osteoporosis is the "thinning" of the bone, which most commonly affects postmenopausal women. The degree and progression of the changes associated with osteoporosis can be measured by the bone-density exam, which compares a patient's test results with the results of younger patients who are disease free.

Domestic Violence Screening and Detection

The efficiency of domestic violence screening and detection is often hampered by the reluctance of the abused individual to report the abuse. Institutions and insurance companies have included routine assessment questions related to a patient's perceptions of personal safety; however, the widespread acceptance and effectiveness of these measures are not known.

High Risk Behaviors

High-risk behaviors can be defined as actions that have a high probability of yielding a negative consequence. Nurses must develop a rapport with patients in an effort to create open communication so the patient will be more likely to reveal conduct that could have detrimental health outcomes. This technique can also encourage patients to ask questions about their risky behaviors. The nurse can then use the established rapport to discern if the patient's level of comfort and commitment to the behaviors is amenable to change.

One of the most effective methods of encouraging open communication with patients is motivational interviewing. Nurses use motivational interviewing to assess, collaborate, plan, and implement treatment with patients. There are five major components of motivational interviewing: express empathy, illustrate incongruity, manage resistance, encourage self-validation, and promote independence. The nurse can employ these steps when combatting ambivalence to change. For example, when working with a patient who is considering smoking cessation, begin with simple statements regarding the difficulties involved with quitting. This often results in the patient remarking about the number of attempts to quit, along with reasons why their prior attempts did not end in success.

Next, draw from earlier statements concerning lifestyle choices, the patient's own reasons for quitting, and the potential for negative outcomes. In the next step, the nurse can tie the elements together, choosing carefully which area of resistance to target. What might the patient gain from quitting? What are the potential barriers to success from the patient's viewpoint? Asking these open-ended questions will help patients draw their own conclusions, validating the ability to self-navigate through possible obstacles. Once able to verbalize how the desired outcome could be achieved, the patient has managed to break through their own resistance, and the groundwork has been set for more internal dialogue.

Lifestyle Choices

Traditionally, nursing interventions are designed to target the **lifestyle choices** that affect disease processes. During every patient encounter, the nurse must ask open-ended questions in order to determine which interventions should be implemented. The acronym **SMART** (specific, measurable, attainable, relevant, and timely) is a concise

69

reference for patients. When it is clearly what the main objective is, the likelihood of achieving that goal is increased.

When addressing multiple issues, choose one area with the highest likelihood of success to build momentum and patient confidence in the process. For example, when discussing diet, it is important for the nurse to first establish what the patient's current diet and exercise plan includes. This dialogue will open the door to likes, dislikes, preferred cooking methods, and diet history. As the discussion expands, inquire about budgetary constraints and access to healthy food options. Once eating habits are known, define daily scheduling conflicts that may become barriers to success. Create a contingency plan, with multiple options. Another major area of importance for lifestyle choices is exercise. Upon reviewing current diagnoses, medications, and any mobility or chronic pain concerns, the nurse can partner with the patient to formulate a reasonable plan. Set a specific goal on the type and duration of exercise; measure steps or activity as accurately as possible with a pedometer. Can they commit to exercise daily? What is an appropriate form of exercise? Maintain the stance of advocate and collaborator to preserve patients' autonomy and validate their experiences whenever possible.

Some types of contraception are not recommended because of the patient's lifestyle choices, agreement level, or a medical condition. For instance, women who smoke and are predisposed to deep vein thrombosis should not use oral contraceptives because they are at risk for blood clots and strokes. Nurses need to be able to identify and convey anticipated consequences of contraception to the patient. These can include being aware of the different family planning methods best suited to the patient's needs and situation, the absence of unplanned pregnancies, the ability to plan a pregnancy until the patient feels the time is appropriate, and participating in a relationship that is sexually satisfying without being afraid of getting pregnant.

When patients exhibit the necessity and wish for contraception, nurses need to remain impartial in their encouragement, no matter their personal thoughts or principles on the topic. Some patients will be eager to discuss the possibility of contraception and others may be hesitant to discuss sexuality and family planning topics. In these circumstances, it is imperative for nurses to develop a level of trust with the patient and encourage them to be able to talk about their viewpoints without feeling judged or ashamed. When discussing these topics with a patient, the nurse needs to convey the advantages, dangers, cost, accessibility, and possible impediments and contraindications of the different types of contraception.

Self-Care

The job of a nurse is physically, mentally, and emotionally stressful. The strain of moving and lifting patients, along with going from room to room constantly answering the needs of the patients for a long shift, can be physically exhausting. One must organize one's time, prioritize tasks, answer questions, and have countless conversations with the healthcare team and patients and their families, all of which can take a mental toll. Dealing with patients who are sick, in pain, suffering, and, in some cases, facing death, can drain a nurse's emotional reserves, which can quickly lead to burnout if left unaddressed. Being aware of this potential for overall fatigue is the first step to managing stress and maintaining one's own health.

It is important that a nurse knows how to cope with the effects of stress positively. **Negative coping mechanisms** include unhealthy eating habits and binging behavior, abusing substances such as alcohol and drugs, acting recklessly with one's own safety, and becoming abusive in personal relationships.

Positive coping mechanisms include finding an activity to engage in to unwind and relieve stress in a healthy way. Activities such as daily exercise, spending quality time with friends and family, cooking, yoga, biking, and hiking are all ways to deal with the stress of a demanding job in a healthy way.

The nurse should be careful not to work too many hours as well. It can be tempting to take on extra shifts continually to earn extra money for gifts, vacations, or simply to pay the bills and support a family. These extra shifts and long hours can put a nurse in a danger zone if they are using up too much mental, physical, and emotional energy. It is better to be well rested and have adequate mental and physical energy for a shift than to put the patient and oneself at risk for harm.

Being properly nourished, getting adequate exercise, and maintaining healthy sleep habits will all positively contribute to a nurse's health. The nurse's health is vital to helping their patients regain or maintain their own health and, thus, should be made a high priority. If one needs help learning healthy eating habits, meal planning, how to get involved in an exercise program or routine, or other methods of managing stress, many facilities have programs to help guide employees toward better health. There are a plethora of available online resources aimed at improving one's health as well.

Practice Quiz

1. When performing HS oral care for a patient with dentures, which action should the nurse take?
    a. Remove the patient's dentures, clean them with cool or tepid water, place them in a denture cup with cool or tepid water or denture cleaning solution, and leave the cup on the bedside table within the patient's reach.
    b. Remove the patient's dentures, clean them with hot water, place them in an empty denture cup, and leave the cup on the bedside table within the patient's reach.
    c. Remove the patient's dentures, wrap them in a paper towel, and place them on the bedside table within the patient's reach.
    d. Remove the patient's dentures, clean them with cool or tepid water, wrap them in a washcloth, and leave them by the sink until the patient is ready for AM care.

2. A nurse is providing AM care to a patient who has suffered a stroke and has right-sided weakness. When dressing the patient, which action should the nurse take?
    a. Before dressing the patient in the new clothing, the nurse should remove all of the patient's old clothing to prevent cross contamination.
    b. The nurse should first undress and redress the patient's upper body, then undress and redress the patient's lower body.
    c. When removing the patient's pants, the nurse should remove the pants from the left leg first and then the right leg.
    d. When redressing the patient in clean pants, the nurse should place the left leg in the pants first and then the right leg.

3. A nurse is assisting a diabetic patient with breakfast. The patient is scheduled for heart surgery in the afternoon. Which breakfast tray is appropriate for this patient?
    a. Coffee, apple juice, lime gelatin, and clear broth
    b. Coffee with sugar substitute, oatmeal, scrambled eggs, and bacon
    c. Coffee with sugar, grits, egg white omelet, and a cup of fresh fruit
    d. This patient should not receive a breakfast tray.

4. A patient is experiencing diarrhea. and complaining of lightheadedness when standing. The patient is normally able to ambulate to the bathroom without assistance. What's the first action a nurse should take?
    a. Encourage the patient to drink lots of fluids to prevent dehydration.
    b. This is normal, and the nurse should do nothing.
    c. Provide the patient with additional washcloths, soap, and towels for perineal care.
    d. Place the call bell within reach and instruct the patient to call for assistance before getting out of bed.

5. A nurse is providing AM care to a comatose patient. The patient has been immobile for several weeks and is at risk for muscle atrophy and contractures. What action should the nurse take in caring for the patient?
    a. Passive range of motion exercises should be done with the patient.
    b. Perineal care should be provided, but a full bed bath should be avoided due to the patient's risk for pressure sores.
    c. Before providing oral care, the head of the patient's bed should be flat, and the patient's head should be turned to the side to prevent aspiration.
    d. The patient should be encouraged to do active range of motion exercises while lying in bed.

See answers on the next page.

Answer Explanations

1. A: The patient's dentures should be removed, cleaned with cool or tepid water, and then stored in a denture cup with cool or tepid water (or denture cleaning solution) within the patient's reach. For Choice *B*, dentures should never be cleaned with or stored in hot water since hot water can damage them. In Choice *C*, a patient's dentures should never be stored in a paper towel because they could accidentally be thrown away. Dentures should always be stored in a denture cup. In Choice *D*, if a patient is unable to put their own dentures in their mouth, or the patient doesn't wish to keep them within reach, storing them by the sink is acceptable. However, they should never be stored in a washcloth. A washcloth can be used to handle dentures while cleaning them to prevent accidental damage, but dentures should always be stored in a denture cup.

2. C: When dressing a patient with a weakness or paralysis on one side, the weak side should always be undressed last and redressed first. In Choice *A*, unless the patient has soiled his clothes, it's unnecessary to remove all of their clothes prior to redressing them. The patient should be covered up as much as possible to avoid discomfort and/or overexposure. For Choice *B*, the order of the upper- and lower-body dressing is unimportant as it relates to the patient's right-sided weakness. There might be a valid reason to start with the upper body, but it isn't related to the right-sided weakness. In Choice *D*, this is the opposite order. The nurse should place the right leg (the weak side) into the pants first.

3. D: A patient scheduled for surgery in the afternoon would be NPO (nothing by mouth) status, so they would not be allowed to have any food or beverage. Choice *A* is an example of a clear liquid diet, which would not be appropriate for a patient with an upcoming surgery. This diet is more appropriate for a patient post-surgery, before progressing to a regular diet. Choice *B* is an appropriate diet for a diabetic patient, but this patient is scheduled for surgery in the afternoon and should be NPO. Finally, Choice *C* is an example of a heart-healthy diet, which may be appropriate for the patient after being cleared to eat solid foods post-surgery.

4. D: The *first* action the nurse should take is to give the call bell to the patient and instruct them to call for assistance. If a patient is experiencing lightheadedness, they're at risk for a fall. Patient safety is the number one priority. In Choice *A*, if not contraindicated, the patient should be encouraged to drink lots of fluids, but this is not the first action the nurse should take. In Choice *B*, the findings should be reported to the nurse; however, the nurse should not leave the room before placing the call bell within reach of the patient and instructing them to call for assistance before getting out of bed. In Choice *C*, the patient might require additional supplies for perineal care, but this isn't the first action the nurse should take.

5. A: "Muscle atrophy" is the weakening of a muscle, and a "contracture" is the shortening of a muscle. Both conditions are due to immobility. Therefore, passive range of motion exercises (unless contraindicated) should be done with the patient. In Choice *B*, patients at risk for pressure sores can have full bed baths, but the nurse must thoroughly dry the patient's skin to prevent breakdown. For Choice *C*, the nurse would be expected to provide oral care to the patient, and the patient's head should be turned to the side (if possible) to prevent aspiration. However, unless contraindicated, the head of the patient's bed should be elevated for oral care. For Choice *D*, active range of motion exercises are those performed by the patient independently. A comatose patient is unable to perform active range of motion exercises, so passive range of motion exercises must be performed by the nurse.

Psychosocial Integrity

Abuse/Neglect

Abuse and neglect can take many forms and affect people of various demographics. Children, women, and the elderly tend to be the vulnerable victim populations. Abuse and neglect cases can often put the victim in the emergency room, so nurses and other medical personnel should be aware that they likely will come across these tragic situations, and intervention may be necessary. It is important to know how to spot abuse and neglect cases for legal and ethical reasons.

In children, abuse and neglect can come from a biological or adoptive parent, guardian, close adult in the child's life, or stranger. Younger children are the most vulnerable individuals in this demographic. This is because they may not be able to speak, defend themselves, or understand that they are being abused, or they may be fearful of reporting a caregiver.

Child abuse can be emotional, such as refusal to provide affection or emotional comfort, criticizing the child in a cruel or unusual manner, or administering humiliation or shame tactics. Child abuse may be hard to detect or penalize legally. Physical abuse of a child involves intentional acts of physical violence that could result in injury. Sexual abuse of a child includes sexual acts or interactions by an adult; even if the child provides consent, it is considered abuse, due to the emotional and mental immaturity of the child. In the United States, legal age of consent varies by state. Signs of abuse in children can include physical indicators, such as cuts, bruises, genital pain or bleeding, and persistent yeast infections. There can also be behavioral indicators, such as slow development, aggression, anxiety, suicidal tendencies, fearful natures, antisocial or awkward behavioral habits, statements describing inappropriate physical or sexual interactions, visibly unusual relationships or interactions with a parent or caregiver, and a lack of desire (or even refusal) to go home.

Child neglect refers to a parent, guardian, or other caretaker's inaction to provide basic care such as food, water, education, medical and dental treatments, safe supervision, and clean and safe living accommodations. Signs of neglect in children can include chronic illness, malnutrition, lack of personal hygiene, above-average school absenteeism, anxiety and depression, and substance abuse.

A single sign may not mean that abuse or neglect is present, but it should be taken seriously by asking further questions and potentially seeking resources, such as legal and social support agencies, to prevent further abuse. Most states require that knowledge of potential abuse or neglect be reported to legal and child protective services. The process of reporting varies by state, and practitioners should familiarize themselves with abuse- and neglect-reporting practices of the state in which their nursing services will be provided.

Domestic violence between adult partners, also known as intimate partner violence and abuse, is also a common form of abuse that can require emergency department visits. While this type of abuse can be experienced by partners of either gender or orientation, it is most commonly inflicted by male partners on female victims. Physical indicators of abuse from a partner include marks such as bruises, black eyes, genital or anal damage, scratches, and welts. Behavioral indicators include a fearful nature, low self-esteem, isolation, anxiety, depression, constant excuses for the abusing partner's dangerous actions, and suicidal tendencies. Again, the presence of one sign may not indicate that abuse is occurring, but it can be a call to action to provide resources for the victim's safety.

Elder abuse and neglect may occur by family members or other caregivers. Elderly people are vulnerable, as they may be physically weak or have other physical and mental limitations, handicaps, or disabilities. Signs of abuse in elders are similar to those seen in children but can also include the occurrence of adult-minded activities that happen without the elder's consent, such as mishandled financial transactions or healthcare fraud. Physical

indicators of abuse in the elderly include bruises, broken bones, and signs of physical restraint. Behavioral indicators include poor relationships with caregivers, anxiety, depression, and a fearful nature. Indicators of neglect in the elderly include missed or improper medication administration, signs of poor hygiene, genital or anal rashes, and malnutrition. Unfortunately, many signs of elder abuse and neglect are similar to signs of dementia, a natural reaction to ailing health, and other behaviors commonly exhibited by this age demographic. Therefore, due diligence by nurses and medical personnel is necessary. All states have elder abuse prevention laws, though procedures for reporting may vary by state, so it is important to know the process for the state in which nursing services will be administered.

Behavioral Interventions

The overall theme of any effective nursing intervention is the implementation of behavioral change to produce healthy outcomes, called **behavioral intervention**. Nursing interventions combine medical and psychosocial interventions to guide patients to live healthier lives. The most successful nursing interventions to promote disease prevention also incorporate the utilization of the patient's support network, stress-management techniques, building effective coping skills, and encouraging healthy lifestyle choices. The best illustration of how all of these components can produce the greatest impact is depicted in the following example.

Consider a nurse providing intensive case management to a morbidly obese patient seeking bariatric surgery. The incidence and prevalence of morbid obesity is rapidly increasing as the number one cause of adverse health conditions in the United States. Despite primary, secondary, and tertiary health promotion efforts, the waistlines of Americans are continuing to grow at exponential rates. Disordered eating, sedentary lifestyle, poor impulse control, and inaccurate perceptions about how to maintain a healthy diet are commonplace. It is essential that the nurse providing case management services to patients seeking morbid-obesity surgery create a specialized treatment plan to help ensure the patient's success.

After conducting the history and physical interview, it is determined that the patient recently received a dual diagnosis of type II diabetes and hypercholesterolemia. With a family history of both parents diagnosed with diabetes and hypertension, there is some concern that the disease will progress rapidly. Newly diagnosed, the patient has not yet been prescribed daily oral medications. Instead, the attending physician has ordered a case management consultation for the patient to discuss morbid-obesity surgery. In this instance, the nurse will assume the role of case manager with the final result being to recommend or deny the request to approve the patient as a candidate for bariatric surgery.

Although the primary mechanism remains under investigation, bariatric surgery has been said to resolve myriad obesity-related comorbidities. As the body mass index of Americans has grown, physicians have observed an inverse relationship with healthy lifestyle choices. Studies have shown that both type II diabetes and hypercholesterolemia are among the main diseases that significantly contribute to the development of cardiovascular disease. These conditions often require extensive, ongoing treatment. Many patients reach a state where traditional medical treatment becomes ineffective in the daily management of their symptoms. As the disease state progresses, dietary interventions also become ineffective. Surgeons who regularly perform bariatric procedures have found that it is the combination of substantial dietary restriction and increased physical activity that can lead to an almost complete resolution of disease. For these reasons, thousands of patients make the decision to pursue bariatric surgery.

Once the initial assessment is completed, the next task for the nurse is to verify the eligibility requirements dictated by the patient's insurance carrier. The nurse will contact the patient's health insurance provider and obtain an explanation of benefits. This information will help the nurse prepare the patient to complete any required criteria. This is an integral step to ensuring that surgery can be approved. Without clear direction, the treatment plan is incomplete. It is customary for the patient to be required to receive diagnostic testing, meet with a dietician, and complete a psychological evaluation to confirm their readiness to succeed after surgery. The nurse will then discuss

the benefit criteria with the patient to assess the patient's commitment to the process. The final step in this preliminary phase is to obtain both written and verbal agreement from the patient to receive and actively participate in medical case management.

During the engagement phase of treatment planning, the nurse will begin to utilize the SMART goal-setting process. This type of behavioral intervention focuses on the presentation of the problem, developing a solution to the problem, and outlining the necessary steps to resolve the problem. Additionally, this technique encourages patients to brainstorm ways to meet their own needs. For this scenario, the nurse will describe the criteria that must be completed in order for the patient to be approved for bariatric surgery, along with any associated timeframes within which those criteria must be met.

In most cases, patients must complete a physician-supervised lifestyle modification program, for a specific number of weeks. The nurse will ask the patient what steps can be taken to adjust their lifestyle in order to satisfy that requirement. Patients can work with a nutritionist, dietician, or their primary care physician. How will those appointments be scheduled, and with whom? What specific lifestyle modifications will the patient need to make and why? What will it look like when the changes have been made? Does the patient believe that they can make the necessary lifestyle modifications? Do the changes seem appropriate, based on the patient's previously stated goals and needs? How long will it take? These questions lead to the development of SMART goals.

SMART goal setting requires a series of question-and-answer sessions. This technique will continue for each objective, in an effort to guide the patient to lead the treatment-planning process. If goals are ambiguous, the patient will not understand what to do. Goals are not measurable if there is no way to track progress. Goals must also be practical in their application. The goal must make sense to the patient and contribute to the overall completion of the desired outcome. The patient must be able to see the big picture and have a clear understanding of how and why all of the tasks are interdependent.

It is also necessary for the nurse to periodically check in with the patient to determine if each task is being completed according to the timeline. Creating a plan in this way will affect how the patient thinks about goal setting in general. It is important for the nurse to allow the patient to take responsibility for completing each task. The patient will monitor their own progress and troubleshoot with the nurse as needed. This technique is self-empowering for the patient and reinforces the self-determination necessary for goal setting in the future.

Behavioral Strategies to Decrease Anxiety

If a patient is showing signs of or exhibiting anxious behavior, a nurse can evaluate their symptoms and come up with a suitable coping strategy. Behavioral strategies to decrease anxiety include:

- Cognitive reframing: educating the patient about how to replace negative thoughts with positive ones
- Deep breathing
- Progressive relaxation: tightening and releasing the body's muscles
- Meditation
- Prayer
- Reminiscence therapy: sharing life remembrances with other people
- Validation therapy: resolving disagreements and concerns through therapy
- Writing their thoughts in a journal
- Guided imagery: visualizing a comforting scene
- Music therapy
- Biofeedback: connecting the patient to a special machine to see various vital statistics when exposed to stress items
- Mindfulness: having an awareness of one's setting

76

- Setting priorities
- Talking positively about one's self
- Medication

Reminiscence Therapy, Validation Therapy, and Reality Orientation

Reminiscence therapy is designed to boost the feelings of self-worth and importance of a person suffering from anxiety. Nurses can help the patient cope with their anxiety by listening to their personal narratives, memories, and other recollections, giving them the chance to go over past events and explain how they experienced and handled stressful incidents.

Nurses can also participate in **validation therapy**, helping patients deal with tension and worry alongside a therapist who specializes in identifying and sympathizing with anxiety-ridden patients, justifying and supporting struggles and concerns.

Reality orientation is meant to help people whose anxiety stems from feelings of confusion or bewilderment gain improved mental and psychomotor function. It helps foster an awareness of various environmental factors impacting the patient, such as their identity, a sense of time, and their surroundings. The nurse can help do this by focusing on factors that are contributing to the patient's disorientation, such as the time of day, month and year, their personal situation, and the current weather. Utilizing items such as calendars, electronic reminders, and clocks can be useful.

Chemical and Other Dependencies

Substance abuse is defined, most simply, as extreme use of a drug. Abuse occurs for many reasons, such as mental health instability, inability to cope with everyday life stressors, the loss of a loved one, or enjoyment of the euphoric state that the overindulgence in a substance causes. Abused substances create some type of intoxication that alters decision-making, awareness, attentiveness, or physical impulses.

Substance abuse results in tolerance, withdrawal, and compulsive drug-taking behavior. Tolerance occurs when increased amounts of the substance are needed to achieve the desired effects. Withdrawal manifests as physiological and substance-specific cognitive symptoms (e.g., cold sweats, shivering, nausea, vomiting, paranoia, hallucinations). Withdrawal not only happens when an individual stops abusing the substance, but also occurs when he or she attempts to reduce the amount taken in an effort to stop using altogether.

Some of the most commonly abused substances include the following:

Tobacco

People abuse tobacco either in cigarette, cigar, pipe, or snuff form. People report many reasons for tobacco use, including a calming effect, suppression of appetite, and relief of depression. The primary addictive component in tobacco is nicotine, but tobacco smoke also contains about seven hundred carcinogens (cancer-causing agents) that may result in lung and throat cancers as well as heart disease, emphysema, peptic ulcer disease, and stroke. Withdrawal indicators include insomnia, irritability, overwhelming nicotine craving, anxiety, and depression.

Alcohol

Some individuals feel the need to have a drink to relax and calm down, as it is a central nervous system (CNS) depressant, which tends to soothe individuals and lower inhibitions. However, it also slurs speech and impairs muscle control, coordination, and reflex time. Alcohol abuse can cause cirrhosis of the liver; liver, esophagus, and stomach cancers; heart enlargement; chronic inflammation of the pancreas; vitamin deficiencies; certain anemias; and brain damage. Physical dependence is a biological need for alcohol in order to avoid physical withdrawal symptoms, which include anxiety, erratic pulse rate, tremors, seizures, and hallucinations. In its most serious form,

withdrawal combined with malnourishment can lead to a potentially fatal condition known as **delirium tremens (DTs)**, which is a psychotic disorder that involves tremors, disorientation, and hallucinations.

Other Prescriptions
Prescription medications, such as anti-anxiety, sleep, and pain medications, are commonly used.

Marijuana
Marijuana is considered the most frequently abused illicit drug in the United States. General effects of marijuana use include pleasure, relaxation, and weakened dexterity and memory. The active addictive ingredient in marijuana is tetrahydrocannabinol (THC). It is normally smoked, but it can also be eaten. The individual withdrawing from marijuana will experience increased irritability and anxiety.

Cocaine
Cocaine is a stimulant that is also known as "coke," "snow," or "rock." It can be smoked, injected, snorted, or swallowed. Reported effects include pleasure, enhanced alertness, and increased energy. Both temporary and prolonged use have been known to contribute to damage to the brain, heart, lungs, and kidneys. Withdrawal symptoms include severe depression and reduced energy.

Heroin
Also known as "smack" and "horse," heroin use continues to increase. Effects of heroin abuse include pleasure, slower respirations, and drowsiness. Overdose and/or overuse of heroin can cause respiratory depression, resulting in death. Use of heroin as an injectable substance can lead to other complications such as heart valve damage, tetanus, botulism, hepatitis B, or human immunodeficiency virus (HIV)/AIDS infection from sharing dirty needles. Withdrawal is usually intense and includes vomiting, abdominal cramps, diarrhea, confusion, body aches, and diaphoresis.

Methamphetamines
Also known as "meth," "crank," and "crystal," methamphetamine use also continues to increase, especially in the West and Midwest regions of the United States. Methamphetamine is categorized as a stimulant that produces such effects as pleasure, increased alertness, and decreased appetite. Similar to cocaine, it can be snorted, smoked, or injected, and it can be taken orally as well. Like cocaine, it shares many of the same detrimental effects, such as myocardial infarction, hypertension, and stroke. Other prolonged usage effects include paranoia, hallucinations, damage to and loss of dentition, and heart damage. Withdrawal symptoms involve depression, abdominal cramps, and increased appetite.

Nursing interventions for the individual addicted to tobacco, alcohol, and other drugs centers around the prevention of relapse, and treatment depends on the individual and the substance that is abused. Behavioral treatment assists with recognition of abuse triggers, habits, and drug cravings, as well as providing the tactics to help one cope with these issues. A physician may prescribe nicotine patches for the tobacco abuser and methadone or Suboxone to manage withdrawal symptoms and certain drug yearnings.

Non-Substance-Related Dependencies
Even some behaviors—such as exercise and work—are recognized as positive behaviors, but when taken to extremes, unpleasant consequences develop. For example, exercise addiction, in its least damaging form, may create anxiety when physical or weather conditions prevent participation. In more extreme cases, certain athletes will continue to train in spite of illness or injury, exacerbating the physical problem and sometimes causing permanent disabilities.

Overworking—sometimes referred to as "workaholism"—may also be viewed as positive by some standards. In the end, however, those working many hours of overtime may result in a life out of balance. They may also be using work as a means to avoid other responsibilities, such as family life. It can create stress and low energy, and it can lead to physical and emotional problems.

Sexual addiction, also known as hypersexuality, involves a preoccupation with sexual pleasures that can manifest itself in a multitude of ways. These behaviors prove harmful to themselves and potentially other people. One example is pornography. Those addicted to pornography find that having close and intimate contact with their long-term partner is less exciting than viewing stimulating films or pictures. This creates intimacy problems and difficulty in one's primary relationship. The Internet has made it easier for people to access these materials, sometimes at no cost, creating a greater number of persons who view it addictively.

Gambling addiction may involve a desire for the adrenaline rush of making bets or a cycle of losing money via gambling and then gambling more to try to make up for previously lost money.

Overeating, based upon the number of obese and overweight persons in our culture, is on the rise. Some people use food much in the same way that others use alcohol or drugs—to feel a sense of pleasure or to numb feelings of depression or anxiety. The consequences of obesity are numerous from a social and physical standpoint, with the most severe of these being the high risk for heart disease or stroke.

Some individuals are addicted to self-harm in the form of cutting, scratching, or mutilating themselves. This is often described as a means to bring relief from emotional pain as one focuses on the physical sensation of pain to distract from the emotional sensation. It may also be a type of self-punishment. Some people have scars from this compulsion. Others may contract infections. It is theorized that persons who self-mutilate are at higher risk of suicide than those who do not, making it a possible precursor to suicidal ideations.

Risk-Taking Behavior

Risk-taking behaviors such as driving fast or engaging in substance use, may lead to car accidents or overdoses, respectively. Yet, they may bring about positive feelings in the moment. This includes the thrill of a fast ride or the high one gets from drug use. Given that risk-taking behavior is potentially dangerous, some people wonder why anyone would take part in such conduct. On one hand, such behavior puts those who engage in it in harm's way, but, on the other, it gives participants the chance to experience an outcome they perceive as positive. Sigmund Freud theorized that this was related to an innate drive within human beings to seek experiences that put them close to death, for the adrenaline high one might feel. Risk-taking behavior can be a singular diagnosis or it can be part of the symptomology of other conditions such as PTSD.

Risk-taking behavior includes having sex with strangers, often with no protection against sexually transmitted diseases or unplanned pregnancies. Risk-takers also enjoy gambling, typically losing more than they can handle. These individuals may also take part in extreme sports or recreational activities.

Some research indicates that men tend to be risk-takers more than women. But both male and female risk-takers share the same personality traits, such as impulsive sensation-seeking, aggression-hostility, and sociability, one study found. Genetics play a role in risk-taking behavior. Identical twins separated at birth tend to engage in risk-taking behaviors at high rates. Testosterone appears to play a role as well, which is why there's a gender imbalance in the people most likely to take part in risk-taking behaviors.

Coping Mechanisms

Unpack **coping mechanisms**, and you will find at their core a whole-hearted but poorly defined resistance to change. Effective stress management combined with adaptive coping skills are directly related to the execution of a

treatment plan. It is the acquisition and application of adaptive coping skills that promotes overall wellbeing. If coping skills are maladaptive, no matter how applicable the treatment plan is, there will be no effect if the patient is ill-equipped to navigate the stages of change. It is essential that the nurse work collaboratively with the patient and other members of the healthcare team to formulate a treatment plan that is based on patient-centered care.

Consider how a nurse working in an inpatient mental health unit would respond during the assessment of a teenage girl admitted for observation after a suicide attempt. The initial physical assessment uncovers evidence of what appears to be a series of self-inflicted cuts, in various stages of healing, on the patient's inner thighs. A thorough interview with the teen reveals that the patient has been cutting herself in response to bullying from fellow residents in her boarding school. The teen also reported that the bullying has occurred for several years and had escalated to threats of physical harm. School officials were notified, and the students were expelled. Despite the fact that the offending students no longer attend the school, the patient has been unable to relinquish cutting herself. Self-injurious behaviors have increased in the last 48 hours, after the teen ended a long-term romantic relationship.

According to the patient, the break-up created feelings of hopelessness and overwhelming depression. In a deep state of depression, the student swallowed a bottle of Tylenol, hoping to end the pain. The admitting diagnosis of the attending physician is depression, with a rule-out diagnosis of bipolar disorder.

On an inpatient unit, there is often an interdisciplinary team assembled to develop a collaborative treatment plan. Although the therapist and social worker will conduct additional interviews with the patient, it will be necessary for the nurse to formulate nursing diagnoses and interventions that complement the overall plan of care. In this case, the most appropriate nursing diagnosis would be: risk for harm associated with feelings of hopelessness secondary to the diagnosis of depression. Suitable interventions would be centered around the application of the adaptive coping skills learned through ongoing individual and group therapies while admitted to the inpatient unit. The nurse will dispense antidepressant medications prescribed by the attending physician, reinforce the techniques demonstrated in therapy, and guide the patient to begin safety planning.

Patients can suffer from poor body image perception due to any number of traumatic incidents such as an accident, physical disability, hair loss due to cancer treatments and body altering surgeries such as a mastectomy or orchiectomy. it is important for nurses and other healthcare team members to help them cope with these thoughts and feelings. The first step involves performing a total evaluation of the patient's perceived body image, then devising a coping strategy. This plan can include reassuring the client to talk about how they feel about the change in their body and their subsequent negative feelings such as despair, rage, desperation, and incompetence, helping educate the patient on fostering body image self-awareness and worthiness, and highlighting the positive attributes, strengths, and capabilities, rather than the changed body element.

Types of Coping Skills

- **Self-Soothing**: Comforting the self through the five senses
- **Distraction**: Taking mind off the problem for a while
- **Opposite Action**: Doing the opposite of the initial impulse that's consistent with a more positive emotion
- **Emotional Awareness**: Tools for identifying and expressing one's feelings
- **Mindfulness**: Tools for centering and grounding the self in the present moment
- **Crisis Plan**: Support and resource information for when coping skills are not enough, such as therapist, family, friends, or a crisis team

The nurse must also remain aware that the stress of managing emotional turmoil can create feelings of powerlessness and depression. The patient may have grown accustomed to denying intense feelings and instincts in an effort to be insulated from the source of pain. The goal is to focus on rebuilding the patient's coping skills from the inside out, in order to promote a sense of hope and self-determination. Discuss the difference between adaptive

and maladaptive coping skills. Encourage the patient to define which behaviors they engage in that they would place into each category. What the patient perceives to be most effective is not necessarily the healthiest response. Educate the patient on how healthier choices lead to healthier outcomes.

Discuss how the self-inflicted wounds could become infected or disfiguring. Offer information on the benefits of aerobic exercise to release endorphins known to naturally elevate the patient's mood. Encourage the patient to consider journaling, writing, or creating art to express suppressed emotions. Pet therapies have also been effective in the treatment of depression, providing much-needed emotional support. Finally, encourage the patient to consider attending local support groups for depressed teens. The communal aspect of a support group is helpful, as other teens battling depression can validate the patient's experience.

The customary discharge plan for depressed patients at risk for suicide includes several components. First, the patient must agree that they will no longer make any attempts to harm themselves in any way. Instead, the patient will create a detailed list of at least two alternatives to self-harm. The nurse must also highlight patients' current coping skills and encourage their ability to support themselves and to utilize their stress management skills. What are alternatives to self-harm that could produce similar feelings of release that the patient can practice? Second, the patient must verbalize understanding that any episodes of self-harm will result in immediate hospitalization. What steps will the patient take when feeling overwhelmed? Does the patient have an accountability partner? Finally, the patient will be equipped with a personalized list of contacts to utilize when stress-relieving techniques are ineffective. This list will include a 24-hour suicide hotline, as well as the contact information for the local therapist assigned prior to the patient's discharge.

Crisis Intervention

Crisis-intervention skills are an essential component of providing exceptional patient care. Crises strike unexpectedly and need immediate intervention. Nurses in particular must have robust crisis-intervention skills in order to address the myriad issues that patients and their caregivers face. Why is crisis intervention so important? Why do nurses need to acquire this dexterity? It is because proper nursing care involves the astute assessment of the patient's overall wellbeing. At some point during the provision of care to patients and families, the nurse will encounter a situation in which they will have no other choice but to intervene. This is primarily because the nurse is often on the front lines of healthcare and the first to interact with the patient. The integration of nursing care, stress-management techniques, and assisting the patient navigate through the stages of grief are of paramount importance. Not unlike every other nursing technique, crisis-intervention skills will be enhanced with repeated use and more progressive problem solving.

Consider the importance of the nurse's adaptability to crises with reference to assisting patients and families impacted by natural disasters. Upon deployment to an area destroyed by torrential rains and subsequent flooding, a nurse could encounter families in need of not only immediate medical care, but ongoing crisis intervention. In conditions such as these, patients are often overwhelmed by their physical pain as well as concerns for how to meet their basic needs for food, shelter, and clean water. Disaster relief relies on medical triage to determine the appropriate level of care needed by patients and is typically assessed based on a four-tier model. Black/blue is reserved for the deceased; red for immediate care such as chest wounds or gunshots; yellow for those with stable wounds or head injuries; green for minor injuries such as fractures or burns.

In this situation, the nurse must be prepared to rapidly assess the patient's level of injury, the most expedient treatment needed for stabilization, and move on to the next case within minutes. Does the patient or anyone in the family maintain a specific medication regimen to manage chronic illnesses? Have any doses of required medications been missed? Are any assistive devices such as hearing aids or canes needed? It is important to note that the nurse will need to focus on the medical stabilization of patients in this stage rather than delving into psychosocial and emotional trauma.

During disaster-relief efforts, nurses are normally dispatched to both acute care and follow-up care zones. Once immediate medical needs are addressed, patients are transferred to a safe holding area. This space is set aside for psychosocial triage, where patients' basic emotional and physical needs are met. Social workers and chaplains are readily available to debrief survivors. Consider the example of a nurse working with a family impacted by the previous illustration. Having lost their home and belongings and facing recovery from minor injuries, they have been transferred to the holding area for processing. The nurse in this example would receive a brief synopsis from triage, but only regarding injuries and treatment. In this stage, the nurse would obtain a brief social history, information on chronic disease, and feasible relocation options.

Then, the nurse will need to begin guiding the patients through processing the emotional trauma of the incident. Are all family members accounted for? Does anyone in the family unit manage any mental health conditions that have been triggered? What, if any, legal or illegal substances are used or abused by anyone in the family unit? These questions are to help determine if the survivors' emotional responses are directly related to the recent trauma.

Responses to acute traumatic events often mirror the typical response of those who have experienced chronic trauma. The nurse must also assess patients for underlying mental health conditions that may have been exacerbated. In this instance, the most appropriate nursing diagnosis would include ineffective coping. Typical nursing interventions would require the nurse to work with the patient to access previous successful navigation through other traumatic events. Present viable options for next steps and allow the patient the time to process the best response to the traumatic event.

Cultural Awareness

Patients will come from all backgrounds and cultures, and medical providers should be aware of the different cultural needs that may present themselves in the emergency department. **Culture** can encompass anything from a person's geographical location, race, ethnicity, age, socioeconomic status, and religious beliefs that influence the behaviors, traditions, and rituals that he or she chooses to engage in each day. It is important to note that cultural considerations will present themselves daily. Some patients may be unable to speak English and will need interpretive services. Some patients may request that only same-sex providers treat them. Respecting and attending to different cultural needs will provide the patient with a better healthcare experience, lead to increased patient satisfaction, and impact overall health outcomes.

Medical providers can show that they consider cultural differences by kindly and compassionately asking patients to share cultural viewpoints, to share aspects of the medical system and services that make them comfortable or uncomfortable, and to continuously create rapport that allows the patient to feel comfortable in voicing their concerns. Medical providers should be mindful of any preconceived notions that they hold of certain cultures, and if possible, actively work to dispel these. Medical providers should also be mindful to not make presumptions, even if those presumptions come from an intention to be empathetic. For example, a patient who looks to be of Asian descent may have been born and raised in the United States and not identify well with any part of Asian culture. Finally, many healthcare organizations offer internal trainings that cover cultural considerations and cultural diversity. For staff that feel their knowledge and experience is limited in this aspect, these trainings can provide an avenue for personal and professional growth.

Having a diverse emergency department staff can be extremely beneficial when servicing a patient demographic that encompasses many cultures. Having a medical provider who is able to relate directly with a patient's culture can make the patient feel more comfortable and open. Additionally, a diverse emergency department staff can overcome common obstacles such as language barriers or lack of patient education. In this regard, healthcare organizations and nursing leadership should work to actively recruit a diverse workforce.

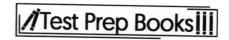

End-of-Life Care

At least once during their career, it is inevitable that a nurse will care for a patient near the end of life. Caring for patients near the end of life can occur in numerous settings. Whether on an inpatient hospice unit or in an outpatient setting, the patient's home, or a skilled nursing facility, the primary objective is to ensure that the nurse provides patient-centered palliative care. There is a stark difference between hospice and palliative care. Both of these, however, fall under the umbrella of end-of-life care. Specifically, end-of-life care includes the care that is received at the end of a patient's illness. While palliative care is considered to be basic comfort care, hospice is the more familiar term, and usually begins once all curative treatments have been stopped.

Hospice can be loosely defined as: primarily palliative and, secondarily, medical care provided to patients deemed by at least two physicians to be terminally ill, with a projected life expectancy of six months or less. This means that the primary objective of hospice care is to provide comfort care to patients. This comfort care is provided under the primary diagnosis. The secondary medical care is typically provided whenever necessary to maintain the patient's comfort. For example, consider a patient who has been receiving hospice care for a primary diagnosis of dementia for four months. Upon admission to the inpatient unit for a weekend of respite, the patient is diagnosed with a kidney infection. The elevated fever, flank pain, nausea, vomiting, and rapid heart rate detract from the patient's overall comfort. The kidney infection is considered to be secondary to the diagnosis of dementia and will be treated. Conditions that are not considered to be comfort care are curative in nature, with the primary objective to prolong life.

It is essential for the nurse to remember that when providing care to a patient who has been placed on hospice, there is always more than one patient to be considered. The spouse or significant other, as well as whomever the patient perceives to be a member of the familial unit, will also be impacted by the patient's diagnosis and subsequent death. The family dynamics will be especially important in these cases, as they must also receive extensive treatment. The nurse can expect to see caregiver burnout, family members struggling with feelings of loss, and anticipatory grief. Most notable is the prospect of funeral planning while the patient is still alive. Although it is not uncommon for the patient or family members to reach end of life without preparing for the funeral, the finality of the task must be worked through. Both the patient and the family may need the intervention of the social worker and/or chaplain in order to facilitate this discussion. It may be necessary to obtain the patient's final wishes separately from the caregiver or family, to be shared upon the patient's demise, if the stress and grief of preparing for death becomes too overwhelming.

Although the patient is still considered to be terminally ill, they will continue to have desires, hopes, and may even want to create a plan for the future. It will be necessary to coordinate the patient's care with the interdisciplinary team (social worker, chaplain, physician, and nurse). All involved will have the opportunity to review the patient's electronic medical records, as well as current diagnosis, medications, and treatment plan. It is usually the nurse who initially notices the beginning of the patient's decompensation. As it is uncommon to accurately predict the precise date of the patient's death, the patient must be guided to prepare advance directives if not completed when enrolled into hospice. The nurse must review these documents carefully, looking for information from the patient's history for evidence of being an organ donor, specific religious affiliations, or stipulations against certain visitors.

A final word regarding the compassionate care of individuals receiving end-of-life care: If the nurse is managing a patient who has specific details in the care plan, or religious beliefs that heavily impact healthcare decisions, additional consultation may be required. For example, for a patient who identifies as Jewish, he or she may prefer to assign an additional family member to sit with the patient once deceased. As this is the religious custom, the nurse must respect this as much as possible. It is imperative that the nurse seek a consultation with the available social worker, chaplain, or member of the hospital/facility ethics board for guidance if any request is questionable. If an internal or professional conflict of interest might prevent the nurse from effectively delivering care to the patient

according to their religious beliefs, the nurse would be best served to recuse herself in the best interests of the patient.

Grief and Loss

Grief Process

Everyone grieves differently after the death of a loved one. Grief, and how it manifests itself, is different in each individual and depends on the relationship with the deceased. For some, grief will be brief, and for others, it will be prolonged. There is a general guideline for the grieving process, but it is descriptive, not prescriptive. Individuals may experience all stages in order, some stages, but not all, or switch between stages out of order at various points in time.

The **Kubler-Ross grieving model** includes five stages: denial, bargaining, depression, anger, and acceptance. For example, when a terminal diagnosis for a loved one is received, the family members may deny what is happening and not acknowledge reality. After this stage of denial, they may begin to bargain, or try to make deals with whoever they believe has the power to change the circumstances for their loved one. This could include long arguments with the healthcare team over care or praying to a higher power for a healing miracle. After bargaining, they may fall into a depression, with feelings of helplessness or powerlessness against the forces of the disease. This may be followed by a stage of anger in which they act outwardly or express frustration that they cannot change the circumstances. The last stage of grief is acceptance, and this is considered the stage in which the grieved person is finally at peace with the circumstances and can begin healing.

As mentioned before, these categories of grief are a rough guideline of what a person may experience. Grief varies in intensity from person to person and depends a great deal on the nature of the relationship with the deceased. The nurse need only be familiar with the stages in order to recognize them in family members and/or the dying person, who may go through these stages as well. If one recognizes the grief process is occurring, one is more sensitive to the needs of the grieving.

Emotional Needs of the Patient, Family, and Caregivers

Grief is a highly emotional process. The range of emotions experienced by those grieving the loss of a loved one is vast. The initial reaction of shock and disbelief may morph quickly into anger, then sadness, and even fear. Sometimes the patient or family may feel such intense emotional pain that physical symptoms such as chest pain, gastrointestinal issues, and shortness of breath may occur.

The best way to help those who are grieving—whether it is the anticipatory grieving the dying patient may feel or the grief that occurs after the patient passes on—is to be there to support the family. It's incorrect to assume that one can imagine or alleviate what the grieving are feeling or thinking. The role of the nurse is to help in any way possible, but not to offer empty optimistic statements or promises, such as "It'll be okay soon," or "You'll move on before you know it." These statements are not helpful and may aggravate the recipient. Instead, focusing on what can be done in the present to assist them is the best approach.

Grief is a process that is different for each individual and is necessary for healing. The nurse can offer a listening ear, a hug, or a hand to hold if welcomed and appropriate, and can inquire how the patient or the family are doing. Simply asking how they are doing shows that the nurse cares and would like to be of assistance in any way possible. Providing for the physical comfort of the grieving by offering a cup of coffee, a warm blanket, or a snack is a way to support them. The emotional pain they are going through may have caused them to ignore their own basic physical needs, such as eating and resting. Helping them focus on something besides their emotional pain can be helpful. The nurse, doctor, and social worker will offer social services, grief counseling, and other resources that will connect the grieving to other forms of support.

Responses to Grief

Not only will each individual respond differently to grief based on personality and relationship with the deceased, but also the response will differ based on their own spiritual beliefs and cultural influences. These beliefs and influences affect how a person thinks they should act during the mourning period, what to wear, what rituals need to be performed, and what happens after a person dies.

Each individual culture will not be gone over in this discussion, as there are a multitude of variations of the death and grieving process. It is not necessary for the nurse to know each and every one, but rather have a general knowledge of differences and be respectful towards them.

Some cultures believe an outward show of emotion is appropriate and necessary. Sometimes, this entails an outward expression of weeping and wailing. Other cultures may be more conservative and think it is appropriate to be stoic, serious, and somber, without crying and losing one's composure. Some have specific rituals before and after the death, involving holy men, priests, or other clergy who prepare the person and/or the body for an afterlife. Some may not have any religious affiliation and may not believe in a life after this one.

Regardless of what cultural and spiritual beliefs are present, the role of the healthcare team is to respect those wishes as much as possible. It is imperative that the team explore the patient and family's wishes in this respect, rather than overlooking or refusing to allow them. It is always appropriate to politely ask how best to respect the patient and family's wishes when performing tasks for the dying or deceased patient. For example, some family members may prefer to clean the body themselves after death, an important ritual to express grief and ensure proper care in their view.

Each member of the healthcare team, including the nurse, needs to assess their own beliefs about death and dying. Self-knowledge on the subject is valuable as it may not be something one has consciously acknowledged. This self-assessment also helps reveal any unfair biases and prejudices towards cultures and people whose worldview is different than one's own. Discovering what one's own beliefs and others' beliefs are leads to a better understanding between groups. These groups can then begin to find ways to work together during the difficult end-of-life period.

Physical Changes and Needs as Death Approaches

As the patient approaches death, the nurse will play an important role in ensuring physical comfort. The patient may have increased pain, skin irritability, decreased control over bowel and bladder, decreased mobility, and decreased consciousness. There are concrete steps that the nurse can take to ensure the patient is as comfortable as possible during the last stage of life.

Monitoring the patient's level of pain is important. Pain medicine as necessary will be used to provide adequate comfort. The nurse should watch for nonverbal signs of pain, such as body tension, moaning, and facial grimacing.

Elimination may become difficult if the patient loses consciousness and mobility. The nurse can make elimination easier for the patient by assisting the patient to a bedside commode or bedpan, and/or checking for incontinence in order to perform perineal care to keep the patient clean and dry.

The patient's skin may become dry and brittle. Breathing through the mouth can cause the oral cavity to dry out quickly, sometimes called **cotton mouth**. Applying lotions, balms, and moisturizers to skin and lips, as well as making sure the oral cavity is well moisturized, are all steps that can relieve skin discomfort. Mouth sponges or swabs can be dipped in water to wet the mouth. Some patients find these sponges comforting to chew on or take a few drops of water from.

Preventing pressure ulcers or preventing existing pressure ulcers from worsening at the end of life is a consideration for nurses to keep in mind. These can cause additional pain and discomfort that might be avoided. Using pillows to

prop and position at-risk areas, such as heels, buttocks, elbows, and the back of the head will help minimize pressure.

The patient will likely have difficulty regulating body temperature and may experience periods of feeling hot, cold, or both. The patient may not be able to verbalize these needs, but the nurse can watch for nonverbal cues such as shivering or sweating. It is important to keep the patient comfortably warm or cool, using blankets and fans. Electric blankets should not be used, as the patient may not be able to verbalize if it is too hot, risking burn injuries.

Breathing may become difficult for the patient. They will likely develop increased secretions in the airway. The patient will likely be too weak to clear these secretions, resulting in a rattling or gurgling sound. Turning the patient's head to the side, providing a cool-mist humidifier (if available), and using suction equipment are all interventions that can alleviate the patient of these secretions. Depending on the facility, the nurse may or may not be able to perform the task of suctioning. The patient may be given supplemental oxygen via nasal cannula for comfort. Monitoring to make sure the prongs of the nasal cannula are in place and not causing discomfort to the patient is important.

The patient may not appear to be awake but still may be able to hear and perceive what is going on around them. Because of this, it is always important for the nurse to identify oneself to the patient when entering the room and tell the patient what they are doing in the room. This courtesy may comfort a patient who is otherwise alone. The nurse aid should talk to the patient, provide quiet music, and keep the lighting low and/or natural. These environmental changes can all soothe the patient and should be guided by the patient and the family's wishes. Some patients may prefer a room full of visitors and others may be more private, preferring only a few close relatives and friends.

The nurse needs to be mindful of the family's needs as well. Again, their grief and emotional response in the moment may cause them to forget their own basic needs, such as eating and getting proper rest. It is important to remind them to rest when they need to, offer them drinks and snacks as appropriate, warm blankets, and any other offering available to comfort them during this difficult time.

The end of life need not be a lonely, miserable experience, lacking warmth, thoughtfulness, and care. The nurse can assist the healthcare team in providing comfort for the patient's physical needs as well as creating a soothing environment around the patient as they approach death.

Post-Mortem Care Procedures

After the patient has passed, the first step the nurse can take is to determine the family's needs. This is a time when spiritual and cultural considerations need to be respected. Some families may linger and talk over the body for hours before leaving the room, while others may say a brief goodbye and leave. The healthcare team should determine if there are any specific burial preparations that need to be done. Funeral and/or burial arrangements, such as cremation or embalmment, will be determined.

Once these considerations are determined, the healthcare team can prepare the body. Generally, the body will need to be cleaned, as bowel and bladder incontinence happens after death. Having an assistant, usually the nurse, is necessary, as the body will be difficult to move by a single person. Any excess tubes or IVs will need to be removed by the nurse, depending on facility policy. The body may need to be placed in a body bag, if in a facility with a morgue. This can be done using the same turning and repositioning techniques used to perform bath care.

The nurse should be aware that there are sights and sounds that one might see in a dead body that might be alarming and unexpected. For example, there may be a release of air from the lungs of the body as the nurse is cleaning or turning that may sound like a gasp or cry. The body may also have muscle twitches and slight

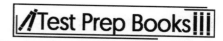

movements as the neurological and muscular systems shut down. Both of these are normal. If the nurse and/or doctor have confirmed official death, post-mortem care can proceed.

After the body has been bathed and placed in a body bag, the body will be transferred to a gurney or some sort of transport stretcher. The body is then transported to the morgue. A morgue refers to the refrigerated room where deceased bodies are held pending funeral and burial arrangements. The cold temperature drastically slows down the decomposition process in the bodies, preserving them for the funeral presentation.

Some nurses may find post-mortem care to be uncomfortable, disturbing, and even depressing. This is an initial reaction, and many adjust to it with time and experience. Dealing with dead bodies is not something that the general public is used to experiencing. The nurse must keep in mind that post-mortem care is a continuation of respecting and caring for the patient. Everyone dies, and their bodies must be taken care of afterwards. Thinking of it as an act of respect and courtesy is perhaps the best perspective. The deceased must be treated with dignity, even in death. The nurse is in the unique position to provide such dignified care to the individual.

The reason that one enters the healthcare field should stem from an earnest desire to help others and care for them in their time of need. This extends beyond their life to their death by taking care of their remains appropriately and respectfully.

Mental Health Concepts

The mental status of a patient has the potential to impact every area of their life, resulting in an inability to respond to any nursing intervention. Compromised mental health has been known to affect a patient's coping mechanisms, lifestyle choices, and ability to manage stress effectively. Nurses who work with patients impacted by mental illness need to maintain awareness of numerous concepts. Chief among them is the nurse's effectiveness in conducting the initial interview. It is essential to assess the patient's mood, affect, body language, and tone. Asking open-ended questions about daily living, employment, relationship status, hobbies, and habits can help the nurse determine if any socialization deficits are present. Once the patient begins to respond, this will create an atmosphere of trust, which is necessary when conducting an assessment for depression.

One of the most frequently diagnosed mental illnesses is clinical depression. Although the vast majority of those diagnosed are women, many men also are seeking help for their own struggles with depression. Once the nurse has completed the depression inventory and determines that some risk for clinical depression does exist, the next step will be to discuss how the patient's symptoms affect daily life. Within the last two weeks, has the patient felt increasingly depressed, hopeless, or helpless? Has the patient struggled to fall asleep, woken up early, or slept longer than expected? Are meal times less or more frequent? Has anyone that knows the patient remarked about a change in their mood? Have there been sudden bouts of tearfulness, sadness, or feelings of worthlessness? Is the patient engaging in self-harm or high-risk behaviors? Has the patient considered hurting themselves? If so, is there a plan? Does the patient have access to weapons or medications, and have there been suicide attempts in the past? This line of questioning will help the nurse to determine if the patient's depression is mild and situational, which is often transient, or if the depressive state is moderate to severe, requiring more immediate intervention.

Once it is determined that the patient is not in imminent danger or planning to commit suicide, the nurse can begin discussing nursing interventions to alleviate the patient's symptoms. If suicidal ideation does exist, safety planning and hospitalization may be necessary. Utilizing motivational interviewing to reveal the patient's readiness for change, the nurse can open the discussion from where the patient sits on the continuum. This type of nursing style is often necessary to confirm the feasibility of proposed nursing interventions.

If the patient is in pre-contemplation, the earliest stage of change, they may have an awareness of the symptoms but not know that those are symptoms of depression. At this stage, information is key. The nurse can explain the

symptoms of depression and should be watchful of worsening symptoms. During the second stage, contemplation, the patient is aware that the symptoms are indicative of depression but remain ambivalent about change. The nurse will continue to provide feedback regarding the patient's own words, reflecting back their statements. The patient may wish for change but is not yet sure if it is possible.

Once the patient reaches perception, the ambivalence has turned into acceptance and the patient feels ready to take the first step. The nurse must have resources readily available regarding how to schedule an appointment with a counselor for talk therapy or to obtain a prescription for antidepressant medications. Be prepared to answer questions about untoward side effects and how quickly the medications become effective. During the action phase, the patient may actually schedule the appointment or fill the prescription, with significant intent to continue. In this instance, the nurse must reinforce the patient's courage and utilize the SMART goal-setting technique to establish a timeline within which to act.

Maintenance occurs once the patient actually takes the medication regularly, attends counseling, and is able to verbalize that change has occurred. The nurse should be able to validate the patient's improvement and continue to offer encouragement regarding the patient's own goals. Finally, during the relapse stage, something has occurred; a substantial stressor or an unexpected disruption creates imbalance. The patient will begin to miss numerous appointments, forget to refill prescriptions, and symptoms will resurface. At this stage, the nurse must realize that the patient may have returned to the preparation phase. They may believe that the counseling or medications were ineffective and be unsure which steps to take next. Outreach is often necessary, as the patient may be hesitant to return; depressive symptoms may also impact their decision-making.

It is important to note that the stages of change are not linear. Patients can move along the continuum; moving between one stage and another frequently or skipping certain stages entirely is not uncommon. It is important for the nurse to remain neutral, mirroring the patient's ambivalence to allow for self-determined action.

Mood Disorders, Depression, Anxiety

A **mood disorder** is a mental health classification for all of the disorders that alter or change a person's mood that are inconsistent with the situation they are experiencing (i.e., depression and bipolar). The following are the most common types of mood disorders:

- **Major depression**: Having less interest in usual activities, feeling sad or hopeless, and other symptoms (as outlined in the DSM 5) for at least 2 weeks.

- **Dysthymia**: A low-grade feeling of depression that lasts for a minimum of two years

- **Bipolar disorder**: a disorder characterized by periods of depression followed by periods of mania.

- **Mood disorder related to another health condition**: Having an acute or chronic medical illnesses can trigger symptoms of depression.

- **Substance-induced mood disorder**: when depression is related to or caused by the use of drugs, alcohol, or other harmful substances.

Mood disorders may be caused by an imbalance of brain chemicals. Life events, abrupt changes in routine, and stress may also contribute to a depressed mood. Mood disorders also tend to run in families and are more intense and harder to manage than normal feelings of sadness. Children, teens, or adults who have a parent with a mood disorder have a greater chance of also having a mood disorder. Rates of depression are nearly twice as high as in women as they are in men. Once a person in the family has this diagnosis, their brothers, sisters, or children have a

higher chance of the same diagnosis. Depending on age and the type of mood disorder, a person may have different symptoms of depression. The following are the most common symptoms of a mood disorder:

- Ongoing sad, anxious, or empty affect
- Feeling hopeless or helpless
- Having low self-esteem
- Feeling inadequate or worthless
- Excessive guilt
- Repeating thoughts of death or suicide
- Loss of interest in usual activities or activities that were once enjoyed, including sex
- Relationship problems
- Trouble sleeping or sleeping too much
- Changes in appetite and/or weight
- Decreased energy
- Trouble concentrating
- A decrease in the ability to make decisions
- Frequent physical complaints that don't get better with treatment
- Very sensitive to failure or rejection
- Irritability, hostility, or aggression

With a mood disorder, these feelings are more intense than what a person may feel occasionally. If these feelings continue over time, interfere with interest in family, friends, community, or work, or if there are thoughts of suicide, medical intervention is needed.

Antidepressant and mood stabilizing medicines, especially when combined with psychotherapy, have been shown to work very well in the treatment of depression. Treatment of bipolar disorder may include mood stabilizers such as lithium and carbamazepine, along with second-generation antipsychotics such as aripiprazole and risperidone. Psychotherapy is focused on changing the person's distorted views of self and the environment. It also helps to improve interpersonal relationship skills, identify stressors in the environment, and assist with avoiding them. Family therapy, electroconvulsive therapy, and transcranial stimulation may also be therapeutic.

Post-Traumatic Stress Disorder (PTSD)

PTSD is a disorder that develops in some people who have experienced a shocking, scary, or dangerous event. People who have PTSD may feel stressed or frightened even when they are not in danger. Fear triggers many split-second changes in the body to help defend against danger or to avoid it. This fight-or-flight response is a typical reaction meant to protect a person from harm. Most people recover from initial symptoms naturally but those who continue to be affected are diagnosed with PTSD.

Symptoms usually begin within 3 months of the traumatic incident, but may occur later. Symptoms must last more than a month and be severe enough to interfere with relationships or work to be considered PTSD. The course of the illness varies, and it may become chronic. Some people recover within 6 months, while others have symptoms that last much longer. Re-experiencing symptoms may cause problems in a person's everyday routine. The symptoms can start from the person's own thoughts and feelings. Words, objects, or situations that are reminders of the event can also trigger re-experiencing symptoms.

To be diagnosed with PTSD, an adult must have all of the following for at least 1 month:

- At least one re-experiencing symptom
    - Flashbacks—reliving the trauma over and over, including physical symptoms like a racing heart or sweating

- o Bad dreams
- o Frightening thoughts
- At least one avoidance symptom
- At least two arousal and reactivity symptoms
- At least two cognition and mood symptoms

Avoidance symptoms include staying away from places, events, or objects that are reminders of the traumatic experience and avoiding thoughts or feelings related to the traumatic event. Things that remind a person of the traumatic event can trigger avoidance symptoms. These symptoms may cause a person to change their personal routine. For example, after a bad car accident, a person who usually drives may avoid driving or riding in a car.

Arousal and reactivity symptoms include being easily startled, feeling tense, having difficulty sleeping, and having angry outbursts. Arousal symptoms are usually constant, instead of being triggered by things that remind one of the traumatic events. These symptoms can make the person feel stressed and angry. They may make it hard to do daily tasks, such as sleeping, eating, or concentrating.

Cognition and mood symptoms include trouble remembering key features of the traumatic event, negative thoughts about self or the world, distorted feelings like guilt or blame, and loss of interest in enjoyable activities. Cognition and mood symptoms can begin or worsen after the traumatic event, but are not due to injury or substance use. These symptoms can make the person feel alienated or detached from friends or family members.

Anyone can develop PTSD at any age. This includes war veterans, children, and people who have been through a physical or sexual assault, abuse, accident, disaster, or many other serious events. According to the National Center for PTSD, about 7 or 8 out of every 100 people will experience PTSD at some point in their lives. Women are more likely to develop PTSD than men, and genes may make some people more likely to develop PTSD than others.

The main treatments for people with PTSD are medications, psychotherapy, or both. Everyone is different, and PTSD affects people differently so a treatment that works for one person may not work for another. It is important for anyone with PTSD to be treated by a mental health provider who is experienced with PTSD. Some people with PTSD need to try different treatments to find what works for their symptoms. As genetic research and brain imaging technologies continue to improve, scientists are more likely to be able to pinpoint when and where in the brain PTSD begins. This understanding may then lead to better targeted treatments to suit each person's own needs or even prevent the disorder before it causes harm.

A 2012 study of 395 military veterans with PTSD found a link between risk-taking behavior and the disorder. In addition to the above forms of riskiness, vets with PTSD have a propensity for firearms play, potentially endangering their lives. People with PTSD have already survived dangerous situations, and risk-taking behavior may give such individuals the feeling that they have more control over their present circumstances than those that led to them developing PTSD. Recognizing this propensity in their personality may help patients with risk-taking behavior, thus being the first step in remediating the problem. Behavioral and cognitive therapy, as well as psychological drugs such as antidepressants, may also aid in the treatment of this behavior.

Suicidal Ideation and/or Behaviors
It is important to take people seriously when they express having suicidal thoughts. Research has shown that about one-fifth of people who die by suicide had talked to their doctor or other healthcare professional about their decision. These types of thoughts may arise in people who feel completely hopeless or believe they can no longer cope with their life situation. Suicidal ideation can vary greatly from fleeting thoughts to preoccupation to detailed planning.

According to the Centers for Disease Control (CDC), for every 25 attempts, there is one suicide death. Suicide is the tenth leading cause of death for all ages in the United States, and the third leading cause of death among 15- to 24

90

year-olds. Patients with borderline personality disorder face an extraordinarily high risk of suicidal ideation and suicide attempts. One study showed that 73% of patients with borderline personality disorder have attempted suicide, with the average patient having 3.4 attempts.

Warning signs may include hopelessness, racing thoughts, insomnia or oversleeping, mania, loss of appetite or overeating, loneliness, alcohol abuse, excessive fatigue or low self-esteem. Research has found a variety of risk factors for suicidal ideation including the following:

- Mood and mental disorders
- Adverse life or family events (divorce, death of a loved one, job loss)
- Chronic illness or pain
- Previous suicide attempt
- Military experience
- Witnessing trauma
- Family violence
- Owning a gun
- Being the victim of abuse or bullying
- Unplanned pregnancy
- Drug or alcohol abuse

An act that is intended to cause injury to one's self but not death is called a non-suicidal self-injury. An example of this type of behavior is when patients cut themselves. It is a method of relieving psychological pain through physical pain. Men are more likely than women to commit suicide, as well as more likely to abuse alcohol and drugs concurrently. Men are less likely to seek help when they are depressed. Veterans have seen an increase in suicides in recent years. It is important to note that despite these risk factors for suicide, it can occur across a wide span of age groups, genders, and life circumstances.

Some patients who are more vocal about their suicidal ideation may be crying out for help and must be taken very seriously. Treatment should include psychotherapy and antidepressants. It should be noted, however, that antidepressants sometimes have the adverse side effect of worsened suicidal behavior. Caregivers should be instructed to be watchful for deepening of depression and thus an increased risk for suicide. Suicide hotlines are available to help suicidal patients in moments of crisis.

Spiritual and Cultural Influences on Health

Religious and spiritual beliefs can heavily influence a patient's decision to receive care. It is important for the nurse to determine if any specific religious or spiritual beliefs exist for the patient, and how those beliefs inform their decisions. Many people value certain dietary customs in accordance with their religion and strictly adhere to them. For example, for those who identify as Jewish, adherence to a strict Kosher diet is non-negotiable. Any attempts by the nurse to suggest any changes to this diet would be viewed as insensitive. It is for this same reason that religious and spiritual beliefs of any kind must be respected.

Congregants of the Church of Scientology have received significant media attention for what some perceive to be controversial beliefs. Some who self-identify as a part of this group have also expressed particular mistrust of mental health practitioners in general. Although they do not forego all medical treatments, a nurse attending to patients following this religion must consider those beliefs when developing interventions and treatment plans. It may be more advantageous to encourage the patient to consult a church advisor and incorporate the tenants of Scientology into direct practice, if permitted.

Another religious group well known for their healthcare choices is Jehovah's Witnesses. Founded by Charles Taze Russell in the late 1800s, this group does not believe in accepting blood transfusions under any circumstances. A nurse caring for a patient who holds this belief must be prepared to discuss any viable options with the patient and church elders. Not all instances of receiving blood products are prohibited, so it will be important to confirm if the patient would consider using plasma, volume expanders, or artificial blood.

Additionally, ethical considerations regarding how to provide sensitive and compassionate care are important to highlight. It is the nurse's responsibility to seek a consultation with the unit chaplain, social worker, or facility ethics board to discuss any areas where there is a potential conflict of interest.

Not only will each individual respond differently to grief based on personality and relationship with the deceased, but also the response will differ based on their own spiritual beliefs and cultural influences. These beliefs and influences affect how a person thinks they should act during the mourning period, what to wear, what rituals need to be performed, and what happens after a person dies.

Each individual culture will not be discussed since there are many variations of how different people handle this process. It is not necessary for the nurse to know each and every one, but rather have a general knowledge of differences and be respectful towards them.

National League for Nursing believes that diversity and quality health care are inseparable and together they create a path to increased access, improved health, and elimination of health disparities. Diversity signifies that each individual is unique and recognizes individual differences such as race, ethnicity, gender, sexual orientation, gender identity, socio-economic status, age, physical abilities, and religious and/or political beliefs. The result is self-awareness and respect for all persons, embracing and celebrating the richness of each individual. It also encompasses organizational, institutional, and system-wide behaviors in nursing, nursing education, and health care.

It is important to note that gender may influence the presentation of certain health problems, such as heart disease and

Sensory/Perceptual Alterations

Nursing interventions include a variety of holistic treatments. Among the most essential elements of nursing techniques that any nurse can employ are those associated with managing **sensory and perceptual alterations**. During the initial assessment or admission, the nurse must be diligent to perform a complete review of the patient's electronic medical record; take note of medications that mask or augment neurological deficits; and observe the patient interacting with family members, caregivers, and other medical staff. Once the nurse has been able to gather the information necessary to form an initial impression, the next step is to evaluate the patient clinically.

It is customary to perform a basic screening neurological exam at every patient encounter. Diagnoses such as Alzheimer's disease and dementia are of special note, and the nurse is to follow facility protocols for treatment of these patients. If neurological decline is detected during the initial screening, it will be necessary to assess the patient periodically and, if not specifically ordered, according to the nurse's clinical judgement.

Once the initial chart review and assessment are completed, the nurse must develop a treatment plan and nursing interventions. All have as their primary objective to maintain patient safety. Some of the most common observations that nurses make concerning these identifying typical safety precautions that these patients often need. Bed alarms, keeping the call light within reach, slip-resistant socks, a writing pad and pen or dry-erase board for communicating, hearing and walking aids within reach, lifting one rail of the bed to allow only one route of access, and rooming the patient closer to the nurse's station are frequently instituted. All interventions are to be provided in a calming manner, being careful not to startle the patient. It will also be necessary to be aware of

distractions to the patient like ambient noise or other patients in the immediate area. Additionally, the nurse must be prepared to teach all caregivers basic diversion tactics to deescalate and soothe the patient's anxieties. Finally, take care to periodically evaluate the effectiveness of all interventions and be prepared to adjust as needed.

Stress Management

Stress management is a crucial piece of overall patient wellbeing. Poorly managed stress has the potential to cause significant health decline. When conducting an assessment, the nurse must carefully approach the topic of stress management. Since many of life's stressors cannot be completely changed, the nurse will be best served to listen actively, remarking about how certain activities or situations can worsen health conditions. Odd work hours, late night shifts, or working multiple jobs can negatively impact sleep patterns. Without restorative sleep, the patient will have difficulties focusing on treatment-plan adherence. As the lack of sleep continues, the patient can begin to lose focus on a previous goal of maintaining healthy lifestyle choices and return to easier high-risk behaviors.

Once the topic of known sources of stress has been initiated, the nurses can go one step further to inquire what steps have been taken to ameliorate those stressors. Next, the patient can be encouraged to state how they have worked to manage the stressors and what has been least effective. It is during this exchange that the patient is more likely to accept recommendations and institute them in daily life. Notably, it is also necessary to uncover sources of stress that are not readily apparent. Ask probing questions about preferred forms of stress relief and relaxation techniques. Encourage patients to seek out trusted members of their support network to communicate their needs and ask for help. Overall, a patient's ability to institute the checks and balances required to alleviate stress is crucial.

Support Systems

Another contributing factor for overall patient wellbeing is a well-functioning **support system**. Even if there is no disease process present, a support system, as defined by the patient, is vital to healthy stress and disease management. During the assessment, the nurse must ask open-ended questions about patients' support systems: What hobbies do they enjoy? How do they spend the holidays, and with whom? Are they married or single? Do they have children? Answers to these few questions will help quickly decide if there are any gaps in socialization and open the discussion on how to fill them.

Whether it's family members, friends, or coworkers, some sort of support network usually exists for most patients. The nurse must make sure to encourage discussion about who the patient confides in and trusts. Those individuals can either add to or subtract from the patient's progression through and whole-hearted commitment to treatment. For those patients who report having no supportive network, the nurse can guide the patient toward viable options. One of the most effective and influential options would be to match the patient to a support group according to any comorbidities that they currently manage. Thousands of independent groups exist to provide a much-needed communal experience. Often run by health professionals or counselors, members of these groups can gain knowledge about their condition, daily symptom management, and possibly gain new supportive friends. Overall, the presence of a network of trusted friends and advisors is an invaluable facet of the therapeutic environment.

Family Dynamics

The term "family" holds a different level of significance to different people. No matter how the nurse chooses to define family, it is imperative that a neutral stance be maintained regarding the patient's familial network. If the nurse cannot maintain a sense of compassionate objectivity, it may cloud the nurse's responsiveness to cultural issues that affect patient care. Whenever possible, the nurse must consider that the **family dynamic** remains as the unseen influence on the patient. Stress-management techniques, as well as the cultural and familial roles assigned in the family, may have an undue influence on the patient's healthcare decisions and adherence to treatment.

A visual assessment of this dynamic can occur within several minutes. Observe how the family members interact; choices of conversation topics and responses can often reveal a great deal about who is the leader in the household. For example, upon the initial assessment of an obese teen and a morbidly obese parent, it can quickly become apparent that the dietary choices made by the teen are a mirror of those made by the primary caregiver. Both may lead a relatively sedentary lifestyle, punctuated by frequent visits to the local fast-food restaurant. As the nurse, it would be necessary to simply ask about their daily vegetable and water consumption, hobbies, or even the teen's favorite meal. During the discussion, the nurse will be better able to discuss SMART goals: specific, measurable, achievable, relevant, and timely. This type of goal setting allows for the patient to set realistic goals, with the opportunity to self-check for progress along the way.

When one member of the family is not performing at peak capacity, the dynamic shifts, causing all others to adopt different roles. If the family dynamic is cooperative, all parties will seek to reach a reasonable state of homeostasis. This means that if there is a recognized deficiency in one member of the family, each member will want to contribute to activities that will restore their health. This informal agreement is one of the ultimate goals of the nursing intervention. If the family dynamic is conflictual, then the parties will seek to satisfy their own needs, rather than help the ill family member achieve better health outcomes. As the nurse, it is important to utilize the familial bond, no matter the type, to influence the best result for the patient.

For the aforementioned example, the nurse would attempt to co-op the conflictual family members and align their needs with those of the patient. Offering healthier alternatives to staple meals, cheaper recipes, and suggestions for more physical activity would likely appeal to all parties. Alternatively, the nurse could propose that the teen prepare healthier meals themselves, allowing a busy parent much-needed respite from cooking daily. During the average professional nursing career, it will become clear that family members' personal health selections can derail patients' lifestyle choices. It is incumbent upon the nurse to incorporate all aspects of the patient's life in order to create the most effective treatment plan.

Therapeutic Communication

Overcoming barriers to communication requires practicing therapeutic communication. **Therapeutic communication** is a type of communication that assists the patient in the healing process rather than hindering it. There are a number of useful communication techniques the nurse can employ to aid in therapeutic communication.

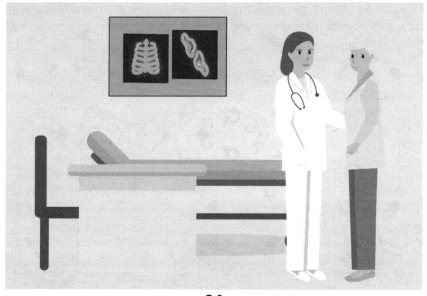

Sometimes, silence is the best way to get clarification from a patient, or simply asking them to clarify when one does not understand. Nurses may offer themselves to support the patient without providing personal details, by sympathizing and saying, "Yes, I have been through something similar." The nurse may ask the patient to summarize their thoughts or identify a theme when stories go on at length. This helps redirect communication in a positive direction.

Asking the patient how certain events made them feel is a way to investigate the patient's emotional status. The nurse may give information about their role and make observations, such as "I noticed you seem tense," to open the door to more fluent conversation. Giving the patient praise and recognition without overt flattery is a way to show support, such as complimenting a noticeable effort during a physical therapy session. The nurse may want to determine the chronological order of events, which can be helpful for reporting information.

Employing therapeutic communication aids smooth collaboration and cooperation between members of the healthcare team. Incorporating smart, simple, therapeutic communication techniques and overcoming barriers to communication are important parts of achieving this goal.

Therapeutic Environment

Within every milieu, the nurse must maintain awareness of the effectiveness of the therapeutic environment of the patient. The nurse must enter into each patient encounter with a plan to develop a rapport as quickly as possible. A warm greeting, using Mr. or Mrs., rather than using a first name, honey, or sweetie, will imply an equal and respectful relationship. The ability to work collaboratively with the patient is the foundation of cooperative treatment planning.

Although the nurse is generally much more comfortable during the assessment, it is important for the nurse to consider that the patient may be hesitant to disclose personal information. If the patient does not trust the nurse or feels unseen, unheard, or hurried through the interaction, the environment may not feel safe. More important, when a patient does not feel safe enough to disclose, they will not share important health information, which could hinder treatment planning and adherence.

Another important aspect of the therapeutic environment for the nurse to be aware of is the treatment setting. For example, a patient in a correctional-facility hospital may be less likely to reveal sensitive information for fear of reprisal from inmates or staff. Alternatively, patients in a mental health or substance abuse treatment center may freely divulge information, as they often seek treatment of their own accord. In either instance, the nurse must utilize critical thinking to determine if the therapeutic environment is negatively impacted by the setting and seek ways to address any barriers to resolution.

Practice Quiz

1. Maya eats a nutrient-rich, balanced diet and exercises vigorously for 30 minutes each day. However, she has gained almost 25 pounds over the course of four months. She has also started growing facial hair and has noticed purple stretch marks on her abdomen and breasts. She visits her primary care provider seeking insight as to what is causing these issues. Maya's blood pressure is 135/90 at the appointment. Maya's physician refers her to an endocrinologist, believing she is showing signs of which of the following?
   a. Hypertension
   b. Gestational diabetes
   c. Chronic kidney disease
   d. Cushing's syndrome

2. Mary is a 7-year-old in second grade. She has been absent from school nine days in one month. When Mary's teacher asks her why she has been absent or contacts her parents to ask about the absences, they all simply say she was sick and don't provide any additional information. Mary looks extremely frightened when asked about her absences. She regularly comes to school in large, baggy clothing that smells unpleasantly, and her hair always looks dirty. She falls asleep often in class, and one day her teacher saw her crying as she prepared to leave for home. Mary's teacher is probably concerned that Mary is dealing with which of the following issues?
   a. She is suffering from a hormonal imbalance or disorder
   b. She is too emotional
   c. She is having a mental breakdown
   d. She is being abused or neglected by a caregiver

3. Which of the following options correctly names the type of common medication used to treat anxiety and depression?
   a. Antipsychotics
   b. Selective serotonin reuptake inhibitors (SSRIs)
   c. Dopamine reuptake inhibitors
   d. Homeopathic options

4. Psychosis is a common side effect of which of the following?
      I. Schizophrenia
      II. Methamphetamine, cocaine, or LSD use
      III. Bipolar Disorder
      IV. HIV antiviral medications
   a. II ad IV only
   b. I and II only
   c. I, II, and III
   d. All of the above

5. Jack and Jill are two nursing students who are on rotation in their county's emergency department. One afternoon, a woman comes into the waiting area and collapses on the floor. She says she cannot breathe and rambles about feeling blindsided. She begins thrashing on the floor and starts to sob. Upon reviewing her intake forms, Jack and Jill notice that the woman's health insurance shows she is employed, and she has not had any notable medical or mental health issues. However, she keeps mentioning that her partner has left her. Jack says, "I think she must have an undiagnosed anxiety disorder; we should look into medication options." Jill disagrees with him, saying that this seems more like which of the following?

    a.   A situational crisis
    b.   A case of cocaine abuse
    c.   A case of intimate partner violence
    d.   A nonemergency situation that they should send to the scheduling department

See answers on the next page.

Answer Explanations

1. D: Cushing's syndrome is characterized by weight gain, purple stretch marks (striae), facial hair growth in women, and high blood pressure. Cushing's syndrome is also associated with the classic signs of a "moon face" or "buffalo hump," which are caused by fat deposits on the face, neck, and upper back. Caused by excessive cortisol in the body which can be the result of overproduction within the body or by long term use of corticosteroids.

2. D: All the signs that Mary is showing, such as poor hygiene, absenteeism, withdrawn behaviors, and crying before going home are red flags for abuse and neglect.

3. B: Selective serotonin reuptake inhibitors (SSRIs) are a class of drugs that can treat both anxiety and depression symptoms. Therefore, brand names of this drug, such as Prozac®, Zoloft®, and Lexapro®, may be prescribed to individuals who are suffering from anxiety, depression, or a combination of both.

4. C: Schizophrenia and bipolar disorder are mental disorders in which hallucinations and delusion (key components of psychosis) are common. These characteristics can also result from mind-altering drugs, specifically methamphetamines, cocaine, and LSD. Antiviral medications used to treat HIV do not normally cause psychosis.

5. A: The patient is having many symptoms of panic, such as struggling to breathe, having difficulty controlling her emotions, and acting agitated. However, she mentions that her partner just left, and there are no other indicators of previous physical or mental health problems in her history. This is a good clue that the patient's partner leaving is a very stressful event for her and a situational crisis that is likely causing these acute, short-term behaviors. Jack and Jill can help this patient by providing comfort, support, and counseling to help her reach a place where they can calmly discuss treatment options needed, if any.

Physiological Integrity

Basic Care and Comfort

Assistive Devices

The nurse may discover during assessment that the client needs an **assistive device**. There are many such devices available for a variety of different client needs. Assistive devices may generally fall into the categories of assisting with sensorial deficits or mobility deficits.

Clients with sensorial deficits may first need a referral to the appropriate party. A client with difficulties seeing may need a referral to an ophthalmologist for evaluation and a prescription for appropriate lenses.

There are four main vision problems that can be treated with corrective eyewear in mild to moderate cases: myopia, presbyopia, hyperopia, and astigmatism. More severe cases may require surgical intervention.

For the client who requires eyeglasses, the nurse must take care to protect the glasses from damage. While in the hospital room, the glasses should be kept in a safe place, such as in their case on the bedside table. Most bedside tables in hospital rooms have pullout drawers underneath that can store items such as glasses, dentures, hearing aids, and other personal effects.

Patients with blindness, who are legally blind, or who have some form of low vision, will need assistive devices to help them navigate their environment. They may also need assistance with written communications such as discharge instructions and other patient education materials. Depending on the facility, the nurse may be able to give the patient access to devices that use Braille for written communication, software for a PC or smartphone that reads aloud written instructions, and magnifiers for computer screens, phone screens, or other devices. The patient with blindness or very low vision may require a special cane, a therapy animal, or a personal assistant to help them ambulate about their room and the facility. The nurse will assess for these needs and ensure the patient has everything they need for clear communication and a safe environment during their stay.

The nurse will further assess the patient with hearing loss for any other needed interventions that might assist with communication and ease of stay. Closed captioning is available on most TV sets for most programs so the patient can fully enjoy what they are watching. The patient may be a lip-reader, in which case the nurse needs to ensure they stand directly in front of the patient, face them, and make solid eye contact when communicating important messages. The patient will need to see the nurse, specifically their lips, to interpret the message. If the nurse's face is turned away or looking down, the patient will have difficulty understanding what is being spoken to them.

The nurse needs to ensure the patient understands the message by asking questions about comprehension. Some patients with chronic, severe hearing loss may have developed a coping mechanism of pretending they understood what was said by nodding or giving a short verbal reply. They may do this because they feel embarrassed or ashamed about their hearing loss. They may also not want the further hassle of admitting they did not hear or understand what was said and needing to have the message repeated. Without further embarrassing the patient, the nurse should gently inquire about comprehension of the medications they are taking, procedures they are to go through, and if they need anything to make their stay better. Patience and thoroughness are key to ensuring the message gets delivered.

A patient with a speech-language deficit may have difficulty forming meaningful communication as well as fully comprehending the messages that are spoken to them. The nurse who assesses such a need can refer the patient to

99

a speech-language pathologist or therapist; most hospitals have a team of these specialists. They will evaluate the patient's speech-language capabilities and recommend assistive devices as needed.

Some such assistive devices include word boards in which the patient can point to a word or picture that helps them communicate a need. The speech-therapy team will work with the patient through exercises aimed at enhancing their abilities to their greatest potential. Patients who have experienced a cerebrovascular accident or stroke often experience speech and language deficits because of the cerebral tissue damage that occurs. Not all function may be restored, depending on the patient and the extent of the stroke.

Patients with difficulties walking may require assistive devices such as a walker, cane, or wheelchair. If the nurse assesses the patient and finds that such a need is there, they may contact the physical and occupational therapy (PT and OT) teams for assistance. PT and OT work to help the patient become mobile to their greatest functioning capability as well as assisting them in performing activities of daily living (ADLs). Common ADLs that PT/OT works with the patient to perform include getting dressed, tying their shoes, and bathing and feeding themselves.

The nurse will work with the patient and encourage them to use their assistive devices as needed. The nurse ensures the patient that they, along with the nursing assistant team, are always a call button away to assist the patient in getting out of bed, walking with the use of a cane or walker, or getting them into a wheelchair. Mobility in patients is always encouraged, as it helps them heal and achieve their fullest sense of wellness, but it must always be done with safety measures in place to prevent falls and injury.

The nurse may advise the patient using a wheelchair to avoid tipping themselves out of the chair by leaning forward. Their feet should be firmly planted in the foot rests to prevent getting caught in the wheels or dragging on the ground. The brakes should be locked at all times that the wheelchair is stopped or not actively rolling to avoid slippage. The patient in the wheelchair should avoid overreaching for objects, as this may also cause them to fall out. The patient's buttocks should be positioned as far back in the seat as possible to avoid falling out.

The nurse may have a patient with a prosthetic limb. Usually these patients arrive at the hospital with their own prosthetic that they have been properly fitted for, educated on, and actively use. If the patient is a new amputee, they will need a referral to the proper prosthetics expert for fitting. Patients with prosthetics should use the proper footwear for their prosthetic as well as adequate support to prevent falls. The patient will be aware that they should not allow their prosthetic limb to become wet. Thus, they will take the limb off when washing or taking a shower. The metal components of the prosthetic will rust if exposed to water. The patient should let the nurse know if their prosthetic device feels uncomfortable, as this may be a sign of misalignment and need adjustment. If the patient is hearing unusual noises from their prosthetic such as squeaks or crunches, this may be a sign of mechanical impairment and that the prosthetic needs repair.

Patients using crutches should start walking by putting all their weight on their good leg. With the crutches firmly situated in the armpits, the patient can then lift the crutches and set them down 6 to 12 inches in front of them, lean their weight into their hands, and then step forward with the good leg. This avoids putting weight on the injured leg, transferring all weight to the hands and the good leg, alternatively.

Elimination

There are many situations in a facility in which the patient is unable to **eliminate**—i.e., defecate and/or urinate—independently. Elimination is a basic and highly personal need for all people, and the nurse needs to be able to assist with this task appropriately and respectfully. Common issues in elimination are incontinence, constipation, and diarrhea. Some patients may have devices to assist with elimination, such as a colostomy, rectal tube, or urinary catheter.

Incontinence is a term meaning the patient cannot control their bladder and/or bowels. Some patients may be said to be incontinent of bowel, incontinent of bladder, or both. This can be for various reasons, including neurological impairment, such as paralysis, or a physical impairment, such as a broken hip. In any scenario of incontinence, it is important to monitor the patient's elimination throughout a shift and assist when possible. If the patient is oriented enough to request help before having a bowel or bladder movement, the nurse should be as available as possible to assist. This may entail assisting the patient to the bathroom or providing a bedside commode or a bedpan.

If the patient is incontinent in bed, a partial bath will be needed along with a linen change. Checking for incontinence frequently is important, as a timely cleanup of a patient who has been incontinent is crucial to preventing skin breakdown. Proper hand hygiene needs to be performed before and after any perineal care to prevent spread of disease.

Constipation refers to a condition in which the bowels have slowed down their movement, preventing normal defecation and potentially causing discomfort to the patient. Immobility and medications may cause constipation as a side effect. Monitoring of output is one way to discover constipation, along with the patient and/or family report of bowel patterns. If constipation is suspected, the healthcare provider may prescribe a stool softener, a laxative, or—in severe cases—an enema. Soap suds and fleets enemas are commonly used types. Each institution has individual policies on who can perform enemas on patients. Other interventions used to alleviate constipation include encouraging mobility, encouraging intake of fluids when possible, and increasing fiber intake.

When the bowels are overly active and amounts of liquid stool are passed frequently, it is called **diarrhea**. Causes of diarrhea include food intolerance or allergy, infection, a medication side effect, or a reaction to a surgical procedure. A major complication of diarrhea is dehydration. Dehydration can occur rapidly in a patient with diarrhea due to loss of fluids. Intake and output need to be vigilantly monitored along with encouragement of fluid intake, if appropriate.

A **colostomy** is a surgically placed opening from the large or small intestines to the abdominal wall as a result of a bowel condition, such as colon cancer. A colostomy bag is attached to the skin around the colostomy to collect stool. Depending on how long the colostomy has been in place and how well developed the colostomy is, the patient may be able to care for their colostomy bag independently or may need varying levels of assistance from the healthcare team. Most colostomy bags are fairly easy to remove, drain, and replace when necessary.

Another assistive device for elimination of the bowels is called a **rectal tube**. A rectal tube is a tube that is inserted into the rectum to collect stool or relieve gas. At the end of the tube is a balloon that can be inflated to anchor it in place as it collects stool. The rectal tube is used in patients who are incontinent, at risk for or have skin breakdown, and/or have diarrhea. Each facility will have specific policies outlining when a rectal tube is needed. Complications, such as atony (loss of muscle tone) of the rectum and internal tissue breakdown, may arise when rectal tubes are in place for extended periods. The rectal tube drains into a bag that the nurse can empty and record as output in the medical record. Perineal care may be required around the site of the rectal tube if any leakage occurs.

The patient may have a urinary catheter for various reasons including immobility and monitoring of output. The catheter has an inflatable balloon at the end filled with normal saline that anchors the catheter in place as it drains

urine from the urinary bladder to a collection bag. The nurse can then empty this bag and record the output in the medical record.

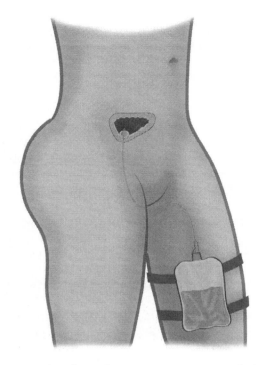

During the patient's daily bath or whenever perineal care is necessary, proper technique must be used to prevent a urinary tract infection (UTI). The nurse must follow the facility's policy regarding proper catheter care, including using warm water around the site to cleanse the urethra and always using a circular motion around the tube moving away from the patient. The nurse should never use a back and forth motion as this could introduce bacteria into the urethra, resulting in a UTI. Signs and symptoms of a UTI include fever, chills, cloudy urine, blood in the urine (hematuria), or a change in mental status. If any of these occur, the nurse should be alerted immediately.

Mobility/Immobility

Promoting Mobility and Proper Positioning

Proper positioning is important for a patient's comfort and safety. Some of the common patient positions are:

- **High Fowler's Position**: The head of the patient's bed is raised 60 to 90 degrees and the knees are either flexed or extended out straight.
- **Fowler's Position**: The head of the patient's bed is raised 45 to 60 degrees.
- **Semi-Fowler's Position**: The head of the patient's bed is raised 30 to 45 degrees.
- **Supine**: The patient is lying on their back.
- **Lateral**: The patient is lying on their side.
- **Prone**: The patient is lying on their stomach, with their head turned to the side.

When positioning a patient in bed, always raise the entire bed high enough to avoid bending over while assisting the patient. Be sure to lower the head of the bed to its lowest position before leaving the patient.

Promoting Function, Including Prosthetic and Orthotic Devices

A nurse should encourage patients to be as mobile as possible and help them correctly use assistive devices such as canes and walkers. Patients with prosthetic limbs should be given assistance with, and access to, these devices. When assisting a patient with a prosthetic limb, always note any redness or irritation that occurs where the prosthetic limb contacts the skin.

Safe Transfer Techniques

When transferring a patient, the safety of the patient and the nurse are of the greatest importance. Incorrectly performed transfers can cause injury to both. Be mindful of proper transfer techniques and body mechanics, such as keeping a straight back, bending at the knees, avoiding twisting at the waist, and, most importantly, asking for additional help if needed.

When assisting a patient out of bed, always make sure that the bed is in the lowest position. Then, assist the patient to sit upright on the side of the bed with both feet on the floor. While the patient remains in this seated position, make sure they aren't lightheaded or dizzy from the position change. If the patient needs significant physical assistance other than stabilization, an assistive device should be considered. To assist the patient in standing, the nurse should stand in front of the patient, place their knees in front of the patient's knees, and hug the patient under the arms for lifting. Then instruct the patient to help as much as possible. If transferring the patient to a chair after assisting them to stand, both the nurse and the patient should take small steps, pivoting around to the chair. Make sure the backs of the patient's knees are touching the front of the seat before lowering them into the chair.

When transferring a patient, make sure that all wheels are locked on the bed and/or chair before moving the patient.

Devices that Promote Mobility (e.g., Braces, Walkers, Wheelchairs, Gait Belt, Trapeze)

A nurse should encourage patients to use available assistive devices, such as canes, walkers, and wheelchairs. Before leaving a patient's room, make sure any assistive device that the patient uses independently is within their reach. Patients with lower-body immobility who still have upper-body strength might have a bed equipped with a trapeze. A **trapeze** is an assistive bar that hangs above the patient's bed and enables self-repositioning. Patients who are able should be encouraged to use the trapeze.

The use of assistive devices such as **gait belts** (also known as transfer belts) benefits both the nurse and the patient. When transferring or walking with a patient who needs assistance, it's advised to use a gait belt to prevent falls. When using a gait belt to assist a patient to walk, fasten the belt around their waist and hold it with both hands while standing to the side and slightly behind the patient. If the patient loses their balance and begins to fall, never attempt to catch them. Instead, continue holding the gait belt, bend at the knees, and slowly lower the patient to the floor.

Range of Motion Techniques

Range of motion exercises involve moving the body's limbs in particular ways to keep the joints healthy and flexible. Active range of motion exercises are performed by the patient independently. Passive range of motion exercises are done for patients who are unable to perform active ones. When performing passive range of motion

exercises, gently guide the patient's limbs through their range of motion. Never force the limbs, as this can harm the patient.

With the patient resting in the supine position, take each joint through its range of motion. **Adduction** is the movement of a limb toward the midline of the body. **Abduction**, the opposite of adduction, is the movement of a limb away from the midline of the body.

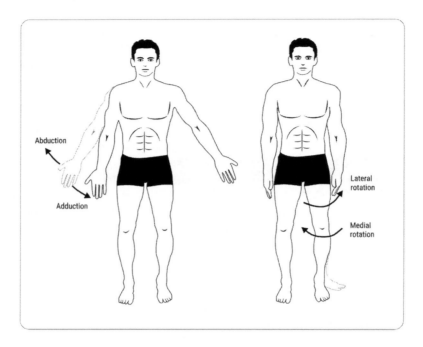

Flexion is the bending of a limb at the joint, while extension is the straightening of a limb at the joint.

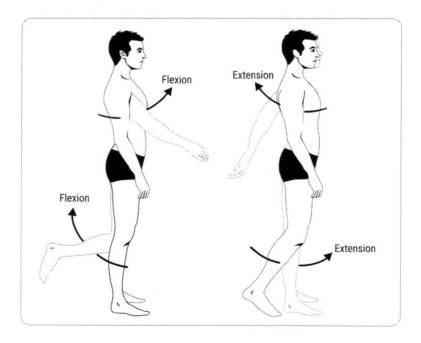

Effects of Immobility

Circulation and Skin Integrity

Patients with limited mobility are at risk for compromised circulation and/or skin breakdown. A nurse helps patients reposition themselves at least once every two hours, which prevents pressure sores and promotes adequate circulation.

Pressure sores (also called bedsores or pressure ulcers) are areas of skin breakdown that manifest when pressure on the skin minimizes circulation in that area. These usually occur over bony prominences such as the heel, ankle, coccyx, elbow, knee, or hip. Patients with pressure sores generally have some degree of immobility and are unable to reposition themselves frequently. Pressure sores are categorized by the following four stages:

- **Stage I**: The skin of the affected area is unbroken, generally red, and warm to the touch. Skin discoloration remains even after the patient is repositioned and the pressure is relieved from the site. Patients may have associated pain. Stage I pressure sores can be difficult to recognize in patients with dark skin.

- **Stage II**: Damage or loss of skin through several layers (partial thickness) with shallow ulceration of the skin, abrasion, or blistering.

- **Stage III**: Full thickness skin loss (epidermal and dermal layers) with ulceration that can be deep enough to expose fatty tissue; however, muscle, bone, and tendon are NOT visible. Tunneling might also be seen in patients with Stage III pressure sores.

- **Stage IV**: Full thickness tissue loss (epidermis, dermis, and underlying tissue damage) with deep ulceration and possible tunneling. Muscle, bone, and/or tendon are visible and palpable with Stage IV pressure sores.

To help prevent pressure sores, keep the patient's skin clean and dry, and reposition the patient at least every two hours. Whenever available, use assistive positioning devices such as pillows and wedges to help relieve pressure on bony prominences. These bony areas should not be massaged in patients who have, or are at risk of having, pressure sores. Clothing and bed linens should be straightened often to avoid wrinkles that can quickly lead to pressure sores in at-risk patients. Report any indication of skin breakdown to the nurse.

Deep vein thrombosis (DVT) refers to a blood clot in the body's deep veins, most commonly in the legs. Redness, swelling, and sometimes pain in an extremity can be signs of DVT. Patients with DVT are at risk for a **pulmonary embolism (PE)**, which occurs when a blood clot in the deep vein breaks off, travels to the lungs, and cuts off blood flow. Do not massage red or swollen areas in the extremities, as this can result in a clot breaking off and causing a pulmonary embolism.

Patients who are immobile are at an increased risk for developing DVT. If possible, patients should be encouraged to ambulate to avoid DVT. If a patient is unable to ambulate, assistance with range of motion exercises should be provided. Anti-embolism stockings (also called thrombo-embolus deterrent hose or TED hose) and sequential compression devices (SCDs) are commonly used for patients who are confined to their beds. Both of these help to promote circulation in the lower legs and prevent blood pooling.

Elimination (Bowel and Bladder)

Immobility can lead to problems with elimination. Patients who are unable to care for their own toileting needs are at risk for incontinence. Be attentive to a patient's toileting needs and attempt to establish a routine with the patient. Immobility can also lead to constipation. If not contraindicated, a patient who is at risk for constipation should be encouraged to increase fluid intake. Patients can be reluctant to increase fluid intake because of their inability to self-toilet, so encourage the patient to increase their intake and be available for their toileting needs.

Sleep and Rest Patterns/Needs

Patients with immobility can have altered sleep patterns because of their limited ability to be physically active. Pain, discomfort, anxiety, stress, and certain medications are also common issues that can disrupt sleep. Older patients, as well as patients who are healing from illness or injury, require frequent rest and sleep periods. However, they should be encouraged to be active when they're able. Assist patients in establishing daily routines and encourage them to participate in daily living activities as much as possible. For instance, if a patient can sit in a chair for a meal rather than remaining in bed, encourage and assist them to do so. As another example, if a patient is able (with assistance) to transfer from using a bedpan to using a bedside toilet, encourage and assist them to do so. Any activities a patient can participate in will benefit their sleep, rest, and overall wellbeing. However, be attentive and careful not to overtire the patient. Any patient complaints of sleeplessness should be reported to the nurse.

Self-Image

When patients lose mobility, they can experience a loss of independence. They can become isolated, depressed, and/or withdrawn and might begin to develop a negative self-image. Encourage these patients to participate in activities of daily living and give them as many opportunities as possible for autonomy.

Strength and Endurance

Patients who experience immobility can begin to lose muscle strength and endurance. If the immobile patient isn't cared for properly and their muscles aren't used, the muscles can begin to atrophy (weaken), the joints can begin to stiffen, and contractures (muscle shortenings) can develop. To prevent this from occurring, a nurse performs passive range of motion exercises with immobile patients during times of care, such as bathing and/or dressing. Patients who are able to perform active range of motion exercises are encouraged to do so.

Activity Tolerance

While patients should be encouraged to participate in activities of daily living as much as possible, be careful not to overtire them. A patient's daily routine should be planned carefully. Activities should be spaced so that there's ample opportunity to participate as well as adequate rest periods in between.

Comfort

A nurse should provide immobile patients with as much comfort as possible. Reposition patients no less than every two hours and use positioning devices such as pillows and wedges to promote proper body alignment and circulation and to reduce issues of skin breakdown.

Changes in Skin Integrity

Patients with illness, altered nutrition, decreased mobilization, and/or incontinence of bowel and/or bladder are at high risk for skin breakdown. There are some important steps a nurse can take to help prevent breakdown and promote healthy skin.

Skin health depends on adequate nutrition—especially protein intake—and proper circulation of nutrients, such as oxygen to the capillary beds near the skin's surface. Immobility and side effects of medications may cause the patients to refrain from repositioning themselves as they normally would in bed to redistribute pressure. When this happens, pressure on certain areas of the skin will cut off the supply of blood to that area. As a result, oxygen and other important nutrients will cease to nourish the area, and a pressure ulcer will begin forming.

Some common areas where pressure ulcers occur are the sacral area/lower back/buttocks and the heels. When turning and bathing, these areas need to be checked for redness, skin breakdown, and blanching, which occurs

when the skin turns white when pressed, then promptly returns to its natural color. Other common areas include the ears, the back of the head, the shoulders, the elbows, and the inner knees.

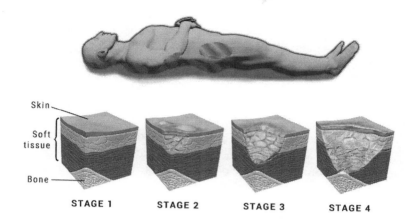

As mentioned in a previous section, there are four main stages of pressure ulcers, ranging from mild pinkness or redness of the skin to severe damage down into the fascia, muscles, and tendons. The nurse does not classify pressure ulcers, but rather observes the skin carefully for changes. Incontinence is a major risk factor for skin breakdown. The nurse may apply lotions or creams to prevent skin breakdown when providing baths and perineal care to the patient. The nurse will also turn and reposition immobile patients every two hours to decrease pressure on bony prominences. Positioning the patient's limbs and back carefully with pillows redistributes pressure.

Any changes in skin such as redness, tearing, or worsening of existing wounds would need to be reported to the nurse immediately. Some facilities may have a skin wound assessment team to oversee the care of the ulcers and recommend interventions.

Pain Management

Pain has been called the fifth vital sign. In addition to heart rate, temperature, blood pressure, and respiratory rate, the patient's experience of pain is just as vital for the healthcare team to assess, monitor, and treat.

The patient may report their pain to the nurse verbally or nonverbally. Nonverbal signs of pain the nurse can look for are facial grimacing, moaning, and tension throughout the body. Behavior that is different for a patient may also be a sign of pain. For example, the nurse may know one patient to normally be very talkative and alert, but they are instead laying silently on the bed for most of the morning, and barely acknowledging anyone entering the room. This may be a sign the patient is experiencing pain and should be investigated and reported to the nurse.

Nonpharmacological Comfort Interventions

When the nurse assesses the patient and finds they need something to alleviate a discomfort, they may first think of pharmacological interventions such as an analgesic. The nurse must also consider nonpharmacological interventions to comfort a patient, as these often come with little to none of the commonly experienced drug side effects.

There are many examples of nonpharmacological interventions the nurse may employ before turning to medication. Repositioning a patient who is feeling uncomfortable may be the first step in relieving a cramp or excessive pressure. This may involve getting the patient in or out of bed, sitting in a chair, or ambulating if appropriate. The nurse may also use pillows to prop and position the patient into a more comfortable position in the bed.

A patient may complain of being too hot or too cold. The nurse may look at what the patient is wearing and decide if additional clothing would help or if the removal of clothing items, as appropriate, would assist. Giving the patient their coat, a warm blanket from the floor's blanket warmer, or socks may comfort a cold patient. Many hospitals do not allow fans, as they are an infection control risk, but the nurse may provide other options to the patient who wishes to cool off. If the patient is not on a fluid restriction, ice chips or ice water may be helpful in refreshing them. Removing excessive blankets may cool them off as well.

The nurse can use heat and cold in even more targeted approaches to relieve pain. Application of heat, such as warm washcloths, electric blankets, and warm baths will increase blood flow to the painful area, reduce muscle spasms, slow down peristalsis, relax the smooth muscles, and even decrease stomach acid production.

Cold application, on the other hand, cannot only decrease the spasmodic activities of muscles but also cause vasoconstriction in the areas where it is applied. The application of cold items such as an ice pack, cool washcloth, and ice cubes can decrease inflammation and increase peristalsis. The application of cold items may have a longer-lasting effect than the application of heat in some patients.

The nurse should not feel uncomfortable offering therapeutic touch where and when appropriate. Most nursing schools train their students in basic massage techniques so that the nurse may use this on clients experiencing muscle tension. Massage should only be applied with the patient's consent and in an appropriate manner. The nurse may use lotion or oil if appropriate to relieve areas of muscle tension. Common areas that become tense include the neck, shoulders, and lower back. By massaging these areas, the nurse may be able to promote healthy blood flow, decrease tension, and maybe even relieve achiness that the client may be experiencing.

Some clients may request alternative therapies for **spiritual needs**. The nurse may refer the client to the appropriate entity for these interventions. For example, most hospitals offer a clergy that will come to the patient and talk with them. Patients may have spiritual issues they may want to discuss. The clergy and spiritual staff available at the hospital can address those needs, talk with the patient, and pray with them.

The nurse may use certain **psychological modalities** for relieving a patient's pain or discomfort. Distraction such as music therapy can be helpful in moving the patient's focus off the discomfort, as pain is perceived in the mind and can sometimes be overcome there as well. The nurse may educate the patient about a topic that is troubling them, thus relieving any anxiety they may feel. Simple strategies aimed at relaxation such as controlled, deep breathing may assist a patient in pain. Deep breathing causes the body to take in far more stress-reducing oxygen and release the waste product carbon dioxide, thus making the patient immediately feel better. Breathing techniques are a hallmark of natural childbirth, as the woman focuses on her breathing to work her way through each contraction. Sometimes the simple act of listening to the patient as they voice their concerns may be all it takes to alleviate their apprehension, working through the inner conflict.

There are certain relaxation strategies that may be used on patients when muscle tension is present. These fall mainly into the categories of progressive muscle relaxation, autogenic training, and biofeedback. **Progressive muscle relaxation** techniques will have the patient alternately tighten and then relax different muscle groups. **Autogenic training** involves the patient training their body to respond to verbal commands, often targeted at the breathing rate, blood pressure, heartbeat, and temperature of the body. **Biofeedback** often includes breathing exercises. The goal of all of these relaxation strategies is to promote relaxation and reduce stress.

Whichever nonpharmacological technique the nurse chooses should be selected very carefully, using critical thinking and sound nursing judgment to best serve the patient's need and alleviate their discomfort.

Nutrition and Oral Hydration

A patient admitted to a facility will often have specific nutritional needs, such as a diet modification or restriction. Conditions, such as nausea or vomiting, and equipment, such as nasogastric tubes, can further complicate the goal of maintaining adequate nutrition. The nurse should also be familiar with intravenous (IV) accesses and how to monitor them.

There are several different dietary restrictions that a patient may have depending on their condition. A cardiac diet, or heart-healthy diet, is for patients with heart conditions. This diet is generally low in sodium, fat, and cholesterol. The nurse will educate the patient about this diet, but it is important for the nurse to ensure the correct meal tray is delivered to the patient. Other dietary restrictions for health reasons include the renal diet—for patients with kidney problems or failure—a diabetic diet, which focuses on controlling carbohydrate intake, and a fluid-restricted diet for patients with heart or kidney failure.

There are cultural and religious considerations to be aware of when it comes to dietary restrictions. Some adherents of the Jewish and Islamic faiths, for example, do not consume pork products. Some Jews also do not consume meat and dairy products in the same meal. Acceptable Jewish meals are referred to as *kosher*, while in the Islamic faith, foods that are acceptable are called *halal*. Some people believe it is wrong to consume any meat and only eat non-animal foods. They are called vegetarians. Vegans do not consume any animal product of any kind, such as milk or honey.

Some patients may be lactose intolerant. Lactose is a sugar found in dairy products that can cause gastrointestinal upset to sensitive individuals. These people may need to abstain from consuming dairy products or take a digestive aid—such as the enzyme lactase—to help them digest the lactose.

There are numerous other dietary restrictions a patient can have for various reasons. The important points for the nurse are to be familiar with the patient's diet order, to ensure the correct tray is delivered, to correct a mistake made by the food service, and to ensure the patient's wishes are respected.

Illness and medications can sometimes bring on side effects of nausea and/or vomiting. The patient experiencing these side effects will likely prefer to abstain from food—called **fasting**—until the nausea and vomiting subsides. If the nausea and vomiting is short-lived, fasting is not a problem. If the fasting is prolonged, however, the patient will experience nutritional deficits and further complications.

The nurse must always assist the healthcare team in carefully monitoring all of a patient's intake and output (I&O) to ensure adequate nutrition and hydration. Any nausea or vomiting must be recorded, as well as the amount of meals eaten. The intake and output record will be tracked by the healthcare team and interventions based upon it. There are medications, such as Zofran (ondansetron), that can alleviate nausea and prevent vomiting. In the case of a patient receiving chemotherapy treatments who has constant nausea and trouble eating, there are medicines that can encourage appetite.

Oral/Sublingual/Buccal

The provider understands that the oral, sublingual, and buccal administration routes are appropriate for agents that will be rapidly absorbed into the bloodstream through the mucous membrane of the gastrointestinal tract. In addition, the sublingual and buccal routes are appropriate if the patient is unable to swallow a medication, or when the medication would be poorly absorbed or inactivated in the stomach. The provider is aware that sublingual and buccal medications are provided in tablet, film, and spray forms.

Oral administration: The provider will assist the patient to swallow oral medications that will be processed in the stomach or small intestine.

Sublingual administration: The provider will place sublingual medications under the tongue to facilitate rapid absorption of the medication into the bloodstream.

Buccal administration: The provider will place buccal medications between the cheek and the gum where the medication will be absorbed through the capillary bed.

Topical

Topical medications are applied to the skin, mucous membrane, or body tissue, and may be provided as transdermal patches; ointments, lotions, and creams; or powders. The provider will assess the administration site for local reaction, and will rotate the site as appropriate for transdermal patches. In addition, the provider will avoid personal contact with the medications that are commonly absorbed rapidly through the skin.

Inhalation

The provider understands that **inhalant drugs** are used to deliver the medication directly to the target organ, which results in more rapid and efficient local absorption of the medication, in addition to decreased systemic exposure to the effects of the medication.

The provider will use medication-specific metered dose inhalers, dry powder inhalers, or nebulizers to administer inhaled agents that may include antimicrobials and corticosteroids. The licensed provider is also responsible for verifying the patient's understanding of the proper use and administration of these medications.

Instillation (eye-ear-nose)

The provider understands that medications may be instilled into the eye, ear, or nose to promote absorption or to treat local irritation of the site. This is called **instillation**.

To instill eye drops, the provider will clear any accumulated secretions, use the nondominant hand to expose the conjunctival sac, instill the prescribed solution into the inner canthus while avoiding any contact with the eye, and use a sterile cotton ball to dry the eyelid.

To instill eye ointment, the provider will clear any accumulated secretions, use the nondominant hand to expose the conjunctival sac, apply the prescribed ointment along the sac from the inner canthus to the outer canthus while avoiding any contact between the eye and the medication container, and use a sterile cotton ball to dry the eyelid.

To instill medications into the ear, the provider will warm the solution to normal body temperature, position the patient with the head turned to the unaffected side, gently pull the ear up and back, instill the medication avoiding contact between the medicine dropper and the ear canal, place a sterile cotton ball loosely in the outer ear and instruct the patient to remain supine for fifteen minutes.

To instill nasal drops, the provider will instruct the patient to gently blow their nose, position the patient supine with the head tilted back, and instill the drops while avoiding contact between the inner nares and the medicine dropper.

Intradermal

The provider will use a 1 milliliter tuberculin syringe with a 5/8 inch 25- to 27-gauge needle to inject the prescribed medication into the dermis level of the skin. The provider must identify the appropriate injection angle for the prescribed treatment; for example, allergy testing requires that the injection is 15 to 20 degrees, while insulin may be injected **intradermally** at 90 degrees. Common intradermal sites include the forearm, shoulder blades, and the chest.

Transdermal

The provider understands that **transdermal medications**, which are absorbed through the skin, provide the continuous release of a precise amount of the medication for a specific period of time. When applying a new dose of the medication, the provider will remove remaining residue from the previous dose, verify that the skin is intact and free of irritation, and sign and date the patch. Birth control pills, smoking cessation medications, pain relief agents, and nitroglycerin are some of the medications that are applied transdermally.

Vaginal

The provider understands that **vaginal medications**, which are available as suppositories, foams, ointments, and sprays, are used to alter the pH of the vagina, treat local infection, and provide comfort. The provider will insert the suppository form into the vaginal vault where it will liquefy as a result of body temperature. The provider will apply the ointment and spray medications according to the manufacturers' directions.

Rectal

Antiemetics, analgesics, and cathartics are commonly available as suppositories. The provider will insert the **rectal suppository** above the internal anal sphincter to prevent displacement.

Injection Site
Site Selection

The provider will select the appropriate **injection site** with consideration of the age and stature of the patient and the administration requirements of the prescribed medication. The provider is aware that injection sites must be systematically rotated for medications such as insulin that are repeated daily.

Needle Length and Gauge

The provider will select the **needle gauge and length** that is consistent with the selected injection site and the administration requirements of the prescribed medication.

Medication Packaging
Multidose Vials

The provider will withdraw the calculated amount of medication from the **multidose vial** using aseptic technique to avoid contamination of the remaining solution.

Ampules

The provider will break the **ampule** using safety precautions related to glass breakage and withdraw the entire contents into the syringe. The provider will then verify that the syringe contains the calculated volume of medication, replace the needle, and administer the medication according to protocol.

Unit Dose

The provider is aware the patient's medications will most often be provided in single-dose amounts, as opposed to multidose amounts, in order to avoid medication errors.

Prefilled Cartridge-Needle Units

The provider is aware that injectable medications may be provided as **prefilled cartridges** with attached needles. Depending on the manufacturer, a nondisposable holder will be provided for the cartridge. The provider must verify that the prefilled cartridge contains the calculated dose.

Powder for Reconstitution

The provider will inject the prescribed amount of diluent into the vial, mix the solution, and withdraw the calculated amount of medication.

Six Rights of Medication Administration

As mentioned above, the **six rights of medication administration** must be addressed for every medication dose. The provider will:

- Use two means of identification (ID) to verify the right patient, which can include the patient's verbal report and the agency ID band

- Verify the prescription and the medication as provided by the pharmacy

- Compare the route of administration documented in the medication record with the original prescription

- Verify the time schedule as documented in the medication record

- Calculate the correct dose and verify the result with another provider as required by agency policy

- Document the administration of the medication and the patient's response in the medication record according to agency policy

Pharmacological Pain Management

Pain is the most commonly seen symptom in the emergency department, as most emergency situations cause patients to have a high level of pain. However, since cases in the emergency department often vary widely in scope and every patient will have a different personal threshold for pain tolerance, best practices are difficult to develop when it comes to **pain management**. It is often done on a case-by-case basis. However, when a patient's pain is not managed in a way that seems appropriate to that individual, it can cause patient and family dissatisfaction in the healthcare organization. As a result, medical staff must try to provide effective and safe pain management options that can make the patient comfortable at the present time, but that also do not cause harm over time. In some cases, like a sprained muscle, ice therapy and time can provide adequate pain management. More serious cases, defined as pain that does not subside after an objectively reasonable period of time for the injury, may require topical, intramuscular, or oral pain medication. These can include stronger doses of common over-the-counter pain medications, or prescription pain medications.

Prescription pain medications, especially opioids and muscle relaxers, are known for causing debilitating addiction, so when prescribing them to a patient, the lowest dose and dosing frequency necessary should be utilized. Additionally, patients should be closely monitored for their reactions to their pain medications. Finally, some individuals who are addicted to prescription pain killers and muscle relaxers may feign injuries in order to receive another prescription. Therefore, all patients' medical histories should be thoroughly evaluated to note their history of pain medication usage. Patients should also be assessed for showing any signs of drug abuse history and withdrawal symptoms (such as damaged teeth, shaking, and agitation).

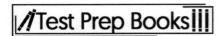

Procedural sedation allows patients to remain somewhat alert during medical procedures that may be uncomfortable but not unbearably painful, such as resetting bones. Unlike general anesthesia, where patients are completely sedated and do not feel any sensations, procedural sedation allows patients to be somewhat conscious and aware of bodily functions. It can be utilized with or without pain-relieving medications. Practitioner awareness is crucial when administering procedural sedation, especially when pain relief is also utilized. Recently, overuse and improper use of common procedural sedation agents, such as propofol, and common pain relief medications that are often used in conjunction, such as fentanyl, have caused high profile deaths.

Reduction of Risk Potential

Changes/Abnormalities in Vital Signs

One of the most basic nursing skills is obtaining and analyzing vital signs. Heart rate, blood pressure, breathing, and temperature are clues that must be interpreted to evaluate a patient's functioning status. Alterations in the vital signs must be carefully monitored to stay on top of the patient's condition and ensure timely and effective interventions take place.

The patient's **heart rate**, measured in beats per minute, tells the nurse a lot about the heart. In an adult, the normal heart rate is 60 to 100 beats per minute.

There are certain points in the body where the pulse can be felt, or palpated. **Palpable pulse points** include the carotid in the neck, the brachial near the elbow, the radial and ulnar on either side of the wrist, the femoral in the groin, the popliteal behind the knee, the posterior tibial behind the ankle, and the dorsalis pedis on top of the foot. The nurse uses these palpable peripheral pulse points to assess and count the heart rate on the patient. The location at which the nurse obtains the pulse is up to their discretion and based on the specific patient's situation. A radial pulse is the most commonly used in a stable, uncomplicated patient. A patient who is in critical condition with weakened blood circulation to the periphery of the body may need a femoral or carotid pulse taken, as these are

closer to the heart and more detectable in situations of lowered cardiac output. The brachial pulse is the one that is measured when blood pressure is taken using an arm cuff.

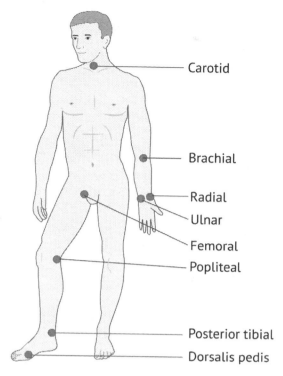

After the location of the pulse is decided and the nurse is palpating with the two-finger technique, the nurse will note the quality of the pulse. Qualities of the pulse can be faint, weak, strong, or bounding. The nurse grades the pulse on a scale of +1 to +4, with 1 indicating a faint pulse and 4 indicating a bounding pulse.

A pulse that is greater than 100 is called **tachycardia** and can arise from any number of causes. Exercise can raise the heart rate above 100 but is not considered abnormal or pathological, as it returns to normal at rest. Tachycardia without exercise and accompanied by other symptoms may be suggestive of a disease state at work and should be investigated.

Common causes of tachycardia include anxiety, medication side effects, street drug use, anemia, overactive thyroid, fear, stress, heart attack, or heart failure, among many others.

Bradycardia is the term for a heart rate that is less than 60 beats per minute. In some patients, this may be a normal finding. Patients who are experienced athletes often run bradycardic. This is because they have strengthened their heart through exercise to the point that their heart beats more efficiently with fewer beats, delivering adequate blood supply to the tissues and organs of the body. Bradycardia noted in a patient without a history of bradycardia, accompanied by other troublesome signs such as a decreased level of consciousness and hypotension, should be evaluated for probable causes and treatment.

Bradycardia may be caused by an underactive thyroid, infections of the heart, coronary artery disease, normal aging processes, medications for heart failure and hypertension, and hyperkalemia, to name a few.

The blood pressure is a vital sign that indicates how strongly the heart is pushing the blood through the circulatory system. **Blood pressure** is measured as a systolic number over a diastolic number. The systolic number represents the pressure at which the heart chambers are contracted, and the diastolic number represents the pressure when

the heart chambers are at rest. Blood pressure is measured in millimeters of mercury (mmHg), as that is what the original sphygmomanometer, or blood pressure cuffs, used to determine a pressure reading.

In general, normal systolic ranges are between 100 and 120 mmHg, and normal diastolic ranges are between 60 and 80 mmHg. Between 120 and 139 mmHg systolic and 80 and 89 mmHg diastolic is considered prehypertensive, and 140 mmHg or greater systolic and 90 mmHg or greater diastolic is considered hypertensive.

Blood Pressure Levels	
Normal	systolic: less than 120 mmHg diastolic: less than 80mmHg
At risk (prehypertension)	systolic: 120–139 mmHg diastolic: 80–89 mmHg
High	systolic: 140 mmHg or higher diastolic: 90 mmHg or higher

Like tachycardia and bradycardia, hypertension and hypotension may arise from many different causes. Accompanying symptoms and patient history are key factors to consider when assessing changes in blood pressure.

Some patients may run a low blood pressure without any other accompanying symptoms, and that is to be noted as their normal, but no treatment is necessary.

Orthostatic hypotension is a special type of hypotension that occurs when the patient changes position. This occurs most commonly when they change from a seated position to standing. The patient will experience profound dizziness and unsteadiness, which is why orthostatic hypotension may lead to falls, and the patient should be cautioned to change positions slowly. Orthostatic hypotension may be measured by taking the patient's blood pressure first when lying down, then sitting up at the edge of the bed, and then a final reading while they are standing. If they are truly experiencing orthostatic hypotension, their blood pressure readings will trend downward significantly over the course of the three readings. Orthostatic hypotension is often a side effect of medications for hypertension.

A severe form of hypotension is shock, in which the body is no longer delivering an adequate supply of blood with its oxygen and nutrients to the vital organs of the body. The patient in shock will need immediate treatment and fluid resuscitation.

Low volume of blood, as occurs with a hemorrhage or a dehydrated state, will lead to low blood pressure. Blood transfusions, fluid resuscitation, and possibly blood pressure-raising medications such as intravenous (IV) dopamine may be necessary to correct hypovolemic hypotension.

A patient's **respiratory rate** should be between 16 and 20 breaths per minute and can be observed and counted simply by looking at the patient's chest for a rise and a fall. Tachypneic patients are those who are breathing at a rate greater than 20 breaths per minute. Patients with bradypnea, on the other hand, are those who are breathing below 16 breaths per minute.

Apnea is an absence of breathing and may occur during a normal sleep cycle, but prolonged and repeated occurrences of apnea are problematic and may suggest a disease process such as obstructive sleep apnea.

A patient may be tachypneic because of a blood clot, pneumonia or other respiratory infection, anxiety, asthma, chronic obstructive pulmonary disease (COPD), or diabetic ketoacidosis. Patients may be bradypneic because of an overdose of alcohol or narcotics, increased intracranial pressure, obesity, an underactive thyroid, a brain lesion, or

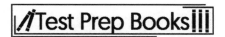

many other causes. The nurse will look for accompanying symptoms and read through the patient history to help accurately evaluate the cause of the breathing abnormality.

The body regulates its temperature through a process called **thermoregulation**. The normal body temperature is right around 98.6 degrees Fahrenheit, give or take a degree depending on the patient's own normal.

Hyperthermia is a temperature that is above normal and may indicate an infection-fighting fever or a heat-induced condition such as heat stroke. Excessive sweating, confusion, and decreased level of consciousness may accompany hyperthermia and should be treated by making efforts to get the patient cooled down.

Hypothermia occurs when the body cannot produce enough heat to replace the heat it has lost, such as if a patient is in a harsh, cold environment without adequate warm clothing or a source of heat such as a furnace. Patients who are older, taking certain medications that interfere with the body's ability to regulate its temperature, have spinal cord injuries, are intoxicated with drugs or alcohol, or are very young are particularly susceptible to hypothermia and should take extra caution when exposed to very low temperatures.

Diagnostic Tests

A **diagnostic test** is one in which the result is hoped to assist in making a diagnosis of the patient's condition. The diagnostic test will reveal the patient's strengths and weaknesses and provide the clinician with data about the patient's condition.

There are many different diagnostic tests available for innumerable patient conditions. Different mediums are used to diagnose conditions, including blood work, ultrasound technology, X-rays, procedures that put cameras in the body to visualize internal structures, and more.

A female patient who has discovered a lump in her breast may be scheduled for a **mammography**. This type of diagnostic procedure is a type of X-ray that visualizes the tissue of the breast. This can help identify lumps that the patient or the practitioner is not able to palpate. The generally agreed-upon guideline for mammography is for it to be performed once every year or two after the age of forty for early breast cancer detection.

Patients with certain heart conditions may have an **echocardiography** performed. An echo, as it is commonly referred to, visualizes the structures and chambers of the heart through ultrasonography. An echo technician will use a small probe called a transducer to emit sound waves into the chest that create a sonographic image of the heart. Gel is applied to the skin of the chest to allow the transducer to easily glide back and forth as different aspects of the heart are visualized. Clots, holes, and any structural abnormalities will be identified during the echo. The official reading and interpretation of the echo images will be performed by a cardiologist after the tech has taken the images.

The **complete blood count (CBC)** is a type of diagnostic test that requires a small vial of blood to be drawn from the patient. The blood is sent to the lab, and the components of the blood are measured. The CBC measures red blood cells (RBCs), white blood cells (WBCs), hemoglobin, hematocrit, and platelets. This simple test can give the clinician a quick look at the body's oxygen-carrying capacity, immune function, and clotting capability all in one go.

For a patient with symptoms related to the gastrointestinal (GI) tract, the endoscope is a handy diagnostic tool to visualize the internal environment of the stomach and intestines. Generally, there are two types of scope: upper endoscopy and lower endoscopy. An **endoscopy** is a procedure in which a flexible tube with a camera, light, irrigation, and instrument ports are inserted for visualization of the GI tract. The patient receiving an upper GI endoscopy will require IV sedation as well as topical anesthetics applied to the throat. Lower endoscopy generally requires anesthesia as well, except for anoscopy and sigmoidoscopy, which do not travel as deeply into the body. Biopsy of tissue may be performed during a scope. As well as diagnosing certain conditions such as colon cancer,

peptic ulcers, and other mucosal lesions, the scope may be performed for therapeutic reasons such as removing foreign bodies, hemostasis of bleeding lesions, debulking of tumors, placement of stents, placing a feeding tube, reduction of volvulus, and decompression of a dilated colon. Common hemostatic methods include placing hemoclips, injecting hemostatic drugs, thermal coagulation, variceal banding, and sclerotherapy.

Look at the image of a **colonoscopy** below:

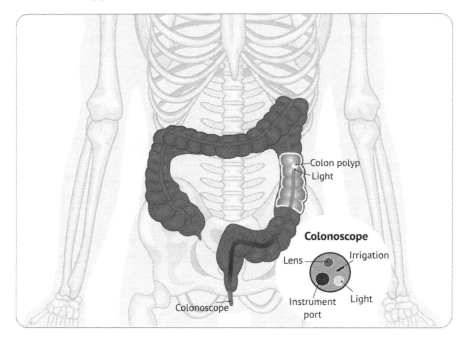

One of the most regularly performed diagnostic tests is the computed tomography scan. It may be referred to as a **CT or CAT scan**, but the meanings are all the same: a test in which a region of the body is scanned and images are obtained using radiography. The patient lays on a sliding table that moves them in and out of a circular opening in which the scanner is housed. As the patient moves through the scanner, an X-ray source and X-ray detector spin around the patient in a circular motion, taking images of the inner structures of the patient's body. These images are then sent to a computer, which makes a composite of all the images into 3-D images to be viewed and interpreted by a qualified radiologist. There are variations on how the CT can be taken, including stopping the patient for each scan or slice or keeping the patient in motion for a spiral CT, but the basic concept is the same.

CT scans may be noncontrast or with contrast. With IV or oral contrast, the patient drinks or is injected with a barium-based solution, targeted at whichever body tissues need imaging, and picked up by the X-ray during the scan. Contrast is often contraindicated in patients with renal failure, as their kidneys are unable to metabolize the substance. Contrast CTs are used to visualize tumors and inflammation and assess the vascular system for pulmonary emboli, aneurysms, or aortic dissection, among many other purposes.

Electrocardiography (EGG/ECG)
To perform a **standard 12-lead EGG/ECG**, the provider will:

- Verify the order and obtain all equipment before approaching the patient.
- Explain the procedure to the patient and assist him/her to a supine position.
- Expose the limbs and the chest, maintaining appropriate draping to preserve patient's privacy.
- Clean the electrode sites with alcohol and remove excess body hair according to agency policy.
- Attach electrodes to appropriate anatomical positions.

- Attach machine cables to the electrodes.
- Enter the patient data and calibrate the machine as necessary.
- Request that the patient does not move or speak.
- Obtain an artifact-free tracing.
- Remove the electrodes and residual conductive gel.
- Return the patient to a position of comfort.
- Submit the tracing for interpretation.

Correct Placement of EKG Leads

The accuracy of the tracing is dependent on correct lead placement; therefore, the provider will position the chest leads as follows:

- V_1 - right sternal border at the level of the fourth intercostal space
- V_2 - left sternal border at the level of fourth intercostal space
- V_3 - centered between V_2 and V_4
- V_4 - the midclavicular line at the level of the fifth intercostal space
- V_5 - horizontal to V_4 at the anterior axillary line
- V_6 - horizontal to V_4 at the midaxillary line

The provider must attach the limb leads to the extremities, not the torso. In addition, the provider must avoid large muscle groups, areas of adipose tissue deposit, and bony prominences when placing the limb leads on the four extremities.

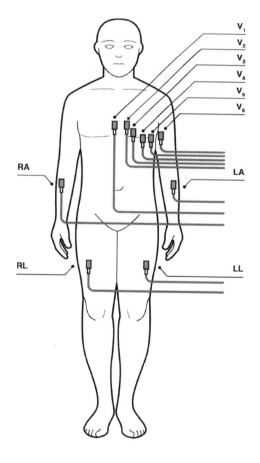

Patient Prep

In order to ensure an accurate tracing, the provider will:

- Explain the procedure to the patient.
- Expose the chest as necessary.
- Clip or shave excess hair as consistent with agency policy.
- Wipe the skin surface with gauze to decrease electrical resistance.
- Remove excess oils with alcohol wipe if necessary.
- Verify that the electrode is intact with sufficient gel.
- Attach the electrodes as appropriate.
- Complete the tracing.

Recognizing Artifacts

An **artifact** is an error produced in the results of a test. Artifacts can emerge for many reasons, including improper technique, faulty or mis-calibrated equipment, or as a normal occurrence in a test that must be accounted for during analysis.

Artifacts during an ECG are most often the result of patient movement while the tracing is being recorded. The provider must be able to differentiate between the artifact and lethal arrhythmias. An ECG artifact is most often evidenced by a chaotic wave pattern that interrupts a normal rhythm, as shown in the figure below.

EKG Artifact

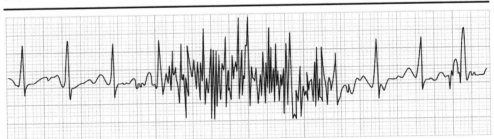

Recognizing Rhythms, Arrhythmias

Normal Sinus: The rhythm originates in the sinoatrial (SA) node as indicated by the presence of an upright p wave in lead 2. A p wave precedes every QRS complex, and the rhythm is regular at 60 to 100 beats per minute.

Normal Sinus Rhythm

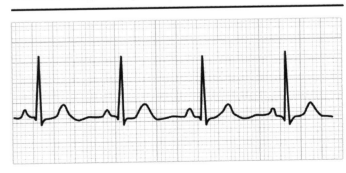

Sinus Tachycardia: The rhythm originates in the SA node as indicated by the presence of an upright p wave in lead 2. A p wave precedes every QRS complex, and the rhythm is regular at a rate greater than 100 beats per minute.

Sinus Tachycardia

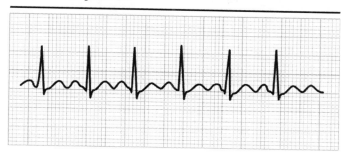

Sinus Bradycardia: The rhythm originates in the SA node as indicated by the presence of an upright p wave in lead 2. A p wave precedes every QRS complex, and the rhythm is regular at less than 60 beats per minute.

Sinus bradycardia

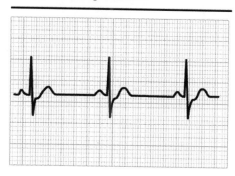

Atrial Fibrillation: Irregular electrical impulses around the heart create disorganized electrical waves in the atria that cause the AV node to fire at irregular intervals. Individual p waves are not visible due to the rapid rate, and the QRS complexes are generally wider than the QRS complexes in the sinus rhythms.

Atrial Fibrillation

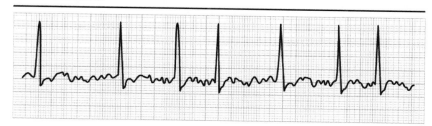

129

Complete Heart Block: The SA node generates a p wave that is not transmitted to the ventricles. The ventricles respond to an impulse from an alternative site, and the resulting complex has no association with the p wave. This condition requires immediate intervention.

Complete Heart Block

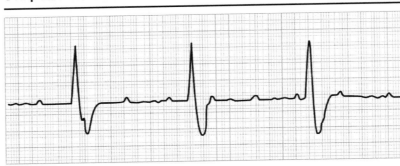

Ventricle Fibrillation: There is only erratic electrical activity resulting in quivering of the heart muscle. Immediate intervention is necessary.

Ventricular Fibrillation

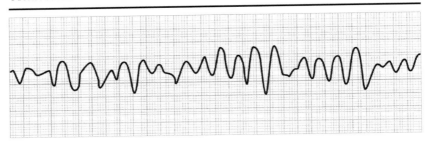

Rhythm Strips

The provider can use a 6- to 10-second strip of cardiac activity to identify the heart rate and rhythm. The ECG paper is standardized to measure time from left to right, with each small box equal to $\frac{4}{10}$ of a second, which means that each large box is equal to 1/5 of a second and the time elapsed between the black ticks is 3 seconds. The provider calculates the heart rate by dividing 300 by the number of large squares between 2 QRS complexes. In the figure below, the heart rate is $\frac{300}{4} = 75$. Alternatively, the provider can identify the heart rate by counting the number of QRS complexes in a 10-second EKG strip and multiplying that result by 10.

The provider will assess the rhythm by comparing the distance between   complexes 1 and 2 with the distance between complexes 2 and 3.

Cardiac Rhythm Strip

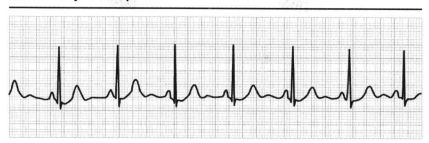

Holter Monitor

The **Holter monitor** is a portable device that is used for monitoring the EKG/ECG. The monitor may be used for routine cardiac monitoring or for diagnosing cardiac conditions that may not be evident on a single EKG/ECG tracing. The provider will attach the leads to the patient's chest, verify the patient's understanding of the process, and provide the patient with a diary with instructions to record all activity and physical symptoms for the duration of the testing period.

Holter monitor with EKG reading

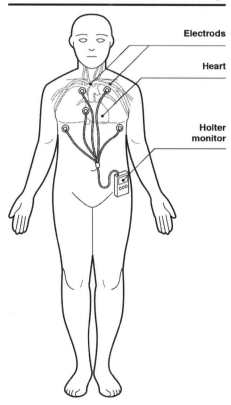

Electrods

Heart

Holter monitor

Cardiac Stress Test

The provider uses the **cardiac stress test** to identify the patient's cardiac response to the stress of exercise. The cardiac activity is recorded after the patient's heart rate reaches a target rate that is equal to 220 minus the patient's age. There are two forms of the test, which include the treadmill test and the pharmacologic test. Patients

who are physically able are asked to walk on the treadmill until the target heart rate is achieved. Patients who are unable to tolerate the exercise will receive medications to raise the heart rate to the desired level. The provider will reverse the effects of these medications as soon as the appropriate tracings are obtained.

Vision Test: Color

The most commonly used test for color blindness is the **Ishihara Color Vision Test**, which is a series of circular images that are composed of colored dots. The identification of the numbers embedded in the colored plates is determined by the patient's ability to identify the red/green numbers and background. There are currently online variations of this test in addition to color testing forms that the provider may use for younger children who are not yet able to identify numbers.

Vision Test: Acuity/Distance

Snellen Chart

The **Snellen chart** contains eleven rows of letters that differ in size from row to row and is viewed from a distance of twenty feet. The resulting numbers, 20/100 for example, indicate that the patient can see objects at a distance of 20 feet that are visible to a person with normal eyesight at a distance of 100 feet.

E Chart

The **E chart** contains nine rows of letters that differ in size from row to row depicting the letter E in alternating positions. The chart is useful for children and others who are not familiar with the English alphabet. The scoring is similar to the Snellen chart.

Jaeger Card

The **Jaeger card** uses six paragraphs in differing font sizes ranging from 14 point to 3 point Times New Roman font to test near vision. The J1 paragraph at 3 point Times New Roman font is considered to equal 20/20 vision per the Snellen chart.

Ocular Pressure

The provider uses a tonometer to touch the surface of the patient's anesthetized cornea in order to record the pressure inside the eye, or **ocular pressure**.

Visual Fields

Visual fields are defined as the total horizontal and vertical range of vision when the patient's eye is centrally focused. The provider may use this test to detect "blind spots" or scotomas.

Pure-Tone Audiometry

The patient's **pure-tone threshold** is identified as the lowest decibel level at which sounds are heard 50 percent of the time.

Speech and Voice Recognition

The speech-awareness threshold (SAT), or **speech-detection threshold (SDT)**, is defined as the lowest decibel level at which the patient can acknowledge the stimuli. The test utilizes spondees—two-syllable words that are spoken with equal stress on each syllable—as the stimuli for this test.

The **speech-recognition threshold (SRT)**, or less commonly speech-reception threshold, measures the lowest decibel level at which the patient can recognize speech at least 50 percent of the time. This test also may be used to validate pure-tone threshold measurements, to determine the gain setting for a patient's hearing aid, or to provide a basis for suprathreshold word recognition testing.

Suprathreshold word recognition is used to assess the patient's ability to recognize and repeat one-syllable words that are presented at decibel levels that are consistent with social environments. Human-voice recordings are used to present the words, and the patient's responses are scored. The provider may use the results of this test to monitor the progression of a condition such as Meniere's disease, to identify improvement afforded by the use of hearing aids, or to isolate the part of the ear that is responsible for the deficit.

Tympanometry

The provider uses a **tonometer** to assess the integrity of the tympanic membrane (ear drum) and the function of the middle ear by introducing air and noise stimuli into the ear. The provider then assesses the resulting waveform and records the results.

Allergy Test: Scratch Test

In a **scratch test**, the provider applies a small amount of diluted allergen to a small wound created in the patient's skin in order to identify the specific allergens that elicit an allergic response in the patient. The allergist will select up to 50 different allergens for testing, which means that the provider will make 50 small incisions or scratches in the patient's skin arranged in a grid system to facilitate the interpretation and reporting of the test results. The provider will observe the patient closely for a minimum of 15 minutes following the introduction of the allergen for the signs of an anaphylactic reaction, in addition to signs of a positive reaction. The provider will document all positive results that are evidenced by a reddened raised area that is pruritic.

Allergy Test: Intradermal Skin Testing

The provider may use intradermal injections of the allergen to confirm negative scratch tests, or as the primary method of allergy testing. Using a 26- or 30-gauge needle, the provider will inject the allergen just below the surface of the skin. The provider must closely observe the patient and record results based on the appearance of raised, reddened wheals that are pruritic.

Pulmonary Function Tests

Pulmonary function tests evaluate the two main functions of the pulmonary system: air exchange and oxygen transport. The specific tests measure the volume of the lungs, the amount of air that can be inhaled or exhaled at one time, and the rate at which that volume is exhaled. The tests are used to monitor the progression of chronic pulmonary disorders, including asthma, emphysema, chronic obstructive lung disease, and sarcoidosis.

Spirometry

Spirometry is one of the two methods used to measure pulmonary function. The provider attaches the mouthpiece to the spirometer and instructs the patient to form a tight seal around its edge. The provider will then demonstrate the breathing patterns that are necessary for successful evaluation of each of the pulmonary measurements. The spirometry device calculates each of the values based on the patient's efforts.

Peak Flow Rate

Peak flow rate is defined as the speed at which the patient can exhale. This measure is commonly used to evaluate pulmonary function in patients with asthma.

Tuberculosis Tests/Purified Protein Derivative Skin Tests

Tuberculosis tests/purified protein derivative (PPD) skin tests are screening tests for the presence of Mycobacterium tuberculosis. The provider will use a tuberculin (TB) syringe to inject 0.1 ml of tuberculin purified protein derivative, the TB antigen, into the interior portion of the forearm. The solution forms a small, round elevation or wheal that is visible on the skin surface. The patient must return to the agency for evaluation of the site between 48 and 72 hours after the injection. The provider will assess the site and document the size of any visible

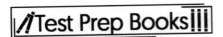

induration or palpable swelling. The provider will not include any reddened areas in that measurement. The provider will refer all results that exceed 5 mm for additional testing and treatment.

Blood Pressure

Technique

To obtain an accurate measurement, the provider will:

- Assist the patient to a seated position.
- Expose the upper arm at the level of the heart.
- Apply the appropriately sized cuff.
- Palpate the antecubital space to identify the strongest pulsation point.
- Position the head of the stethoscope over the pulsation point.
- Slowly inflate the cuff to between 30 and 40 mm Hg above the patient's recorded blood pressure (BP). If this information is unavailable, the cuff may be inflated to between 160 and 180 mm Hg.
- Note the point at which the pulse is initially audible, which represents the systolic BP.
- Slowly deflate the cuff and record the point at which the pulse is initially audible as the systolic BP.
- Record the point at which the sounds are no longer audible as the diastolic BP.

Equipment

The **stethoscope** is a Y-shaped, hollow tube with earpieces and a diaphragm that transmits the sound to the earpieces when the provider places the diaphragm against the patient's body.

The **sphygmomanometer** includes the cuff, the mercury-filled gauge, or manometer that records the patient's pressure, and the release valve that regulates the air pressure in the cuff.

Pulse

Technique

To assess the pulse the provider will:

- Expose the intended pulse point.
- Palpate the area for the strongest pulsation.
- Position the middle three fingers of the hand on the point.
- Count the pulse for one full minute.

The provider will identify the pulse points that include the radial artery in the wrist, the brachial artery in the elbow, the carotid artery in the neck, the femoral artery in the groin, the popliteal artery behind the knee, and the dorsalis pedis and the posterior tibialis arteries in the foot.

The provider will assess the pulse rate by counting the number of pulsations per sixty seconds. In addition to the pulse rate, the provider will document the regularity or irregularity and strength of the pulsations.

Height/Weight/BMI

Technique

To record an accurate height, the provider must instruct the patient to:

- Remove all footwear.
- Stand straight with the back against the wall.
- Remain still until the height is recorded.

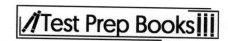

To record an accurate weight, the provider must first zero the scale and then instruct the patient to:

- Remove all heavy objects from the pockets.
- Stand on the scale facing forward.
- Remain still until the weight is recorded.

The BMI (body mass index) is equal to:

- Imperial English BMI Formula: weight (lbs) $\times$ 703 $\div$ height (in^2)
- Metric BMI Formula: weight (kg) $\div$ height(m^2)

For example:

The BMI of a patient who weighs 150 pounds and is 5'6" is equal to:

$$150 \times 703 = 105,450 = 24.2 \text{ or } 24.0$$

$$66 \times 66 = 4,356$$

Equipment
Bodyweight scales may be mechanical or digital. Some digital scales also provide detailed metabolic information including the BMI in addition to the weight. Other scales can accommodate patients who are confined to bed.

Body Temperature
There are five possible assessment sites for **body temperature**, including oral, axillary, rectal, tympanic, and temporal. The route will depend on the patient's age and the agency policies. Assessment of oral temperatures requires the provider to verify that the patient has had nothing to eat or drink for five minutes before testing in order to avoid inaccurate readings.

Thermometers may be digital with disposal covers for the probe, wand-like structures that use infrared technology and are moved across the forehead to the temporal area, or handles with disposable cones that measure the tympanic temperature.

Oxygen Saturation/Pulse Oximetry
When every hemoglobin molecule in the circulating blood volume is carrying the maximum number of four oxygen molecules, the **oxygen saturation rate** is 100 percent. The normal oxygen saturation level is 95 percent to 100 percent, and levels below 90 percent must be treated.

The provider measures oxygen saturation noninvasively by the application of a pulse oximetry device, which the provider will attach to the patient's finger. The device may be used for continuous or intermittent monitoring of the saturation rate.

The **pulse oximeter** is a foam-lined clip that attaches to the patient's finger and uses infrared technology to assess the oxygen saturation level, which is expressed as a percentage.

Respiration Rate
The **respiratory rate** is counted, and the breathing pattern is assessed. The provider should ensure that the patient is unaware that the breathing rate is being counted by leaving the fingers resting on the radial pulse site while the respiratory rate is assessed.

Age-Specific Normal and Abnormal Vital Signs

Age	Temperature Degrees Fahrenheit	Pulse Range	Respiratory Rate Range	Blood Pressure mmHg
Newborns	98.2 axillary	100–160	30–50	75–100/50–70
0–5 years	99.9 rectal	80–120	20–30	80–110/50–80
6–10 years	98.6 oral	70–100	15–30	85–120/55–80
11–14 years	98.6 oral	60–105	12–20	95–140/60–90
15–20 years	98.6 oral	60–100	12–30	95–140/60–90
Adults	98.6 oral	50–80	16–20	120/80

Examinations

- **Auscultation** refers to listening to the sounds of body organs or processes, such as blood pressure, using a stethoscope.

- **Palpation** refers to using the hand or fingers to apply pressure to a body site to assess an organ for pain or consistency.

- **Percussion** refers to tapping on a body part to assess for rebound sounds. It may be used to assess the abdomen or the lungs.

- **Mensuration** refers to the measurement of body structures, such as measuring the circumference of the newborn's head.

- **Manipulation** refers to using the hands to determine motion and flexibility of a body part or to correct a defect such as realigning the bones after a fracture.

- **Inspection** refers to the simple observation of the color, contour, or size of a body structure.

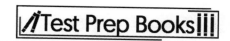

Body Positions/Draping

The provider will use proper draping to maximize the patient's privacy and to facilitate the planned procedures.

Draping Body Position

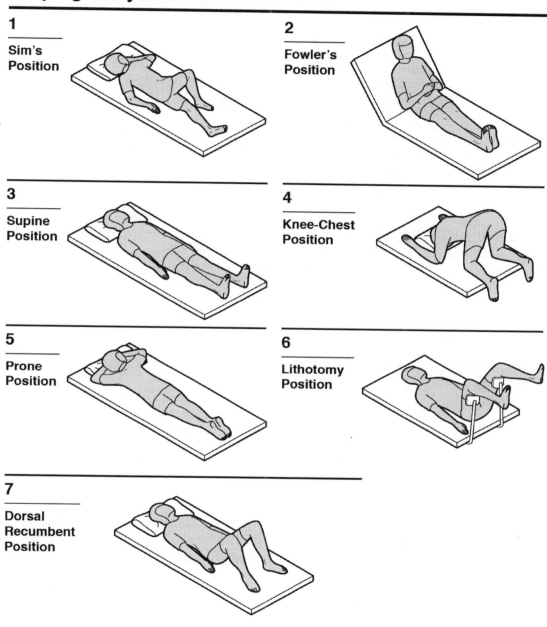

1 Sim's Position

2 Fowler's Position

3 Supine Position

4 Knee-Chest Position

5 Prone Position

6 Lithotomy Position

7 Dorsal Recumbent Position

Pediatric Exam

The purpose of the **pediatric exam** is to assess the child's growth and development and to provide family counseling regarding behavioral issues, nutrition, and injury protection. In addition, providers screen children for specific conditions at various ages to ensure that appropriate treatment is not delayed. For instance, newborns are tested

for phenylketonuria and hearing loss. Children between three and five years old are tested for alterations in vision, and school-aged children are screened for obesity.

Growth Chart

The **growth chart** is a systematic assessment of a child's growth pattern that can be compared to gender-specific norms.

The head circumference, height, and body weight are measured in children from birth to three years of age. In children older than three, the BMI is measured in addition to height and weight.

The head circumference is measured from birth to three years of age. The provider will measure the head circumference by placing a flexible measuring tape around the widest circumference of the child's head, which most commonly is above the eyebrows and the top of the ears. The provider will weigh infants lying down without clothes or diapers, and older children on mechanical or digital scales. To assess an infant's height, the provider will lay the child on a flat surface with the knee straightened and extend the flexible tape from the top of the infant's head to the bottom of the foot. The provider will position older children with their backs to a wall for an accurate measurement of their height.

Pelvic Exam/ Papanicolaou (PAP) Smear

The **pelvic exam** is done to assess the organs of the female reproductive system. The ovaries and the uterus are assessed by palpation, and the cervix is assessed by inspection. The **PAP smear** sample is a screening test for cervical cancer. The sample, obtained from the opening of the cervix, is transferred to glass slides for processing.

Prenatal/Postpartum Exams

The provider performs the **prenatal pelvic exam** to assess the development of the fetus and the status of the maternal reproductive system. The pelvic exam is done at the first visit, but is not repeated with every visit. In a normal pregnancy, it may not be repeated until the third trimester. The provider performs the postpartum exam to assess the return of the maternal reproductive organs to the nonpregnant state.

Laboratory Values

The nurse will need a savvy knowledge of common lab tests performed, why they are performed, and the normal values that are expected from the tests. These values will indicate if a disease process is at work in a body system. The nurse will need to be able to interpret that abnormality to report it to the ordering physician.

One commonly taken lab test is the serum electrolyte panel. In the body, the electrolytes work to maintain healthy cellular functions and metabolism. Electrolytes provide the structure in cell walls, generate energy for metabolic activity, transport fluid, cause muscle cell contraction, and even generate electrical impulses in the cardiac cells. Electrolytes that are often measured and assessed in the patient include sodium, potassium, magnesium, phosphorus, chloride, and calcium. The normal values of these electrolytes are listed below:

- Sodium: 135–145 mEq/L
- Potassium: 3.5–5.1 mEq/L
- Magnesium: 1.6–2.6 mg/dL
- Phosphorus: 2.5–4.5 mg/dL
- Chloride: 98–107 mEq/L
- Calcium: 8.5–10.0 mg/L

Values outside of these normal parameters may suggest an electrolyte imbalance. Hyper/hypokalemia, hyper/hyponatremia, hyper/hypomagnesemia, hyper/hypochloremia, hyper/hypocalcemia, and

hyper/hypophosphatemia are all conditions that should be immediately reported to the ordering physician if they are newly developed or worsened since the last reading. Signs and symptoms accompanying these electrolyte abnormalities should also be noted and treated as appropriate.

The CBC, as noted earlier in the Diagnostic Tests section, is useful for giving the clinician a picture of the health of the circulatory system. The CBC will show if the patient is anemic, leukemic, or lacking the necessary platelets for clotting and maintaining hemostasis. The following list shows normal, expected values for each component of the CBC:

- Red blood cells: 4–5 million cells/mcL for women, 5–6 million cells/mcL for men
- White blood cells: 4500–10,000 cells/mcL
- Hemoglobin (Hbg): 14–17 gm/dL
- Hematocrit (Hct): 41%–50% for men, 36%–44% for women
- Platelets: 140,000–450,000 cells/mcL
- Mean corpuscular volume (MCV) (the size of red blood cells): 80–95

The **comprehensive metabolic panel (CMP)** is a group of lab values that are often taken together that measure how well the kidneys and liver are functioning and levels of blood sugar, cholesterol, calcium, and protein in the body. The electrolytes may be measured using the CMP or as part of a smaller lab test called a **basic metabolic panel (BMP)**. Though it varies based on facility, the CMP generally consists of fourteen separate lab tests, while a BMP may only contain eight separate lab tests. The practitioner will determine which of these tests to perform.

The following are normal levels found on a CMP:

- Blood glucose: 70–110 mg/dL
- Albumin: 3.4–5.4 g/dL
- Alkaline phosphatase: 44–147 IU/L
- Alanine aminotransferase (ALT): 7–40 IU/L
- Aspartate aminotransferase (AST): 10–34 IU/L
- Blood urea nitrogen (BUN): 6–20 mg/dL
- Creatinine: 0.6–1.3 mg/dL
- Total bilirubin: 0.3–1.0 mg/dL
- Total protein: 6.0–8.3 g/dL

The final lab test the nurse will need to be able to interpret is the **arterial blood gas (ABG) sample**. A commonly performed test in patients with respiratory disorders or on mechanical ventilation in the intensive care unit (ICU), this test shows the pH balance, carbon dioxide level, and bicarbonate level in the patient's blood. This test will show how well the patient's respiratory processes are performing. Adjustments to respiratory and other therapies may be made based on it. The arterial sample is usually obtained from the radial, femoral, or brachial arteries. The following are normal ABG ranges:

- Oxygen (O_2) saturation (SaO2): 94%–100%
- Arterial blood pH: 7.35–7.45
- Partial pressure of oxygen (PaO2): 75–100 mmHg
- Partial pressure of carbon dioxide (PaCO2): 38–41 mmHg
- Bicarbonate (HCO3): 22–28 mEq/L

Abnormalities in the ABGs could suggest an alkalotic or acidotic state of the patient's blood that will need correction. Reporting abnormal values to the physician and the respiratory therapist will be part of the nurse's expected duties.

139

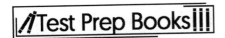

Urinalysis

- **Physical (urinalysis):** The provider will perform a visual assessment of the color and turbidity of the urine sample.

- **Chemical (urinalysis):** The provider will use the reagent strip to assess the specific gravity, the pH, and the presence and quantity of protein, glucose, ketones, hemoglobin and myoglobin, leukocyte esterase, bilirubin, and urobilirubin.

- **Microscopic (urinalysis):** The provider will separate the urine sediment from the fluid volume to microscopically identify the presence of RBCs, WBCs, epithelial cells, bacteria, yeasts, and parasites.

- **Culture (urinalysis):** The provider will assess the presence of infectious agents in the urine sample by inoculating the agar plates, incubating sample at body temperature, and observing and documenting any growth at 24 and 48 hours after inoculation of the sample.

Hematology Panel

- **Hematocrit (HCT):** The provider will assess the RBC count as defined by the hematocrit—amount of red blood cells in the blood—by placing the anticoagulated blood sample into the microhematocrit centrifuge and documenting the results.

- **Hemoglobin:** The provider will assess the amount of the hemoglobin protein that is present in the red blood cells by placing the anticoagulated blood sample into the microhematocrit centrifuge and documenting the results.

- **Erythrocyte Sedimentation Rate (ESR):** The provider will assess the ESR, which is a nonspecific indicator of inflammation, by placing the anticoagulated sample in the Westergren tube and recording the height of the settled RBCs after one hour.

- **Automated Cell Counts:** The provider will use the automated device to assess RBC, WBC, and platelet counts by preparing the sample, obtaining, and documenting the results.

- **Coagulation testing/international normalized ratio (INR):** The provider will calculate the INR, which is used to assess blood-clotting levels in patients being treated with Warfarin, according to laboratory protocol after verifying that the sample was not drawn from a heparinized line.

Chemistry/Metabolic Testing

Glucose
The provider will identify the **blood glucose sample**, which measures the amount of glucose in the circulating blood volume, as fasting or nonfasting before processing and documenting the results.

Kidney Function Tests
Kidney function is assessed by measuring the levels of metabolic waste products, including blood urea nitrogen (BUN) and creatinine, and by calculating the **glomerular filtration rate (GFR)**, which corresponds with the clearance of waste products from the blood by the kidneys. The provider will process the sample to obtain the BUN and creatinine levels. The provider will then use the creatinine level and the patient's age, body size, and gender to calculate the GFR according to the agency-approved equation for GFR. There are four equations that may be used to calculate the GFR in adults that include the Modification of Diet in Renal Disease (MDRD), the Study equation (IDMS-traceable version), and the Chronic Kidney Disease Epidemiology Collaboration (CKD-EPI) equation.

Liver Function Tests

Elevated levels of alanine transaminase (ALT) and aspartate aminotransferase (AST), two liver enzymes, indicate acute/chronic hepatitis, cirrhosis, or liver cancer. Decreased levels of these enzymes may be due to Vitamin B-12 deficiency. Albumin, a protein synthesized by the liver that is necessary for the maintenance of osmotic pressure in the vasculature, is decreased in liver failure due to cirrhosis or cancer. The liver processes bilirubin, a waste product resulting from the normal destruction of old red blood cells, for excretion by the gastrointestinal system; however, elevated levels may be due to liver failure or transfusion reactions. The provider will verify a 10-minute centrifuge time, process the sample, and document results.

Lipid Profile

Excess dietary intake of animal fats can result in elevated total cholesterol and low-density lipoprotein (LDL) or "bad cholesterol" levels, while elevated high-density lipoprotein (HDL) or "good cholesterol" levels are the result of appropriate nutrition or the effect of cholesterol-lowering medications. Elevated triglyceride levels may result from diabetes, obesity, liver failure, or kidney disease. The provider will verify that the fasting sample was obtained before the administration of N-Acetylcysteine (NAC) or Metamizole, if indicated. The provider will then process the sample per protocol within two hours of the venipuncture and document the results.

Hemoglobin A1c

A **Hemoglobin A1c** test measures the percentage of hemoglobin molecules that are coated or glycated with glucose. Hemoglobin molecules are located in the red blood cell, which has a lifespan of 110 to 120 days; therefore, the hemoglobin A1c test measures the average blood sugar for a four-month period. The normal A1c level is less than 5.7 percent; levels between 5.7 percent and 6.4 percent indicate prediabetes and levels greater than 6.5 percent indicate diabetes. Elevated HGB A1c levels must be confirmed with additional testing before treatment is initiated. The provider will inform the patient that fasting is not required, process the sample, and document results.

Immunology

Mononucleosis Test

The immune system produces heterophile proteins in response to the presence of the Epstein-Barr virus (EBV), the causative agent of mononucleosis. Specific tests include the analysis of the viral capsid antigen (VCA), the early antigen (EA), or the EBV nuclear antigen (EBNA). The Monospot test detects antibodies that are not specific for mononucleosis, leading to false positive and false negative results. In addition, the Monospot test may be insensitive to the heterophile antibodies produced by children with mononucleosis. The provider will freeze the sample if processing is delayed beyond 24 hours after preparation.

Rapid Group A Streptococcus Test

Identification of the beta-hemolytic bacterium **Streptococcus pyogenes**, the most common cause of acute pharyngitis in adults and children, is obtained by using isothermal nucleic acid amplification technology. The provider will transfer the sample to the testing device adhering to proper wait-times, process the sample, and document the results.

C-Reactive Protein (CRP)

C-reactive protein (CRP) is an indicator of inflammation that is released into the bloodstream in response to tissue injury or the onset of an infection. The provider will verify that all reagents and the serum sample are at room temperature, assess the processed sample for agglutination, and document the results.

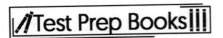

HCG Pregnancy Test

Serum levels of human chorionic gonadotropin hormone detect the presence of a pregnancy. Elevated levels may indicate a normal pregnancy, either single or multiple, chorionic cancer, or hydatidiform mole. The provider will centrifuge the clotted sample for ten minutes at room temperature, and document the results.

H. pylori

There are three testing methods for the *Helicobacter pylori* organism, including histological examination and culture of samples obtained by endoscopic biopsy, the urea breath test (UBT) that measures CO_2 levels on exhalation, and the fecal antigen test that identifies antibodies to the organism. The provider will verify that the patient has avoided antibiotics and bismuth preparations for two weeks prior to the testing. The provider will process all samples according to the specific test requirements and document the results.

Influenza

Influenza testing methods include the Rapid Influenza Diagnostic Test (RIDT), and the Real Time Polymerase Chain Reaction, and the viral culture, which identify   the genetic material of the virus in secretions obtained from a nasal or throat swab. The provider will process all samples according to the specific test requirements and document the results.

Fecal Occult Blood Testing

Occult bleeding is not visibly apparent, which means that detection methods rely on the chemical reaction between the blood and the testing reagents for identification of blood in a sample. For home sample collection with guaiac testing, the provider will instruct the patient to collect three samples on three different days to optimize results. The patient will secure the test card and submit it to the provider for testing. The provider will apply a guaiac solution to the sample to identify a bluish tinge in the test area, which is considered positive for the presence of occult blood.

Potential for Alterations in Body Systems

The nurse will work with patients who are at risk for an alteration in their body systems. The nurse identifies compromising patient situations that have the potential to lead to complications. These complications could include aspiration, skin breakdown, insufficient vascular perfusion, and the devastating problems that may occur when a patient has been sedentary for too long.

There are many conditions that may cause a patient to be at risk for aspiration. A patient who has suffered a stroke and has developed dysphagia, or difficulty swallowing, is immediately considered at risk for aspiration. This is because the mechanical difficulty they experience when they try to swallow can sometimes lead to leakage of the substance they are trying to swallow into their airway instead of the esophagus. Foreign substances in the airway lead to immediate difficulty breathing and respiratory distress. At this point, aspiration has occurred, and the patient needs emergent intervention to restore proper respiratory faculties.

A client with a feeding tube in place, whether nasogastric (NG) or placed via gastrostomy, is at risk for aspiration. **Aspiration** is, in fact, one of the most common complications of enteral feedings. The stomach becomes quite full with the feedings, causing gastric contents to reflux, and secretions accumulate in the pharynx where they are then aspirated. The integrity of the upper and lower esophageal sphincters may become compromised over time, contributing to aspiration risk. The patient receiving tube feedings also has the potential to have a weakened swallowing and gag reflex, contributing to aspiration risk. Clients on tube feedings should be carefully monitored for fullness of the stomach and signs of fluid buildup such as wet-sounding coughs and a rattle-like sound when breathing.

Patients who are sedated are at risk for aspiration due to their altered level of consciousness. The head of the bed should remain elevated at least 45 degrees to 90 degrees if the patient has recently received an enteral feeding to promote digestion and stomach emptying. Laying the patient flat on their back puts them at risk of aspiration.

All patients who have been immobilized by an illness are at risk for skin breakdown while in bed. The increased pressure on bony prominences that a prolonged period spent in bed creates can easily compromise skin integrity and lead to an ulceration. The nurse works to prevent pressure ulcers by keeping the client on a "turn every two hours" repositioning schedule. Every two hours, the client will be repositioned in bed, from the left side to the right side and then back again. The patient should only be positioned on their back for feedings, as this position can put quite a bit of pressure on the sacrum, an area especially vulnerable to breakdown.

There are many patient situations that may put them at risk for insufficient vascular perfusion. Patients with impaired circulation may be at risk because of hypervolemia, hypovolemia, a low amount of circulating oxygen associated with low hemoglobin counts, low blood pressure, immobilization of a limb, decreased cardiac output as seen in heart failure, and diabetes. After the nurse has identified that the client has a compromise of vascular perfusion, efforts will be made to intervene and restore normal circulation. Early mobility, in which the client is encouraged to get out of bed and get moving as soon as they are able, is vital to maintaining healthy circulation. Compression stockings are commonplace in immobile patients to artificially maintain healthy circulation.

Certain factors put a patient more at risk for developing cancer. A patient who uses tobacco or is exposed to secondhand smoke on a regular basis is at a greater risk for developing cancers of the lung, mouth, larynx, and esophagus. Patients with a family history of a certain type of cancer such as breast, colon, ovarian, and uterine are more at risk for developing these types of cancers. The nurse will review and record a client's risk factors for developing cancers when performing the initial admission assessment.

Potential for Complications of Diagnostic Tests/Treatments/Procedures

When a client undergoes a procedure or diagnostic test at the hospital, things do not always go according to plan. The nurse is there to assess the client when they return from their procedure to monitor them for complications. When a complication is noted, the nurse is quick to intervene, alert the attending physician, and take care of the patient to get them stabilized.

One common diagnostic procedure performed regularly at hospitals is the cardiac catheterization. Patients returning from a cardiac catheterization are at risk for developing complications such as bleeding and dysrhythmias. Most facilities have protocols and checklists in place post-procedure that the nurse will follow strictly. These checklists include regular vital-sign monitoring, checking the access site for bleeding or hematoma, and cardiac monitoring for dysrhythmias. The client will be made to lay flat for a predetermined amount of time, usually six hours, so that blood flow to the accessed artery is not compromised and the access point can fully heal. Bleeding around the puncture point as well as formation of an aneurysm are other possible complications. Any abnormality will be reported to the cardiologist.

A patient who has a limb with a cast placed will be monitored for compartment syndrome. The nurse pays close attention to the limb, especially the more distal end, to ensure that adequate circulation is maintained and is not cut off by the cast placement. Assessment of pulses, whether radial or ulnar in the upper limbs or dorsalis pedis or posterior tibial in the lower limbs, will be performed to assess that circulation is not compromised.

After any test that involves incision, puncture, or any other access to the client's circulatory system, bleeding and infection are always major risks. Patients with thrombocytopenia, or a low platelet count, are at an increased risk for bleeding, as they lack the necessary component for proper hemostasis. Blood pressure monitoring is an excellent way to monitor the patient's hemodynamic status. A lowered blood pressure that is trending downward is

an ominous sign that the client may be losing blood internally. Hypotension is the first step toward any sort of shock state and can lead to an interrupted delivery of oxygen to vital organs and tissues. Identifying if the client is bleeding and where the source of the bleed is will require an advanced interventional team such as a rapid-response team, usually headed by an intensivist or ICU doctor.

Along with bleeding, infection is a common complication of invasive diagnostic procedures. The nurse works to prevent infection by performing meticulous handwashing before and after client care, observing infection prevention precautions such as donning gloves and gowns in patients with communicable diseases and disinfecting equipment after use. The disposal of medical supplies in the appropriate receptacle, such as sharps in the sharps container, will assist in the goal of preventing the spread of infections. The nurse takes care to perform certain tasks using an aseptic or sterile technique, such as dressing changes, insertion of urinary catheters, insertion of NG tubes, and obtaining IV accesses.

System Specific Assessments

The nurse will need to perform a **body system-specific assessment** on clients who have undergone a diagnostic procedure or a treatment. This is when a nurse examines a specific area of the body to check for any new complications, to see if the procedure went as planned, or to see what else may need to be done to resolve the issue.

Knowledge of peripheral pulse assessment is necessary to evaluate the patient's circulatory status. Strong pulses at a normal rhythm are good; faint pulses that are either too fast or too slow are worrisome and need further evaluation. Pulses are graded on a scale of 0 to 4, 0 being absent, 1 being weak, 2 being normal, 3 being increased volume, and 4 being a bounding pulse. The pulse is assessed and documented with further action being taken if necessary.

Another way to evaluate the health of the circulatory system is to assess for and grade edema. **Edema**, a fluid accumulation in the peripheral tissues of the body, can get to a point where, when pushed down upon with a finger, the impression stays in the skin. These impressions can be graded by their depth, ranging from +1 to +4 as shown in the diagram below.

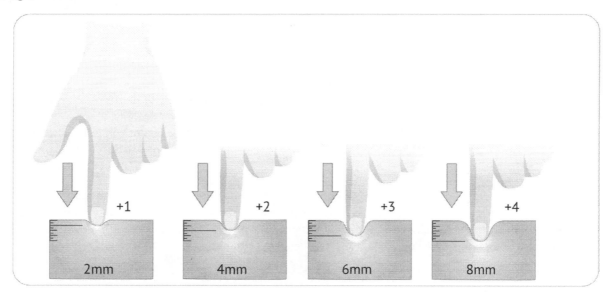

The neurological system may need specific evaluation requiring the nurse's keen assessment skills. The nurse will start by evaluating the client's level of consciousness, which is measured by interviewing the client and their

knowledge of who they are, where they are, and the time. A client oriented to all three of these components is said to be oriented times three, while a client who only knows their name, for example, is only oriented times one. Commonly, this is noted in the nurse's notes as "A&OX3" or something similar. The "A" stands for "alert," as opposed to obtunded, drowsy, sleepy, difficult to arouse, and other altered levels of consciousness.

Other components of the neurological assessment include assessment of the cranial nerves, usually used on stroke assessments, motor and sensory function, pupillary response, reflexes, cerebellar function, and vital signs.

The following are the **"Five P's" of Neurovascular Assessment**:

- Pain
- Pulse
- Pallor
- Paresthesia
- Paralysis

The nurse can assess the client's musculoskeletal system by testing for bilateral strength and equality of movement. Muscular strength can be graded on a 0 to 5 scale. A patient with no visible muscle contraction is graded as a 0, a patient who has visible contraction but still no movement is graded as a 1, a patient that is contracting and trying to move but cannot overcome gravity is graded as a 2, the same without the ability to push against resistance is a 3, the same with only a limited effect of resistance on their effort is a 4, and finally, a full contraction with movement that can overcome elevated levels of resistance is a 5.

Diabetic patients have a constant battle maintaining a healthy level of blood sugar. The nurse taking care of a diabetic patient keeps a close eye on not only the patient's blood sugar but also their diabetic medications, the fluids they are receiving, and their mealtime habits. The classic symptoms of hyperglycemia are polydipsia and polyuria, where the patient drinks copious amounts of fluid and produces massive amounts of urine. Hypoglycemia symptoms reflect the interruption of blood glucose to the brain, resulting in neurological symptoms such as confusion, lowered level of consciousness, slurred speech, lightheadedness, and dizziness.

Potential for Complications from Surgical Procedures and Health Alterations

During the **surgical consent process**, surgical risks and potential complications are explained to the patient by the surgeon. The risk of complications depends on the type of surgical procedure being performed, as well as the condition and comorbidities of the patient. The perioperative environment predisposes the patient to risk of hypothermia. Per best practice guidelines, the operating room temperature should be kept between sixty-eight and seventy-three degrees Fahrenheit. Depending on the procedure, the patient may be partially clothed or fully naked. If the procedure is one hour or greater in duration, thermoregulation measures should be taken to prevent hypothermia. These measures can include warming blankets and warm intravenous fluid administration. Methods for monitoring patient temperature in the perioperative environment include temporal, esophageal, bladder, rectal, and via thermodilution catheter, which is inserted into the pulmonary artery.

Hypothermia places the patient at greater risk for developing **surgical site infection (SSI)**. Although the signs of SSI may not be apparent for several weeks postoperatively, steps in preventing SSI are implemented in the preoperative period. The Joint Commission's **Surgical Care Improvement Project (SCIP)** outlines standards around preoperative antibiotic prophylaxis and other measures to decrease risk of SSI. Major surgical procedures involving the vascular system, such as abdominal aortic aneurysm repair and open-heart surgical procedures, present the risk for high amounts of blood loss.

Hemodynamic changes often occur as a result of blood loss. **Hemodynamic changes** during the surgical procedure can include hypotension, hypertension, cardiac arrhythmias, and decreased oxygen saturation. Changes in

hemodynamic stability can create the need for blood transfusion. Blood loss can lead to cardiac complications, especially in those with coronary artery disease. Patients with cardiac disease are at risk for myocardial infarction (MI) due to the surgical process. In vascular procedures, the clamping of vessels can release calcified areas or plaque into circulation, which can cause an MI or a stroke.

Venous thromboembolism (VTE) is another potential complication from surgery. VTE prophylaxis measures are implemented preoperatively to reduce this risk. Depending on the patient, these measures can include application of **sequential compression devices (SCDs)** to bilateral lower extremities. SCDs work by creating mild, intermittent compression to the extremities to prevent pooling of blood while the patient is not ambulatory. The physician may choose to order a medical VTE prophylaxis protocol. For example, the patient may receive enoxaparin (Lovenox®), a blood thinner, for a set number of doses postoperatively.

A rare yet life-threatening complication of surgery is **malignant hyperthermia (MH)**. MH is a genetic disorder that presents after exposure to anesthetic gases and/or paralytic drugs. Since MH is a genetic disorder, the preoperative interview should include questions that assess family history of MH and complications of anesthesia. If the patient indicates a history of MH or a family history of difficulty with anesthesia, the perioperative team should be prepared for MH crisis and discuss this risk with the entire perioperative team. Symptoms of MH crisis include muscle rigidity, tachycardia, rising body temperature, and rising levels of end-tidal carbon dioxide (ETCO2).

Finally, death is a potential complication of the surgery process. Risk of surgical death is related to the type of surgery and patient comorbidities. Adverse perioperative events such as dissecting a major blood vessel can also lead to death. Emergency procedures generally carry a higher risk of death than routine procedures.

Therapeutic Procedures

The nurse will need to be able to assess a client who has recently undergone a **therapeutic procedure**, apply their knowledge regarding the procedure, educate the client about aftercare, and monitor the patient post-procedure, observing the proper precautions.

Many therapeutic procedures will use anesthesia, whether local, regional, or general. **Local anesthesia** includes topical and injected anesthetics such as lidocaine and benzocaine and are common in minimally invasive procedures such as external biopsies, removals of skin lesions and moles, and dental surgeries. A **regional anesthetic** only provides analgesia to a certain part of the body and includes epidural, spinal, or paravertebral nerve blocks. **General anesthesia** renders the patient completely unconscious using medical gas or IV transfusion.

There are four stages of anesthesia: induction, excitement, surgical anesthesia, and emergence. The anesthetist carefully monitors the patient as they travel throughout these stages, maintaining them in the appropriate state of consciousness while the procedure occurs. During these stages, the client is closely monitored using pulse oximetry, blood pressure readings, measurement of heart rate and rhythm, and body temperature. The patient airway will be monitored, especially if under general anesthesia, and an artificial airway is being used such as an endotracheal tube.

All three levels of anesthesia come with their own potential complications. With local anesthetics, the patient may get too high off of a dose, or the anesthetic may be administered too rapidly. Potential complications of a local anesthetic include excitability, seizure activity, depression of the central nervous system, and respiratory and cardiac distress. Regional anesthetics can cause headache, soreness at the injection site, infection, bleeding, bruising, and low blood pressure. General sedation complications range from mild to severe, including sore throat, fatigue, and dizziness, all the way to malignant hyperthermia, respiratory arrest, cardiac arrest, and cerebrovascular accident or stroke.

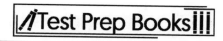
Before and after the procedure, the nurse will assess the client's knowledge of the therapeutic intervention being performed, answer questions within their scope of practice, refer to the performing physician where appropriate, and educate the patient regarding the procedure. Each facility will have client education literature that can be accessed and printed out for the client and nurse's use. Informed consent will need to be obtained for most serious interventions, so this information will be useful to have on hand to answer the client's questions.

The nurse will ensure that the patient's preoperative orders are followed, such as the observance of NPO (nothing by mouth), in which the patient is not to eat or drink anything preprocedure. Any medications that are required before the procedure will be administered and documented in a timely manner. Many procedures have a pre- and postprocedure checklist that the nurse will ensure gets filled out.

The nurse will need to identify the client before and after the procedure following the two-identifier technique. Usually this involves having the client state their name and date of birth, along with a scanning of their identification band for additional identification.

The client who is to go home following a procedure will need home care instructions, such as taking care of an incision site. The nurse will educate the patient about their posthospital care. Usually, if an incision is present, there will be specific instructions as to how to keep the site clean, when the client can shower and bathe again, and how to do dressing changes. Follow-up appointments will be made to ensure the client's progress and healing.

Methods of Collection
Blood
For a venipuncture process, the provider will:

- Identify the patient, review the order, and label the collection tubes.
- Assess the nondominant hand to identify a vein that is straight and palpable.
- Wash hands and apply PPE.
- Clean the selected site with an alcohol swab per agency policy.
- Inspect the test-specific vacuum tubes and needles to verify that:
  - The tube is securely sealed and vacuum has been maintained.
  - Appropriate additives such as anticoagulants or other fixatives that may be required to maintain the sample are present in the tube.
  - The chosen needle size is appropriate to the selected vein.
- Complete the venipuncture per agency policy.
- Apply pressure and a sterile dressing to the venipuncture site.
- Submit the sample for processing per agency policy.

The provider will use a capillary/dermal puncture to obtain blood from small children or when only a small volume of blood is necessary as in finger-stick puncture for blood glucose analysis.

Urine
The provider can collect a random urinalysis any time the patient voids.

To obtain a midstream/clean catch urine sample, the provider will instruct the patient to first clean the urinary meatus with the appropriate antiseptic solution, void without collecting the initial volume, and then deposit the remaining output into the container.

Before beginning the collection of a timed 24-hour collection, the provider must obtain a storage container containing any necessary preservative from the laboratory, and confirm the accommodations for refrigeration of the sample if required. The first time the patient voids, the provider will discard the specimen and record the time.

All urine collected in the following 24-hour period will be collected by the provider and stored in the prepared container at the prescribed temperature.

Catheterization may be used to obtain a sterile specimen. The provider will pass the sterile catheter into the bladder to drain the urine into a sterile container, which must then be labeled and transported to the lab according to agency policy.

The pediatric urine collector is a plastic pouch attached to a foam adhesive-backed base. The provider will verify that the skin around the urinary meatus is clean, dry, and free of powder or lotions. The provider will adhere the adhesive section of the collection device over the urinary meatus and replace the patient's diaper.

Fecal Specimen
The provider will place the fecal specimen in a clean, leak-proof, properly labeled container, and promptly transport the sample to the laboratory for processing.

Sputum Specimen
The sputum specimen must contain sputum, not saliva, and it is best obtained early in the morning.

Throat Swab
After assisting the patient to a seated position in a chair or bed, the provider will use sterile swabs to remove the sample from the back of the throat while avoiding contact with the uvula and tongue. The provider will then break the tips of the swabs and secure them in the labeled collection sleeve, transport the sample to the lab according to agency policy, and document the sample collection time and site.

Genital
The provider will position the patient according to the site being sampled. The provider will use sterile swabs to sample the top of the vaginal vault for a vaginal swab, the center of the cervical os for a cervical swab, or the urinary meatus for a urethral swab. The provider will then break the tips of the swabs and secure them in the labeled collection sleeve, transport the sample to the lab according to agency policy, and document the sample collection time and site.

Wound
The provider will position the patient according to the site being sampled. The provider will remove and discard the existing dressing, use sterile swabs to obtain the sample from the center of the wound, then break the tips of the swabs and secure them in the labeled collection sleeve. Once the swabs are secured, the provider will dress the wound, ensure that the sample is delivered to the laboratory, and document the wound assessment and the sample collection time and site.

Nasopharyngeal
The provider will position the patient in a seated position with the head tilted back. After verifying the patency of the nares, the provider will insert the sterile swab 3 to 4 inches into the nasopharynx, rotate the swabs to obtain the sample, remove the swabs, break the tips of the swabs to secure them in the labeled collection sleeve, transport the specimen to the laboratory, and document the collection site and time.

Physiological Adaptation

Alterations in Body Systems

Nurses must have the ability to assess a client for alterations in their body systems. This is an inevitable occurrence, as a body system alteration is precisely the reason the client is at the hospital in the first place. The nurse will identify the body system alteration and draw up a plan of care based on their findings.

Intake and output are items that are closely monitored by the nurse to discover if an alteration in a body system has occurred. There are several types of drainage a client may experience that fall into the category of input and output. The nurse measures the drainage where appropriate and notes its appearance. Color, quantity, consistency, and any other notable characteristics are observed and documented. Types of drainage the nurse may encounter in client care include feeding tube drainage, respiratory secretions, drainage from a chest tube, rectal tube output, and urinary catheter output.

Clients with cancer may be put on radiation therapy to target and destroy cancerous tumors. This client may develop alterations in certain body systems as a result. The client is likely to become quite fatigued, as their energy is sapped by the intensity of the therapy. Weakness often accompanies fatigue. They may experience skin reactions such as a rash. The skin may become red, looking like a sunburn. The skin above the targeted location for radiation absorbs a bit of the radiation, which is why the reaction occurs. Other radiation therapy side effects may be specific to the area in which the therapy is targeted. If therapy occurs near the stomach or abdomen, for example, stomachache, nausea, vomiting, and diarrhea may occur.

If the nurse is caring for a woman who is pregnant, they will be mindful of certain body alterations associated with the prenatal period. One such complication is high blood pressure during pregnancy, called **preeclampsia**. The woman's blood pressure is carefully monitored during the prenatal period to watch for the development of this condition, which could lead to complications for both the mother and the baby. Gestational diabetes is another prenatal complication of which the nurse is mindful. Somewhere between 24 and 28 weeks, pregnant women are screened for gestational diabetes by performing the oral glucose tolerance test (OGTT). This glucose screening will identify if the woman is at risk, and treatment will follow if necessary.

Patients who are developing an infection will often have some telltale symptoms that the nurse will be watchful for. The classic signs of a localized infection on the outer surface of the body will be redness, inflammation, heat, and swelling. If the infection is systemic, within the body, the patient may have a fever, increased WBC count (or decreased if the infection has been prolonged), prodromal malaise, fatigue, chills, elevated heart rate, and even altered level of consciousness and orientation. Some infections will have specific symptoms related to the organ or tissue of the body affected. For example, a urinary tract infection (UTI) will cause the patient to have pain or burning while urinating, called **dysuria**, possibly blood in the urine, and frequent urges to void. A respiratory infection, on the other hand, will have respiratory-specific symptoms such as cough, difficulty breathing, and adventitious breath sounds on lung auscultation.

Nurses must also be aware that certain medical interventions and devices, such as indwelling long-term dialysis catheters, could increase the risk of infections such as endocarditis. In addition to watching for signs of infection, nurses can help prevent infection through proper treatment of patients with elevated risk.

Having a basic knowledge of how an infection works, from start to finish, is advantageous to the nurse when trying to understand what is going on within the client's body. The causative organism must enter the body through some entryway: respiratory tract, break in the skin, urinary tract, IV access, GI tract, and so on. The organism then goes through what is called the "incubation period," which refers to the time that elapses between the organism entering the body and when symptoms actually begin occurring. During the incubation period, the organism is usually

149

multiplying until it starts to have a noticeable effect on the body. Some pathogens will have a longer incubation time, while others will have shorter. Depending on the pathogen, there may be some communicability of the disease involved, in which the disease can be spread from one person to another. Therefore, observing universal precautions is vital to prevent the spread of disease. Meticulous handwashing by the nurse and all members of the healthcare team, as well as patients and family, is vital.

A full-blown infection occurs when the body's natural defenses cannot overcome the organism effectively and symptoms occur, compromising overall body function. The patient may have an elevated WBC count on the CBC, indicating the body is bolstering its immune defenses to try and overcome the infection. The final stage of the infection is when the body's immune system plus the help of medication and therapeutic interventions destroy the organism, restoring the body to natural, normal functioning ability.

Patient education is an important aspect of care that the nurse diligently performs when body system alterations occur. Helping the patient understand what is going on in their body and answering their questions is an excellent way to reduce anxiety and promote calm and understanding. Anxiety, the nurse knows, only causes additional stress in the body, which will not be conducive to healing.

When educating the patient, the nurse will talk about the body system alteration they are experiencing, using their knowledge of pathophysiology, anatomy, and physiology as well as incorporating lessons about the pharmacological interventions being used on the patient. Discussion of risk factors related to the body alterations and side effects of medication is important to include. The nurse will discuss factors that will promote healing, such as the patient getting adequate rest and early mobility. The nurse will encourage the patient to call on the healthcare team whenever a need arises, whether the need is for the nurse's aide, the nurse, or the physician. The patient should be encouraged to ask their questions and raise their concerns, as they are an important member of the healthcare team. The nurse will include information about helpful resources that the client may access such as community groups for the client's specific condition or illness, social services, and community meal or ride programs.

The following detail the basics of the body systems and their normal functions.

Integumentary

The skin or **integumentary body system** is the largest organ of the body in surface area and weight. It is composed of three layers, which include the outermost layer or epidermis, the dermis, and the hypodermis. The thickness of the epidermis varies according to the specific body area. For example, the skin is thicker on the palms and the soles of the feet than on the eyelids. The dermis contains the hair follicles, sebaceous glands, and sweat glands. Melanin is the pigment that is responsible for skin color.

The main function of the skin is the protection of the body from the outside environment. The skin regulates body temperature, using the insulation provided by body fat and the secretion of sweat, which acts as a coolant for the body. Sebum lubricates and protects the hair and the skin, and melanin absorbs harmful ultraviolet radiation. Special cells that lie on the surface of the skin also provide a barrier to bacterial infection. Nerves in the skin are responsible for sensations of pain, pressure, and temperature. In addition, the synthesis of Vitamin D, which is essential for the absorption of calcium from ingested food, begins in the skin.

Vernix caseosa is a thick, protein-based substance that protects the skin of the fetus against infection and irritation from the amniotic fluid from the third trimester until it dissipates after birth. Several childhood illnesses, such as measles and chicken pox, are associated with specific skin alterations. Acne related to hormonal changes is common in adolescents, and the effects of sunburn are observed across the lifespan. In the elderly, some of the protections provided by the skin become less effective; decreases in body fat and altered sweat production affect cold tolerance, loss of collagen support results in wrinkling of the skin, and decreased sebum secretions lead to changes in hair growth and skin moisture content.

Musculoskeletal

The **musculoskeletal system** consists of the bones, muscles, tendons, ligaments, and connective tissues that function together, providing support and motion of the body. The layers of bone include the hard exterior compact bone, the spongy bone that contains nerves and blood vessels, and the central bone marrow. The outer compact layer is covered by the strong periosteum membrane, which provides additional strength and protection for the bone. Skeletal muscles are voluntary muscles that are capable of contracting in response to nervous stimulation. Muscles are connected to bones by tendons, which are composed of tough connective tissue. Additional connective tissues called ligaments connect one bone to another at various joints.

In addition to providing support and protection, the bones are important for calcium storage and the production of blood cells. Skeletal muscles allow movement by pulling on the bones, while joints make different body movements possible.

The two most significant periods of bone growth are during fetal life and at puberty. However, until old age, bone is continually being remodeled. Specialized cells called osteoclasts break down the old bone, and osteoblasts generate new bone. In the elderly, bone remodeling is less effective, resulting in the loss of bone mass, and the incidence of osteoporosis increases. These changes can result in bone fractures, often from falling, that do not heal effectively. Muscle development follows a similar pattern with a progressive increase in muscle mass from infancy to adulthood, as well as a decline in muscle mass and physical strength in the elderly.

Nervous

The two parts of the **nervous system** are the central nervous system, which contains the brain and spinal cord, and the peripheral nervous system, which includes the ganglia and nerves. The cerebrospinal fluid and the bones of the cranium and the spine protect the brain and spinal cord. The nerves transmit impulses from one another to accomplish voluntary and involuntary processes. The nerves are surrounded by a specialized myelin sheath that insulates the nerves and facilitates the transmission of impulses.

The nervous system receives information from the body, interprets that information, and directs all motor activity for the body. This means the nervous system coordinates all the activities of the body.

The fetal brain and spinal cord are clearly visible within six weeks after conception. After the child is born, the nervous system continues to mature as the child gains motor control and learns about the environment. In the well-elderly, brain function remains stable until the age of 80, when the processing of information and short-term memory may slow.

Cardiovascular, Hematopoietic, and Lymphatic

The **cardiovascular system** includes the heart, the blood vessels, and the blood. The heart is a muscle that has four "chambers," or sections. The three types of blood vessels are: the arteries, which have a smooth muscle layer and are controlled by the nervous system; the veins, which are thinner than arteries and have valves to facilitate the return of the blood to the heart; and the capillaries, which are often only one-cell thick. Blood is red in color because the red blood cells (RBCs) contain hemoglobin, which is a red pigment as well a protein that transports oxygen.

The deoxygenated blood from the body enters the heart and is transported to the lungs to allow the exchange of waste products for oxygen. The oxygenated blood then returns to the heart, which pumps the blood to the rest of the body. The arteries carry oxygenated blood from the heart to the body; the veins return the deoxygenated blood to the heart, while the actual exchange of oxygen and waste products takes place in the capillaries.

The fetal cardiac system must undergo dramatic changes at birth as the infant's lungs function for the first time. Cardiovascular function remains stable until middle age, when genetic influences and lifestyle choices may affect the cardiovascular system. Most elderly people have at least some indication of decreasing efficiency of the system.

The hematopoietic system, a division of the lymphatic system, is responsible for blood-cell production. The cells are produced in the bone marrow, which is soft connective tissue in the center of large bones that have a rich blood supply. The two types of bone marrow are red bone marrow and yellow bone marrow.

The red bone marrow contains the stem cells, which can transform into specific blood cells as needed by the body. The yellow bone marrow is less active and is composed of fat cells; however, if needed, the yellow marrow can function as the red marrow to produce the blood cells.

The red bone marrow predominates from birth until adolescence. From that point on, the amount of red marrow decreases, and the amount of yellow marrow increases. This means that the elderly are at risk for conditions related to decreased blood-cell replenishment.

The lymphatic system includes the spleen, thymus, tonsils, lymph nodes, lymphatic vessels, and the lymph. The spleen is located below the diaphragm and to the rear of the stomach. The thymus consists of specialized lymphatic tissue and lies in the mediastinum behind the sternum. The tonsils are globules of lymphoid tissue located in the oropharynx. The lymphatic vessels are very small and contain valves to prevent backflow in the system vessels. The vessels that lie in close proximity to the capillaries circulate the lymph. Lymph is composed of infectious substances and cellular waste products in addition to hormones and oxygen.

The main function of the lymphatic system is protection against infection. The system also conserves body fluids and proteins and absorbs vitamins from the digestive system.

The spleen filters the blood in order to remove toxic agents and is also a reservoir for blood that can be released into systemic circulation as needed. The thymus is the site of the development and regulation of white blood cells (WBCs). The tonsils trap and destroy infectious agents as they enter the body through the mouth. The lymphatic vessels circulate the lymph, and the lymph carries toxins and cellular waste products from the cell to the heart for filtration.

There is rapid growth of the thymus gland from birth to ten years. The action of the entire system declines from adulthood to old age, which means that the elderly are less able to respond to infection.

Respiratory

The **respiratory system** consists of the airway, lungs, and respiratory muscles. The airway is composed of the pharynx, larynx, trachea, bronchi, and bronchioles. The lungs contain air-filled sacs called alveoli, and they are covered by a visceral layer of double-layered pleural membrane. The intercostal muscles are located between the ribs, and the diaphragm separates the thoracic cavity from the abdominal cavity.

On inspiration, the airway transports the outside air to the lungs, while the expired air carries the carbon dioxide that is removed by the lungs. The alveoli are the site of the exchange of carbon dioxide from the systemic circulation with the oxygen contained in the inspired air. The muscles help the thoracic cavity to expand and contract to allow for air exchange.

The respiratory rate in the infant gradually decreases from a normal of 30 to 40 breaths per minute, until adolescence when it equals the normal adult rate of 12 to 20 breaths per minute. Pulmonary function declines after the age of 60 because the alveoli become larger and less efficient, and the respiratory muscles weaken.

Digestive

The **digestive system** includes the mouth, pharynx, esophagus, stomach, small intestine, large intestine, and sigmoid colon. The entire system forms a 24-foot tube through which ingested food passes. Digestion begins in the mouth, where digestive enzymes are secreted in response to food intake. Food then passes through the esophagus to the stomach, which is a pouch-shaped organ that collects and holds food for a period of time. The small intestine begins at the distal end of the stomach. The lining of the small intestine contains many villi, which are small, hair-like projections that increase the absorption of nutrients from the ingested food. The large intestine originates at the distal end of the small intestine and terminates in the rectum. The large intestine is 4 feet long and has 3 segments, including the ascending colon along the right side, the transverse colon from right to left across the body, and the descending colon down the left side of the body, where the sigmoid colon begins.

The enzymes of the mouth, stomach, and the proximal end of the small intestine break down the ingested food into nutrients that can be absorbed and used by the body. The nutrients are absorbed by the small intestine. The large intestine removes the water from the waste products, which forms the stool. The muscle layer of the large intestine is responsible for peristalsis, which is the force that moves the waste products through the intestine.

The function of the digestive system declines more slowly than other body systems, and the changes that most often occur are the result of lifestyle issues or medication use.

Urinary

The **urinary system** includes the kidneys, ureters, bladder, and urethra. The kidneys are a pair of bean-shaped organs that lie in the peritoneal cavity just below and toward the rear of the liver. The nephron is the functional unit of the kidney, and there are about 1 million nephrons in each of the two kidneys. The ureters are hollow tubes that allow the urine formed in the kidneys to pass into the bladder. The urinary bladder is a hollow mucous lined pouch with the ureters entering the upper portion, and the urethra exiting from the bottom portion. The urethra is a tubular structure lined with mucous membrane that connects the bladder with the outside of the body.

In addition to the formation and excretion of the waste product urine, the nephron of the kidney also regulates fluid and electrolyte balance and contributes to the control of blood pressure. The ureters allow the urine to pass from the kidneys to the bladder. The bladder stores the urine and regulates the process of urination. The urethra delivers the urine from the bladder to the outside of the body.

The lifespan changes in the urinary system are more often the result of the effects of chronic disease on the system, rather than normal decline.

Reproductive

The major organs of the **female reproductive system** include the uterus, cervix, vagina, ovaries, and fallopian tubes.

The uterus is a hollow, pear-shaped organ with a muscular layer that is positioned between the bladder and the rectum. The uterus terminates at the cervix, which opens into the vagina, which is open to the outside of the body. The ovaries, supported by several ligaments, are oval organs 1- to 2-inches long that are positioned on either side of the uterus in the pelvic cavity. The fallopian tubes, which are 4 inches long and .5 inches in diameter, connect the uterus with the ovaries.

The **male reproductive system** includes the penis, scrotum, testicles, vas deferens, seminal vesicles, and the prostate gland. In addition to the urethra, the penis contains 3 sections of erectile tissue. The scrotum is a fibromuscular pouch that contains the testes, the spermatic cord, and the epididymis. The pair of testes is suspended in the scrotum and each one is approximately 2 inches by 1 inch long. The vas deferens is a tubular pathway between the testes and the penis, and the seminal vesicles are small organs located between the bladder and the bowel. The prostate gland surrounds the proximal end of the urethra within the pelvic cavity.

The main function of the male reproductive system is the production of sperm. Several million immature sperm are produced every day in the testes. The sperm are transported through the vas deferens to the penis, and the prostate gland and seminal vesicles contribute fluids that support the activity of the sperm after ejaculation.

At puberty, egg maturation, menses, and sperm production begin, and the secondary sex characteristics appear. Female fertility declines at 30 years of age, and the maturation of eggs in the ovaries ceases at menopause, which occurs at 50 years of age. Sperm production continues from puberty until death; however, after 60 years of age, the ability of the sperm to travel to the fallopian tube to fertilize an egg is decreased.

Endocrine

The glands of the **endocrine system** include the pituitary, thyroid, parathyroid, adrenal, and reproductive glands, as well as the hypothalamus, the pancreas, and the pineal body. The function of the system is to synthesize and secrete hormones that control body growth, sexual function, and metabolism, which is the production and use of energy by the body. The thyroid gland, located on either side of the trachea, regulates energy production, or the rate at which the body uses ingested food to support body functions. The parathyroid, located on the upper margin of the thyroid gland, regulates calcium levels by the activation of Vitamin D, which increases intestinal absorption of calcium, and by regulating the amount of calcium that is stored in the bones or excreted by the kidneys. The adrenal glands, located on the upper margin of the kidneys, consist of the adrenal cortex and the adrenal medulla.

The hormones secreted by the adrenal cortex are necessary for life and include: cortisol, or hydrocortisone, which regulates the breakdown of proteins, carbohydrates, and fats for energy production and the body's response to stress; corticosterone, which works with cortisol to regulate the immune system; and aldosterone, which contributes to blood-pressure control. The adrenal medulla secretions, including adrenaline, regulate the body's reaction to stress known as the fight-or-flight response. The ovaries secrete estrogen and the testes secrete testosterone, which regulate sexual maturation and function. The pancreas, located in the right upper quadrant of the abdomen, secretes the insulin that regulates blood sugar, in addition to other hormones that regulate water absorption and secretion in the intestines. The pineal gland, located in the center of the brain, secretes melatonin, which regulates the circadian rhythm or sleep cycle.

The nervous system connects each of these glands to the hypothalamus and the pituitary gland. The hypothalamus senses alterations in hormone secretions in all of these organs and conveys those messages to the pituitary gland, which then stimulates each specific organ to either increase or decrease secretion of the relevant hormone. This feedback system is necessary for homeostasis.

Sensory

The **sensory organs** include the eyes, ears, nose, tongue, and skin, and they contain special receptor cells that transmit information to the nervous system. The eyes receive and process light energy. The ears process sound waves and also contribute to the maintenance of equilibrium. The nose senses odors and the tongue senses taste. The skin responds to tactile stimulation, including pain, hot, cold, and touch. Internal organs also sense pain and pressure. The brain is responsible for processing all of these sensations.

The senses of touch and smell are active in the fetus and continue to mature after birth. Touch is especially important for infants. The elderly experience a decline in the acuity of all of the senses; however, eyesight and hearing are most commonly affected due to the effects of chronic diseases such as hypertension and diabetes.

Respiratory Problems

Some patients experiencing respiratory issues may receive supplemental oxygen. Oxygen can be administered in several different ways. The most common and minimal administration technique is via nasal cannula. The oxygen will flow through the nasal cannula into the patient's nose, and the tubing will be connected into either a mobile

oxygen tank or an oxygen supply on the wall of the patient's room. Depending on the facility, there will often be a respiratory therapy team in charge of caring for patients' respiratory issues.

The picture demonstrates oxygen being administered via nasal cannula. The two prongs are placed into the nostrils of the patient.

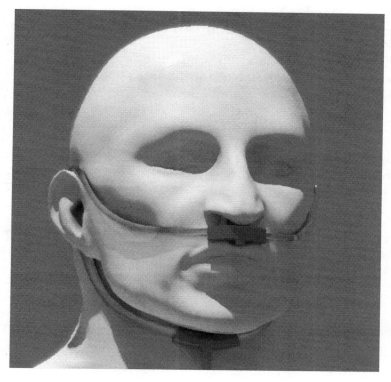

Part of the nurse's normal vital signs collection will include oxygen saturation readings. This is especially important in patients receiving supplemental oxygen and/or with identified respiratory issues. Normal values are generally considered to be 93 to 100 percent, but some patients with COPD may have a baseline saturation in the high 80s.

It is important that the aide understand the flow rate of supplemental oxygen that the patient is receiving. A typical rate is 2 to 4 liters per minute (LPM). The nurse should look for signs of hypoxia—a lack of oxygen in the body. These include decreased level of consciousness, shortness of breath, bluish lips or blueness of the extremities/nail beds (cyanosis), or unresponsiveness. Any change in respiratory status or suspected issues with oxygen administration should be reported to the nurse or respiratory therapist immediately.

Finally, the nurse must be familiar with IV (intravenous) accesses. IVs are used to administer medicine and fluids. Signs that an IV access is compromised are redness around the site, patient discomfort, bruising, and leakage. Any changes in IV access, IV pump alarms, and patient complaints should be reported to the nurse immediately.

Basic Pathophysiology

Pathophysiology refers to changes in the body due to a disease process. The patient's history of chronic and acute disease is discovered during the preoperative patient interview and chart review. Understanding the pathophysiology of the patient's disease process (or processes) empowers the nurse to know if assessment findings are congruent with the disease process or if findings are indicative of something else. For example, if a patient has 2+ pitting edema with a history of congestive heart failure (CHF), the nurse may suspect the edema is secondary to a

CHF exacerbation and investigate further by auscultating lung sounds and consulting with a cardiologist. It is also important for the nurse to consider the pathophysiological processes associated with the patient's scheduled procedure. The nurse should note that although the scheduled procedure may be minor, the patient's diagnosis may be quite serious. If the patient is having a PowerPort insertion, the surgery process is minor. However, the patient may have a diagnosis of stage IV lung cancer, and this is quite serious. Understanding this, the nurse may allow more time for the patient to verbalize feelings and provide emotional support for the patient.

Illness Management

There are certain client situations that indicate a worsening of their illness. The nurse needs to be prepared to identify this worsening and report it immediately to the attending practitioner. A solid knowledge of disease processes must be applied when managing patients' illnesses. The nurse must also be able to educate the patient regarding their condition and the management thereof. Certain interventional skills such as gastric lavage may be required for management of the patient's illness.

Any patient condition that involves a sudden compromise of airway, breathing, or circulation must be reported immediately. Swift intervention is needed to prevent long-term damage or fatality. Airway, breathing, and circulation are referred to as the patient's "ABCs" for short, and their management is at the top of the nurse's assessment checklist.

In addition to addressing the patient's ABCs, the nurse will also prioritize their care based off Maslow's hierarchy of needs. The nurse will recall that, according to this hierarchy, the patient must have physiological needs, such as hunger and thirst, met before higher priorities such as safety, esteem, and self-actualization may be met.

Determining the type of illness is key to creating a strategy to manage it. The client may suffer from chronic diseases such as heart failure, COPD, or diabetes. They may be engaged in a battle with mental illnesses such as anxiety, depression, and bipolar disorder. Depending on the client's unique profile, the nurse will identify their needs and determine a care plan that will assist them in managing their illness effectively.

A change in the client's baseline functioning status is any symptom, blood test, or behavior that trends significantly different from their normal. Some clients have abnormalities as their normal, such as a low blood pressure, low pulse oxygenation, heart dysrhythmia such as prolonged QT segment, or a "normal" level of confusion in dementia patients. The nurse goes off their initial assessments of the patient as well as the patient's medical record and family reports to determine if a notable change is taking place and needs reporting.

The nurse closely monitors the patient's response to interventions that are intended to be therapeutic. The patient may have an unexpected and unwanted response to medications and other therapies. Side effects, adverse reactions, and allergic responses all fall into this category of unwanted response to a pharmacological therapy. A patient receiving mechanical ventilation via an endotracheal tube may become agitated and aggressive, as this type of therapy can be highly irritating. The nurse sees this unwanted response and uses tools such as sedation, within the ordered parameters, to soothe the patient and return them to the therapeutic response.

Using their knowledge of pathophysiology, the nurse works to effectively manage the client's care and prevent complications. Using the example of the patient with diabetes, the nurse knows that tight management of blood glucose is a high priority. The nurse knows that these patients, depending on the cause of their diabetes, have a tough time using the body's insulin to regulate glucose in the bloodstream. The nurse monitors the client's intake at mealtimes, measures blood glucose regularly, administers diabetic medications in a timely manner so they will have maximal effectiveness, and keeps a close eye on the patient when they must be NPO or off the floor for procedures, as these are prime occasions for the patient to have a hypoglycemic event.

The nurse must manage not only one client's illness but often is working to manage an entire caseload of clients all at the same time, depending on what type of unit they are working in. Caseloads of patients require exceptional time management and organizational skills from the nurse. The nurse must be able to prioritize client needs effectively to meet them in a timely manner.

Client education performed by the nurse is a way the nurse may enable the patient to become independent in their own illness management. The patient can then feel more comfortable making informed decisions and speaking up about their care. The nurse answers the client's questions, addresses their concerns, and informs them about therapies and medications. Part of this patient education is assessing what specific education the patient needs. Some clients are very much informed about their condition and treatment modalities, while others may be healthcare illiterate, meaning they do not know very much about their condition or their options in managing it. Based on the nurse's assessment of the client's educational needs, the nurse will formulate their educational plan.

There are certain cases of client illness in which the nurse will need to perform **gastric lavage**. *Lavage* means a cleaning or rinsing out, while *gastric* refers to the stomach. The patient will be placed in high Fowler's position while an NG tube is inserted. This tube is carefully measured from the nose of the client to their earlobe and then to the tip of the xiphoid process. This point is then marked on a piece of tape. Water-soluble gel is applied to the tip of the tube before insertion for lubrication. The client will be instructed to look upward to create a hyperextension of the neck. The tube is advanced into the nares until resistance is met at the nasopharynx.

The nurse expects that the client's gag reflex will kick in as well as watering of the eyes. The client will take small sips of water to open the epiglottis at which point the nurse will then be able to advance the tube all the way down to the stomach. Placement is assessed via pH test of aspirated gastric contents from the tube and/or obtainment of chest X-ray. The nurse will secure the NG tube using tape to the client's nose and a safety pin to the client's gown. After correct placement is confirmed, the nurse may use the tube to lavage the client's stomach. This will be done according to the ordering gastroenterologist's preferred method but usually includes the instilment of a solution, clamping of the tube for a determined amount of time, and then removal of the fluid later.

Fluid and Electrolyte Imbalances

Electrolytes are minerals that, when dissolved, break down into ions. They can be acids, bases, or salts. In the body, different electrolytes are responsible for specific cellular functions. These functions make up larger, critical system-wide processes, such as hydration, homeostasis, pH balance, and muscle contraction. Electrolytes typically enter the body through food and drink consumption, but in severe cases of imbalance, they may be medically-administered. They are found in the fluids of the body, such as blood.

Key electrolytes found in the body include the following:

Sodium and Chloride

Sodium (Na+) is mainly responsible for managing hydration, blood pressure, and blood volume in the body. It is found in blood, plasma, and lymph. It is important to note that sodium is primarily found outside of cells and is accessed by a number of different systems and organs to tightly regulate water and blood levels. For example, in cases of severe dehydration, the circulatory and endocrine systems will transmit signals to the kidneys to retain sodium and, consequently, water.

Sodium also affects muscle and nerve function. It is a positively-charged ion and contributes to membrane potential—an electrochemical balance between sodium and potassium (another electrolyte) that is responsible for up to 40 percent of resting energy expenditure in a healthy adult. This balance strongly influences the functioning of nerve impulses and the ability of muscles to contract. Healthy heart functioning and contraction is dependent on membrane potential.

Sodium is available in large quantities in the standard diets of developed countries, especially in processed foods, as it is found in table salt. Consequently, sodium deficiencies (hyponatremia) are possible, but rare, in the average person. Hyponatremia can result in endocrine or nervous system disorders where sodium regulation is affected. It can also result in excessive sweating, vomiting, or diarrhea, such as in endurance sporting events, improper use of diuretics, or gastrointestinal illness. Hyponatremia may be treated with an IV sodium solution. Too much sodium (hypernatremia) is usually a result of dehydration. Hypernatremia may be treated by introducing water quantities appropriate for suspending the sodium level that is tested in the patient's blood and urine.

Chloride (Cl-) is a negatively-charged ion found outside of the cells that works closely with sodium. It shares many of the same physiologic responsibilities as sodium. Any imbalances (hypochloremia and hyperchloremia) are rare but may affect overall pH levels of the body. Chloride imbalances usually occur in response to an imbalance in other electrolytes, so treating a chloride imbalance directly is uncommon.

Potassium

Potassium (K+) is mainly responsible for regulating muscular function and is especially important in cardiac and digestive functions. In women, it is believed to promote bone density. It works in tandem with sodium to create membrane potential. Potassium is a positively-charged ion and is usually found inside cells. It plays a role in maintaining homeostasis between the intracellular and extracellular environments.

Potassium is found in all animal protein and animal dairy products and in most fruits and vegetables. Low potassium levels (hypokalemia) may be caused by dehydration due to excessive vomiting, urination, or diarrhea. In severe or acute cases, hypokalemia may be a result of renal dysfunction and may cause lethargy, muscle cramps, or heart dysrhythmia. It may be treated by stopping the cause of potassium loss (e.g., diuretics), followed by oral or IV potassium replenishment.

High potassium levels (hyperkalemia) can quickly become fatal. **Hyperkalemia** is often the result of a serious condition, such as sudden kidney or adrenal failure, and may cause nausea, vomiting, chest pain, and muscle dysfunction. It is treated based on its severity, with treatment options ranging from diuretic use to IV insulin or glucose. IV calcium may be administered if potentially dangerous heart arrhythmias are present.

1.

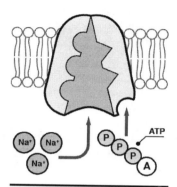

The sodium-potassium pump binds three sodium ions and a molecule of ATP.

2.

The splitting of ATP provides energy to change the shape of the channel. The sodium ions are driven through the channel.

3.

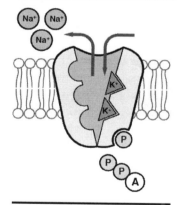

The sodium ions are released to the outside of the membrane, and the new shape of the channel allows two potassium ions to bind

4.

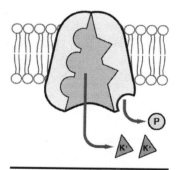

Release of the phosphate allows the channel to revert to its original form, releasing the potassium ions on the inside of the membrane

Calcium and Phosphorus

Calcium (Ca++) is plentiful in the body, with most calcium stored throughout the skeletal system. However, if there is not enough calcium in the blood (usually available through proper diet), the body will take calcium from the bones. This can become detrimental over time. If enough calcium becomes present in the blood, the body will

159

return extra calcium stores to the bones. Besides contributing to the skeletal structure, this electrolyte is important in nerve signaling, muscle function, and blood coagulation. It is found in dairy products, leafy greens, and fatty fishes. Many other consumables, such as fruit juices and cereals, are often fortified with calcium.

Low calcium levels (hypocalcemia) can be caused by poor diet, thyroid or kidney disorders, and some medications. Symptoms can include lethargy, poor memory, inability to concentrate, muscle cramps, and general stiffness and achiness in the body. Supplementation can rapidly restore blood calcium levels. In cases where symptoms are present, IV calcium administration in conjunction with an oral or IV vitamin D supplement may be utilized.

High calcium levels (hypercalcemia) is usually caused by thyroid dysfunction but can also be the result of diet, limited mobility (such as in paralyzed individuals), some cancers, or the use of some diuretics. Symptoms can include thirst, excess urination, gastrointestinal issues, and unexplained pain in the abdominal area or bones. Severe or untreated hypercalcemia can result in kidney stones, kidney failure, confusion, depression, lethargy, irregular heartbeat, or bone problems.

There is an intricate balance between calcium levels and the levels of phosphorus, another electrolyte. Phosphorus, like calcium, is stored in the bones and found in many of the same foods as calcium. These electrolytes work together to maintain bone integrity. When too much calcium exists in the blood, the bones release more phosphorus to balance the two levels. When there is too much phosphorus in the blood, the bones release calcium. Therefore, the presence or absence of one directly impacts the presence or absence of the other. Indicators of hypocalcemia and hypercalcemia usually also indicate low levels of phosphorus (hypophosphatemia) and high levels of phosphorus (hyperphosphatemia), respectively.

Magnesium

Magnesium (Mg++) is another electrolyte that is usually plentiful in the body. It is responsible for an array of life-sustaining functions, including hundreds of biochemical reactions such as oxidative phosphorylation and glycolysis. It is also an important factor in DNA and RNA synthesis, bone development, nerve signaling, and muscle function. Magnesium is stored inside cells or within the structure of the bones. It can be consumed through leafy greens, nuts, seeds, beans, unrefined grains, and most foods that contain fiber. Some water sources may also contain high levels of magnesium.

Low levels of magnesium (hypomagnesemia) are primarily caused by chronic alcohol or drug abuse and some prescription medications and can also occur in patients with gastrointestinal diseases (such as celiac or Crohn's). Symptoms of hypomagnesemia include nausea, vomiting, depression, personality and mood disorders, and muscle dysfunction. Chronically depleted patients may have an increased risk of cardiovascular and metabolic disorders.

High levels of magnesium (hypermagnesemia) are rare and usually result in conjunction with kidney disorders when medications are used improperly. Symptoms include low blood pressure that may result in heart failure. Hypermagnesemia is usually treated by removing any magnesium sources (such as salts or laxatives) and may also require the IV administration of calcium gluconate.

Magnesium imbalance can lead to calcium or potassium imbalance over time, as these electrolytes work together to achieve homeostasis in the body.

Hydration is critical to fluid presence in the body, as water is a critical component of blood, plasma, and lymph. When fluid levels are too high or too low, electrolytes cannot move freely or carry out their intended functions. Therefore, treating an electrolyte imbalance almost always involves managing a fluid imbalance as well. Typically, as fluid levels rise, electrolyte levels decrease. As fluid levels decrease, electrolyte levels rise. Common tests to determine electrolyte fluid imbalances include basic and comprehensive metabolic panels, which test levels of sodium, potassium, chloride, and any other electrolyte in question.

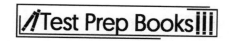

Hemodynamics

A crucial part of patient assessment and monitoring is their hemodynamic profile. **Hemodynamics** are the forces that cause blood to circulate throughout the body, originating in the heart, branching out to the vital organs and tissues, and then recirculating back to the heart and lungs for reoxygenation and pumping. There are at least three different aspects of hemodynamics that can be focused on: the measurement of pressure, flow, and oxygenation of the blood in the cardiovascular system; the use of invasive technological tools to measure and quantitate pressures, volumes, and capacity of the vascular system; and the monitoring of hemodynamics that involves measuring and interpreting the biological systems that are affected by it.

Hemodynamics can be assessed using noninvasive or invasive measures. Noninvasive measures would include the nurse's assessment of the patient's overall presentation, heart rate, and blood pressure. Invasive measurements would include inserting an arterial blood pressure monitor directly into an artery or the insertion of a Swan-Ganz catheter. The Swan-Ganz catheter, also known as a pulmonary artery catheter (PAC) or right-heart catheter, is threaded into the patient's subclavian vein, down the superior vena cava, right up to the pulmonary artery (PA). This type of catheter is used quite commonly in ICU patients. PACs give information about the patient's cardiac output and preload. Preload is obtained by estimating the pulmonary artery occlusion pressure (PAOP). Another way to assess preload is determining the right ventricular end-diastolic volume (RVEDV), measured by fast-response thermistors reading the heart rate. There is some question as to whether the use of PACs helps patients or not. Some studies suggest that the use of PACs does not reduce morbidity or mortality but rather increases these occurrences. Their use, therefore, should be weighed carefully according to the physician's discretion.

There are many different parameters to consider when assessing a patient's hemodynamics. Blood pressure is the measurement of the systolic pressure over the diastolic pressure, or the pressure in the vasculature when the heart contracts over the pressure when the heart is at rest.

Mean arterial pressure (MAP) shows the relationship between the amount of blood pumped out of the heart and the resistance the vascular system puts up against it. A low MAP suggests that blood flow has decreased to the organs, while a high MAP may indicate that the workload for the heart is increased.

Cardiac index reflects the quantity of blood pumped by the heart per minute and per meter squared of the patient's body surface area.

Cardiac output measures how much blood the heart pumps out per beat and is measured in liters.

Central venous pressure (CVP) is an estimate of the RVEDP, thus assessing RV function as well as the patient's general hydration status. A low CVP may mean the patient is dehydrated or has a decreased amount of venous return. A high CVP may indicate fluid overload or right-sided heart failure.

Pulmonary artery pressure measures the pressure in the PA. An increase in this pressure may mean the patient has developed a left-to-right cardiac shunt, they have hypertension of the PA, they may have worsening complications of COPD, a clot has traveled to the lungs (pulmonary embolus), the lungs are filling with fluid (pulmonary edema), or the left ventricle is failing.

The **pulmonary capillary wedge pressure (PCWP)** approximates the left ventricular end-diastolic pressure (LVEDP). This number, when increased, may be a result of LV failure, a pathology of the mitral valve, cardiac sufficiency, or compression of the heart after a hemorrhage, such as cardiac tamponade.

The resistance that the pulmonary capillary bed in the lungs puts up against blood flow is measured via **pulmonary vascular resistance (PVR)**. When there is disease in the lungs, a pulmonary embolism, hypoxia, or pulmonary vasculitis, this number may increase. Calcium channel blockers and certain other medications may cause the PVR to be lowered because of their mechanism of action.

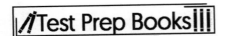

A hemodynamic measurement used to assess RV function and the patient's fluid status is the RV pressure. When this number is elevated, the patient may have pulmonary hypertension, failure of the right ventricle, or worsening congestive heart failure.

The stroke index measures how much blood the heart is pumping in a cardiac cycle in relation to the patient's body surface area.

Stroke volume (SV) measures how much blood the heart pumps in milliliters per beat.

The systemic vascular resistance parameter reflects how much pressure the vasculature peripheral to the heart puts up to blood flow from the heart. Vasoconstrictors, low blood volume, and septic shock can cause this number to rise, while vasodilators, high blood levels of carbon dioxide (hypercarbia), nitrates, and morphine may cause this number to fall.

The following is a list of commonly measured hemodynamic parameters and their normal values:

- Blood pressure: 90–140 mmHg systolic over 60–90 mmHg diastolic
- Mean arterial pressure (MAP): 70–100 mmHg
- Cardiac index (CI): 2.5–4.0 L/min/m^2
- Cardiac output (CO): 4–8 L/min
- Central venous pressure (CVP) or right arterial pressure (RA): 2–6 mmHg
- Pulmonary artery pressure (PA): systolic 20–30 mmHg (PAS), diastolic 8–12 mmHg (PAD), mean 25 mmHg (PAM)
- Pulmonary capillary wedge pressure (PCWP): 4–12 mmHg
- Pulmonary vascular resistance (PVR): 37–250 dynes/sec/cm^5
- Right ventricular pressure (RV): systolic 20–30 mmHg over diastolic 0–5 mmHg
- Stroke index (SI): 25–45 mL/m^2
- Stroke volume (SV): 50–100 mL/beat
- Systemic vascular resistance (SVR): 800–1200 dynes/sec/cm^5

Medical Emergencies

In the event of a medical emergency, there are specific steps to take depending on the situation. There will be written policies for these types of emergencies in the workplace that are used for patients, staff, and/or visitors.

Below are some examples of medical emergencies:

- Choking
- Unresponsive or unconscious person or patient
- Excessive bleeding
- Head injury
- Broken bones
- Severe burns
- Seizures
- Chest pain
- Difficulty breathing
- Allergic reactions that cause swelling and/or breathing difficulties
- Inhalation or swallowing of a toxic substance
- Accidental poisoning

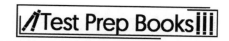

Choking

If someone is **choking**, the victim will most likely grab at their throat, or they may have a cough that eventually stops, indicating blockage of the airway. If the airway is blocked, they will need the **Heimlich maneuver** to be performed immediately. Oftentimes people cough and may leave the room to get a drink or to avoid disrupting others. It is best to follow that person to ensure they are not choking.

When someone is choking and conscious, the responder, or person at the scene who witnesses and intervenes, should:

- Ask the victim if they are choking and tell them help is here.
- Assist the victim to a standing position.
- Stand behind the victim and wrap the arms around the victim's waist.
- Make a fist with one hand and place the thumb against the victim's stomach just above their belly button.
- Place the other hand on top of the fisted hand.
- Thrust quick, hard, and upward on the victim's stomach.
- Continue this until the food or object comes out of the victim's mouth.
- Do *not* swipe the victim's mouth with one finger, as this could push the blockage further down the airway.

If the victim is still choking and goes unconscious:

- Lower the victim to the floor, shout for help, and have someone call 911.
- Begin cardiopulmonary resuscitation (CPR) by following the basic life support steps until emergency medical services (EMS) arrives.

Unconsciousness or Unresponsiveness

If someone is **unconscious**, first try to arouse the person by shaking or tapping them. If they are indeed unresponsive, call for help, have someone call 911, and proceed to:

- Make sure the patient is lying flat and place a backboard under them for CPR.
- Follow basic life support (BLS) protocol.
- Look and listen for breathing (chest rise).
- Check for a pulse in radial artery (wrist).
- If patient is breathing, stay with them until EMS arrives. If there is a pulse but no breathing, begin rescue breaths. Give one breath every 5 or 6 seconds. Check pulse every 2 minutes.
- If no pulse, begin CPR and continue until EMS arrives.
- Direct someone else to get the automated external defibrillator (AED) as CPR is continued.
- CPR: 30 chest compressions then 2 breaths, repeat for 2-minute cycles.
- Chest compressions should be firm and deep, to the rhythm of the disco song "Stayin' Alive," about 100 beats per minute. This ensures adequate perfusion of organs with blood since the heart is not pumping on its own.
- When the AED arrives, turn it on and follow the prompts for use.

If the patient recovers, turn them onto their left side and continue to monitor them until EMS arrives. Healthcare workers will be trained and certified on BLS, CPR, and AED use.

Excessive Bleeding

For **excessive bleeding**, call for help and call 911. Then:

- Have the patient sit down or lie down.
- Use a towel or shirt to hold continuous pressure on the bleeding area.

- Elevate the area above their heart. For example, if the leg is bleeding, have the patient lie down and put their leg on a chair.
- Talk to the patient and monitor their responsiveness. Stay with them until EMS arrives.

Head Injury

Concussions, contusions, and skull fractures are all common types of traumatic brain injuries. **Concussions** occur when the brain is jarred against the skull, usually during sports, hard contact with another person, or hitting the head on the ground. Concussions can cause mental confusion and lead to disruptions in normal brain functioning. The effects of a concussion can show up immediately, or they may not show up for hours or days. Normally, concussions do not cause a loss of consciousness, so it is important to pay attention to other possible symptoms. Another type of traumatic brain injury is a contusion, which is a bruise on the brain. This bruise can swell in the brain and cause a hematoma, or bleeding in the brain. A skull fracture is a break in the skull bone and can occur with or without brain damage. The following list includes symptoms of traumatic brain injuries:

- Confusion
- Depression
- Dizziness or balance problems
- Foggy feeling
- Double vision or changes in vision
- Tiredness
- Headache
- Memory loss
- Nausea
- Sensitivity to light
- Trouble remembering and concentrating

If a patient has a known head injury, or they stated that they hit their head, stay with the patient and call for a supervisor. Monitor the patient for mild symptoms from the list above. If the symptoms are not serious, the patient may require a visit from the physician. If the patient is elderly or has other serious health issues, hospitalization may be required to rule out more serious consequences from the head injury. The pie chart below depicts the leading causes of traumatic brain injury, with falls being the largest percentage.

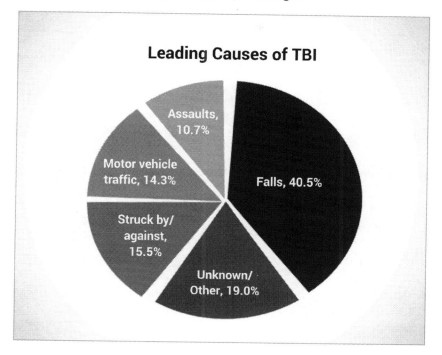

Leading Causes of TBI

- Falls, 40.5%
- Unknown/Other, 19.0%
- Struck by/against, 15.5%
- Motor vehicle traffic, 14.3%
- Assaults, 10.7%

Symptoms of a head injury that are more serious and require immediate emergency treatment include:

- Unequal pupils
- Convulsions
- Fracture of the skull or face
- Inability to move legs or arms
- Clear or bloody fluid coming from the ears, nose, or mouth
- Loss of consciousness
- Persistent vomiting
- Severe headache
- Slurred speech and distorted vision
- Restlessness and irritability

If any of the above symptoms appear after a head injury, call for help and call 911.

Broken Bones (Compound Fractures)

A **compound fracture** is a fracture in which the bone is protruding through the skin. Other symptoms include pain, swelling, deformity in the fractured area, and bruising. This is the most serious type of fracture and requires immediate attention. The following comprises first aid for fractures:

- Call for help and call 911, especially if a fracture in the head, back, or neck is suspected.
- Don't move the patient unless they are in danger of further injury.
- Keep the injured area still and stay with the patient.
- Treat any bleeding by holding pressure with a towel or gauze.
- Look for signs of shock in the patient (shallow, fast breathing, or feeling faint) and lay them down with their feet elevated.

- Wrap ice packs in a towel and ice the injured area.
- Wait for EMS to arrive.

Burns

Burn injuries can range from mild to severe, but the initial treatment for all burns is the same. First-degree burns affect the top layer of the skin, second-degree burns affect two layers, and third-degree burns affect all three layers. Call for an emergency response if:

- The burn is through all the skin layers.
- The person is a baby or elderly and the burn is severe.
- The hands, feet, face, or genitals are burned.
- The burn is larger than two inches or is oozing.
- The burn is charred and leathery, or has white, brown, or black patches.

Initial treatment for all burns includes:

- Remove the source of the burn, put out the fire, smother the burning area, or have the person stop, drop, and roll.
- Remove any hot or burned clothing.
- Remove clothing that is tight and remove jewelry (burns can swell very quickly).
- Hold the burned area under cool, running water for 20 minutes.
- Use two cold cloths if running water is not available. Alternate holding them on the area every 2 minutes.
- Do not put ice on the burn.
- Keep the patient warm by covering the rest of the body.
- Wrap or cover the burn loosely with gauze, or a use a sheet for large areas.
- If EMS has been called, stay with the patient and keep them warm until help arrives.

Seizures

Seizures have many symptoms depending on the type of seizure. Some symptoms include jerking motions, shaking, unconsciousness, stiffness, and blank staring. If someone is having a violent seizure, the steps to follow include:

- Protect the victim's head by moving hard objects out of the way and placing a blanket under their head.
- Loosen clothing around their neck.
- Do not try to hold them down and do not try to put something in their mouth.
- Get help to control bystanders so that the victim has some space.
- When the seizure is over, have the victim lie on their side and make sure their airway is open.
- Call 911 if the seizure lasts more than 5 minutes, if the victim has other medical conditions, or if the person has never had a seizure before.
- People with known epilepsy may have seizures that are short and frequent, so calling 911 may not be necessary.

Chest Pain

Chest pain can be a symptom of a heart attack or other serious heart or lung condition. Prompt attention is necessary so that the person can be treated before serious heart damage or death occurs. Chest pain can also be a result of a lung infection, excessive coughing, broken ribs from an injury, anxiety, indigestion, or muscular injury. If the patient has not fallen or does not have any outward physical signs of injury to the chest area, assume that the chest pain is cardiac related. When someone complains of chest pain, do the following:

- Have the person sit down and ask where the pain is located.
- Call for the supervisor immediately.

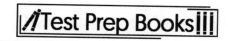

- Assess if they have any injuries on or near their chest.
- Call 911 (if not in a medical facility) if the pain lasts more than a few minutes, or they have the following symptoms:
- Pain in the arms, shoulders, back and chest
- Difficulty breathing
- Fatigue
- Nausea
- Sweating
- Dizziness
- If there is oxygen available, a respiratory therapist or nurse will place a nasal cannula in their nose and give between two and four liters of oxygen.
- If available and the person is not allergic or taking any blood-thinner medication, the nurse will have the person chew a regular-strength aspirin. Aspirin helps the blood flow to the heart.
- Stay with the person until EMS arrives.
- If the person becomes unconscious, follow BLS guidelines and initiate CPR.

Difficulty Breathing

Breathing difficulties or shortness of breath can be caused by many factors, such as asthma, bronchitis, pneumonia, heart conditions, pulmonary embolism, anxiety, or exercise. People may occasionally have shortness of breath because of an underlying condition that is being monitored by a physician. They may take medication for this symptom and be able to continue to live relatively normal lives. However, if a person has sudden difficulty catching their breath, and it is not relieved with rest, change of position, or their inhaler medication, immediate attention is required. Do the following if a person begins to struggle with breathing:

- Call for help and have the person sit up in their chair or in their bed.

- Instruct the person to try to take slow breaths, inhaling though their nose and exhaling out of their mouth.

- Continue to talk to them reassuringly and soothingly. Anxiety can actually make breathing even more difficult.

- If their breathing becomes easier and they seem to calm down, have a physician see them as soon as possible, especially if this is something new for this person.

- If breathing continues to be difficult, call 911 (if not in medical facility).

- Place oxygen on the patient with a mask or nasal cannula, if available.

- Stay with the patient until help arrives and monitor their level of consciousness and breathing rate.

Allergic Reactions

Allergies can cause many symptoms from mild to severe. Some examples of mild symptoms might include itching, redness on the skin, hives, sneezing, runny nose, and itchy eyes. Wheezing may occur and may be treated with a prescribed inhaler. Life-threatening allergic reactions include swelling of the tongue or throat, difficulty breathing, and anaphylaxis, which is a systemic reaction. Anaphylaxis is rare but can lead to death if it is not recognized and treated quickly. Allergies to foods, medications, latex, and insect bites can cause anaphylaxis. Normally a person who has serious allergic reactions will have an epinephrine pen, or "epi-pen," with them at all times, to be administered in case of a reaction. If the following symptoms associated with anaphylaxis are observed outside of a medical facility, call 911. Otherwise, report any of the following symptoms to the nurse:

- Difficulty breathing
- Swollen tongue or throat tightness

- Wheezing
- Nausea and vomiting
- Fainting or dizziness
- Low blood pressure
- Rapid heart beat
- Feeling strange or sense of impending doom
- Chest pain

Call 911 even if an epi-pen has been administered for the allergic reaction. Reaction symptoms can continue to occur or can reoccur later.

Poisoning

Poison can be something eaten, inhaled, or absorbed in excess, or exposure to toxic substances. This type of emergency can happen to patients and employees. If there is an accidental poisoning and the person is awake and alert, call the poison-control hotline at 1-800-222-1222. Stay on the phone with poison control and stay with the victim. Try to have the following information available for the responders:

- Weight and age of the victim
- The label or bottle of the substance taken
- The time of exposure to the substance (how long it has been)
- The address of where the victim is located

If the person goes unconscious or is not breathing, call 911.

Many chemical labels, such as cleaning supplies, have warning labels and instructions for dealing with toxic exposure. The eyes may need to be flushed with water, for example. Read labels but also call for help. In healthcare facilities, protocols for chemical spills or exposure exist so that clean up and injury can be dealt with quickly. Always follow the policy provided by the facility or workplace.

Unexpected Response to Therapies

There are a vast multitude of unexpected responses that may occur during a patient's therapy. With every desired effect, there are many undesired effects that may develop. The nurse works with the healthcare team to prevent, watch for, and treat unexpected patient responses right away.

One of the most dangerous complications for a woman who has just given birth is a postpartum hemorrhage. This occurs when the uterus continues to bleed excessively, losing more than 500 mL after the baby has been delivered. An accompanying signal of postpartum hemorrhage is a drop in the hematocrit by more than ten percentage points. A postpartum hemorrhage may be primary, occurring shortly after childbirth, or secondary, occurring within twelve weeks postpartum. Postpartum hemorrhage arises from many different causes, including abnormal uterine contractility, placental complications, injury due to caesarean section or uterine rupture, or congenital coagulation disorders.

The nurse assesses the mother for potential postpartum hemorrhage by taking vital signs, massaging the uterine fundus, and preventing bladder distention by encouraging the mother to empty her bladder regularly. Heart rate and blood pressure readings will let the nurse know whether the mother is hemodynamically stable or not. Massage of the uterine fundus encourages continued uterine contractions and prevents bleeding associated with a boggy fundus. **Boggy** means that the uterus is soft, not firm as when palpating a contracted muscle. Bladder distention can cause a displacement of the woman's uterus, which can interfere with proper contractions.

168

A patient receiving **total parenteral nutrition (TPN)** is at risk for the unexpected development of a pneumothorax. When the physician is inserting the catheter that will deliver the TPN, there is a potential for the catheter to enter the pleural space, causing air, fluids, or blood to leak into the pleural cavity. The potential development of pneumothorax, hemothorax, and hydrothorax is one of many reasons why checking the placement of lines in patients is a crucial first step to take before using them.

Observing a sterile technique when placing central lines, dialysis catheters, and other invasive devices into patients is critical. The nurse, as part of the healthcare team, works to ensure that a proper sterile technique is observed each time a sterile procedure is to occur. This helps to prevent infections from happening in patients during the placement of such lines. The nurse also supervises the process of disposing sharps such as needles into the proper sharps receptacle, placed in each patient's room in most facilities. Needlesticks from contaminated syringes can spread bloodborne infections such as HIV/AIDS, hepatitis B, and hepatitis C.

Practice Quiz

1. What are the blood vessels called that carry blood back to the heart from the rest of the body?
   a. Capillaries
   b. Arteries
   c. Ventricles
   d. Veins

2. The nurse is taking a manual blood pressure reading from a patient who is seated in an armchair. Which of the following body positions should the nurse ask the patient to change in order to get the most accurate reading?
   a. Crossed legs
   b. Holding remote with hand not getting blood pressure reading
   c. Resting head on headrest
   d. Slouching

3. When giving an intramuscular injection of the pneumococcal vaccine, the nurse selects the deltoid muscle as the site of injection. What technique can the nurse use to avoid leakage of the injected fluid into the subcutaneous tissue?
   a. Aspiration
   b. Injection at a 45-degree angle
   c. Z-track
   d. Massaging the site

4. The nurse is assessing a patient for possible risk factors for developing cancer. The patient reports a longtime smoking habit that she has struggled to kick. The nurse knows that this risk factor puts the patient most at risk for developing all except which of the following cancers?
   a. Larynx
   b. Esophagus
   c. Lung
   d. Breast

5. The nurse is caring for a woman who is 3 hours postpartum. The nurse takes all EXCEPT which of the following actions to prevent and monitor for postpartum hemorrhage?
   a. Massage the uterine fundus.
   b. Obtain regular vital signs, including heart rate and blood pressure.
   c. Ensure that the woman avoids bladder distention.
   d. Encourage the woman to perform her Kegel exercises.

See answers on the next page.

Answer Explanations

1. D: The blood vessels that carry blood back to the heart are called veins. Capillaries are where arteries and veins meet to exchange oxygen and carbon dioxide at the tissue level. Arteries carry blood away from the heart to the tissues of the body. Ventricles are a type of blood pumping chamber in the heart, although there are also ventricles in the brain that serve a different purpose.

2. A: The nurse should politely ask the patient to uncross her legs to get the most accurate blood pressure reading. Crossed legs can affect the blood pressure reading, since blood vessels can be compressed. Holding a remote, slouching, and resting the head will not compress any major arteries or veins and affect the blood pressure reading, so there is no need for the nurse to correct these positions.

3. C: The Z-track technique is used to avoid medication leakage into the subcutaneous tissue. The nurse pulls the skin downward or upward, injects the medication at a 90-degree angle, and then releases the skin to create the zigzag track. Aspiration is a technique that may be used to ensure the nurse has not accidentally accessed a vein or artery when injecting but is not necessary for routine injections into the deltoid where there are no large vessels. Massaging the injection site may cause leakage and irritation.

4. D: Breast cancer is not usually highly correlated to smoking cigarettes, although there is some evidence that smoking does not help a person avoid breast cancer. Cancers of the mouth, throat, esophagus, and lungs are all closely correlated with a smoking habit due to their contact with the toxic inhaled smoke. The nurse notes the patient's risk factor for developing cancer in the patient medical record.

5. D: Kegel exercises are performed to strengthen the pelvic floor and prevent urinary incontinence, among many other benefits. They are not specifically targeted at preventing postpartum hemorrhage, however. All three of the other options are correct. Massaging the uterine fundus will encourage uterine contractions, which will help prevent excessive bleeding. A boggy fundus is a worrisome sign. The nurse wants to feel a firm uterus, signaling healthy contractions. Monitoring vital signs, especially heart rate and blood pressure, will keep the nurse informed about the woman's hemodynamic stability. The nurse will encourage the patient to empty her bladder regularly, as bladder distention can displace the uterus and interfere with proper uterine contractions.

NCLEX-PN Practice Test #1

1. When preparing a patient for the insertion of a central venous access device (CVAD), the nurse explains that the benefits of a CVAD include all except which of the following?
   a. Easier-to-obtain frequent blood draws
   b. Administration of large amounts of medications and fluids
   c. Decreased peripheral sticks and peripheral inflammation
   d. Decreased risk of infection

2. Which statement best describes the evaluation phase of the nursing process?
   a. Subjective, objective, and psychosocial data are gathered in this phase.
   b. Nursing diagnoses are formulated during the evaluation phase.
   c. Evaluation happens across the continuum of the nursing process.
   d. This phase often begins with educating the patient on expected outcomes.

3. Which of the following items rules a person out for being an organ donor?
   a. Elderly
   b. Overweight
   c. Substance use
   d. Resolved case of depression

4. Which ocular positioning aligns with the patient's diagnosis of exotropia?

   a.

   b.

   c.

   d.

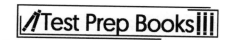

5. Of the following patients, which one has the highest risk for skin injury?
    a.   An elderly woman in an assisted-living facility who ambulates with a cane
    b.   An eighty-year-old man in the hospital recovering from hip surgery
    c.   A seventy-year-old man hospitalized for pneumonia
    d.   An elderly woman who is incontinent of stool and is showing signs of confusion

6. The nurse is providing telephonic guidance to a 31-year-old patient who is 36 weeks pregnant regarding distinguishing between true and false labor. Which contraction findings does the nurse explain are likely due to false labor? Select all that apply.
    a.   Consistently regular and closer together
    b.   Cease with walking
    c.   Felt in abdomen above umbilicus
    d.   Radiate to lower abdomen from lower back
    e.   Temporarily regular

7. By definition, competent bacteria can do which of the following?
    a.   Transformation
    b.   Transduction
    c.   Conjugation
    d.   Form a sex pilus

8. The nurse is providing patient instruction on obtaining a sterile specimen, also known as a clean catch, for an uncircumcised male patient. Arrange the following steps in the order the nurse should instruct the patient to perform them. Include all options.
    a.   Clean meatus
    b.   Retract foreskin
    c.   Catch urine stream in cup uninterrupted
    d.   Void a small amount into toilet

9. What is the last stage in Freud's model of the five stages of human development?
    a.   Latent stage
    b.   Adult stage
    c.   Genital stage
    d.   Self-actualization stage

10. Which of the following statements is correct?
    a.   Self-destruction ideation is characterized by thoughts of harming oneself, while global destruction ideation is characterized by thoughts of harming others.
    b.   Suicidal ideation is characterized by thoughts of harming oneself, while homicidal ideation is characterized by thoughts of harming others.
    c.   Internal ideation is characterized by thoughts of harming oneself, while external ideation is characterized by thoughts of harming others.
    d.   Intrinsic ideation is characterized by thoughts of harming oneself, while extrinsic ideation is characterized by thoughts of harming others.

11. Which of the following terms refers to a state in which the client has a lower than normal count of platelet cells?
    a.   Neutropenia
    b.   Anemia
    c.   Thrombocytopenia
    d.   Leukopenia

12. The action created by a drug is known as what?
    a. Pharmacology
    b. Side effect
    c. Adverse reaction
    d. Intended effect

13. Upon analysis of the following fetal heart rate and maternal contraction readings gained from electronic fetal monitoring, which fetal heart pattern does the nurse determine?

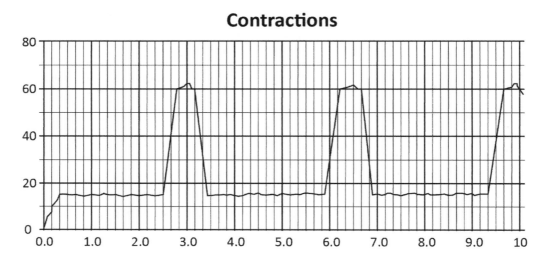

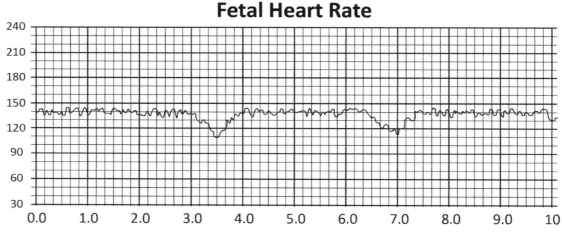

    a. Early deceleration
    b. Adequate acceleration
    c. Late deceleration
    d. Prolonged acceleration

14. Which intervention should the nurse NOT include while maintaining seizure precautions for a patient with epilepsy?
    a. Padded side-rails
    b. Suction by the bedside
    c. Side-rails down
    d. Ambu bag in room

15. Where should the nurse place the bell or diaphragm of their stethoscope to auscultate the pulmonic area during a focused cardiac assessment? Place an X to mark your answer.

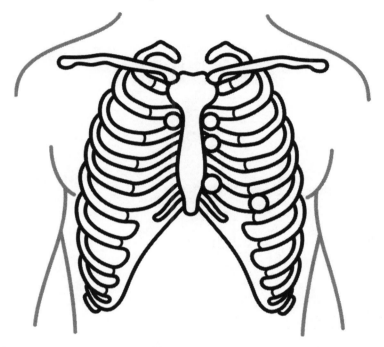

16. While caring for a pediatric patient, the nurse is providing discharge instructions to the patient and family regarding the oral administration of a liquid treatment, which is available as 5 mg/mL. The patient is prescribed 40 mg. How many mL should the patient's parent plan to administer?

_____ mL

17. The nurse is providing patient education when the patient inquires, "What is the plan to help with my fatigue, hair thinning, and weight gain?" Which medication from the patient's electronic medication administration record does the nurse identify as supporting targeted relief for the patient's symptoms of hypothyroidism?

Electronic Medication Administration Record (EMAR)

Tab 1, Morning	Levothyroxine 88 mcg po qam Lithobid 300 mg BID Simethicone 150 mg po TID after meals (0800)
Tab 2, Afternoon	Simethicone 150 mg po TID after meals (1300) Simethicone 150 mg po TID after meals (1800)
Tab 3, Night	Lithobid 300 mg po BID Zolpidem tartrate 5 mg po qhs

    a. Levothyroxine
    b. Simethicone
    c. Lithobid
    d. Zolpidem tartrate

18. Which of the following ECG strips indicates atrial flutter?

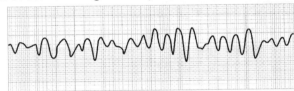

a.

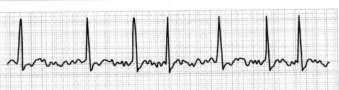

b.

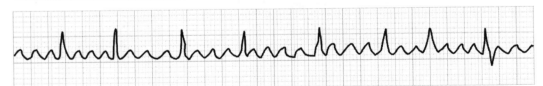

c.

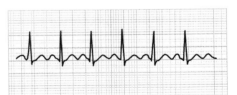

d.

19. Which of the following choices illustrates the prone position?

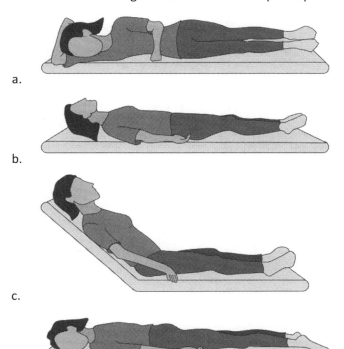

a.

b.

c.

d.

20. In Erikson's eight stages of development, Identity versus Role Confusion begins at age 12 and contains all EXCEPT which of the following challenges?
   a. Working through and understanding multiple changes and demands placed upon the child as he or she moves toward adulthood
   b. Increasing understanding of sexual, hormonal, and other physical changes that are occurring
   c. Finding a long-term partner and starting a family
   d. Assessing one's talents, sexual preferences, and vocational interests

21. When reviewing their knowledge of the stages of infections, the nurse knows that which period precedes the first symptoms of the infection?
   a. Prodromal period
   b. Colonization of organism
   c. Incubation period
   d. Convalescent period

22. When taking a history from a pregnant woman with placenta previa, the nurse would expect the patient to report which of the following?
   a. Maternal age of twenty-eight years
   b. First pregnancy
   c. Previous C-section
   d. One previous vaginal delivery

23. The nurse reviews the following cardiac telemetry strips during physiotherapy. Which, if any, displays traces of chest wall clapping?

CARDIAC STRIP 1

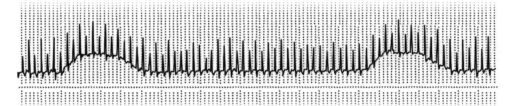

CARDIAC STRIP 2

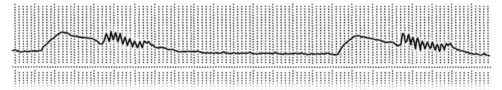

CARDIAC STRIP 3

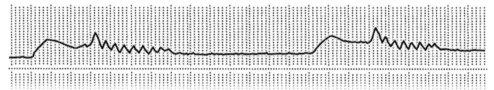

    a.   Chest wall clapping is not noted
    b.   Cardiac strip 1
    c.   Cardiac strip 2
    d.   Cardiac strip 3

24. Which type of law deals with misdemeanors and felonies?
    a.   Criminal law
    b.   Constitutional law
    c.   Common law
    d.   Stationary law

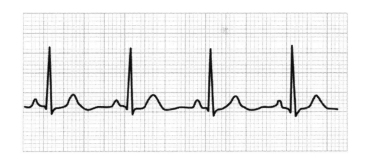

25. How should the nurse evaluate the following cardiac rhythm noted on a patient's electrocardiogram?

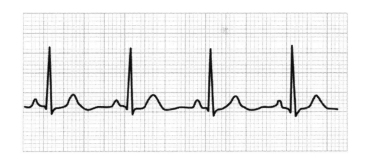

    a. Normal sinus rhythm
    b. Sinus bradycardia
    c. Sinus tachycardia
    d. Supraventricular tachycardia

26. The patient reports that he feels dizzy and lightheaded when he stands up after sitting for a long time. What would be the appropriate intervention performed by the nurse to assess the cause of these symptoms?
    a. Taking the patient's temperature
    b. Observing the patient's rate of breathing and effort of breathing
    c. Assessing bilateral radial pulses and comparing strength
    d. Lying/sitting/standing blood pressure readings

27. Which of the following are vulnerable populations at high risk of being abuse and neglect victims?
    a. Men, women, and children
    b. Immigrants, women, and minority races
    c. Children, women, and the elderly
    d. Children, pets, and immigrants

28. The nurse is caring for a patient struggling with changes to their behavior, memory, speech, hearing, and vision secondary to a traumatic brain injury sustained during a motor vehicle accident. Which lobe does the nurse understand to be the site of injury causing these symptoms? Place an X to mark your answer.

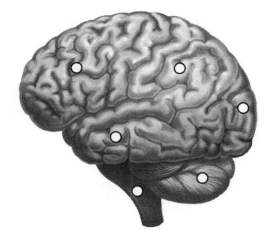

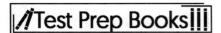
29. Which statement is typical of data the nurse collects on a woman hospitalized with abruptio placenta?
   a. "I am a smoker."
   b. "I am twenty-five years old."
   c. "I do not drink alcohol."
   d. "I have no history of placental abruption."

30. There is an interruption in the patient's care when their case is shifted from one health care environment to another in a way that causes ambiguity over who is responsible for care. What is this called?
   a. Continuity of care
   b. Fluidity of care
   c. Fragmentation of care
   d. Division of care

31. In receiving a new patient upon admission to an inpatient room, the nurse delegates appropriate tasks to the unlicensed assistive personnel (UAP). What equipment is appropriate for the UAP to safely start on the patient?
   a. Cervical traction
   b. Ventilator
   c. Hemovac drain
   d. Sequential compression device

32. According to Piaget, the process by which old ideas or beliefs must be replaced with new ones due to obtaining new and more factual information is called which of the following?
   a. Schemas
   b. Assimilation
   c. Object permanence
   d. Accommodation

33. Following a traumatic brain injury during a sporting event, the patient reports loss of their sense of smell. Which cranial nerve is responsible for the sense of smell? Place an X to mark your answer.

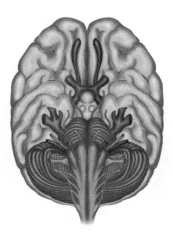

34. What part of supervision involves the nurse giving the staff member tips for a better performance, using utmost respect and professionalism?
   a. Delegation
   b. Follow-up
   c. Documentation
   d. Coaching

35. A state board of nursing has a set amount of continuing education requirements that the nurse must fulfill each year to maintain their license. Which type of law is this?
   a. Statutory law
   b. Administrative law
   c. Constitutional law
   d. Common law

36. The nurse caring for a patient postcardiac catheterization will perform which specific intervention to monitor for the development of life-threatening dysrhythmias?
   a. Keep the patient flat on their back for at least six hours postprocedure.
   b. Take regular vital signs, especially heart rate and blood pressure.
   c. Regularly observe the patient's ECG via cardiac monitoring, according to facility protocol.
   d. Regularly observe the incision site, looking for bruising, swelling, and redness.

37. A patient needs invasive hemodynamic monitoring as they are being admitted to the ICU for hemorrhagic shock. The nurse will expect an order for which type of line to be inserted?
   a. PICC line
   b. Port-a-cath
   c. Dialysis catheter
   d. Right-heart catheter

38. A patient presents to the emergency department via ambulance after experiencing a fire accident while camping. The nurse is assisting with determining the percentage of surface area directly impacted by the burns. What region of the patient's body, when affected anteriorly and posteriorly, combines to a total 36% surface area? Place an X to mark your answer.

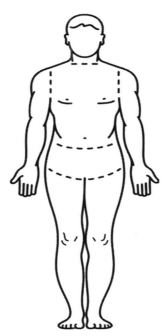

181

89. Which of the following lab values suggests the client is experiencing hypokalemia?
    a. 3.2 mEq/L
    b. 3.5 mEq/L
    c. 5.0 mEq/L
    d. 5.5 mEq/L

90. You suspect that your patient who is receiving a blood transfusion is experiencing a transfusion reaction. List the order in which the following things should occur:
    a. Notify RN.
    b. Notify MD.
    c. Stop transfusion.
    d. Check vital signs.

91. You present information on advanced directives to your patient. Your patient states that they do not want to be resuscitated in the event their heart should stop. That is, they have a "do not resuscitate" order, or DNR. What actions should you take? Select all that apply.
    a. Enter an order for DNR status.
    b. Give the patient medication to keep them comfortable.
    c. Notify the physician.
    d. Provide support using therapeutic communication.
    e. Put a "do not resuscitate" sign in the patient's room.

92. The nurse identifies a patient care safety risk while rounding on the unit at the start of shift. Which member of the care team should the nurse elevate this concern to?
    a. Director of nursing
    b. Charge nurse
    c. Chief nursing officer
    d. Nursing supervisor

93. The nurse has a patient who reports that he is 155 pounds. The nurse needs to record the patient's weight in kilograms. Knowing that 1 kilogram is equal to 2.2 pounds, the nurse then calculates the patient's weight to be what in kilograms?
    a. 60 kg
    b. 70 kg
    c. 341 kg
    d. 300 kg

94. Which heart rate does the nurse consider within normal range for the two-week-old patient?
    a. 54 beats per minute
    b. 171 beats per minute
    c. 198 beats per minute
    d. 62 beats per minute

95. Which of the following is NOT a preventative measure for pressure-ulcer formation?
    a. Padding bony areas on the body
    b. Repositioning the patient at least every two hours
    c. Keeping the patient in a sitting position while in their bed
    d. Changing soiled linens and clothing promptly

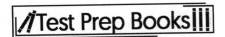

96. As the nurse is receiving reports on her patients for the day, she knows that which patient will take top priority in being assessed and treated?
    a. 33-year-old female who is nauseous and needs an antiemetic administered
    b. 49-year-old female who is scheduled for a cardiac catheterization and needs to sign the informed consent
    c. 55-year-old male who is being discharged later today and has a question about his care at home
    d. 78-year-old male who is complaining of shortness of breath

97. Which body surface correlates to an 18% burn percentage in an adult patient?

a.

b.

c.

d.

98. A patient calls the doctor's office asking how many milliliters of ibuprofen she should give her nine-month-old baby. The baby weighs 18 pounds. The ibuprofen comes in drops with a concentration of 50 mg/1.25 mL. The dose is 75 mg. The nurse tells the patient to give her baby how many milliliters? Round to the nearest tenth of a decimal.

_____ mL

99. A nursing student is interested in becoming a case manager. Which of the following will be required to attain this nursing role?
    a. Additional case management training, certification, and clinical hours
    b. Passing the NCLEX licensure exam
    c. Graduating with an associate's or baccalaureate degree in nursing
    d. Obtaining the required clinical hours before graduating with a nursing degree

100. The nurse looks for which of the following signs that the patient is having an allergic reaction after administering a drug?
    a. Aching and stiffness
    b. Coughing and fever
    c. Fever and chills
    d. Itching and rash

101. Which scores from the Norton Scale for Assessing Risk of Pressure Ulcers indicate that the patient is susceptible to ulcers? Select all that apply.
    a. 5
    b. 7
    c. 10
    d. 14
    e. 19

102. High levels of dopamine are associated with which of the following?
    a. Parkinson's disease
    b. Alzheimer's disease
    c. Schizophrenia
    d. Personality disorders

Case Study #1

The med-surg nurse is caring for a 68-year-old male patient following a partial cystectomy for bladder cancer.

Physician Orders:

- Discharge home after providing education and completing med rec
- Provide home health referral to company of patient's choice
- Provide education on self-catheterization of the urinary tract

Question #1: Once the nurse has provided self-catheterization education, which of the following statements from the patient that would indicate that he understood the education provided.

Patient Statement	Understanding	No Understanding
"I will self-catheterize on or near the toilet to make the process easier."	☐	☐
"I need to insert the catheter slowly and remove the catheter quickly when urine stops."	☐	☐
"I should aim my penis upward toward my abdomen to make the insertion easier."	☐	☐
"Once I see urine flow coming from the catheter, I should stop immediately and allow the catheter to fully drain."	☐	☐
"I can insert the catheter in the shower to be sure I am clean."	☐	☐

Nurses' Notes:

0913: Discharge orders received. Patient is to be educated on self-catheterization and provided with home health referral information.

0956: Urinary catheter from post-op removed with no resistance and catheter tip intact. 100 mL of opaque urine with mild odor. Patient was provided with education on self-catheterization with medication reconciliation completed. Case manager assisted the patient with setting up home health. Patient is waiting for his wife to come pick him up for discharge.

1047: Called to the bedside. Patient asks why he is still here and appears agitated. Nurse asked if the patient would like his wife to be contacted, but the patient states that he hasn't spoken to her in weeks, as she is out of town for business.

Question #2: What are the appropriate next steps for the nurse to take in this situation? Select all that apply.

☐ Contact the medical provider

☐ Contact the next-of-kin since the wife is out of town

☐ Set up transport and contact home health for a same-day visit

☐ Reinsert urinary catheter for drainage

☐ Assess vital signs

☐ Place the patient in bed with side rails up and reduce stimuli

Nurses' Notes:

0913: Discharge orders received. Patient is to be educated on self-catheterization and provided with home health referral information.

0956: Urinary catheter from post-op removed with no resistance and catheter tip intact. 100 mL of opaque urine with mild odor. Patient was provided with education on self-catheterization, with medication reconciliation completed. Case manager assisted the patient with setting up home health. Patient is waiting for his wife to come pick him up for discharge.

1047: Called to the bedside. Patient asks why he is still here and appears agitated. Nurse asked if the patient would like his wife to be contacted, but the patient states that he hasn't spoken to her in weeks, as she is out of town for business.

Question #3: After notifying the physician, the nurse received orders to D/C the discharge order. Based on the acute-onset delirium, the medical team is ruling out the common causes of delirium in the geriatric population. Which medical conditions MOST COMMONLY cause delirium in a geriatric patient? Select all that apply.

☐ Pneumonia

☐ Herpes zoster

☐ UTI

☐ Osteopenia

☐ Dehydration

☐ Macular degeneration

The MICU nurse is caring for a 68-year-old male patient with altered mental status following a five-day observational period postoperative for a partial cystectomy.

Physician Orders:

- D/C discharge order
- Transfer to ICU for additional monitoring
- Obtain urinalysis, chest X-ray
- Labs: CBC, CMP, D-dimer, lactate

Nurses' Notes:

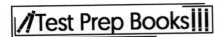

1201: Patient transferred to MICU with altered LOC. Wife present upon transfer and said this was "very abnormal" behavior for her husband. Patient diaphoretic and combative upon physical assessment and when obtaining vitals. Vital signs: T 101.4 °F, HR 98 and regular, BP 101/72, RR 19 and non-labored, O2 97% on RA. I&O catheter inserted for urine sample collection with 30 mL of opaque, foul urine obtained. Labs obtained, awaiting results.

Question #4: Based on the clinical data obtained thus far and using nursing judgment, select if the following potential nursing interventions are indicated or not indicated.

Potential Nursing Interventions	Indicated	Not Indicated
Ensure someone is with the patient at all times	☐	☐
Administer lorazepam per standing orders	☐	☐
Initiate intravenous access	☐	☐
Reorient the patient	☐	☐
Encourage multiple friends and family to visit for familiarity	☐	☐

Nurses' Notes:

1310: Patient currently resting with his wife present but remains confused. Peripheral IV 22G placed in RUA after two attempts (patient removed the first one before the securement device was in place) with 0.9% normal saline flowing at 50 mL/hr. IV piperacillin-tazobactam started for suspected UTI while awaiting cultures. Facial grimacing noted during lower abdominal palpation with no bladder distention noted. Discomfort noted upon CVA percussion.

Vital Signs:

1310:   T: 101.2 °F

   HR: 122 and regular

   BP: 92/58

   RR: 14 and unlabored

   O2: 95% on RA

Lab Results:

   WBC: 11,000/mm3 (normal: 4,500–10,000/mm3)

   BUN: 42 mg/dL (normal: 14–23 mg/dL)

   Creatinine: 1.1 mg/dL (normal: 0.7–1.3 mg/dL)

   Sodium: 147 mEq/L (normal: 135–145 mEq/L)

   Lactate: 3.6 mmol/L (normal: <2 mmol/L)

   D-dimer: <0.5 mg/L (normal: <0.5 mg/L)

Question #5: Highlight the findings or results that would require the nurse to contact the medical provider for the worsening of the patient's suspected UTI.

The MICU nurse is caring for a 68-year-old male patient with altered mental status following a five-day observational period postoperative for a partial cystectomy.

Nurses' Notes:

1310: Patient currently resting with wife, but remains confused. Peripheral IV 22G placed in RUA after two attempts (patient removed the first one before the securement device was in place) with 0.9% normal saline flowing at 50 mL/hr. IV piperacillin-tazobactam started for suspected UTI while awaiting cultures. Facial grimacing noted during lower abdominal palpation, with no bladder distention noted. Discomfort noted upon CVA percussion.

Vital Signs:

1310:   T: 101.2 °F

   HR: 122 and regular

   BP: 92/58

   RR: 14 and unlabored

   O2: 95% on RA

Lab Results:

WBC: 11,000/mm3 (normal: 4,500–10,000/mm3)

BUN: 42 mg/dL (normal: 14–23 mg/dL)

Creatinine: 1.1 mg/dL (normal: 0.7–1.3 mg/dL)

Sodium: 147 mEq/L (normal: 135–145 mEq/L)

Lactate: 3.6 mmol/L (normal: <2 mmol/L)

D-dimer: <0.5 mg/L (normal: <0.5 mg/L)

Question #6: Based on the clinical data obtained, select the medical condition that the patient will likely be treated for that also requires close monitoring. Based on that medical condition, select the most appropriate potential nursing interventions and the most appropriate things to closely monitor.

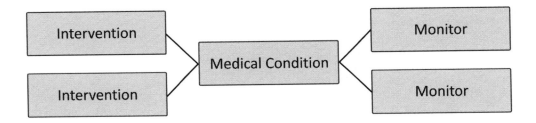

Potential Interventions	Potential Medical Condition	What to Assess/Monitor
Increase flow rate of IV fluids	Pyelonephritis	Costovertebral angle discomfort
Insert indwelling urinary catheter	Acute kidney failure	WBC & serum sodium levels
Initiate supplemental oxygen	Cystitis	Hemodynamics
Initiate vasopressors	Urosepsis	Lactate & urine output

Case Study #2

The ED nurse is caring for a 57-year-old female patient.

Nurses' Notes:

0956: Patient presents to the ED with left-sided hemiparesis and altered speech. Patient's daughter is present and states that this came on very suddenly. Vital signs: T 98.1 °F axillary, HR 102, RR 24 and labored, BP 151/92, and O2 97% on RA. Lung sounds CTA. PERRLA 4 mm. Unable to determine orientation due to aphasia.

Question #1: Based on the initial nursing assessment, select the appropriate next steps the nurse should anticipate.

☐ STAT blood glucose level

☐ Initiate tPA via IV infusion immediately

☐ Get the specific time that symptoms started

☐ STAT non-contrast CT

☐ STAT CMP, CBC, troponin, PTT, PT/INR

☐ Perform a gait assessment

Nurses' Notes:

0956: Patient presents to the ED with left-sided hemiparesis and altered speech. Patient's daughter is present and states that this came on very suddenly. Vital signs: T 98.1 °F axillary, HR 102, RR 24 and labored, BP 151/92, and O2 97% on RA. Lung sounds CTA. PERRLA 4 mm. Unable to determine orientation due to aphasia.

Physician Orders:

STAT bedside glucose

STAT non-contrast CT

STAT CMP, CBC, troponin, PTT, PT/INR

Chest X-ray

ECG

Question #2: For each specific assessment finding, select whether the finding is consistent with the following disease processes: ischemic stroke, hemorrhagic stroke, and TIA. Each row must have at least one selection but can have more than one selection per row.

Assessment Findings	Ischemic Stroke	Hemorrhagic Stroke	Transient Ischemic Attack (TIA)
Aphasia	☐	☐	☐
Shortened aPTT	☐	☐	☐
Neuronal cell death	☐	☐	☐
Hemiparesis	☐	☐	☐
Cerebral edema	☐	☐	☐

Nurses' Notes:

0956: Patient presents to the ED with left-sided hemiparesis and altered speech. Patient's daughter is present and states that this came on very suddenly. Vital signs: T 98.1 °F axillary, HR 102, RR 24 and labored, BP 151/92, and O2 97% on RA. Lung sounds CTA. PERRLA 4 mm. Unable to determine orientation due to aphasia.

1034: Obtained ECG. Awaiting radiology transport for non-contrast CT. BG 185. Obtained and sent labs via STAT order.

Physician Orders:

STAT bedside glucose

STAT non-contrast CT

STAT CMP, CBC, troponin, PTT, PT/INR

Chest X-ray

ECG

Question #3: Based on the following ECG strip obtained, which type of stroke is the patient most likely experiencing? Select the correct answer from the options below.

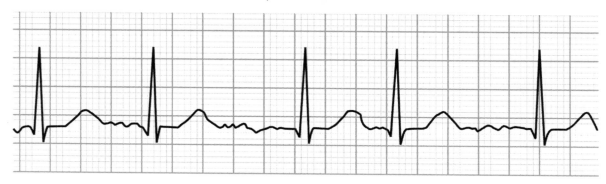

200

a. Thrombotic stroke
b. Intracerebral hemorrhagic stroke
c. Embolic stroke
d. Subarachnoid hemorrhage
e. Transient ischemic attack (TIA)

Radiology Report

CT BRAIN W/O CONTRAST - 02/23/2019 - 1046

Impression: Hyperdensity noted in middle cerebral artery (consistent with visualization of thromboembolism). No intracranial hemorrhage observed.

Question #4: Considering the radiology report shows the patient is likely experiencing an ischemic stroke, the administration of tPA is now a priority. What should the nurse recognize as contraindications to the administration of tPA? Select all that apply.

☐ Age >70 years old
☐ Moderate thrombocytopenia
☐ Stroke symptoms are present for longer than 30 minutes
☐ History of subarachnoid hemorrhage(s)
☐ Use of warfarin
☐ Patient is prehypertensive

The Neuro ICU nurse is caring for a 57-year-old female patient recovering from an ischemic stroke.

Nurses' Notes:

0645: Patient is resuming PO meds per provider orders and passing bedside swallow study.

Medication Administration Record:

0700 Medications: ☐ Lisinopril 20 mg PO

☐ Alendronate 10 mg PO

☐ Clopidogrel 75 mg PO

☐ Estradiol 2 mg PO

☐ Atorvastatin 20 mg PO

Question #5: After reviewing the medications to be administered, which medication should the nurse hold until consulting with the medical provider?

a. Lisinopril
b. Alendronate
c. Clopidogrel
d. Estradiol
e. Atorvastatin

The med-surg nurse is caring for a 57-year-old female patient recovering from an ischemic stroke. The nurse is preparing the patient for discharge.

Question #6: Determine whether the following discharge plans are appropriate or inappropriate for this patient.

Discharge Plans	Indicated	Not Indicated
Reduce activity to decrease the likelihood of a fall	☐	☐
Reduce the intake of red meats	☐	☐
Ensure the patient and all caregivers/loved ones are aware of the signs/symptoms of a stroke	☐	☐
Reduce alcohol intake and if smoking, stop immediately	☐	☐
Encourage daily intake of black/oolong/green tea for antioxidant purposes	☐	☐

Case Study #3

The primary care nurse is caring for a 28-year-old female patient with no reported PMH.

Progress Note:

Patient presents to the clinic with a CC of fatigue. General appearance is well groomed, but she wears multiple layers of clothing in the middle of summer. Patient states that she has been cold lately, especially in her hands and feet. Upon further assessment, the patient states a reduced appetite, typically only eating a few snacks throughout the day. Mild facial erythema noted with malar rash. Bilateral lung sounds CTA. Oral thrush with mild geographic tongue. Vital signs: T 99.1 °F oral, HR 122 and regular, BP 116/76, RR 19 and unlabored, O2 98% on RA.

Question #1: Based on the clinical presentation of the patient and objective data, which TWO specialty blood tests should the nurse expect to obtain? Write the correct answers in the slots provided.

- Lipid profile
- Antinuclear antibody test (ANA)
- Arterial blood gas (ABG)
- Coagulation factor tests
- Thyroid panel with TSH

Progress Note:

Patient presents to the clinic with a CC of fatigue. General appearance is well groomed, but she wears multiple layers of clothing in the middle of summer. Patient states that she has been cold lately, especially in her hands and feet. Upon further assessment, the patient states a reduced appetite, typically only eating a few snacks throughout the day. Mild facial erythema noted with malar rash. Bilateral lung sounds CTA. Oral thrush with mild geographic tongue. Vital signs: T 99.1 °F oral, HR 122 and regular, BP 116/76, RR 19 and unlabored, O2 98% on RA.

Lab Values:

Lab Test	Result	Reference Range
ANA	POSITIVE	—
T3	105 ng/dL	60–180 ng/dL
FT4	1.2 ng/dL	0.7–1.9 ng/dL
TSH	4.9 mIU/L	0.5–5 mIU/L

Question #2: Considering the patient has a positive ANA titer, the patient requires further assessment/diagnostics for a potential autoimmune dysfunction. Click to specify which assessment findings/symptoms below would be

commonly associated with the autoimmune dysfunctions listed. Each row must have at least one selection, but each row can have more than one selection.

Assessment Findings/Symptoms	Systemic Lupus Erythematosus (SLE)	Rheumatoid Arthritis (RA)	Multiple Sclerosis (MS)
Paresthesia	☐	☐	☐
Malar rash	☐	☐	☐
Swan neck deformity (phalanges)	☐	☐	☐
Anasarca	☐	☐	☐

Progress Note:

Patient presents to the clinic with a CC of fatigue. General appearance is well groomed, but she wears multiple layers of clothing in the middle of summer. Patient states that she has been cold lately, especially in her hands and feet. Upon further assessment, the patient states a reduced appetite, typically only eating a few snacks throughout the day. Mild facial erythema noted with malar rash. Bilateral lung sounds CTA. Oral thrush with mild geographic tongue. Vital signs: T 99.1 °F oral, HR 122 and regular, BP 116/76, RR 19 and unlabored, O2 98% on RA.

Lab Values:

Lab Test	Result	Reference Range
ANA	POSITIVE	–
T3	105 ng/dL	60–180 ng/dL
FT4	1.2 ng/dL	0.7–1.9 ng/dL
TSH	4.9 mIU/L	0.5–5 mIU/L

Question #3: Based on the information present, select the medical condition that the patient will MOST LIKELY be diagnosed with. In the event of a diagnosis, what potential education might be provided and what would the medical team need to monitor?

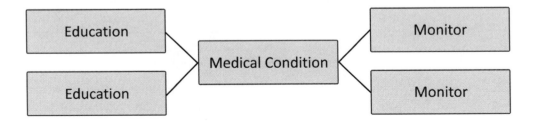

Potential Education	Potential Medical Condition	What to Assess/Monitor
Encourage the patient to remove excess clothing to thermoregulate.	Hyperthyroidism	Weight
Encourage the patient to follow a balanced diet and track dietary intake.	Systemic lupus erythematosus (SLE)	Thyroid stimulating hormone (TSH)
Encourage the patient to closely track temperature during a flare.	Rheumatoid arthritis (RA)	White blood cell (WBC) count
Encourage sedentary activities to conserve energy for daily activities.	Fibromyalgia	Thyroid peroxidase antibodies (TPO)

Progress Note:

Patient presents to the clinic with a CC of fatigue. General appearance is well groomed, but she wears multiple layers of clothing in the middle of summer. Patient states that she has been cold lately, especially in her hands and feet. Upon further assessment, the patient states a reduced appetite, typically only eating a few snacks throughout the day. Mild facial erythema noted with malar rash. Bilateral lung sounds CTA. Oral thrush with mild geographic tongue. Vital signs: T 99.1 °F oral, HR 122 and regular, BP 116/76, RR 19 and unlabored, O2 98% on RA.

Lab Values:

Lab Test	Result	Reference Range
ANA	POSITIVE	–
T3	105 ng/dL	60–180 ng/dL
FT4	1.2 ng/dL	0.7–1.9 ng/dL
TSH	4.9 mIU/L	0.5–5 mIU/L

Physician Orders:

- Administer triamcinolone 60 mg IM one-time dose for symptom relief.
- Refer to rheumatology for follow-up.

Question #4: What is the patient at risk for developing once an immunosuppressive medication is started? Select all that apply.

- Malignancy
- Hypoglycemia
- Infection
- Vitamin D toxicity
- Osteoporosis

The rheumatology clinic nurse is caring for a 28-year-old female patient with an active diagnosis of systemic lupus erythematosus (SLE).

Question #5: After the rheumatologist provides education on SLE and a general overview of autoimmune disorders, the nurse discusses all remaining information with the patient regarding follow-up and medical compliance. Select the following statements from the patient that would indicate she understood the education provided.

Patient Statement	Understanding	No Understanding
"I can only have one active autoimmune disorder."	☐	☐
"I should avoid excess sun exposure."	☐	☐
"I need to increase my medication dosage during a flare."	☐	☐
"I should remain active as much as possible."	☐	☐
"I need to consult with my rheumatologist before starting any OTC or herbal medications."	☐	☐

Question #6: In addition to providing lifestyle and medication education, the nurse also needs to ensure the patient understands when to seek a higher level of care. Under what circumstances should the patient immediately seek emergency care? Select all that apply.

- Increased fatigue
- Sharp pain in neck/shoulder area
- Purpura
- Aphthous ulcers
- Scleral icterus
- Hip pain with decreased ROM

NCLEX-PN Answer Explanations #1

1. D: Though there are many benefits to the CVAD, it still poses a risk for infection to the patient, even more so than a peripheral device, as it is more centric to the patient's circulatory system and vital organs. The CVAD has many benefits, including being able to provide easy access for blood draws; the capacity to deliver large amounts of blood, drugs, and fluids to the patient; and decreasing peripheral sticks and the inflammation that goes along with those. The use of the CVAD must be carefully decided, weighing the pros against the cons.

2. C: The final phase of the nursing process is evaluation; however, evaluation happens across the continuum of the nursing process, not just at the end. The nurse frequently evaluates the effectiveness of care plans, adjusts as necessary, and reevaluates. Data is collected during the assessment phase. Nursing diagnoses are formulated in the diagnosis phase. The implementation phase often begins with educating the patient on expected outcomes.

3. C: Substance use, as well as chronic disease, alcohol abuse, and communicable diseases potentially rule out a person from being an organ donor. A strict list of criteria must be met for organ donation to occur. These criteria ensure the health and viability of the organs and tissues to be donated. Age, weight, and previous psychiatric illness do not necessarily rule a person out for organ donation.

4. B: Choice *B* aligns with the ocular positioning that accompanies a diagnosis of exotropia with an outward turn. Choice *A* aligns with esotropia, with an inward turn. Choice *C* aligns with hypertropia, with an upward turn. Choice *D* aligns with hypotropia, with a downward turn.

5. D: An elderly woman who is incontinent of stool will need frequent linen changes and cleansing of her bottom. The constant moisture has a very high potential for causing skin breakdown. She is also showing signs of confusion, which means she may become agitated and unaware of her surroundings, leading to potential bruises or tears on her extremities. The other patient scenarios described are also at risk for skin injury. However, with the information given, *D* is the patient with the highest risk.

6. B, C, E: Choices *B, C,* and *E* typically align with false labor, which also includes cessation of contractions when comfort measures are included. Choices *A* and *D* typically indicate true labor, which becomes more intense while walking and continues regardless of comfort.

7. A: Competent bacteria can perform the process of transformation, wherein they can absorb and incorporate foreign DNA from their environment into their own chromosomal DNA. Some bacteria are naturally competent, while others, under certain laboratory conditions, can become competent. Transduction is a term used with viral replication and is the process by which some portion of the host cell's chromosome gets packaged and transferred out of the cell in the new copy of the virus, and then gets incorporated into the next host cell when the virus delivers its viral DNA.

8. B, A, D, C: The nurse should instruct the patient to perform the steps for collecting a sterile specimen in the following order to maintain aseptic technique so that testing is accurate and reliable. The patient should retract the foreskin, clean the meatus, void a small amount into the toilet, and then catch the urine stream in a cup uninterrupted.

9. C: The Genital stage starts in adolescence and lays the groundwork for future life relationships. As one enters adolescence, sexual identity and orientation begin to develop. Values regarding sexuality, views about the opposite sex, and the process of interacting with others on a more intimate level occur. These more mature elements of relationship-building lay the foundation for future relationships, but not only from a sexual standpoint. Choice *A,* the Latent stage, occurs from age 6 to puberty, and it is a time when the child's sexual energy becomes somewhat dormant. Choices *B* and *D* are not included in Freud's model of human development.

10. B: Suicidal ideation is characterized by recurrent thoughts of suicide, ranging from passive ideation to active ideation. Homicidal ideation is characterized by thoughts or plans to kill another person or a group of people.

11. C: Thrombocytopenia means that there are a lower than normal number of platelets in the blood. The term comes from the root word "thrombocyte." The prefix "thrombo-" means clot, and the suffix "-cyte" means cell. These cells are responsible for the body's ability to stop bleeding by forming a clot. Neutropenia and leukopenia are used interchangeably to refer to a lowered white blood cell count. *Neutrophils,* the root word for *neutropenia,* are the largest portion of the white blood cells. If the neutrophils are significantly lowered, then leukopenia results, thus the interchangeability of the words. Anemia refers to a lower than normal count of red blood cells and reduces the body's ability to carry and deliver oxygen.

12. A: The nurse should review the pharmacology, or the action created by a drug, of the patient's current medications. Knowing the pharmacological effects of these medications and those of the scheduled preoperative medications can help keep the patient safe. Side effects and adverse reactions are included in the pharmacology. The intended effect does not include possible side effects or adverse reactions.

13. C: Choice *C* aligns with the deceleration seen of the fetal heart rate after the maternal contractions are witnessed. Choice *A* would involve deceleration before the contractions. Choices *B* and *D* would both involve acceleration instead of the deceleration indicated by the depressions on the reading.

14. C: Choice *C* should NOT be implemented for a patient with epilepsy. Side-rails should be up to discourage patient falls during seizure activity. Choice *A* provides additional protection from injury. Choices *B* and *D* include equipment that should be ready for use in case it is needed during a seizure. The nurse should support the patient into a side-lying position and maintain their airway.

15. The pulmonic valve is located at the second intercostal space to the left sternal border. The nurse should place the bell or diaphragm of their stethoscope at this location to engage in pulmonic valve auscultation.

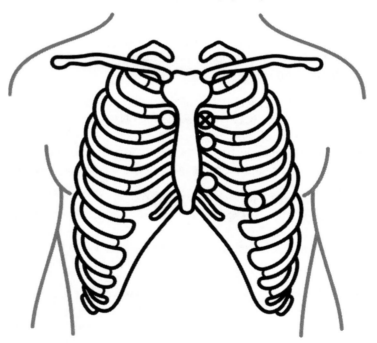

16. 8 mL: The nurse should instruct the patient and family to use the dosage calculation of "dose ordered" divided by "dose on hand." In this case, the parent should divide 40 mg by 5 mg/mL to yield 8 mL.

17. A: Choice *A* is a synthetic hormone replacement prescribed for hypothyroidism, which targets symptoms such as fatigue, hair thinning, and weight gain. Choice *B* promotes a reduction in flatulence. Choice *C* is prescribed for mood disorders. Choice *D* targets poor sleep.

18. C: Choice *C* is correct. Atrial flutter is a type of supraventricular tachycardia, often indicated by flutter waves at a high rate between 200 and 300 BPM, as seen in Choice *C*.

19. D: Choice *D* is correct. The patient is laying on their front, which is the prone position. Choice *A* is the side position, Choice *B* is supine, and Choice *C* is semi-Fowler's.

20. C: Developing a long-term relationship and starting a family are concepts more closely associated with stage six of Erikson's model, Intimacy versus Isolation, which occurs from age 18 through age 40. During this period, one is faced with the challenge of coming to terms with sexual preference, choosing a career path, and determining where, with whom, and how one plans to live. Long-term, future-oriented thinking is required. This phase is important, in that if not successfully mastered, the following phases—Generativity versus Stagnation and Ego Integrity versus Despair—may lead to emotional pain and anxiety in later life.

21. C: The incubation period is the point in time where the organism has already invaded the person's body through a portal of entry, is multiplying, and is getting ready to manifest the first symptoms of infection. The colonization period occurs right after entry into the body where the organism takes up residence in the host and prepares to multiply. The prodromal period is when the person develops general signs or symptoms (such as fatigue, headache, fever, etc.) before developing more specific signs and symptoms that help point towards a diagnosis. The convalescent period is when the person is recovering from the illness.

22. C: Placenta previa is the abnormal placement of the placenta over the internal cervical os or within 2 centimeters of the internal cervical os. The risk factors for placenta previa are previous C-section, maternal age greater than thirty-five years, and increased number of previous pregnancies. Other risk factors include infertility treatments, multiple births, previous abortions, and smoking or cocaine use.

23. B: Choice *B* shows traces of chest wall clapping. Choice *A* is incorrect as chest wall clapping is visibly present. Choice *C* indicates vibration. Choice *D* indicates shaking.

24. A: Criminal law has to do with the arrest, prosecution, and incarceration of those who commit misdemeanors and felonies. Constitutional law has to do with the laws set forth by the Constitution of the United States of America. Common law is based on legal precedents. Stationary is not a term used to describe laws. Stationary sounds similar to "statutory," which has to do with laws passed down by legislative bodies such as a state's legislature. There are statutes criminalizing certain acts, such as assault.

25. A: Choice *A* aligns with the patient's electrocardiogram as it shows a regular rhythm and rate with each QRS complex preceded by a normal P wave and constant PR interval. Choices *B*, *C*, and *D* all fall outside of normal and do not correlate to the characteristics of the normal sinus rhythm seen on this strip.

26. D: The nurse should assess for orthostatic hypotension by performing lying/sitting/standing (LSS) blood pressure readings. If the readings trend downward significantly, up to twenty points in mmHg on the systolic side, the patient probably has orthostatic hypotension. Assessing for the patient's temperature and rate of breathing and comparing bilateral radial pulses can all be performed for the sake of having additional data but do not follow the symptoms this specific patient reported.

27. C: Children, women, and the elderly are vulnerable populations due to tendencies to be physically weaker than their attackers, possibly disabled, unable to communicate, or dependent in some other way.

28. A traumatic injury to the temporal lobe causes changes to behavior, memory, speech, hearing, and vision. This lobe is located anterior to the occipital lobe and posterior to the frontal lobe, beneath the lateral fissure.

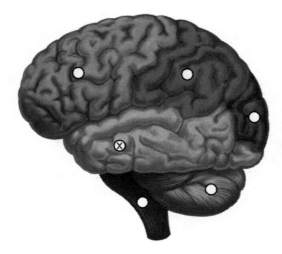

29. A: Abruptio placenta is the premature separation of the placenta from the wall of the uterus. Common risk factors for this condition are smoking, maternal hypertension, trauma (such as car accidents, falls, or assaults), cocaine or alcohol abuse, maternal age greater than thirty-five or less than twenty-years-old, and previous history of abruptio placenta. Therefore, Choices *B*, *C*, and *D* are not correct.

30. C: Fragmentation of care occurs when the patient's case is shifted from one health care environment to another, in such a way that ambiguity over who is responsible for the patient's overall case results. This leads to errors and prolonged inaction as well as patient frustration. Continuity of care is the opposite of fragmentation of care and is the ideal. Continuity of care means the plan of care stays consistent across many different health care environments that the patient may find themselves in. Choices *B* and *D*, fluidity and division, are not terms used for these concepts.

31. D: The unlicensed assistive personnel (UAP) is able to assist with patient equipment by supporting placement of the sequential compression devices (SCDs). It would not be within the UAP's scope to apply cervical traction (Choice *A*), a hemovac drain (Choice *C*), or a ventilator (Choice *B*).

32. D: Accommodation occurs when one recognizes that previous beliefs were incorrect or no longer beneficial, based upon learning and integrating new information. Accommodation should occur throughout one's life as new information enters the consciousness and the process of assimilation occurs. If one is unable to accommodate new ideas, then it is difficult to grow emotionally and intellectually. If an individual continues to insist that using a yellow legal pad and an encyclopedia is just as efficient as using a computer to complete a complex research project, accommodation has failed to occur. This forces the person to work at a "snail's pace" in comparison to using technology to more quickly and accurately complete the task. Choice *A* is incorrect in that schemas are a set of thoughts and ideas that fit together and present the person with a belief, or even a script, for life. Choice *B* is incorrect because assimilation refers to the process of integrating the new information gained through accommodation. Choice *C* refers to object permanence, a process in which an infant learns that even though a person or object leaves the room, that person still exists, and this understanding reduces anxiety and fear of abandonment.

33. The olfactory nerve, one of twelve cranial nerves, represents a more frequently injured nerve and is characterized by a loss of smell. Injury to this nerve prevents the transmission of the sensation of smell to the patient's brain. It is the first and shortest cranial nerve.

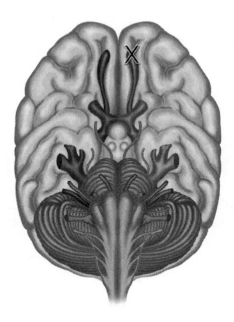

34. D: Sometimes the supervising nurse must coach the staff member to whom they have delegated a task to ensure a better performance the next time. The nurse should use the utmost professionalism and respect during these encounters, ensuring the staff member is receptive and the criticism is constructive. Follow-up is investigating that the task was done. Delegation is handing out a task to an appropriate staff member. Documentation needs to occur following each task that is performed, and the delegating nurse needs to ensure this is performed for all care activity.

35. B: Administrative law is the type of law given by administrative bodies such as a state's nursing board. Constitutional law is specific to the United States Constitution and does not rule on nursing administrative issues. Common law is based on legal precedents. Statutory law involves legislative bodies such as a state's legislature.

36. C: Observing and recording the patient's heart rhythm via ECG is the specific intervention necessary to monitor for the development of dysrhythmias postcardiac catheterization. All of the other interventions listed are correct postcardiac catheterization care but not specific to dysrhythmias. The nurse will keep the patient flat to assist with incision healing, take regular vital signs. such as heart rate. and blood pressure., and monitor for bleeding and hematoma at the incision site to evaluate the patient's overall stability.

37. D: A right-heart catheter., also called a Swan-Ganz catheter. or pulmonary artery catheter., is threaded through a patient's central veins. into the superior vena cava, terminating at the pulmonary artery. This type of catheter is used for hemodynamic monitoring, giving information about the patient's preload. and cardiac output.. A PICC line., or peripherally inserted central catheter, can be used for medication and fluid administration but does not give information about hemodynamics.. A port-a-cath is another type of central line used for similar purposes as the PICC line and can be kept in the patient for an extended period. A dialysis catheter is a long-term access device for patients receiving regular treatments of dialysis but is not used for hemodynamic monitoring.

38. The anterior and posterior aspects of the patient's torso cover 18% surface area each, thus totaling to 36% when both aspects are affected. Additionally, the anterior head accounts for 4.5%, the posterior head 4.5%, the anterior leg 9%, the posterior leg 9%, the anterior arm 4.5%, the posterior arm 4.5%, and finally the perineum 1%.

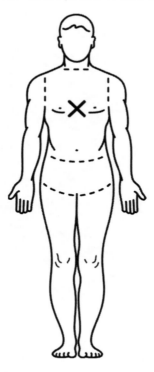

39. B: The patient's physiological needs must be met first and foremost, before any other level of the hierarchy can be addressed. Maslow's description of the physiological needs include hunger, thirst, breathing, sleep, and homeostasis. Safety is the next level; it addresses morality, family, and security of the body. Love comes next in Maslow's hierarchy, involving relationships with family and friends. Esteem is one level higher than love, involving self-esteem, confidence, achievement, and respect of others.

40. B: Right medical facility is not part of the six patient medication administration rights. The six rights are the following: right medication, right route, right time frame, right patient, right dosage, and right documentation.

41. 240 mg: The medication includes 40 mg of caffeine per tablet, therefore the nurse should multiply 40 mg/tablet by 6 tablets to yield 240 mg, which is the daily maximum total of caffeine consumption as ordered.

42. B: Nurses are legally mandated to report gunshot wounds, dog bites, communicable disease, neglect, and abuse. Marital status, religious beliefs, and urinary tract infections are not legally mandated items for the nurse to report.

43. C: Even if no pressure sores are present, all immobile patients should be repositioned at least once every two hours. For Choice A, the patient should be repositioned at least once every two hours to prevent pressure sores from developing. Again in Choice B, an immobile patient should be repositioned at least once every two hours. However, if the patient expresses discomfort, the nurse can reposition the patient even if they were repositioned less than two hours ago. For Choice D, while it might be appropriate to coordinate care in this manner, again the patient should be repositioned at least once every two hours whether or not any other care is being provided.

44. B: Changing behavior through rewards for approximation of desired behavior is the correct answer. Skinner demonstrated that behavior can be learned by rewarding actions that are similar to the desired behavior. If one wants to teach a dog to chase and catch a Frisbee thrown to the end of a field, the dog must first be rewarded for

212

sniffing the Frisbee, then grasping the Frisbee, and then catching it when thrown four feet, then six, then ten. This process is called successive approximation. Choice A refers to a form of behavioral change through punishment. Choice C refers to superstitions, meaning that one can sometimes be confused as to which behavior is soliciting the reward. Some athletes wear the same pair of "lucky" socks each game, thinking this behavior leads to the reward of winning. In reality, the behavior that leads to the win can be anything from practicing harder to playing a team that is not highly skilled; therefore, the behavior is superstitious. Choice D is a poor form of teaching a person to learn a new behavior because it may take much trial and error before perfection is achieved.

45. C: Treatment of Alzheimer's disease, a chronic progressive form of dementia, is supportive; however, cholinesterase inhibitors and N-Methyl-D-aspartate (NMDA) receptor antagonists have been demonstrated to slow the disease progression if they are started early in the course of the disease. Choices A and B are incorrect since early use of these medications will not cure the disease or cause it to enter remission. Choice D is incorrect because these medications have been shown to work for a limited time, if started early in the disease.

46. D: Culture is a complex and multi-faceted concept and is related to when, where, and with whom one was raised. Those in the metal health field should always consider and discuss a client's cultural practices because these strongly impact beliefs, ethics, and behavior. The other three answer choices are all important elements in understanding cultural background, but it is the combination of these and other factors that make up one's cultural background.

47. A: A leakage of air into the pleural cavity outside of the lungs is called a *pneumothorax*. This may happen as a complication of central line placement for TPN. Hemothorax results when blood is leaked into the pleural cavity. *Hydrothorax* refers to a leakage of water into the pleural cavity. Pneumonia is an infection that forms in the lungs as the result of an infectious organism and may cause fluid to accumulate in the bases of the lungs.

48. A: The nurse assessing a stable, uncomplicated patient will most likely go for the radial pulse. The femoral pulse, found in the groin, would be an invasion of the patient's privacy and not appropriate for this type of routine checkup. The popliteal pulse, found behind the knee, would be an unusual and hard-to-reach spot for a routine pulse assessment. The carotid pulse is reserved for emergency situations such as cardiac arrest to assess for pulselessness before starting cardiopulmonary resuscitation (CPR).

49. C: The rhythm shown demonstrates sinus tachycardia. Sinus tachycardia originates from the sinus node but has a faster rate than normal sinus rhythm.

50. C: Population density, which is the total number of people divided by the total land area, generally tends to be much higher in urban areas than rural ones. This is true due to high-rise apartment complexes, sewage and freshwater infrastructure, and complex transportation systems, allowing for easy movement of food from nearby farms. Consequently, competition among citizens for resources is certainly higher in high-density areas, as are greater strains on infrastructure within urban centers.

51. D: The patient-centered medical home (PCMH) is a model of care that promotes wellness for the patient through proactivity, care coordination, and patient-centered planning. PCMH is a model that seeks to combat fragmentation of care and the problems that come with it. The other three terms are not applicable to the description, though community and public health organizations do play a role in promoting community wellness.

52. B: The blood sugars represented on this graph are under control.

53. B: Choice B indicates the most supportive splint for a patient struggling with a Colles fracture post fall. This fracture-type involves falling on an outstretched hand, which fractures and displaces distal radius. Choice A is indicated for a thumb dislocation. Choice C is indicated for a 4th or 5th metatarsal fracture. Choice D is indicated for a wrist sprain.

54. C: This type of seizure with muscle rigidity, convulsions, and unconsciousness is called a grand mal seizure. An absence seizure involves a brief loss of consciousness where the patient may stare into space. A myoclonic seizure involves the body making jerking movements. A tonic seizure is characterized by rigidity and stiffness of the muscles.

55. B: The patient must have a chest x-ray to confirm correct placement of the PICC line. Correct placement will show that the PICC line tip is resting in the distal end of the superior vena cava, right at the cavoatrial junction. The other three imaging studies are not routinely ordered to confirm PICC line placement.

56. B: The patient with a pH value of 7.25 is still very much acidotic and needs further therapy to return them to normal. The other values listed fall in the normal range of 7.35 to 7.45 or in the alkalotic range, which is greater than 7.45.

57. B: A subclavian catheter is an example of a non-tunneled central venous access device. Jugular and femoral lines are other examples of non-tunneled catheters. Examples of tunneled catheters include Groshong's, small-bore, Hickman's, and Broviac's.

58. C: Choice *C*, passive leg raise, supports proper positioning for a patient with vital signs indicative of shock. The patient is supine with the legs elevated 8-12 inches. It is the nurse's priority to enhance circulation and assess the need for additional interventions. Choice *A* aligns with a raised upper body, while Choice *B* is side lying, and Choice *D* is face down, none of which support improved vital signs and symptom management of shock for the patient at this time.

59. B: The patient with Meniere's disease, an inner ear vestibular condition, struggles with symptoms of tinnitus and severe vertigo. A shower chair, Choice *B*, is crucial for this patient in order to prevent falls while showering. The patient should be encouraged to use the shower chair during every shower, and if available, grab bars as well, as symptoms can exacerbate in the shower and may lead to unsteady balance. A leg lifter is not a necessary device to offer this patient at this time, as it does not correlate with the patient's condition; thus, Choice *A* is incorrect. Button hooks and voice boxes, Choices *C* and Choice *D*, while supportive, do not align with symptoms of this condition.

60. B: The reflex arc is the simplest nerve pathway. The stimulus bypasses the brain, going from sensory receptors through an afferent (incoming) neuron to the spinal cord. It synapses with an efferent (outgoing) neuron in the spinal cord and is transmitted directly to muscle. There is no interneuron involved in a reflex arc. The classic example of a reflex arc is the knee-jerk response. Tapping on the patellar tendon of the knee stimulates the quadriceps muscle of the thigh, resulting in contraction of the muscle and extension of the knee.

61. C: Patients respond favorably to positive intrapersonal communication between their attending nurses and physicians. The other options may be nice for patients, but studies indicate that nurse and physician relationships have the most impact on a patient's overall experience.

62. C: The patient has given implied consent. There is neither verbal nor written confirmation of consent; rather, both parties silently agree without a formal conversation about the topic. Assumed is not a term used for consent, though both parties are assuming that consent is given. Written consent involves a signed legal document by the patient and usually follows a conversation about the plan of care or procedure with the physician performing it. Verbal consent is given by the patient, affirming verbally their consent to the procedure to be done.

63. B: Based on the symptoms of stomach pain and bloody emesis that the patient reported, they will likely be scheduled for an upper endoscopy. An upper endoscopy, also called an esophagogastroduodenoscopy (EGD), visualizes the internal mucosa of the upper gastrointestinal (GI) tract. A sigmoidoscopy visualizes the sigmoid portion of the colon. An anoscopy is performed to visualize the area just inside the anus. A colonoscopy is performed to assess and intervene within the entire colon, usually used for early detection of colon cancer.

64. C: The mammography test is a type of x-ray, not computed tomography. While CT scans may be performed, x-rays are the gold standard for early detection of breast cancer. The patient is recommended to get the test once every year after the age of forty for early breast cancer detection. The test can pick up masses that may not be manually palpable to the patient or the practitioner.

65. 3 doses: 2 grams of acetaminophen are equal to 2000 mg. 2000 mg (total) divided by 650 mg (per dose) is equal to 3.077, or 3 doses.

66. C: When an unconscious patient is brought in for emergency care, they are agreeing to the care by way of implied consent. However, it is important to note that implied consent could never overrule a patient's denial to receive care. It is implied that an unconscious patient brought to the emergency room would want to be treated. Therefore, Choice *A* is incorrect. A patient would need to be conscious and verbal to provide explicit or expressed consent, so Choices *B* and *D* are incorrect. A patient's action and conduct to willingly receive the medical care, even if not expressed verbally, functions as the basis for implied consent.

67. B: Hyperthyroidism occurs when there is an overproduction of T4 and/or T5 by the thyroid gland. Women under age 40 are most likely to be diagnosed with this disorder. This makes Choices *A*, *C*, and *D* incorrect.

68. A: The correct answer is 7.5 mL. The answer is obtained by using the desired dose divided by the amount on hand multiplied by the volume, or the D/H x V formula. By taking the desired dose (240 mg), dividing it by the amount on hand (160mg), and multiplying it by the volume the drug is formulated in (5 mL), the nurse will then arrive at the correct dose of 7.5 mL.

69. A: The cardiac index reflects the quantity of blood pumped by the heart per minute per meter squared of the patient's body surface area. Cardiac output measures how much blood the heart pumps out per minute in liters. The mean arterial pressure, or MAP, shows the relationship between the amount of blood pumped out of the heart and the resistance the vascular system puts up against it. The stroke volume measures how much blood the heart pumps in milliliters per beat.

70. A: *Parenteral* is the term that refers to any route outside of the gastrointestinal tract, also referred to as the *alimentary canal*. *Motor* is not a viable answer choice. *Enteral* also refers to the GI tract or intestines. *Buccal* refers to the cheeks, or inner oral cavity.

71. C: The sympathetic nervous system initiates the "fight-or-flight" response and is responsible for body changes that direct all available energy towards survival. Digestion is completely sacrificed so that energy can be diverted to increase heart rate and breathing (thus, bronchiole dilation). The liver is stimulated to release glycogen to provide available energy. The parasympathetic system is responsible for stimulating everyday activities like digestion.

72. A, B, C, E: It is important to know what the patient's other vital signs are before proceeding. The physician must be notified for a heart rate of 150 bpm. The administration of oxygen is appropriate for an SpO2 of 88 percent. It is important to stay with this patient until the patient has stabilized. Choice D is incorrect because this unstable patient takes priority.

73. C: The nurse must consider the strengths and weaknesses of a particular CNA before delegating a task to them. This will best assist the nurse in making a sound decision. The school that the CNA received their training from, the other staff members they associate with, and what time they get off work are irrelevant to their performance as a CNA. The nurse must be aware of and careful of their own personal bias and prejudice when deciding to whom to delegate tasks. Each person must be judged fairly based on their merit, attitude, and performance.

74. C: Metabolic syndrome, also called Syndrome X, is the presence of comorbid cardiovascular and insulin-related conditions. Those with metabolic disease may have excess belly fat, not excess fat on the upper back. Choices *A* and

B are incorrect since patients with metabolic syndrome must have three or more of the following conditions: hypertension, elevated fasting blood glucose levels, low HDL cholesterol, high triglycerides, and excess belly fat. Patients with this disorder are typically overweight or obese and are at an increased risk for organ failure, heart attack, and stroke, making Choice *D* incorrect.

75. C: Gloves and a disposable mask are all that are required for droplet precaution; however, additional PPE may be used if desiring extra protection. The key word in this question is *minimum*. Choice *A* is not correct because an N-95 mask is not required. Choice *D* is not correct because sterile gloves are not needed and eyewear is optional. Choice *B* would give the most coverage for protection but it is not the minimum PPE required.

76. D: The oral glucose tolerance test is performed between the twenty-fourth and twenty-eighth week of pregnancy to screen for gestational diabetes. Hyperemesis gravidarum is a severe form of morning sickness that occurs in the first trimester but sometimes continues until the third trimester. Preeclampsia is detected through blood pressure monitoring. Iron-deficiency anemia may be detected first through symptoms of fatigue, weakness, and dizziness and then confirmed with a blood test showing a low hemoglobin and hematocrit count. These components of the red blood cells are responsible for carrying oxygen to the organs and tissues of the body and can drop during pregnancy.

77. D: Severe allergies can be life-threatening and lead to anaphylaxis. An epinephrine injection pen is the first line of defense if a person comes into contact with an allergen to which he or she has a serious or life-threatening reaction.

78. A, C, D, E: Educating the patient and setting the alarm are appropriate interventions, as the patient has a history of falling. The RN should be included in the plan of care for this patient. The patient should be checked on frequently to make sure they are safe and are following instructions. Choice *B* is incorrect because writing a plan of care is not within the LPN's scope of practice.

79. C: The liver is a solid organ located in the right upper quadrant of the abdomen. When a penetrating wound such as a gunshot has occurred to the abdomen, it is important to be mindful of organ damage underneath the point of penetration. The small intestine, stomach, and colon are all hollow organs located in different areas of the abdomen.

80. D, C, B, A: The nurse prepares to don personal protective equipment (PPE) via steps performed in the following order to ensure infection control is maintained by safely applying equipment in layers to later avoid contamination of equipment or self. The nurse should don the gown, mask, goggles, and lastly, gloves.

81. B: Choice *B* indicates the proper instrument selection for the nurse to use for debridement, as this tool supports irrigation. Choice *A* supports suctioning, such as of vomit and mucus. Choice *B* supports sampling, such as of blood and bodily fluids. Choice *D* supports injections, such as of medication.

82. D: Negligence, along with malpractice, is a type of unintentional tort. Intentional torts include false imprisonment, batter, and assault. Libel and slander, in which false statements are made as a form of defamation, both fall under the category of intentional tort.

83. D: The hypothalamus is the link between the nervous system and endocrine system. It receives information from the brain and sends signals to the pituitary gland, instructing it to release or inhibit the release of hormones. Aside from its endocrine function, it controls body temperature, hunger, sleep, and circadian rhythms, and it is part of the limbic system.

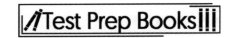

84. D: The nurse could appropriately make a speech therapy referral in this child's case, connecting the child and the child's family to needed services. The other three options of a dietician, physical therapist, and social services are not appropriate for this specific scenario.

85. A: Approximately 20-25 percent of the population in the United States struggles with a mental disorder in any given year. That is 1 out of every 4 or 5 people. It is estimated that a smaller percentage, 4-8 percent, struggle with a severe or serious mental illness. The United States has a high level of mental disorders as compared to other countries.

86. D: Bipolar disorder was formerly called manic-depressive disorder and is characterized by fluctuations in mood, from bouts of depression to periods of mania or euphoria. There are different types of bipolar disorder, some types having milder forms of mania or depression than others. Anxiety disorders are characterized by persistent worry, anxiety, or fear. Trauma-related disorders develop in reaction to stressful and traumatic experiences that a person has endured.

87. A: Choice A should be assessed using the bell of the stethoscope for detection. Choices B, C, and D should be auscultated with the diaphragm of the stethoscope. The bell supports auscultation of low frequency sounds, while the diaphragm filters low sounds out. The bell is helpful for detecting abnormal heart sounds and bruits.

88. B: Choice B represents the normal range for white blood cells in a healthy adult patient. Choices A, C, and D are outside of the normal range and would indicate a potential problem requiring further assessment by the nurse at this time. Choice A is below normal range. Choices C and D are above normal range.

89. A: A normal range for serum potassium is between 3.5 and 5.1 mEq/L; thus, 3.2 is the correct answer. 3.5 and 5.0 mEq/L suggest a normal serum potassium. A level of 5.5 mEq/L suggests a hyperkalemic state. The nurse should report hypokalemia and will prepare to administer potassium supplementation if ordered by the physician.

90. C, A, D, B: The transfusion should be stopped immediately to ensure that the patient is safe and the reaction is minimized. The RN should be made aware so that the team of nurses can collaborate. Vital signs should be taken before notifying the physician, so that you can inform the physician about them.

91. C, D: The physician should be notified of the patient's wishes so they can direct care appropriately. The LPN can answer questions about advance directives. Choice A is incorrect because only physicians can order a DNR. Choices B and E are incorrect because the patient is not a DNR until the physician orders it.

92. B: Choice B indicates the appropriate team member for the nurse to elevate a patient care safety risk to. Choices A, C, and D fall higher in the nursing chain of command; therefore, they should not yet be prompted to handle this concern.

93. B: The correct conversion of the patient's weight is 70 kilograms. This answer is found by dividing the weight in pounds, 155, by the number of kilograms that are found in a pound, 2.2, which gives the nurse the correct answer. The other three answers are incorrect.

94. B: Choice B indicates a normal assessment finding for a two-week-old patient. Choices A, C, and D are outside of the normal range for the age of this patient, as the heart rate should be between 70 and 190 beats per minute. This rate is applicable for the first month of life. At one month of age, the normal heart rate adjusts to 80 to 160 beats per minute.

95. C: Keeping a patient in a sitting position in their bed puts extra pressure on their coccyx and bottom due to gravity; therefore, this option is not a preventative measure for pressure-ulcer formation. Choices A, B, and D are interventions that should be done to help prevent pressure ulcers.

96. D: The nurse will see the patient who is complaining of shortness of breath first. Airway, breathing, and circulation are always the highest priority for the nurse to address, as they can quickly become life-threatening situations. Maintaining proper respiration is a vital function to the patient's well-being, and stabilization is necessary immediately. The woman who is nauseous and needs antiemetics such as Zofran is the second priority, as she is actively ill and there is something the nurse can do to help her symptoms. The nurse's third priority will be the patient who needs to sign the informed consent. The nurse needs to ensure she gets that signed before the patient leaves the floor, although there are nurses in the cardiac catheterization lab who can obtain the consent if need be. The patient who has a question about discharge is the last priority, as there is no immediate threat to his health and the doctor will need to see the patient before he is discharged anyway.

97. D: Choice *D* correlates to an 18% burn percentage in an adult patient. Choice *A* correlates to a 4.5% burn percentage. Choice *B* correlates to a 9% burn percentage. Choice *C* correlates to a 4.5% burn percentage. The nurse applies burn percentage to patient care and triage of thermal injuries.

98. 1.88 mL: If the drops come in a concentration of 50 mg/1.25 mL, then 1.875 is the correct mL for 75 mg. 1.875 rounded to the nearest hundredth is 1.88 mL.

99. A: To become a case manager, the nurse needs to fulfill requirements beyond their initial nursing degree. These requirements include case management–specific training, clinical hours following the case management team, and passing a case management certification exam. The initial passing of the NCLEX, clinical hours required for the nursing degree, and the nursing degree itself are all required before beginning case management training.

100. D: Itching and the development of a rash are signs that the patient is having an allergic reaction to a medication. These two symptoms are signs that the body's inflammatory response has been kicked into overdrive because of a drug allergy. The other symptoms listed are not commonly associated with an allergic reaction.

101. A, B, C, D: Choices *A, B, C,* and *D* indicate that the patient is susceptible to ulcers. When using the Norton Scale for Assessment Risk of Pressure Ulcers, a score of 14 or less indicates susceptibility. Choice *E* is outside of the susceptibility range. This scale rates five criteria that include: physical condition, mental condition, activity, mobility, and incontinence.

102. C: Schizophrenia is highly genetic and is associated with high levels of dopamine in the brain. Parkinson's disease is correlated to low levels of dopamine, so treatments for schizophrenia can sometimes cause Parkinson's disease. Alzheimer's disease is associated with a deficit in the neurotransmitter acetylcholine rather than dopamine. There has been no strong link connecting dopamine to personality disorders.

Case Study #1

Question #1:

Patient Statement	Understanding	No Understanding
"I will self-catheterize on or near the toilet to make the process easier."	☒	☐
"I need to insert the catheter slowly and remove the catheter quickly when urine stops."	☐	☒
"I should aim my penis upward toward my abdomen to make the insertion easier."	☒	☐
"Once I see urine flow coming from the catheter, I should stop immediately and allow the catheter to fully drain."	☐	☒
"I can insert the catheter in the shower to be sure I am clean."	☐	☒

The patient demonstrates understanding of safe self-catheterization when he states that he will be on or near the toilet for the procedure and that he should aim his penis upward for the insertion of the urinary catheter. Being on or near the toilet allows the patient to drain the urine directly rather than collecting it in a container and disposing of it after. Aiming the penis upward allows the patient to adequately visualize the urethral opening for insertion, helping ensure a clean insertion.

The patient does not understand the process of self-catheterization if he states that he should remove the catheter quickly, that he should not advance the catheter slightly after seeing urine flow upon insertion, and/or that he should insert the catheter in the shower. The catheter should be removed slowly to prevent urethral trauma. The catheter should be advanced slightly after seeing urine flow with insertion to ensure the tip of the urinary catheter is fully in the bladder. Lastly, the urinary catheter should not be inserted in the shower, as both the catheter and the urethral opening should be completely dry.

Question #2: Based on the patient's recent medical history and prolonged postoperative use of a urinary catheter, the patient is likely experiencing delirium related to a urinary tract infection (UTI). For this reason, the nurse should contact the medical provider and assess the vital signs. Contacting the medical provider is always the answer for an acute change in LOC, while assessing the patient's vital signs is important in checking for a fever or a hemodynamic response to an infection. The nurse would need to contact the wife directly for the change in LOC. The nurse would not need to reinsert the urinary catheter unless directly ordered to by the physician and would never place the patient in the bed with all side rails up, as that is considered entrapment (a form of restraint).

219

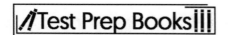
Question #3: Based on the options provided, the medical conditions that most commonly cause delirium in the geriatric population are pneumonia, UTIs, and dehydration. Additional conditions that cause delirium in the geriatric population include dementia, influenza, polypharmacy, cerebrovascular accidents, and head injuries (sustained from falls/injuries).

Question #4:

Potential Nursing Interventions	Indicated	Not Indicated
Ensure someone is with the patient at all times	☒	☐
Administer lorazepam per standing orders	☐	☒
Initiate intravenous access	☒	☐
Reorient the patient	☒	☐
Encourage multiple friends and family to visit for familiarity	☐	☒

The correct nursing interventions based on the patient's current clinical presentation include ensuring someone is with the patient at all times, initiating intravenous access, and reorienting the patient. Ensuring the patient has a family member or sitter with him throughout the delirium is important for patient safety. IV access is critical in getting IV fluids and IV antibiotics initiated per the medical provider's order. Lastly, calmly reorienting the patient is important for reminding the patient where he is and why he is there.

A benzodiazepine should not be administered in this situation, even with standing orders, without medical provider guidance. Clinical evidence shows that benzos can cause or worsen delirium in the non-alcoholic delirious patient. Also, while it is important to provide the patient with comforting things (e.g., familiar music, pictures of family and friends), overstimulation with multiple family members and friends can worsen the delirium. The goal of nursing interventions with a delirious patient is safety.

Question #5:

Nurses' Notes:

1310: Patient currently resting with wife present, but remains confused. Peripheral IV 22G placed in RUA after two attempts (patient removed the first one before the securement device was in place) with 0.9% normal saline flowing at 50 mL/hr. IV piperacillin-tazobactam started for suspected UTI while awaiting cultures. Facial grimacing noted during lower abdominal palpation, with no bladder distention noted. Discomfort noted upon CVA percussion.

Vital Signs:

1310: T: 101.2 °F

HR: 122 and regular

BP: 92/58

RR: 14 and unlabored

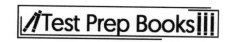

O2: 95% on RA

Lab Results:

WBC: 11,000/mm3 (normal: 4,500–10,000/mm3)

BUN: 42 mg/dL (normal: 14–23 mg/dL)

Creatinine: 1.1 mg/dL (normal: 0.7–1.3 mg/dL)

Sodium: 147 mEq/L (normal: 135–145 mEq/L)

Lactate: 3.6 mmol/L (normal: <2 mmol/L)

D-dimer: <0.5 mg/L (normal: <0.5 mg/L)

Considering the medical provider is already aware of the symptoms present with the suspected UTI, the nurse would need to focus on symptomatology that suggests a worsening of the condition. Discomfort during CVA percussion would indicate retroperitoneal inflammation, meaning the infection could have spread to the kidneys (pyelonephritis). Tachycardia, hypotension, and elevated lactate would need to be relayed to the medical provider immediately, as these results in conjunction with an active infection could mean urosepsis, a life-threatening condition.

Abdominal palpation discomfort and elevated WBC count are common symptoms with a standard UTI. The patient was febrile with the last medical provider assessment, so that would not be a new or worsening symptom. Elevated BUN (without a change in serum creatinine) and mild hypernatremia are common with dehydration and can also be present with UTIs.

Question #6:

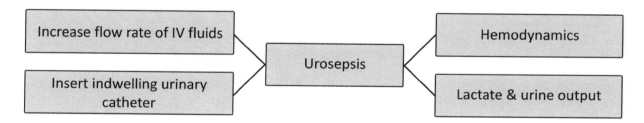

Based on the clinical data obtained, the patient is likely experiencing urosepsis. While the patient is likely experiencing pyelonephritis due to the CVA tenderness/discomfort, the increased lactate would be more concerning due to the potential for urosepsis. When serum lactate is elevated, perfusion becomes an issue. The most likely interventions would be to increase the flow rate (30 mL/kg administered in the first three hours is a standard order for sepsis—that will be MUCH higher than a 50 mL/hr flow rate) and to insert an indwelling urinary catheter. While infection source control would indicate the removal of an indwelling catheter, the importance of urine drainage related to the retention from the previous surgery, as well as the close monitoring of urine output with the septic patient, would require the patient to have an indwelling urinary catheter (with infection control taking precedence regarding insertion and maintenance). The nurse should also closely monitor the patient's hemodynamics, lactate, and urine output. CVA discomfort, WBC count, and serum sodium levels would be still monitored but would not be as critical in monitoring the worsening of sepsis as hemodynamics, serum lactate, and urine output.

221

Case Study #2

Question #1: Based on the initial nursing assessment, the nurse should expect the patient to be worked up for a stroke. The next steps that the nurse should anticipate are a STAT blood glucose level, getting the specific time that symptoms started, and a STAT non-contrast CT, STAT CMP, CBC, troponin, PTT, PT/INR. The most important aspects the nurse should understand regarding interventions for an acute stroke are time and type. If the patient is having an ischemic stroke, the tPA should be initiated within 90 minutes of the start of symptoms. That is why having a detailed timeline and ruling out a hemorrhagic stroke are of critical importance in the treatment of this patient.

Immediately initiating tPA is inappropriate. If the patient is having a hemorrhagic stroke, the tPA would worsen the bleeding. While time is of the essence, the result of the CT will need to be received before starting any clot-busting medications. Lastly, a gait assessment would be inappropriate, as the patient is experiencing notably obvious left-sided hemiparesis, which increases the risk for a fall.

Question #2:

Assessment Findings	Ischemic Stroke	Hemorrhagic Stroke	Transient Ischemic Attack (TIA)
Aphasia	☒	☒	☒
Shortened aPTT	☒	☐	☐
Neuronal cell death	☒	☒	☐
Hemiparesis	☒	☒	☒
Cerebral edema	☒	☒	☐

Symptoms such as aphasia and hemiparesis can present with ischemic strokes, hemorrhagic strokes, and TIAs. Since clotting is the hallmark in an ischemic stroke, aPTT (partial thromboplastin time) will be shortened. Neurological deficits such as cerebral edema and neuronal cell death are found with ischemic strokes and hemorrhagic strokes, but not TIAs. TIAs mimic stroke symptoms but do not cause actual neurological damage.

Question #3: Because the ECG strip shows that the patient is in atrial fibrillation, the patient is most likely experiencing an embolic stroke. Fibrillation in the atria results in the pooling of blood; stagnant blood is more likely to clot. Remember that an embolism is a blood clot that has broken off or traveled through the bloodstream and blocked a vessel, while a thrombus is a clot formation within the vessel that can impede or restrict blood flow.

Question #4: Contraindications to the administration of tPA include moderate thrombocytopenia, a history of subarachnoid hemorrhage(s), and the use of warfarin. Moderate thrombocytopenia is a platelet count of <100,000, which increases the risk for bleeding. A history of a subarachnoid hemorrhage and anticoagulation treatment (warfarin) also increases the risk for bleeding with thrombolytic therapy. Being over 70 years old is not a contraindication. Stroke symptoms being present for greater than 90 minutes, not 30 minutes, is the timeline for tPA. Lastly, prehypertension would not be a contraindication for tPA, but uncontrolled hypertension would be.

Question #5: Considering the patient experienced an ischemic stroke, the nurse should question anything that would increase the likelihood of clot formation. Estrogen increases the risk of both arterial and venous thrombosis formation. Holding the estradiol and consulting the medical provider is appropriate in this situation. Lisinopril

223

(treating HTN), alendronate (treating osteoporosis), clopidogrel (antiplatelet), and atorvastatin (treating hyperlipidemia) are all appropriate for a patient who recently experienced an ischemic stroke.

Question #6:

Discharge Plans	Indicated	Not Indicated
Reduce activity to decrease the likelihood of a fall.	☐	☒
Reduce the intake of red meats.	☒	☐
Ensure patient and all caregivers and loved ones are aware of the signs and symptoms of a stroke.	☒	☐
Reduce alcohol intake and if smoking, stop immediately.	☒	☐
Encourage daily intake of black/oolong/green tea for antioxidant purposes.	☐	☒

A patient that has experienced an ischemic stroke will receive detailed discharge information with follow-up appointments, referrals for certain therapies (PT, OT), and new medication orders. General discharge education includes reducing the intake of red meats, ensuring the patient and all caregivers and loved ones are aware of the signs and symptoms of a stroke, reducing alcohol intake, and smoking cessation if applicable. The discharge plan should not include reducing activity due to the likelihood of a fall. An activity plan will be established with the medical team, but the patient should not avoid activity due to a fall; rather, they should have safeguards in place for safe activity. The discharge plan should also not include the promotion of additional caffeine intake, as black/oolong/green teas are all high in caffeine.

Case Study #3

Question #1:

Antinuclear antibody test (ANA)	Thyroid panel with TSH

The patient is presenting with symptoms consistent with autoimmune dysfunction and/or an underactive thyroid. While a positive ANA test doesn't always mean autoimmune dysfunction, a positive ANA combined with autoimmune-related symptoms would indicate the presence of an autoimmune disorder. Also, a thyroid panel would be important to get an overall view of the thyroid gland's ability to secrete sufficient amounts of hormones. Obtaining a TSH in conjunction with a basic thyroid panel is important to detect any compensation by the thyroid. For example, if T3 and T4 levels are normal, but the thyroid stimulating hormone (TSH) is elevated, the patient is suffering from a form of hypothyroidism that wouldn't be detected without obtaining a TSH level.

Question #2:

Assessment Findings/Symptoms	Systemic Lupus Erythematosus (SLE)	Rheumatoid Arthritis (RA)	Multiple Sclerosis (MS)
Paresthesia	☒	☒	☒
Malar rash	☒	☐	☐
Swan neck deformity (phalanges)	☐	☒	☐
Anasarca	☒	☐	☐

Paresthesia (pins and needles sensation in the extremities) is a common characteristic of SLE, RA, and MS due to inflammation and, in the case of MS, neurologic dysfunction. A malar rash, or "butterfly rash," is consistent with a diagnosis of SLE. Swan neck deformity in one or more phalanges is consistent with worsening RA, as joints become permanently deformed. Lastly, anasarca (generalized edema) is typically associated with conditions that affect kidney function. Considering the kidneys can be heavily affected by SLE, anasarca could be seen with the SLE patient. Edema will be seen with the RA and potentially MS patient, but it will almost always be localized.

Question #3:

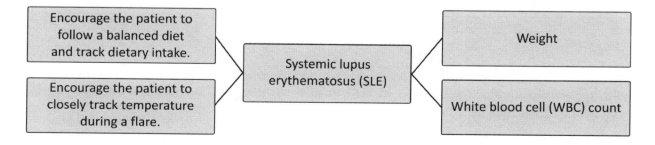

225

The diagnosis for a patient experiencing fatigue and coldness can be a number of disease processes. In the event of a malar rash, sometimes known as a butterfly rash, the medical team will likely closely assess the patient for systemic lupus erythematosus (SLE). A malar rash is a hallmark sign of SLE.

If the patient is diagnosed with SLE, the medical team should educate the patient on following a well-balanced diet while tracking dietary intake and closely tracking body temperature during an SLE flare. The patient would not need to remove clothing, as that would not result in thermoregulation and the patient would still be cold. The patient would also not need to perform sedentary activities to conserve energy for daily activities. Rather, the patient would need to perform exercise as tolerated and manage their daily activities accordingly to conserve energy.

Things to monitor in the SLE patient would include WBC count and weight, as the patient is at a higher risk of infection and a higher risk of fluid retention with potential kidney dysfunction.

Question #4: Immunosuppression increases the risk for developing malignancy, infection, and osteoporosis. Hyperglycemia, not hypoglycemia, is typically a concern, since corticosteroids are an immunosuppressive medication that results in elevated blood sugars. The patient taking immunosuppressive medications will also potentially be educated on vitamin D supplementation, as immune dysfunction typically results in lower serum levels of vitamin D.

Question #5:

Patient Statement	Understanding	No Understanding
"I can only have one active autoimmune disorder."	☐	☒
"I should avoid excess sun exposure."	☒	☐
"I need to increase my medication dosage during a flare."	☐	☒
"I should remain active as much as possible."	☒	☐
"I need to consult with my rheumatologist before starting any OTC or herbal medications."	☒	☐

Avoiding excess sun exposure, remaining active as much as possible, and consulting the rheumatologist prior to starting any new OTC or herbal medications would all indicate an understanding of the education provided. Excess sun exposure can worsen any skin condition related to SLE. Also, remaining active as much as possible is important for improving immune function—that being said, the patient will need to avoid excessively strenuous exercise, as that can reduce immune function.

Statements that the patient can only have one autoimmune disorder and needs to increase medication dosage during a flare are incorrect and would warrant further education. Patients can have multiple autoimmune disorders, which are sometimes difficult to differentiate because they can look very similar. While medication dosages will

226

likely be titrated during a flare, the patient should never adjust/alter medication dosages without the medical provider's order.

Question #6: A patient with an autoimmune disorder, especially SLE, will need to seek emergency care with a sharp pain in the neck/shoulder area, purpura, and scleral icterus.

A sharp pain in the neck/shoulder area can be referred pain resulting from pericarditis. Pericarditis is the most common cardiac dysfunction resulting from SLE. Purpura and petechiae would also warrant emergency treatment because the SLE patient is at a higher risk of developing systemic vasculitis, a life-threatening condition that results from the inflammation of blood vessels. Lastly, scleral icterus (yellowing of the sclera) can be a medical emergency for the SLE patient, as it can indicate autoimmune hepatitis or thrombotic thrombocytopenic purpura (TTP).

Increased fatigue by itself would not warrant an emergency department visit, along with aphthous ulcers (mouth ulcers) and hip pain with decreased ROM. While these symptoms can indicate a flare, they do not indicate an emergency condition.

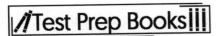

NCLEX-PN Practice Test #2

1. When reducing the risk of infection transmission, which personal protective equipment (PPE) should the nurse don first?
   a. Gloves
   b. Mask
   c. Gown
   d. Goggles

For the following question, please refer to this chart.

Patient Information	Initials: E. F. Age: 67 Sex: Male Height: 5'10" Weight: 300 lbs.		
Problems	Hypertension, obesity, atrial fibrillation, pre-diabetes		
Medications	COUMADIN, METAPROLOL SUCCINATE, METFORMIN, HCTZ		
Labs	RBCs: 6.0 WBC: 8.6 Triclycerides: 100 Glucose: 253	Hgb: 11.5 HDL: 70 Total cholesterol: 200 BUN: 30	Hct: 39 LDL: 130 A1c: 8.4 Creat: 1.2

2. The MD is starting insulin for this patient. You provide him with education about his insulin regimen for his diabetes. Appropriate education on side effects of insulin would include monitoring for signs and symptoms of what?
   a. Infection
   b. Electrolyte abnormalities
   c. Stroke
   d. Hypoglycemia

3. How should the nurse document the finding of a patient's elevated respiratory rate?
   a. Tachypnea
   b. Orthopnea
   c. Tachycardia
   d. Hyperthermia

4. A patient started having a reaction to a blood transfusion after approximately $\frac{1}{3}$ of the 500 cc of blood had been transfused. Approximately how many cc of blood had the patient received? Round to the nearest whole number.

_____ cc

5. What is an example of health promotion? Select all that apply.
    a. Collecting a thorough and accurate health history
    b. Obtaining accurate vital signs
    c. Providing information on smoking cessation
    d. Setting the bed alarm
    e. Educating patient on a healthy diet

6. The nurse is receiving reports at the beginning of the shift. One of the patients has been admitted to the hospital and is awaiting transfer to the ICU with an admitting diagnosis of obstructive shock. Which of the following findings are characteristic of obstructive shock?
    a. Jugular vein distention, peripheral edema, and pulmonary congestion
    b. Decreased urine output, increased BUN, and increased creatinine
    c. Chest pain, fatigue, and lightheadedness
    d. Problems with coordination, blurred vision, and partial paralysis

7. The nurse is caring for a sixty-two-year-old woman with myalgia, fever, dyspnea, and decreased breath sounds. To assist with a more rapid diagnosis for possible viral pneumonia, the nurse should prepare the patient for which of the following tests?
    a. Pulmonary function tests
    b. Blood cultures
    c. CT scan
    d. Rapid antigen testing

8. What defense mechanism, characterized by unconsciously inhibiting thoughts and transferring symptoms, is associated with conversion disorder?
    a. Projection
    b. Repression
    c. Reaction formation
    d. Intellectualization

9. The nurse is looking to locate the lower margin of the liver for assessment. Which abdominal quadrant should the nurse palpate? Place an X to mark your answer.

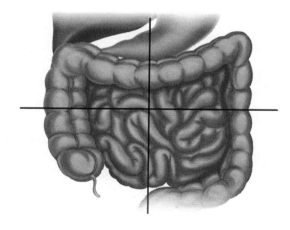

229

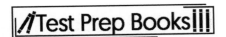

10. The nurse is caring for a patient with multiple medical issues and asks the patient if he has a signed advance directive. The patient wants to know how the nurse is involved with fulfilling his wishes. Which statement is most accurate concerning the nurse's role with an advance directive?
   a. The nurse supports the healthcare surrogate in deciding a choice not expressed by the patient.
   b. The nurse asks the next-of-kin to sign the advance directive when the patient is incapacitated.
   c. The nurse determines the patient's end-of-life wishes when he can reason and problem-solve.
   d. The nurse ensures that the advanced directive overrides the ability for medical care.

11. A patient with dementia periodically becomes restless and sets off the bed alarm due to attempts to get out of bed. The nurse is concerned that the patient will fall. What is the priority action for the nurse?
   a. Administering a benzodiazepine medication
   b. Ambulating the patient to the toilet
   c. Turning on the television as a diversion method
   d. Applying non-violent soft wrist restraints

12. Which of the following are examples of therapeutic communication? Select all that apply.
   a. Active listening
   b. Checking to see what time it is
   c. Folding your arms across your chest
   d. Asking clarifying questions
   e. Acknowledging the patient's feelings

13. Which of the following statements is true?
   a. As fluid levels decrease, electrolyte levels increase.
   b. As fluid levels increase, electrolyte levels increase.
   c. As fluid levels osmose, electrolyte levels diffuse.
   d. As fluid levels homogenize, electrolyte levels dissipate.

14. During an abdominal physical assessment of a patient with gastrointestinal distress, which action should the nurse perform second?
   a. Percussion
   b. Auscultation
   c. Inspection
   d. Palpation

15. The nurse percusses the patient's lungs during a focused assessment. Which sound aligns with a normal finding?
   a. Tympany
   b. Hyperresonance
   c. Dullness
   d. Resonance

16. The LPN/LVN is caring for a patient admitted for a left hip fracture under the supervision of a registered nurse (RN). The patient is experiencing severe pain. Select the response that best describes the role of the LPN/LVN in the plan of care.
   a. Collecting and documenting the patient's pain by asking the patient to describe duration, location, and severity
   b. Establishing a nursing diagnosis of acute pain related to left hip fracture as evidenced by a report of 8/10 pain and crying
   c. Determining the appropriate pharmacological and non-pharmacological pain measures required
   d. Initiating patient teaching of pain management when discharged to home

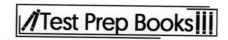

17. During morning report, the oncoming nurse learns from the outgoing night nurse that a 38-year-old patient has been requesting discharge all night. Upon walking into the patient room to meet them after report, the patient exclaims, "I want to go home now!" Which action should the nurse implement first?
   a. Page the physician for a consult for potential discharge
   b. Report suspected patient neglect to the nurse manager
   c. Administer a PRN medication for anxiety
   d. Explore the patient's reasoning for requesting discharge

18. Which fasting blood sugar level is considered within normal range for a healthy client?
   a. 54 mg/dL
   b. 82 mg/dL
   c. 110 mg/dL
   d. 123 mg/dL

19. Which infection control precautions should the nurse implement to reduce the risk of transmission for a patient diagnosed with active tuberculosis?
   a. Standard
   b. Contact
   c. Droplet
   d. Airborne

20. The nurse has an order to give 40 mEq of KCl IV to a patient over 4 hours. The KCl comes in bags with a concentration of 20 mEq/50mL. How many mL/hour should be given?

_____ mL/hr

21. Which graphic illustrates the PR interval of the ECG strip?

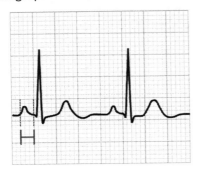

a.

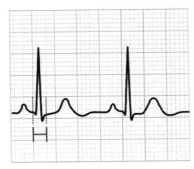

b.

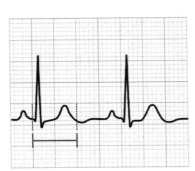

c.

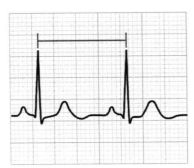

d.

22. What diet is best for the patient diagnosed with phenylketonuria (PKU)?
    a.   Low protein
    b.   High protein
    c.   Low folic acid
    d.   High folic acid

23. All of the following ethnic groups are at increased risk for sickle cell anemia EXCEPT?
    a.   African
    b.   Asian
    c.   Eastern European
    d.   Middle Eastern

24. While completing a physical assessment for suspected aortoiliac occlusive disease on a 68-year-old patient, which locations should the nurse assess blood pressure and pulse to detect a blockage? Select all that apply.
    a.   Thigh
    b.   Arm
    c.   Calf
    d.   Foot
    e.   Wrist

25. Which test should the nurse anticipate in a patient who reports excessive fatigue, depression, and weight gain?
    a.   Cortisol level
    b.   T4 and TSH levels
    c.   Blood glucose level
    d.   Aldosterone level

26. The nurse is caring for a client who recently underwent radiation therapy to his abdomen. Based on the location of the radiation, the nurse expects which of the following side effects?
    a.   Diarrhea
    b.   Fatigue
    c.   Trembling
    d.   Muscle aches

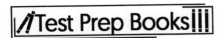

27. The nurse reviews the following ventilator strips. Which, if any, displays tidal volume?

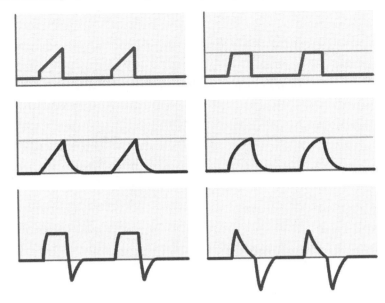

    a.   Tidal volume is not displayed
    b.   Ventilator strip 1 (top)
    c.   Ventilator strip 2 (middle)
    d.   Ventilator strip 3 (bottom)

28. Which type of consent provides the nurse with the opportunity to conduct cardiopulmonary resuscitation on an unaccompanied unconscious patient?
    a.   Expressed consent
    b.   Opt-out consent
    c.   Implied consent
    d.   Informed consent

29. Which medication does the nurse expect the patient with hyperthyroidism, an overactive thyroid condition, to be prescribed for disease management?
    a.   Synthroid® (levothyroxine)
    b.   Armour® Thyroid (thyroid desiccated)
    c.   Cytomel® (liothyronine sodium)
    d.   Tapazole® (methimazole)

30. Your patient's urine sample is positive for a multi-drug resistant organism (MDRO). Which of the following should you do? Select all that apply.
    a.   Prepare for Foley catheter insertion.
    b.   Use airborne precautions.
    c.   Notify the physician.
    d.   Use standard precautions.
    e.   Expect an order for antibiotics.

31. During a code, the nurse is retrieving equipment to collaborate with the physician to provide airway support for a 10-year-old pediatric patient that weighs 32 kg. Which equipment should the nurse collect? Select all that apply.
    a. Endotracheal tube, 6.5 cuffed
    b. Chest tube, 16
    c. Laryngoscope blade, 1 straight
    d. Endotracheal tube, 3.5 cuffed
    e. Laryngoscope blade, 4 straight/cuffed

32. Nurses are responsible for which of the following elements of informed consent?
    a. Identification of alternatives to the planned procedure
    b. Description of associated risks and benefits
    c. Explanation of the planned procedure or diagnostic test
    d. Assessment of the patient's understanding of the information that is provided

33. The nurse is caring for an 8-year-old patient who just received a diagnosis of a greenstick fracture. Which of the following does the nurse recognize as correlating with this diagnosis?

a.

b.

c.

d.

34. The nurse must always provide truthful engagements with patients. This is ethically substantiated by what principle?
    a. Fidelity
    b. Veracity
    c. Autonomy
    d. Distributive justice

35. In guiding practice, the nurse is aware of the nursing science and philosophy of law. What is this practice referred to as?
    a. Fundamentals of nursing
    b. Basic human rights
    c. Nursing process
    d. Nursing jurisprudence

36. Which of the following is NOT a risk factor for falls in the elderly?
    a. Using a cane to walk
    b. Inadequate lighting in a room
    c. Muscle weakness
    d. Slower reflexes

37. During breakfast, a patient with dysphagia states, "Well, I haven't choked yet," then knocks on the wooden side-table. The nurse educates the unlicensed assistive personnel regarding this behavior. What is knocking on wood an example of?
    a. Cultural norm
    b. Undoing
    c. Repetitive behavior
    d. Compulsion

38. Which routine treatment for cystic fibrosis facilitates movement of secretions from small to large airways for subsequent expulsion?
    a. Antibiotics
    b. The six-foot rule
    c. Pulmonary function tests
    d. Chest physiotherapy

39. Upon retiring from practice after forty years, the nurse shares with their novice colleagues that they have experienced numerous healthcare documentation methods throughout their career. What is new technology that replaces a previously established technology identified as?
    a. Protocol
    b. Disruptive
    c. Gateway
    d. Recovery

40. The nurse is caring for a patient with bacterial meningitis. Which classic findings of this disease should the nurse expect to find on assessment?
    a. Fever, nuchal rigidity, headache
    b. Fever, vomiting, photophobia
    c. Confusion, decreased level of consciousness, photophobia
    d. Fatigue, muscle aches, decreased appetite

41. When caring for a patient with autoimmune gastritis, the nurse should assess the patient for manifestations of which vitamin deficiency?
   a. Vitamin B-1
   b. Vitamin B-12
   c. Vitamin D
   d. Vitamin K

42. While implementing a plan of care for a patient experiencing alcohol withdrawal, which supplement should the nurse include?
   a. Calcium
   b. Magnesium
   c. Vitamin D
   d. Thiamine

43. During a level of consciousness assessment, the nurse finds no articulated verbal response with limited moaning, accompanied by arousal only after vigorous stimulation. How should the nurse document these findings?
   a. "The patient is lethargic."
   b. "The patient is obtunded."
   c. "The patient is stuporous."
   d. "The patient is comatose."

44. The nurse is reviewing the interpretation of the cardiac rhythm strip as sinus bradycardia. For this interpretation to be accurate, which heart rate must correlate with these findings?
   a. Below 60 beats per minute
   b. Above 150 beats per minute
   c. From 90–120 beats per minute
   d. From 121–150 beats per minute

45. The patient must make a decision regarding the next steps in their plan of treatment and in doing so, is weighing out two significantly different care options. Which ethical provision does the nurse practice when ensuring that the patient has the right to make self-directed decisions?
   a. Beneficence
   b. Autonomy
   c. Non-Maleficence
   d. Justice

46. Which position should the nurse help a patient into for pain management of acute appendicitis?
   a. High Fowler's position
   b. Fetal position
   c. Prone position
   d. Supine position

47. While working with a patient struggling with schizophrenia and paranoid symptoms, which non-pharmacological therapeutic aid should the nurse suggest to support symptom management?
   a. Book
   b. Television
   c. Instrumental music
   d. Food

48. The nurse case manager requests extra paid days from the third party payer for the patient's length of stay in order to continue providing covered treatment. What is this process an example of?
    a. Concurrent review
    b. Prior authorization
    c. Retrospective review
    d. Prospective review

49. What ethical principle sets forth that the nurse must maintain truthful engagements with their patient?
    a. Justice
    b. Veracity
    c. Nonmaleficence
    d. Beneficence

50. The nurse applies a condom catheter. Arrange the following steps in the order the nurse should perform them. Include all options.
    a. Assist patient to low Fowler's position
    b. Roll condom catheter onto penis
    c. Put urinary drainage bag on bed
    d. Place elastic adhesive around top of condom catheter

51. An aide enters a patient's room in response to the call light and sees a fire behind the television. What is the aide's first action?
    a. Activate the fire alarm.
    b. Use the nearest fire extinguisher.
    c. Move the patient to a safer location away from the room.
    d. Smother the fire with a blanket.

52. While caring for a patient with impaired renal function, the medical surgical nurse assesses ascites and dependent edema. Which electrolyte imbalance does the nurse suspect may be present?
    a. Hyperkalemia
    b. Hypokalemia
    c. Hypernatremia
    d. Hyponatremia

53. A nurse identifies that many collaborative peers have contributed to a possible sentinel event. Does the accredited hospital have to report the sentinel event to The Joint Commission after the nurse elevates their report of the incident?
    a. Yes, always report it.
    b. No, these are always internal only.
    c. Yes, in some cases.
    d. No, but it is encouraged.

54. The nurse prepares to suction nasopharyngeal secretions. Arrange the following steps in the order the nurse should perform them. Include all options.
    a. Attach catheter to suction tubing
    b. Don sterile gloves
    c. Assess breath sounds
    d. Power on suction device

55. While implementing a plan of care for a patient with heart failure, how should the nurse address activity?
   a. Increase activity and limit time in bed.
   b. Remain on bed rest.
   c. Alternate rest and activity.
   d. Ambulate to the bathroom only.

56. What color stool does the nurse expect to note from a patient struggling with a bile duct blockage?
   a. White
   b. Green
   c. Black
   d. Red

57. Which of the following patients is NOT at increased risk for the development of an embolism?
   a. A twenty-four-year-old with a broken femur
   b. An eighty-five-year-old female with a history of a stroke
   c. A sixty-two-year-old male with first-degree heart block
   d. A nineteen-year-old female two weeks postpartum

58. While working with a female patient 25 years older than the male nurse, the nurse notices that the patient repeatedly shames him and questions his intentions during interventions. After elevating this concern, the nurse case manager discussed this occurrence with the patient. During the discussion, the patient reported that the nurse reminds her of her son, who has ongoing struggles with honesty and maintaining commitments. What is this skewed engagement an example of?
   a. Regression
   b. Countertransference
   c. Transference
   d. Repression

59. A nurse is using standard precautions when caring for his patients. Standard precautions are best described as which of the following measures?
   a. Placing soiled linen in a designated container
   b. Using dedicated patient care equipment
   c. Ensuring that the patient is placed in a single patient room
   d. Reducing the transmission risk of airborne, droplet, and contact pathogens

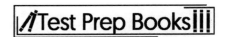

For the following question, please refer to this chart:

Name	Monica Latte
Problems	DIABETES MELLITUS (ICD-250.) HYPERTENSION, BENIGN ESSENTIAL (ICD-401.1)
Medications	HUMULIN INJ 70/30 20 u ac breakfast PRINIVIL TABS 20 MG 1 qd
History	Hyperglycemic Symptoms
Vital Signs	**Height**: 64 in. **Weight**: 140 lbs. **Temperature**: 98.0 deg F **Temperature site**: oral **Pulse**: 72 **Rhythm**: regular **Respiratory rate**: 16 **Blood pressure**: 158/90
Physical Exam	**General Appearance**: well developed, well nourished, no acute distress **Eyes**: conjunctiva and lids normal, PERRLA, EOMI, fundi WNL **Ears, Nose, Mouth, Throat**: TM clear, nares clear, oral exam WNL **Respiratory**: clear to auscultation and percussion, respiratory effort normal **Cardiovascular**: regular rate and rhythm, S1-S2, no murmur, rub or gallop, no bruits, peripheral pulses normal and symmetric, no cyanosis, clubbing, edema or varicosities **Skin**: clear, good turgor, color WNL, no rashes, lesions, or ulcerations **Problems** (including changes): Blood pressure is lower. Feet are inspected and there are no callouses, no compromised skin. No vision complaints. **Impression**: Sub optimal sugar, control with retinopathy and neuropathy, high glucometer readings. Will work harder on diet. Will increase insulin by 2 units.

Metabolic Panel			
	ALK PHOS	72	35-100
	BG RANDOM	125 mg/dl	70-125
	BUN	16 mg/dl	7-25
	CALCIUM	9.6 mg/dl	8.2-10.2
	CHLORIDE	101 mmol/l	96-109
	CO2	27 mmol/l	23-29
	CREATININE	0.7 mg/dl	0.6-1.2
Metabolic Panel	**PO4**	2.9 mg/dl	2.5-4.5
	POTASSIUM	4.5 mmol/l	3.5-5.3
	SGOT	31 U/L	0-40
	BILI TOTAL	0.7 mg/dl	0.0-1.3
	URIC ACID	4.8 mg/dl	3.4-7.0
	LDH, TOTAL	136 IU/L	0-200
	SODIUM	135 mmol/l	135-145

HbA1c Test	HbA1c level 6.0%
Lipid Profile	Cholesterol, Total: 210 mg/dl Triglycerides: 236 mg/dl HDL Cholesterol: 36 LDL Cholesterol: 107

60. You are seeing the patient M.L. in a physician's office. You take her blood pressure, chart it, and confirm that she is taking her daily prescribed medications. What action should you anticipate from the physician?
   a. They will increase the dose of the current blood pressure medication.
   b. They will admit the patient to the hospital for blood pressure control.
   c. They will make no medication changes; the patient is already taking a blood pressure medication.
   d. They will discontinue the blood pressure medication because the blood pressure has improved since the last visit.

61. The nurse is attending an in-service on the safe administration of high-risk medications. In order to reduce the risk of patient harm, what is an important concept of high-risk medications?
   a. The patient should have specific prescribers according to each drug class.
   b. Transitions of care promote safety due to increased communication by the healthcare team.
   c. Medication workarounds incorporate a streamlined approach to nursing workflow.
   d. Separate storage areas are designated if the medication needs to be refrigerated.

62. A patient is admitted with a diagnosis of heart block. The nurse is aware that the pacemaker of the heart is which of the following?
   a. AV node
   b. Purkinje fibers
   c. SA node
   d. Bundle of His

63. A fifty-five-year-old male is undergoing an endoscopy to discover the source of his hematemesis. The gastroenterologist encounters an active, bleeding lesion. What procedure using the application of heat to seal the lesion will probably be used next?
   a. Banding
   b. Biopsy
   c. Angioplasty
   d. Cauterization

64. What score represents the degree to which a patient's psychological symptoms impact their daily life?
   a. Apgar score
   b. AIMS score
   c. GAF score
   d. Withdrawal protocol score

65. The nurse is educating a patient regarding their anemic state. Which organ is the source of the bone's failure to produce red blood cells?
   a. Stomach
   b. Kidney
   c. Gallbladder
   d. Hypothalamus

66. The nurse is administering total parenteral nutrition (TPN) to the patient for the first time. He knows that he should administer the medication at which of the following rates?
   a. Slowly, at 50 percent of the prescribed dosage
   b. Quickly, at double the prescribed dosage
   c. Quickly, at three times the prescribed dosage
   d. Slowly, at 25 percent of the prescribed dosage

242

67. The nurse is looking over the patient's lab values for the day. He notices that one lab parameter has gone up significantly, signaling a possible infectious process at work. Which lab parameter is he likely drawing this conclusion from?
    a. Blood urea nitrogen
    b. Hematocrit
    c. Neutrophils
    d. Sodium level

68. A patient walks into the emergency department and collapses. The nurse identifies the condition as cardiopulmonary arrest, and resuscitation efforts are started. The nurse understands that, in addition to CPR, defibrillation, and the ACLS protocol, the most important factor for patient survival is which of the following?
    a. Administration of oxygen
    b. Establishing IV access
    c. Inserting a Foley catheter
    d. Time between the collapse and the start of resuscitation efforts

69. The nurse is reviewing new medication orders for a patient with multiple diagnoses, including pernicious anemia. As the nurse has a clear understanding of this type of anemia, which treatment do they suspect to see ordered via subcutaneous injection for this patient?
    a. Iron
    b. Vitamin B-12
    c. Packed RBCs
    d. Stem cells

70. The doctor has ordered a nasogastric (NG) tube to be placed by the nurse for gastric lavage. After placing the NG, the nurse expects which of the following tests to be performed to confirm the placement of the tube?
    a. Aspiration of laryngeal secretions for pH testing
    b. Chest radiograph
    c. Abdominal ultrasound
    d. Manual palpation of the gastric body for the catheter tip

71. During the morning community meeting for the adult intensive outpatient program, the clients are identifying their personal goals for the week. Which goal identified by the client struggling with substance abuse does the nurse recognize as realistic?
    a. Use the substance of choice in moderation.
    b. Stop needing to connect with their sponsor.
    c. Avoid places where they typically have used substances in the past.
    d. Use self-control to prevent all cravings.

72. The nurse is educating a 43-year-old patient regarding their fracture, which has resulted in the fragmentation of the bones in their right hand after a motor vehicle accident. Which type of fracture represents this finding?
    a. Compound fracture
    b. Oblique fracture
    c. Comminuted fracture
    d. Greenstick fracture

73. Identify the ulna.

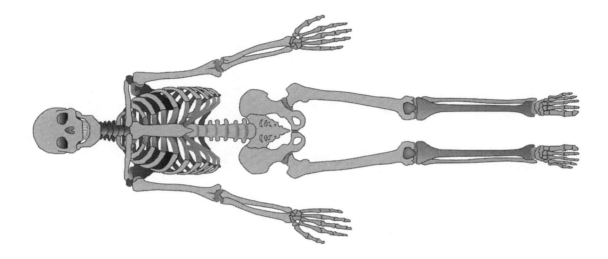

74. The nurse is facilitating a community pediatric health course and including Erikson's Psychosocial Theory to describe stages of development. Arrange the following stages in ascending order by typical age of experience. Include all options.
   a. Autonomy vs. shame
   b. Trust vs. mistrust
   c. Initiative vs. guilt
   d. Industry vs. inferiority

75. Of the following tasks, which one is NOT considered "dirty"?
   a. Changing a diaper
   b. Assisting with oral care
   c. Changing a wound dressing
   d. Helping a patient get dressed

76. The nurse auscultates the patient's heart sounds and notes both an S3 and an S4 sound. Which rhythm aligns with this finding?
   a. Still's Murmur
   b. Regular Rhythm
   c. Summation Gallop
   d. Systolic Murmur

77. The nurse notices a patient's medication list contains a drug that is likely to lower her pulmonary vascular resistance. Which type of medicine is the nurse likely looking at to draw this conclusion?
   a. Diuretic
   b. Morphine
   c. Nitrate
   d. Calcium channel blocker

78. The community health nurse understands that which child is most at risk for developing bronchiolitis?
   a. A six-month-old child
   b. A two-year-old child
   c. A child in kindergarten
   d. A high school student

79. The pediatric nurse is caring for a child who has had three seizures lasting five to eight minutes over a thirty-minute period. The nurse understands that the child is experiencing which of the following conditions?
   a. Generalized seizures
   b. Focal seizures
   c. Status epilepticus
   d. Postictal state

80. The nurse is caring for a thirty-eight-year-old male who presents with marked left-sided scrotal swelling and distention of the abdomen. The nurse understands that which of the following is NOT an expected finding in this patient?
   a. Diarrhea
   b. Tachycardia
   c. Rebound tenderness
   d. BUN 27

81. The nurse recognizes that a patient is having a severe reaction to Enoxaparin. What medication should be given to neutralize this medication and inhibit this reaction?
   a. Pilocarpine
   b. Romazicon
   c. Naloxone
   d. Protamine

82. Before administering Catapres® (clonidine), which action does the nurse delegate to the unlicensed assistive personnel (UAP)?
   a. Assist the patient with eating their meal.
   b. Ask the patient for the time of their last bowel movement.
   c. Take the patient's vital signs.
   d. Deliver a heated blanket to the patient's lower extremities.

83. A 57-year-old male comes in for an annual check-up. Current medications include HCTZ 25 mg PO daily. You anticipate that the provider will prescribe what medication for this patient?

Patient Information	Name: Glen Delaney Age: 57 Sex: Male
Vital Signs	HR: 70 Respiratory Rate: 20 BP: 122/75 SpO2: 99%
Labs	RBC 5.0, Hgb 13.5, Hct 45, WBC 8, HDL 60, LDL 165, Triclycerides 200, Total Cholesterol 225, A1c 6.2, BUN 20, Creat 0.6
Medications	HCTZ 25 mg PO daily

    a.   Lovastatin 20 mg PO daily
    b.   Sliding scale insulin
    c.   Metoprolol 25 mg PO daily
    d.   Ferrous sulfate 325 mg PO TID

84. The nurse is caring for a four-patient assignment. Which nursing activity is most appropriate to delegate to the nursing assistant?
    a. Determining whether the patient can hold a toothbrush to provide oral care
    b. Providing a bed bath to a cognitively impaired patient with a stage 3 sacral pressure injury
    c. Explaining the importance of a turning schedule to the family
    d. Feeding a patient whose diet was advanced from NPO after aspirating

85. Patients on the cusp of respiratory failure may exhibit which of the following early signs and symptoms?
    a.   Decreased respiratory rate
    b.   Unconsciousness
    c.   Cyanosis
    d.   Agitation

86. The nurse is caring for a patient with myasthenia gravis. Altered transmission of which of the following neurotransmitters would the nurse understand guides the care of this patient?
    a.   Serotonin
    b.   Dopamine
    c.   Acetylcholine
    d.   Norepinephrine

87. Your patient is complaining of pain at their IV site. You note phlebitis at the insertion site. What else should you do? Select all that apply.
   a. Tell the patient you will assess them again later.
   b. Discontinue the IV.
   c. Start IV fluids.
   d. Apply a warm compress.
   e. Start a new IV in a different location.

88. An English-speaking nurse is completing a history and physical on a newly admitted patient. How should the nurse communicate with a Spanish-speaking patient?
   a. Speak loud and slowly
   b. Use a monotone voice to avoid inflection
   c. Phone the interpreter line for assistance
   d. Request that a family member translate the discussion

89. The nurse is caring for a patient with diabetic ketoacidosis. Which of the following statements is consistent with the cause of this disorder?
   a. This condition results from having excess insulin in the body.
   b. Poor management of diabetes can cause this disorder.
   c. Reduced glucose ingestion can lead to this disorder.
   d. Taking too much oral anti-diabetic medication can cause this disorder.

90. What stage is this pressure ulcer?

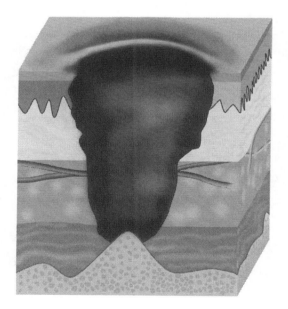

   a. Stage 1
   b. Stage 2
   c. Stage 3
   d. Stage 4

91. Which communication technique hinders the discussion between the nurse and the patient?
    a. Empathetic engagement
    b. Open-ended questions
    c. Nurse-focused answers
    d. Restating

92. The nurse is viewing a record that contains diverse information from all providers involved in the patient's care. What type of communication system is the nurse using?
    a. Electronic health record (EHR)
    b. Electronic medication administration record (EMAR)
    c. Electronic medical record (EMR)
    d. Personal health record (PHR)

93. While providing education to a new graduate nurse, the senior nurse details the progression of intestinal obstruction leading to death. Arrange the following steps in the order the nurse should teach them. Include all options.
    a. Necrosis
    b. Ischemia
    c. Shock
    d. Mechanical obstruction

94. You are preparing to go into a patient's room to administer their morning medications. List the order in which the following things should occur:
    a. Confirm the patient's name and date of birth.
    b. Administer the medication.
    c. Confirm the five rights of medication administration.
    d. Educate the patient about medication side effects.

95. A patient calls the office to ask how many tablespoons of liquid cough syrup to give her child. The dose is 45 mL. How many tablespoons should she give? Round to the nearest tenth.

_____ Tbsp

96. Which type of social norm is characterized by a moral or ethical component?
    a. Taboos
    b. Group norms
    c. Folkways
    d. Mores

97. Where should the nurse place the diaphragm of their stethoscope to assess the patient's apical pulse? Place an X to mark your answer.

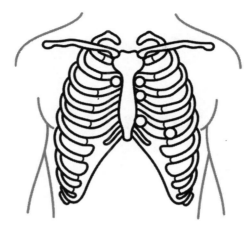

98. Which area of the body is the most distal to the heart? Place an X to mark your answer.

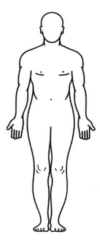

99. Which stage of disease is a patient noted to be experiencing when they are asymptomatic following exposure to a pathogenic organism?
    a. Incubation period
    b. Prodromal period
    c. Acute period
    d. Convalescence period

100. During a respiratory physical assessment of a patient with shortness of breath, which action should the nurse perform second?
    a. Inspection
    b. Percussion
    c. Palpation
    d. Auscultation

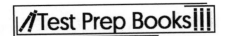
101. Which image of the heart should the nurse use to provide patient education on atrioventricular septal defect?

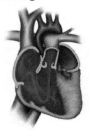

a.

b.

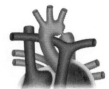

c.

d.

102. Review the electronic medication administration record. Which medication, if any, should be administered for pain management?

Electronic Medication Administration Record (EMAR)

Tab 1, EMAR Order 1 Carbamazepine 800 po qam

Tab 2, EMAR Order 2 Tramadol 50 mg po q6h

Tab 3, EMAR Order 3 Valsartan 80 mg po qam

    a. The patient needs a medication order for pain management.
    b. Carbamazepine
    c. Tramadol
    d. Valsartan

103. While looking through the orders for his patients, the nurse sees that his eighty-seven-year-old patient has been discharged by the provider. All the statements about the patient discharge are true EXCEPT which of the following?

a. Early patient discharge planning decreases the risk of falling after hospitalization.

b. The medication reconciliation process at discharge decreases the risk of medication error.

c. A multidisciplinary approach in patient discharge increases the risk of readmissions.

d. A delayed discharge increases the risk of hospital-acquired infections.

Case Study #1

A nurse in the ED is caring for a 26-year-old male presenting with delusional behavior and hallucinations.

Nurses' Notes:

2114: Patient presents to the ED following an altercation with law enforcement, during which the patient stated that the police officers were talking about him and trying to follow him home. When the officers attempted to calm him down, the patient became combative and yelled that they were a part of the New World Order and wanted to kill him and his family. Upon arrival, the patient is incoherent with occasional word salad. The patient has no pertinent medical history, and his next of kin (patient's mother) answered PMH and medication related questions.

2120: Patient refuses any assessments or treatment. Unable to obtain vital signs or start an IV. Patient states, "No one is touching me because you all work for them."

Question #1: While the patient is experiencing acute psychosis with an unknown etiology, which psychiatric condition are these symptoms consistent with that would require additional evaluation? Which medication should the nurse anticipate administering? Choose one answer from each column.

Psychiatric Condition		Medication(s)
Dissociative identity disorder		Haloperidol
Schizophrenia		Meperidine
Bipolar disorder		Diphenhydramine
Histrionic personality disorder		Lithium

Nurses' Notes:

2114: Patient presents to the ED following an altercation with law enforcement, during which the patient stated that the police officers were talking about him and trying to follow him home. When the officers attempted to calm him down, the patient became combative and yelled that they were a part of the New World Order and wanted to kill him and his family. Upon arrival, the patient is incoherent with occasional word salad. The patient has no pertinent medical history, and his next of kin (patient's mother) answered PMH and medication related questions.

2120: Patient refuses any assessments or treatment. Unable to obtain vital signs or start an IV. Patient states, "No one is touching me because you all work for them."

Question #2: During the psychiatric workup, the medical team needs to rule out any differential diagnoses. What are the differential diagnoses that should be ruled out prior to further treatment? Select all that apply.

- Fibromyalgia
- Substance abuse or withdrawal
- Hypermagnesemia
- Intracranial space-occupying lesion

- Hypoglycemia
- Trauma

Nurses' Notes:

2114: Patient presents to the ED following an altercation with law enforcement, during which the patient stated that the police officers were talking about him and trying to follow him home. When the officers attempted to calm him down, the patient became combative and yelled that they were a part of the New World Order and wanted to kill him and his family. Upon arrival, the patient is incoherent with occasional word salad. The patient has no pertinent medical history, and his next of kin (patient's mother) answered PMH and medication related questions.

2120: Patient refuses any assessments or treatment. Unable to obtain vital signs or start an IV. Patient states, "No one is touching me because you all work for them."

Question #3: While a patient cannot be diagnosed with schizophrenia with one occasion of acute psychosis, the psychiatric team is establishing a follow-up and treatment plan that is appropriate for schizophrenia. Considering schizophrenia is diagnosed off of an assessment of symptoms, the psychiatric team will need to be prepared to group the schizophrenic symptoms accordingly. Click to specify the type of each schizophrenic symptoms listed. Each row must have one selection.

Schizophrenia Symptom	Positive	Negative	Cognitive
Hallucinations	☐	☐	☐
Anhedonia	☐	☐	☐
Impaired memory	☐	☐	☐
Word salad	☐	☐	☐
Apathy	☐	☐	☐

Nurses' Notes:

2114: Patient presents to the ED following an altercation with law enforcement, during which the patient stated that the police officers were talking about him and trying to follow him home. When the officers attempted to calm him down, the patient became combative and yelled that they were a part of the New World Order and wanted to kill him and his family. Upon arrival, the patient is incoherent with occasional word salad. The patient has no pertinent medical history, and his next of kin (patient's mother) answered PMH and medication related questions.

2120: Patient refuses any assessments or treatment. Unable to obtain vital signs or start an IV. Patient states, "No one is touching me because you all work for them."

2125: Per MD order, attempted to administer haloperidol IM, but the patient became extremely combative and threatened to stab the next person that came into his room.

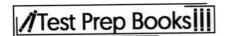

Question #4: Complete the following sentences by selecting the most appropriate option.

The nurse should request assistance and immediately:

- a. Obtain an order to place the patient in confinement.
- b. Obtain an order to restrain the patient.
- c. Use therapeutic communication to reorient the patient.

The nurse should:

- a. Obtain a transfer order to the psychiatric unit.
- b. Notify the medical provider or designated staff to assess the patient.
- c. Obtain a STAT psychiatric evaluation.

The nurse should obtain this within:

- a. One hour
- b. Four hours
- c. Eight hours

Nurses' Notes:

2114: Patient presents to the ED following an altercation with law enforcement, during which the patient stated that the police officers were talking about him and trying to follow him home. When the officers attempted to calm him down, the patient became combative and yelled that they were a part of the New World Order and wanted to kill him and his family. Upon arrival, the patient is incoherent with occasional word salad. The patient has no pertinent medical history, and his next of kin (patient's mother) answered PMH and medication related questions.

2120: Patient refuses any assessments or treatment. Unable to obtain vital signs or start an IV. Patient states, "No one is touching me because you all work for them."

2125: Per MD order, attempted to administer haloperidol IM, but the patient became extremely combative and threatened to stab the next person that came into his room.

Physician Orders:

1/24 @2131: Apply four-point soft restraints for violent behavior.

Question #5: With the patient physically restrained, the nurse must be prepared to follow strict guidelines for patient safety while restrained. Select the following statement(s) that are correct regarding caring for a patient in physical restraints. Select all that apply.

- A new order is needed every time restraints are discontinued and restarted.
- Toileting should be offered every four hours.
- Restraints are to be removed for ROM exercises every two hours.
- PRN restraint orders can be used for consistently combative/violent patients.
- A new order is needed every 24 hours.
- Circulation of restrained extremities should be assessed every hour.

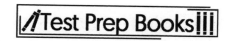

Nurses' Notes:

2114: Patient presents to the ED following an altercation with law enforcement, during which the patient stated that the police officers were talking about him and trying to follow him home. When the officers attempted to calm him down, the patient became combative and yelled that they were a part of the New World Order and wanted to kill him and his family. Upon arrival, the patient is incoherent with occasional word salad. The patient has no pertinent medical history, and his next of kin (patient's mother) answered PMH and medication related questions.

2120: Patient refuses any assessments or treatment. Unable to obtain vital signs or start an IV. Patient states, "No one is touching me because you all work for them."

2125: Per MD order, attempted to administer haloperidol IM, but the patient became extremely combative and threatened to stab the next person that came into his room.

2135: Per MD order, the patient was placed in four-point soft restraints for violent behavior. IM haloperidol administered via right ventrogluteal. Restraint protocol initiated to ensure patient comfort/safety and removal of restraints as soon as medically appropriate.

Restraint Documentation:

2148: Bilateral radial and dorsalis pedis pulses remain +2. Passive ROM performed with no discomfort or resistance.

2200: Bilateral radial and dorsalis pedis pulses remain +2. Passive ROM performed with no discomfort or resistance.

2211: Bilateral radial and dorsalis pedis pulses remain +2. Passive ROM performed with no discomfort, but mild resistance.

2224: Bilateral radial and dorsalis pedis pulses remain +2. Passive ROM performed with no discomfort, but mild resistance.

2238: Bilateral radial and dorsalis pedis pulses remain +2. Passive ROM performed with no discomfort, but mild resistance.

2305: Bilateral radial and dorsalis pedis pulses remain +2. Passive ROM performed with moderate resistance.

2330: Bilateral radial and dorsalis pedis pulses remain +2. Restraints removed to perform active ROM and allow the patient to void. When the restraints were removed, rigidity noted with resistance in bilateral upper extremities. While the patient remains incomprehensible, he also appears drowsy.

Vital Signs:

2145:   T: 97.2 °F axillary

HR: 97 and regular

BP: 134/78

RR: 20 and unlabored

O2: 98% on RA

2252:   T: 101.1 °F axillary

        HR: 122 and regular

        BP: 142/89

        RR: 21 and shallow

        O2: 95% on RA

Question #6: Based on the new symptoms the patient is experiencing, select what the patient is MOST LIKELY experiencing:

- Septic shock
- Normal side effects of haloperidol
- Progression of acute psychosis
- Neuroleptic malignant syndrome
- Panic/anxiety attack
- Malignant hyperthermia

Case Study #2

The nurse in the pediatric clinic is providing care to a three-year-old female with the child's mother present.

Nurses' Notes:

9/26 - 0930: Patient is a three-year-old female present for a sick visit with reported vomiting and a low-grade fever (all subjective data obtained from the child's mother). According to the child's mother, the patient began vomiting 48 hours ago and has had a fever for the past "day or so." Upon assessment, a non-blanchable maculopapular rash is noted on the sacrum. The mother states that the child (who is potty trained) has had to go back to wearing diapers for the past two days since she has been mostly bedbound. Patient's mother stated she noticed the rash earlier this morning, but it was slightly smaller.

Patient appears lethargic, but responsive and able to follow age-appropriate commands. Mild pallor noted with cap refill <3 seconds. Mother states that the patient has had two wet diapers in the past 12 hours, but she has been unable to keep fluids down. Vital signs: T 101.1 °F oral, HR 114 and regular, BP 99/67, RR 42 and unlabored but shallow, O2 96% on RA.

Question #1: Select the assessment findings that the nurse should report to the pediatrician. Select all that apply.

- The rash is maculopapular.
- Vomiting
- Mild pallor
- Cap refill
- The rash is non-blanchable.
- Temperature
- Heart rate
- Urine output

Nurses' Notes:

9/26 - 0930: Patient is a three-year-old female present for a sick visit with reported vomiting and a low-grade fever (all subjective data obtained from the child's mother). According to the child's mother, the patient began vomiting 48 hours ago and has had a fever for the past "day or so." Upon assessment, a non-blanchable maculopapular rash is noted on the sacrum. The mother states that the child (who is potty trained) has had to go back to wearing diapers for the past two days since she has been mostly bedbound. Patient's mother stated she noticed the rash earlier this morning, but it was slightly smaller.

Patient appears lethargic, but responsive and able to follow age-appropriate commands. Mild pallor noted with cap refill <3 seconds. Mother states that the patient has had two wet diapers in the past 12 hours, but she has been unable to keep fluids down. Vital signs: T 101.1 °F oral, HR 114 and regular, BP 99/67, RR 42 and unlabored but shallow, O2 96% on RA.

Question #2: Which symptom would require the pediatric office to refer the patient to the ED immediately?

- Increased temperature
- Diarrhea
- Limited neck flexion
- Rash spreading to back
- Chills/shivering

Question #3: Based on the clinical presentation of the patient, for which condition should the medical team further assess? Also, what are the potential nursing assessments/interventions for the specific medical condition?

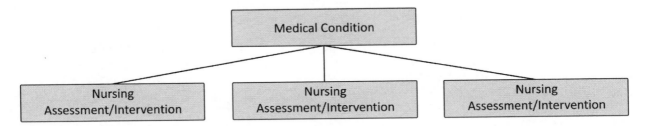

Medical Condition	Nursing Assessment/Intervention
Lyme disease	Keep the patient's head elevated and midline
Meningitis	Assess for nuchal rigidity
Respiratory syncytial virus (RSV)	Apply cool compress to maculopapular rash
Cystic fibrosis	Place the patient in a supine position
Coxsackie viral infection (HFMD)	Initiate supplemental oxygen via nasal cannula
Gastroenteritis	Reduce external stimuli

Nurses' Notes:

9/26 - 0930: Patient is a three-year-old female present for a sick visit with reported vomiting and a low-grade fever (all subjective data obtained from the child's mother). According to the child's mother, the patient began vomiting 48 hours ago and has had a fever for the past "day or so." Upon assessment, a non-blanchable maculopapular rash is noted on the sacrum. The mother states that the child (who is potty trained) has had to go back to wearing diapers for the past two days since she has been mostly bedbound. Patient's mother stated she noticed the rash earlier this morning, but it was slightly smaller.

Patient appears lethargic, but responsive and able to follow age-appropriate commands. Mild pallor noted with cap refill <3 seconds. Mother states that the patient has had two wet diapers in the past 12 hours, but she has been unable to keep fluids down. Vital signs: T 101.1 °F oral, HR 114 and regular, BP 99/67, RR 42 and unlabored but shallow, O2 96% on RA.

9/26 - 0942: Mother reports to nurses' station saying she forgot to say the patient just got off antibiotics for a bilateral ear infection. She reported that the patient had to have two rounds of antibiotics, as the first round didn't clear the infection.

Question #4: Using nursing judgment based on the clinical presentation of the patient and reported data, select what the nurse should be closely monitoring for that would indicate the specific medical condition is worsening. Select all that apply.

- Stupor
- Muscular atrophy
- Seizure
- Paralysis
- Acute hypervigilance
- Hyperphagia

The patient is being transferred to a pediatric ED for further evaluation and treatment. The pediatric ED nurse has received the transfer report from the pediatric clinic and just received a verbal plan of care from the ED physician that included the following:

- Lumbar puncture for CSF collection (if not contraindicated)
- Initiate empiric antimicrobial therapy and dexamethasone (if not contraindicated)
- Assess for increased intracranial pressure (ICP)
- Obtain blood cultures, CBC, CMP, coag test

Question #5: Now that the nurse is prepared with the general plan of care to be provided upon arrival, what is the correct order of steps that should be taken?

Lumbar puncture for CSF collection (if not contraindicated)		1.
Initiate empiric antimicrobial therapy and dexamethasone (if not contraindicated)		2.
Assess for increased intracranial pressure (ICP)		3.
Obtain blood cultures, CBC, CMP, and coag test		4.

The patient is being discharged home after seven days of IV ampicillin q6h for a diagnosis of *H. influenzae* bacterial meningitis.

Question #6: Once the nurse has provided discharge education, select the following statements from the patient's mother that would indicate she understood the education provided.

Statement	Understanding	No Understanding
"The best way to stop the spread of infection is hand hygiene."	☐	☐
"Antibiotics are the only cure for meningitis."	☐	☐
"Routine childhood vaccines can help prevent certain types of meningitis."	☐	☐
"Meningitis is not serious in the adult population due to developed immune function."	☐	☐
"She may have some temporary hearing issues from the swelling."	☐	☐

Case Study #3

The nurse on the med-surg unit is discharging a 68-year-old male patient following a transmetatarsal amputation of the left foot. The patient will be placed on home health services for wound care.

Past Medical History

Surgical History:

- Tonsillectomy est. 1982
- Wisdom tooth extraction est. 1990

Medical History:

- Diagnosed with HTN in 2013—prescribed amlodipine 10 mg daily—patient reports taking medication inconsistently
- MVA leading to spinal cord injury resulting in paraplegia
- Diagnosed with T2DM in 2017—currently noncompliant with scheduled and sliding-scale insulin regimen

Admission Note:

Patient admitted for scheduled transmetatarsal amputation of the left foot following diabetic complications. Patient reports noncompliance with diabetes medications, also states that he doesn't check his blood sugar daily. He reports only checking his blood sugar once a week or when he "feels off." Patient is also noncompliant with dietary standards, stating he eats one to two small meals a day that consist mostly of refined carbs and/or fast food. BMI is 27. Patient reports short spurts of activity throughout the day, but he is able to resituate in bed/recliner. Patient also reports frequent stress incontinence, requiring him to wear incontinence underwear consistently.

Question #1: Highlight the FOUR statements/diagnoses/medical observations that significantly increase the patient's risk of a pressure injury.

Question #2: Once the discharge education has been provided by the nurse, determine which of the following statements from the patient indicate he understood the education provided.

Patient Statement	Understanding	No Understanding
"I need to make sure I eat minimal protein."	☐	☐
"I need to make positional changes at least every two hours in the daytime."	☐	☐
"I need to report to the ED if I notice any signs of a sacral wound."	☐	☐

Patient Statement	Understanding	No Understanding
"I need to contact the home health agency if I notice a bad smell coming from my amputation site."	☐	☐
"If I don't follow my daily diabetic medication schedule, I need to at least follow my sliding-scale orders."	☐	☐

The home health nurse is admitting a 68-year-old male patient following a transmetatarsal amputation of the left foot for daily wound care.

Question #3: What would be early indicators of a pressure injury? Select all that apply.

- Keloids at site
- Clammy skin at site
- Erythema
- Petechiae
- Induration
- Skin appears shiny at site
- Pallor

Progress Notes - Skin Assessment

10/23 @0934: Amputation site cleaned and dressed per MD order. Incision is well approximated with no erythema, edema, drainage, or odor. Patient tolerated wound care with minimal pain, reporting a verbal pain scale of 2/10. Percocet 7.5 mg/325 mg administered 30 minutes prior to wound care. Upon general skin assessment, non-blanchable erythema and mild induration noted on sacrum. Wound measurements are: L 10.1 cm/W 6.8 cm/D <0.1 cm. Awaiting further orders from MD regarding wound care.

Question #4: After consulting with the medical provider, the stage 1 pressure injury requires treatment to prevent the progression of the wound. Select if the following medical interventions below are indicated or not indicated for this stage of wound.

Potential Medical Interventions	Indicated	Not Indicated
Clean site daily with hydrogen peroxide.	☐	☐
Remove pressure from the site at all times.	☐	☐
Wet-to-dry dressing changes BID	☐	☐
Apply skin barrier.	☐	☐
Assess for negative pressure wound therapy.	☐	☐

Potential Medical Interventions	Indicated	Not Indicated
Pack the wound with iodoform.	☐	☐

Progress Notes - Skin Assessment

10/23 @0934: Amputation site cleaned and dressed per MD order. Incision is well approximated with no erythema, edema, drainage, or odor. Patient tolerated wound care with minimal pain, reporting a verbal pain scale of 2/10. Percocet 7.5 mg/325 mg administered 30 minutes prior to wound care. Upon general skin assessment, non-blanchable erythema and mild induration noted on sacrum. Wound measurements are: L 10.1 cm/W 6.8 cm/D <0.1 cm. Awaiting further orders from MD regarding wound care.

10/24 @0821: Amputation site cleaned and dressed per MD order. Incision site maintains well approximated with no erythema, edema, drainage, or odor. Patient reported forgetting to take his pain medication, so Percocet 7.5 mg/325 mg administered upon arrival. Patient reported a verbal pain score of 6/10 during wound care, but reduced it to 2/10 prior to the end of the skilled nursing visit. Upon assessment of stage 1 sacral pressure injury, non-blanchable erythema and mild induration maintain with blistering present. Patient reports that site occasionally itches. Warmness noted on injury. Wound measurements are: L 10.6 cm/W 7.2 cm/D <0.1 cm. Periwound blanchable erythema present with barrier cream in place.

Question #5: Highlight all of the clinical data that would indicate the stage 1 pressure injury worsening.

10/24 @0821: Amputation site cleaned and dressed per MD order. Incision site maintains well approximated with no erythema, edema, drainage, or odor. Patient reported forgetting to take his pain medication, so Percocet 7.5 mg/325 mg administered upon arrival. Patient reported a verbal pain score of 6/10 during wound care, but reduced it to 2/10 prior to the end of the skilled nursing visit. Upon assessment of stage 1 sacral pressure injury, non-blanchable erythema and mild induration maintain with blistering present. Patient reports that site occasionally itches. Warmness noted on injury. Wound measurements are: L 10.6 cm/W 7.2 cm/D <0.1 cm. Periwound blanchable erythema present with barrier cream in place.

Question #6: What is the patient at HIGHEST risk of developing with a stage 2 sacral pressure injury?
   a. Dehiscence
   b. Osteomyelitis
   c. Hematoma
   d. Localized wound infection
   e. Tissue necrosis
   f. Squamous cell carcinoma

NCLEX-PN Answer Explanations #2

1. C: The first piece of personal protective equipment the nurse should don is a gown, Choice *C*. Choice *A*, gloves, are donned next, followed by Choice *B*, mask, and ultimately, Choice *D*, goggles, are donned last. The nurse must follow this sequence to ensure protection against infection transmission.

2. D: The patient is currently on insulin. Choices *A, B,* and *C* are not correct because they are not potential adverse effects of insulin.

3. A: Tachypnea, Choice *A*, describes an elevated respiratory rate. Tachypnea can be witnessed in a variety of patient presentations and must be carefully assessed. Rapid breathing is not always overt or labored, so taking the time to count respirations and complete a thorough examination is key. Orthopnea, Choice *B*, represents labored breathing, while tachycardia, Choice *C*, correlates to a rapid heart rate. Hyperthermia, Choice *D*, involves an elevated body temperature.

4. 167 cc: The patient received $\frac{1}{3}$ of 500 cc. 500 divided by $\frac{1}{3}$ is 166.666, which, rounded to nearest whole number, is 167 cc.

5. A, B, C, E: Collecting a thorough health history, collecting accurate vital signs, providing smoking cessation information, as well as information on a healthy diet are examples of health promotion and maintenance. Choice *D*, setting the bed alarm, is an example of providing a safe and effective care environment.

6. A: Jugular vein distention, peripheral edema, and pulmonary congestion are characteristics of blood volume backing up due to an obstruction. Decreased urine output, increased BUN, and increased creatinine are signs of renal failure. Chest pain, fatigue, and lightheadedness are signs of an MI. Problems with coordination, blurred vision, and paralysis are symptomatic of a stroke.

7. D: Viral pneumonia, commonly caused by RSV, parainfluenza virus, and adenovirus, may be diagnosed by chest x-ray and viral cultures. Rapid antigen testing is now also being used for diagnosis and has the advantage of shortening the time for diagnosing this infection. Choices *A, B,* and *C* are incorrect, as these tests are not used to either diagnose viral pneumonia or shorten the diagnostic time.

8. B: Conversion disorder is the transformation of emotional distress into physical manifestations. These physical manifestations initially appear to be linked to the nervous system, but they have no medical explanation and really originate in the psyche. Conversion disorder is often associated with repression (Choice *B*), a defense mechanism that is characterized by inhibiting or forgetting thoughts the patient does not want to acknowledge. Conversion disorder represents the expression of the disavowed thoughts in the form of transferred symptoms. Projection, reaction formation, and intellectualization, while they are defense mechanisms, are not associated with conversion disorder. Therefore, Choices *A, C,* and *D* are incorrect.

9. The lower margin of the liver can be found in the right upper quadrant of the abdomen. During palpation, the nurse should ask the patient to take a deep breath; this causes the liver to be displaced downward, and it can be further palpated in the right lower quadrant.

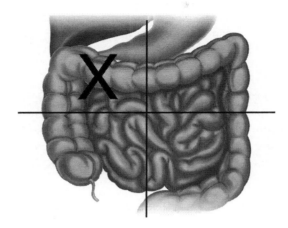

10. C: Choice *C* is correct. The nurse begins the discussion about end-of-life wishes when the patient has normal cognition, including reasoning and problem-solving, and can still make decisions. An advance directive is a legal document that describes the patient's wishes when they become incapacitated. Choice *A* can be eliminated. Ethically, the nurse advocates for the patient by supporting decisions made by the healthcare surrogate that are based on the patient's wishes. Choice *B* can be eliminated because the patient determines end-of-life decisions before becoming incapacitated. Choice *D* is not correct because an advanced directive does not override the ability to receive medical treatment.

11. B: Choice *B* is correct. Ambulating the patient to the toilet is the priority nursing action. Agitation and restlessness are often non-verbal signs that patients with dementia need to use the toilet. Immobility can also increase the risk of falling. Choice *A* is incorrect because administering a benzodiazepine may worsen cognition. Choice *C* can be eliminated because turning on the television provides a diversion yet does not address the underlying cause of restlessness. Toileting the patient is the better choice. Choice *D* is not correct because applying wrist restraints should always be performed when all other efforts to calm the patient have been exhausted.

12. A, D, E: Active listening, asking clarifying questions, and acknowledging the patient's feelings are examples of therapeutic communication. Choices *B* and *C*, checking the time and folding your arms across your chest, do not encourage communication.

13. A: Since electrolytes need to be suspended in a certain amount of liquid to move optimally and carry out their intended function, fluid level in the body is important. As fluid levels increase beyond a state of fluid-electrolyte balance, electrolyte levels will decrease, since there is too much fluid present. If fluid levels are too low, such as in a state of dehydration, there will be too many electrolytes per unit of fluid, which also prevents the electrolytes from carrying out their intended function.

14. B: Auscultation, Choice *B*, is the second step of an abdominal physical assessment. The nurse should first perform Choice *C*, inspection, then Choice *B*, auscultation, followed by Choice *A*, percussion, and finally Choice *D*, palpation. This sequence of techniques is unique to an abdominal physical assessment to promote accuracy in findings by not interfering with the results.

15. D: Choice *D* demonstrates a normal finding when auscultating the patient's lungs. Choice *A* is not a normal finding over the lungs, rather normal over the stomach. Choice *B* is not a normal finding, as it is indicative of air

265

hyperinflation, such as with asthma. Choice *C* is not a normal finding over the lungs, rather normal over dense areas such as the liver.

16. A: Choice *A* is correct. In this scenario, the licensed practice nurse/licensed vocational nurse (LPN/LVN) supports the plan of care best by data collection of subjective information when interviewing the patient. Choice *B* of establishing a nursing diagnosis, Choice *C* of implementing interventions, and Choice *D* of initiating patient teaching are specific roles pertaining to the registered nurse (RN). The LPN/LVN would collaborate with the RN during these phases of the nursing care plan.

17. D: Choice *D* designates the appropriate first action to be implemented by the nurse in response to the patient's request for discharge. Exploring the patient's reasoning for discharge is patient-centered and allows the nurse to gather additional information to formulate a clear understanding of the present issue(s) before deciding on next steps. Choice *A* may be an appropriate second step, depending on the patient's response to the original inquiry in step one. Choices *B* and *C*, while potential actions that may be necessary at some point, are not priorities in this situation.

18. B: Choice *B* represents a fasting blood sugar level that is within normal range, which is considered to be between 60-99 mg/dL. Choice *A* is a below normal finding. Choice *C* and Choice *D* are above normal findings and indicate the possible presence of pre-diabetes.

19. D: Choice *D* indicates the appropriate level of infection control to reduce the risk of transmission for a patient diagnosed with active tuberculosis. Choices *A*, *B*, and *C* would not provide enough protection in reducing this risk. Tuberculosis is an airborne disease; therefore, transmission of the bacillus, *Mycobacterium tuberculosis*, must be minimized.

20. 25 mL/hr: A total of 40 mEq of KCl will be given, for a total of 100 mL. 100 mL divided by 4 hours equals 25 mL/hr.

21. A: Choice *A* is correct. The PR interval, sometimes also termed the PQ interval, ranges from the start of the P wave (atrial depolarization) to the start of the QRS complex. Choices *B*, *C*, and *D* illustrate the QRS complex, QT interval, and RR interval, respectively.

22. A: A low protein diet, Choice *A*, is the best diet for the patient diagnosed with phenylketonuria, as protein processing is affected in this condition. A high protein diet, Choice *B*, should be avoided. The amino acids found within protein can exacerbate symptoms and lead to risky disease management. Folic acid levels are not closely correlated with phenylketonuria management. Thus, Choices *C* and *D* are incorrect.

23. C: Choice *C* does NOT represent an ethnic group at an increased risk for sickle cell anemia. Choices *A*, *C*, and *D* are all ethnic groups that have a heightened risk for developing this inherited red blood cell disorder.

24. A, C, D: Choices *A*, *C*, and *D* all represent the locations where the nurse should assess the patient's blood pressure and pulse to detect a blockage for a patient with suspected aortoiliac occlusive disease. This disease affects the iliac and femoral arteries. The blood pressure and pulse are taken in the thigh, calf, and foot to assess for inadequate blood flow that happens during a blockage. Choices *B* and *E* do not support the assessment of this lower body condition and therefore are not relevant for the nurse's physical assessment of the patient at this time.

25. B: Hypothyroidism occurs when there is an underproduction of T3 and/or T4 hormones. Low levels of these hormones may cause depression, excessive fatigue, chills, dry skin, lowered heart rate, constipation, and unexplained weight gain. Therefore, the nurse anticipates that the physician will order serum T4 levels. Cortisol, blood glucose, and aldosterone levels are not used in the diagnosis of hypothyroidism, making Choices *A*, *C*, and *D* incorrect.

26. A: Based on the abdominal location of the radiation therapy, it is likely that the patient will experience gastrointestinal symptoms, including diarrhea, nausea, and vomiting, as a side effect. Fatigue, trembling, and muscle aches are possible with radiation therapy but not specific to the organs of the abdomen.

27. C: Choice *C* displays tidal volume, which involves the volume of air moving in and out of the lungs during respiration. Choice *A* is incorrect as the volume is noted within the reading of strip two. Choice *B* indicates pressure. Choice *D* indicates flow.

28. C: Implied consent, Choice *C,* allows for the nurse to properly administer cardiopulmonary resuscitation to an unconscious patient. Implied consent is not expressly granted, though it is supported by the circumstance and inaction against the intervention. Choices *A, B,* and *D* are not appropriate because regardless of the terms of each type of consent, the patient is unable to consciously, therefore competently, engage in them, rendering them invalid.

29. D: Tapazole® (methimazole), Choice *D,* is a medication used for disease management in hyperthyroidism, an overactive thyroid condition. This condition occurs when the thyroid gland secretes an abundance of hormone and medication is used to reduce this process. Some symptoms of hyperthyroidism include weight loss, rapid heartbeat, diaphoresis, and irritability. Choices *A, B,* and *C* are all medications used to treat the underactive thyroid condition known as hypothyroidism.

30. C, D, E: The physician must be notified so that appropriate antibiotics are ordered for the patient. A patient with an MDRO infection only requires standard precautions. Choice *A,* inserting a Foley catheter, should be avoided in most cases and is not indicated for infection. Choice *B,* airborne precautions, are not warranted as the MDRO is not an airborne infection.

31. A, E: Choices *A* and *E* indicate appropriate equipment for the nurse to retrieve to provide airway support for a 10-year-old patient that weighs 32 kg. Choices *B, C,* and *D* indicate appropriate equipment for a younger, smaller pediatric patient.

32. D: While the physician is legally responsible for satisfying all elements of informed consent, nurses are ethically responsible for assessing the patient's ability to process and understand the implications of informed consent. Nurses protect the patient's autonomy by raising these questions and concerns. The remaining elements of informed consent are required of the physician, rather than the nurses.

33. C: Choice *C* identifies the fracture view of a greenstick fracture, which is commonly found in young pediatric patients. This fracture-type involves the bone bending and cracking on one side. Choice *A* indicates a longitudinal fracture. Choice *B* indicates a compound fracture. Choice *D* indicates a comminuted fracture.

34. B: The ethical principle of veracity is grounded in truth. Ethical practice is integrated into all aspects of nursing care. The nurse should be honest and tell the truth to patients and caregivers, as this is the basis to building trust in the relationship and supporting fair, autonomous, informed decision making.

35. D: Nurses must practice with consideration to nursing science and philosophy of law. These laws stem from both state and federal statutes and guide practice consideration. Nursing jurisprudence is the act of navigating nursing practice with these considerations as the managing foundation for care. Choice *A* involves basic nursing care. Choice *B* includes basic rights that all humans hold, whereas nursing process, Choice *C,* involves sequential steps of the nursing practice.

36. A: Use of a cane is not a risk factor for falls in the elderly. A cane would actually benefit a person by giving them extra stability when walking. Poor lighting is a risk factor because it could cause someone to stumble over items on

the floor or cause an imbalance by bumping into unseen furniture. Muscle weakness and slower reflexes are also risk factors for falls in the elderly.

37. B: Choice *B* indicates the patient's behavior to undo something that they hope will not take place. Undoing involves a sense of magic. Choices *A*, *C*, and *D* are not present in the patient's actions.

38. D: Chest physiotherapy, Choice *D*, is a supportive treatment routinely used for the care of individuals with cystic fibrosis to facilitate movement of secretions from small to large airways. Once the secretions have mobilized, they are much more readily expressed via coughing. Chest physiotherapy involves postural drainage, followed by percussion and vibration to loosen thick mucus and mobilize secretions. Choice *A*, antibiotics, while used for those with cystic fibrosis who develop infections, are not prescribed for routine care to mobile secretions. The six-foot rule, Choice *B*, signifies the practice of two individuals with cystic fibrosis maintaining a minimum 6-foot distance between one another to reduce the likelihood of spreading respiratory infections. Pulmonary function tests, Choice *C*, are done to assess pulmonary function.

39. B: Disruptive technology involves a modern technique that replaces and renders a previous technology obsolete. The current use of electronic health record (EHR) and electronic medical record (EMR) systems are examples of disruptive technologies. Choices *A*, *C*, and *D* do not involve technology that replaced previous technology.

40. A: The classic manifestations of bacterial meningitis include fever, nuchal rigidity, and headache. Other manifestations may include nausea, vomiting, photophobia, confusion, and a decreased level of consciousness; therefore, Choices *B* and *C* are incorrect. Manifestations of viral meningitis may include fatigue, muscle aches, and decreased appetite, making Choice *D* incorrect.

41. B: In autoimmune gastritis, there is a deficiency of intrinsic factor, which is responsible for the absorption of vitamin B-12. Therefore, the patient with autoimmune gastritis will have a vitamin B-12 deficiency. As a result, Choices *A*, *C*, and *D* are incorrect.

42. D: Choice *D*, a vitamin found in food and supplements, is a key element of an alcohol withdrawal protocol. Thiamine is typically deficient in those with alcohol abuse and dependence and is replaced during treatment. Choices *A*, *B*, and *C*, while all potentially helpful supplements across a variety of conditions, are not specifically associated with the needs of the patient at this time.

43. C: Choice *C* identifies a stuporous patient exhibiting no articulated verbal response with limited moaning, accompanied by arousal only after vigorous stimulation. Lethargic, Choice *A*, describes a patient who appears drowsy and arouses with gentle stimulation. Obtunded, Choice *B*, describes a patient who responds to repeated external stimulation to maintain attention. A patient that is comatose, Choice *D*, indicates they have no discernable response to stimulation. The levels of consciousness proceed with increasing severity from confused, to lethargic, to obtunded, to stuporous, and finally to comatose.

44. A: A diagnosis of bradycardia indicates the patient is experiencing a heart rate below 60 beats per minute, so Choice *A* is correct. Choices *B*, *C*, and *D* are within normal to high limits. The normal resting heart rate for adults is between 60 and 100 beats per minute.

45. B: Autonomy, Choice *B*, protects the patient's right to self-directed, independent decisions. Once the patient has received the information they need to make an informed selection of treatment, the patient, or proxy when indicated, autonomously makes the final decision for care. Beneficence, Choice *A*, morally encourages the nurse to do right by the patient. Non-maleficence, Choice *C*, supports not causing harm to the patient. Justice, Choice *D*, stimulates ethical fairness for the patient.

46. B: Choice B should be supported by the nurse, as it brings the knees to chest and typically encourages some pain relief in acute appendicitis. Choices A, C, and D represent positions that would likely exacerbate the patient's pain symptoms and should not be encouraged at this time.

47. C: Instrumental music, Choice C, encourages symptom management in reducing psychotic and paranoid symptoms for a patient struggling with schizophrenia, as instrumental music does not contribute to disturbed thought patterns and soothes the ill mind. Books, television, and food all carry the capacity to encourage worsening symptoms and should be avoided. Patients with schizophrenia may worry that their food is poisoned or be influenced to expand on delusional or paranoid thinking when influenced by stories in a book or on television.

48. A: The nurse case manager engages with third-party payers during a patient's inpatient stay in order to review current treatment, cost, and plans for additional care. This process, known as concurrent review, is a standard activity of the inpatient stay. Choice B, prior authorization, is specific to medication or individual intervention. Choice C, retrospective review, takes place after discharge to seek coverage for care. Choice D, prospective review, happens before admission.

49. B: Choice B aligns with the ethical principle to maintain truthful engagements. Choice A aligns with ethical fairness. Choice C aligns with refraining from harm. Choice D promotes doing right by the patient.

50. A, C, B, D: The nurse applies a condom catheter via steps performed in the following order to ensure proper positioning of the patient and equipment for safe and effective placement. The nurse should assist the patient to low Fowler's position, put urinary drainage bag on bed, roll condom catheter onto penis, and then place elastic adhesive around top of condom catheter.

51. C: Use the acronym RACE to answer this question. The information given in the question suggests that the patient is in the room and there is probably an electrical fire. The first action should be to rescue the patient by removing them from the room. Next, activate the fire alarm and then contain the fire by closing the door to the room. Extinguish the fire with the appropriate extinguisher if available. Choice D, smothering the fire, is not appropriate for an electrical fire.

52. D: Choice D is correct as this imbalance can cause a buildup of fluid in the form of edema and ascites for patients with impaired renal function. Low sodium levels alter the fluid balance of the body, encouraging the retention seen in these findings. Choices A, B, and C, while significant imbalances to measure, do not directly influence the development of ascites and dependent edema secondary to impaired renal function.

53. D: Choice D correctly aligns with the Joint Commission's standards, as sentinel events are not mandatory to report but are encouraged. Choices A, B, and C are inaccurate interpretations of the Joint Commission's role in accredited organization reporting of sentinel events.

54. C, D, B, A: The nurse prepares to suction nasopharyngeal secretions by carrying out steps in the following order to ensure thorough removal of excess secretions. Assess breath sounds. Power on suction device. Don sterile gloves. Attach catheter to suction tubing.

55. C: Choice C represents the appropriate level of activity for the patient with heart failure. Alternating rest with activity supports a reduced cardiac workload. Choice A would encourage a higher level of activity than the patient's condition can maintain. Choices B and D place unnecessary restrictions on the patient's activity.

56. A: A reduction in bile can also produce stool that is tan or clay-colored. As less bile is present, the stool becomes paler in color. Thus, Choice A, white stool, is seen when a patient is struggling with a bile duct blockage. Green stool, Choice B, is indicative of a high vegetable intake or antibiotic use. Black stool, Choice C, can be seen with upper

269

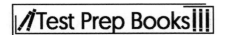

gastrointestinal bleeds or iron supplementation, whereas red stool, Choice *D*, can be observed with lower gastrointestinal bleeds or foods with red dyes.

57. C: A first-degree heart block is NOT a direct risk factor for the development of an embolus. Women during pregnancy and in the postpartum period, individuals with a history of a previous stroke, and patients with fractures that involve long bones are all at risk for the development of an embolus.

58. C: Choice *C*, transference, is observed when one member of an interaction transfers thoughts or feelings that were originally about one person onto someone else. In this case, the patient is reminded of her son while interacting with the nurse, and she transfers the negative association she has with her son onto the nurse. Choice *B*, countertransference, occurs when the clinician displaces their feelings onto the client. Choice *A*, regression, involves reverting to an earlier version of the self, while Choice *D*, repression, manifests itself through reducing emotions.

59. A: Choice *A* is correct. Standard precautions best pertain to placing soiled linen in a designated container and not holding the contents close to the body. Standard precautions are infection prevention measures used for all patients. Choice *B* of using dedicated patient care equipment, Choice *C* of ensuring that the patient is placed in a single patient room, and Choice *D* of reducing the risk of pathogen transmission all describe transmission-based precautions. Transmission-based precautions decrease the spread of an infectious agent.

60. A: The patient's blood pressure is still elevated. Choices *C* and *D* are incorrect because the patient's blood pressure is currently high. Choice *B* is incorrect because the patient's blood pressure is elevated but is not considered a medical emergency.

61. D: Choice *D* is correct. A high-risk medication is a medication that bears heightened risk due to the potential to create significant harm. One way to mitigate harm is to designate a separate storage area for these medications. The other selections may lead to harm. Choice *A* can be eliminated because patients should have limited providers to prevent polypharmacy. Choice *B* is not correct because transitions of care are one of the most vulnerable times for a patient. Because patients' medications are often changed, a lack of communication by the healthcare team can cause harm. Choice *C* can be eliminated because medication workarounds compromise patient safety when they deviate from the standard performance of care.

62. C: The SA, or sinoatrial, node is the heart's natural pacemaker. The AV node, which is positioned between the atria and ventricle, receives the impulse from the SA node. The Purkinje fibers are the end point of the conduction system. These fibers spread out across the ventricles after receiving the impulse through the Bundle of His. The Bundle of His receives the impulse from the AV node.

63. D: The gastroenterologist will likely use cauterization, an application of heat, to seal the bleeding lesion. Banding is a procedure used to help stop bleeding in esophageal varices. Biopsy is where tissues are removed for histological analysis. Angioplasty is performed in cardiac catheterizations and involves balloon inflation and stent placement to open up occluded blood vessels.

64. C: During a psychiatric evaluation, the clinician will determine the degree to which a patient's psychological symptoms impact their daily life. This score is then represented in the evaluation as a GAF score, which stands for Global Assessment of Functioning (Choice *C*). An Apgar score measures a neonate's general condition at birth (Choice *A*), and an AIMS score measures side effects of antipsychotic medication use (Choice *B*). The withdrawal protocol (Choice *D*) concerns symptoms that, in a patient struggling with substance abuse, must be controlled with medication, typically a benzodiazepine.

65. B: The kidney, Choice *B*, is the source of the bone's failure to produce red blood cells leading to their current anemic state. The kidney is responsible for stimulating this activity. The organs in Choices *A*, *C*, and *D* do not directly affect the bone's failure to produce red blood cells.

66. A: The TPN should be administered slowly, at 50 percent of the prescribed dosage, when beginning therapy. TPN comes with many possible complications as the body adjusts to this different source of nutrition, so starting slowly is recommended. The other three answers are incorrect.

67. C: Neutrophils are the major component of the white blood cells. When their count is elevated, that means the white blood cells are hard at work fighting an infectious process. The nurse would need to investigate this conclusion further, possibly getting an order to draw some blood cultures if appropriate. Blood urea nitrogen is a waste product of the body. An elevated level would suggest failing kidneys but not an infection. Hematocrit is a component of red blood cells and is not part of the body's immune system. A high sodium level is an electrolyte abnormality that may have to do with the renal system or overall patient fluid status but not an infectious process.

68. D: Time between the collapse and the start of resuscitation efforts is the most important factor in patient survival. Administering supplemental oxygen is a component of resuscitation efforts. Establishing IV access is an essential component of resuscitation efforts. Inserting a Foley catheter to drain the urinary bladder is not related to survival.

69. B: Only vitamin B-12, Choice *B*, should be an expected subcutaneous treatment for the patient with pernicious anemia. However, iron, packed RBCs, and stem cells are involved in various other forms of anemia. Multiple forms of anemia exist including iron-deficiency anemia, hemolytic anemia, and aplastic anemia, to name a few. In this case, the patient is suffering from pernicious anemia, an autoimmune condition in which the body is unable to absorb the vitamin B-12 consumed in one's diet, leading to deficiency. Vitamin B-12 injections are required to form healthy red blood cells.

70. B: A chest radiograph is the test of choice to confirm the placement of a nasogastric tube. The x-ray will show whether the catheter tip is in the gastric body or not. Aspiration of stomach contents, not laryngeal secretions, with a pH test is another, less preferred way to confirm placement. The pH test may be misleading, as there may be gastric contents farther up the esophageal canal and not necessarily within the stomach in some patients with weakened sphincters. An abdominal ultrasound may show the catheter tip, but it is not the preferred method of evaluating placement. Manual palpation of the gastric body is not a way to confirm placement, as it would be very difficult to actually feel the catheter within the stomach.

71. C: For an individual struggling with substance abuse, avoiding places where they have typically used substances in the past is a realistic goal for intensive outpatient therapy (Choice *C*). It would not be realistic for the client to use their substance of abuse in moderation (Choice *A*), stop requiring connection with their sponsor (Choice *B*), or prevent all cravings via self-control (Choice *D*) during the week they are engaged in intensive treatment for substance abuse.

72. C: In a comminuted fracture, Choice *C*, the bones break into multiple fragments, as they would have done during the motor vehicle accident. Comminuted fractures typically occur in the hands and feet in response to severe trauma. The nurse would educate the patient regarding the specific fracture that they are suffering from and plan treatment options in response. A compound fracture, Choice *A*, involves a fracture where the bones break through the skin. An oblique fracture, Choice *B*, involves a fracture that breaks at an angle. A greenstick fracture, Choice *D*, involves a fracture where the bones do not break all the way through.

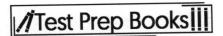

73. The ulna is the medial long bone between the elbow and wrist.

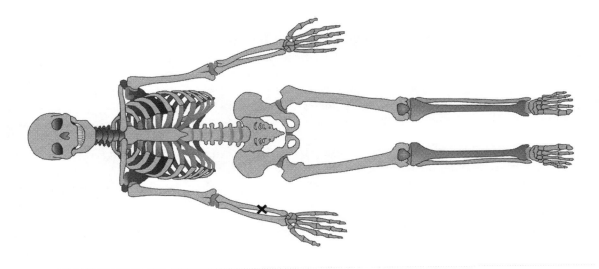

74. B, A, C, D: The nurse educates on the following stages in ascending order according to Erikson's Psychosocial Theory to describe the age stages of development. The nurse educates that development ascends from trust vs. mistrust, to autonomy vs. shame, to initiative vs. guilt, to industry vs. inferiority.

75. D: Helping a patient get dressed is not considered a dirty task unless the clothing is soiled with any bodily fluid. *A*, *B*, and *C* are all tasks that involve bodily fluids and are considered dirty. Clean tasks should be performed first, followed by dirty tasks.

76. C: Choice *C* is correct as audible S3 and S4 sounds upon cardiac auscultation indicate summation gallop. Choice *A* sounds musical or vibratory. Choice *B* contains two audible heart sounds, S1 and S2. Choice *D* is heard as a sound between the S1 and S2 heartbeat cycle.

77. D: A calcium channel blocker can lower the pulmonary vascular resistance in a patient. Diuretics, morphine, and nitrates all have potent lowering effects on the systemic vascular resistance, as opposed to the pulmonary vasculature. Knowing the hemodynamic effects certain medications have is helpful in anticipating unwanted side effects and potential drug interactions.

78. A: Bronchiolitis, an inflammation of the small airways in the lung, most commonly affects children under the age of two, with the greatest incidence between three and six months old. Children age two and older, including children entering kindergarten or in high school, are less likely to be affected, making Choices *B*, *C*, and *D* inappropriate choices.

79. C: Status epilepticus is prolonged seizure activity involving multiple seizures, each lasting five minutes or more, over a thirty-minute period of time. A generalized seizure is a seizure that originates in two or more networks of the brain. A focal seizure is one that originates in a single area of the brain. The postictal state follows a seizure and is characterized by alterations in consciousness and awareness, as well as increased oral secretions.

80. A: The patient's manifestations are consistent with an incarcerated or strangulated hernia that is progressing to a small-bowel obstruction as evidenced by the abdominal distention. This complication is associated with decreased peristalsis and eventual absence of bowel activity, which means that diarrhea would be an uncommon manifestation. Tachycardia and a BUN of 27 are related to fluid volume losses resulting from the accumulation of

fluid proximal to the obstruction in the small bowel; therefore, Choices B and D are incorrect. Rebound tenderness is also an expected finding in a bowel obstruction due to the trapped gas and fluid proximal to the obstruction; therefore, Choice C is incorrect.

81. D: Choice D is the antidote given to counteract the effects of Enoxaparin. Choices A, B, and C represent medications used as antidotes for a wide variety of medications but will not neutralize this medication and inhibit the reaction.

82. C: The nurse should ensure that the patient's vital signs are taken before administering Catapres® (clonidine), Choice C, as this medication often reduces blood pressure and pulse. While this medication is indicated to treat hypertension, it also is used outside of this indication, such as in the management of attention deficit hyperactivity disorder, anxiety, and sleep. Taking patient vital signs is an appropriate task to delegate to the unlicensed assistive personnel (UAP). Assisting the patient with eating their meal and asking about the time of their last bowel movement (Choices A and B), while important interventions in daily patient care, do not directly influence the administration of Catapres® (clonidine); therefore, they are not current priorities. Delivering a heated blanket, Choice D, does not directly impact the administration of this medication and is typically reserved to support circulatory concerns.

83. A: Choice A is correct. Lovastatin is used to lower cholesterol and triglycerides. Choice B, sliding scale insulin, is not currently indicated as the patient does not have a diagnosis of diabetes. Choice C, metoprolol, a beta blocker, is used to lower heart rate and blood pressure and is not indicated. Choice D, ferrous sulfate, is a supplement used to treat iron deficiency anemia. The patient is not anemic, making Choice D incorrect.

84. B: Choice B is correct. The nursing activity most appropriate to delegate to the nursing assistant is providing a bed bath to the patient with a pressure injury. The response does not indicate that an assessment, nursing intervention, or evaluation is required. The other activities are reserved for the nurse. In Choice A, the nurse assesses the patient's ability to hold a toothbrush. In Choice C, the nurse teaches the family about the turning schedule. In Choice D, the nurse evaluates the outcome of feeding a high-risk patient who recently aspirated.

85. D: An early sign of respiratory distress is agitation, along with confusion and oxygen hunger. Later signs of respiratory distress occur when the patient has become fatigued because of the respiratory effort they have put forth. These signs include decreased respiratory rate, unconsciousness, and cyanosis.

86. C: Myasthenia gravis is an autoimmune disease caused by the altered transmission of the neurotransmitter acetylcholine at the neuromuscular junction due to antibody formation. Therefore, Choices A, B, and D are incorrect.

87. B, D, E: The IV should be removed and a warm compress should be applied as soon as possible to prevent further damage and for the patient's comfort. A new IV should be started in a different vein. Choice C, starting IV fluids, would further damage the vessel with phlebitis. Choice A, telling the patient you will assess them again later, is not helpful.

88. C: Choice C indicates the appropriate professional response by the nurse to address the present language barrier. Choices A and B would not directly support communication that is free from misunderstanding and should be omitted. Choice D would not rely on a professional, non-biased party for translation and should be avoided if possible.

89. B: Diabetic ketoacidosis is an acidotic metabolic state that can be caused by poor diabetic management, leading to hyperglycemia. Diabetic management involves regular visits to the healthcare provider, taking insulin or oral anti-diabetic agents as ordered, following a healthy diet, exercising regularly, and monitoring blood glucose levels at home. Hyperglycemia can occur when the patient does not have enough insulin in the body, making Choice A an

273

incorrect answer. Since ingesting high glucose levels leads to hyperglycemia, not reduced glucose levels, Choice *C* is not the correct answer. It can also occur when the oral anti-diabetic management is not sufficient to control high blood glucose levels, making Choice *D* an incorrect answer.

90. D: This patient has a stage 4 pressure ulcer. The skin breakdown goes down to the level of muscle and bone. Choices *A*, *B*, and *C* are pressure ulcers that are not as deep.

91. C: Choice *C* represents a hindrance to the development of a therapeutic nurse-to-patient discussion and should be avoided. Choice *A* displays understanding, Choice *B* encourages deeper dialogue, and Choice *D* shows comprehension of what the patient communicated.

92. A: The electronic health record (EHR) is a document containing charted documentation from multiple providers across specialties supporting patient care. Choice *C*, the medical record (EMR), is a charting system used by one provider, while the patient uses a personal health record (PHR) system (Choice *D*). Choice *B*, electronic medication administration record (EMAR), involves documentation of medication only.

93. D, B, A, C: The nurse details the progression of intestinal obstruction leading to death by teaching steps in the following order to demonstrate the physiological tissue breakdown and subsequent system-wide failure. The progression is as follows: mechanical obstruction, ischemia, necrosis, and shock.

94. A, C, D, B: The correct order is A, C, D, and B. The patient's identity should be obtained before anything else is done. The other rights included in the five rights should be verified next. The patient can then be educated on the medication. Lastly, the medication is administered.

95. 3 Tbsp: 1 Tbsp is equal to 15 mL, so 45 mL is equal to 3 Tbsp.

96. D: Mores are social norms that are particularly characterized by a moral component. They are often established through religious systems, and violations of mores are likely to lead to formal or informal sanction. Folkways are the daily customs and traditions of a society. Taboos are the behaviors that are so strictly forbidden by a society that ostracism may occur if a person violates them.

97. The apical pulse can be assessed at the apex of the heart, which is located at the fourth intercostal space at the midclavicular line. This location is the point of maximal impulse (PMI).

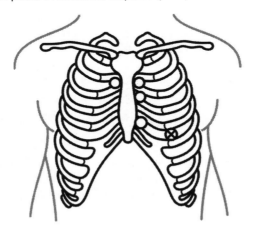

274

98. Distal locations indicate areas of the body that are further away from either the trunk or a given reference point, in this case the heart. The foot is the most distal area of the body from the heart. Conversely, proximal is closer to the trunk or a given reference point.

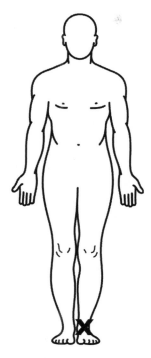

99. A: The incubation period, Choice *A,* is the stage of disease where the individual often does not yet realize that they have been exposed to a pathogenic organism, as they are asymptomatic. This stage makes up the period of time from exposure to when symptoms become apparent. The prodromal period, Choice *B,* represents the stage during which symptoms are first noted and may be vague in presentation. The acute period, Choice *C,* represents the stage of disease that has progressed to include a worsening of symptoms that are specific to pathogen and illness. The convalescence period, Choice *D,* signifies the stage involving a gradual reduction of symptoms and recovery of health after illness.

100. C: Palpate, Choice *C,* represents the second step of a respiratory physical assessment. The nurse should first perform Choice *A,* inspect, then Choice *C,* palpate, followed by Choice *B,* percuss, and finally Choice *D,* auscultate. This sequence of techniques is standard for physical assessments—except when performing an abdominal assessment—to promote accuracy in findings.

101. D: Choice *D* represents the image of the heart that the nurse should use to provide patient education on atrioventricular septal defect. Choice *A* displays an image of hypoplastic left heart syndrome. Choice *B* displays an image of patent ductus arteriosus. Choice *C* displays an image of coarctation of the aorta. Providing an image to correlate with verbal discussion supports the patient to visualize their condition.

102. C: Choice *C* represents an analgesic medication prescribed for pain management. Choice *A* is incorrect, as the patient currently has an order for a medication that supports pain management. Choice *B* targets seizure disorders. Choice *D* targets hypertension.

103. C: Choice *C* is correct. A multidisciplinary approach to patient discharge decreases the risk of hospital readmission. Healthcare team members are the nurses, providers, case managers, social workers, and others who communicate to establish patient goals and coordinate care based on needs. The other choices are incorrect. Choice

A can be eliminated because early discharge planning allows for patient teaching and the validation of patient understanding, along with the identification of functional needs. Choice *B* can be eliminated because the medication reconciliation process decreases the risk of error. Choice *D* can be eliminated because a delayed discharge may increase the risk of hospital-acquired infections.

Case Study #1

Question #1:

Schizophrenia	⟶	Haloperidol

The psychiatric disorder closely associated with paranoid delusions, hallucinations, and word salad is schizophrenia. While there would be a workup for differential diagnoses, the patient would be treated with an antipsychotic, haloperidol. The use of benzodiazepines to treat acute psychosis in the healthcare setting varies due to the level of sedation and slight potential for worsening psychosis; however, it can also be a first or second line of treatment. Narcotics, such as meperidine, and antihistamines, such as diphenhydramine, should not be given to the patient in acute psychosis. While lithium is a popular treatment for bipolar disorder, it is not effective in cases of acute psychosis.

Question #2: Differential diagnoses for this patient include substance abuse/withdrawal, intracranial space-occupying lesions, hypoglycemia, and trauma, as all of these conditions can cause acute psychosis. Fibromyalgia is not linked to acute psychosis, and low levels of magnesium, rather than high levels, are associated with psychiatric dysfunction, including psychosis and seizures.

Question #3:

Schizophrenia Symptom	Positive	Negative	Cognitive
Hallucinations	☒	☐	☐
Anhedonia	☐	☒	☐
Impaired memory	☐	☐	☒
Word salad	☒	☐	☐
Apathy	☐	☒	☐

For the schizophrenic patient, positive symptoms are additional behaviors that are either new or distorted, such as hallucinations, delusions, word salad, and movement disorders. Negative symptoms are absent or severely blunted behaviors, such as anhedonia, apathy, depression, and flat affect. Cognitive symptoms are related to the cognitive function that is affected by the psychiatric dysfunction, such as impaired memory, altered attention, and impaired decision making.

Question #4: Because the patient is now a threat to the safety of the staff and potentially himself, the patient should be restrained as a safety measure. The goal with any form of restraint is to start with the least restrictive restraints and remove them as soon as possible while maintaining safety. Confinement would be moving to a higher level of restraint and would not help with the issue of medication administration. While therapeutic communication is a great nursing practice, safety needs to be strongly considered once a verbal threat has been made.

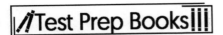

The nurse should then immediately notify the medical provider or designated staff (some advanced practice nurses or physician assistants can assess the patient if approved by that specific facility) to assess the patient within one hour. This involves checking the appropriateness of the restraints, how the patient is tolerating the restraints, and whether removing them is appropriate.

Ensure there is an order in place for the use of restraints prior to restraining the patient. Restraining a patient without an active order is considered false imprisonment.

Question #5: The correct statements regarding restraint regulations include needing a new order every time restraints are discontinued and restarted, restraints needing to be removed every two hours for ROM exercises, and needing a new order every 24 hours.

Along with ROM exercises, toileting should be offered every two hours, not every four hours. PRN restraint orders are not appropriate, and restraint orders should be on a patient specific basis only. Lastly, the circulation of restrained extremities should be assessed every 15 minutes within the first hour, then every 30 minutes from there on out.

Question #6: Considering the patient was given haloperidol, an antipsychotic/neuroleptic medication, and is now experiencing rigidity, elevated temperature, tachycardia, and hypertension, the patient is most likely experiencing neuroleptic malignant syndrome. Tachypnea with shallow respirations can also be related to the generalized rigidity. This is a psychiatric emergency and will require the nurse to notify the medical provider immediately.

Case Study #2

Question #1: The nurse should report vomiting, mild pallor, non-blanchable rash, temperature, and urine output to the pediatrician. A maculopapular rash just means the rash is both raised and flat, but a non-blanchable rash can be indicative of vascular damage or meningitis. The patient's cap refill is normal and would not need to be reported. For the three-year-old patient, a heart rate of 114 beats per minute is normal. Lastly, two wet diapers in 12 hours would indicate the patient is dehydrated.

Question #2: If the patient exhibited limited neck flexion, or nuchal rigidity, the patient would need emergency medical treatment for the likelihood of meningitis. While viral meningitis can resolve on its own within one to two weeks, bacterial meningitis can become life threatening if not treated rapidly. While fungal and bacterial meningitis are rarer than the viral type, the patient is symptomatic and will likely require fluid restoration and close monitoring. A positive Brudzinski's sign or Kernig's sign is also a physical demonstration of meningitis.

Kernig Sign

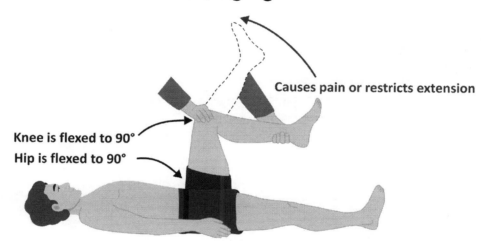

Causes pain or restricts extension

Knee is flexed to 90°
Hip is flexed to 90°

Brudzinski Sign

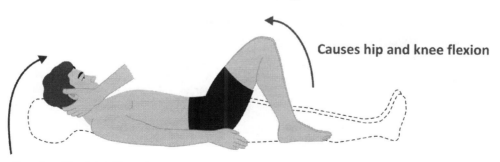

Causes hip and knee flexion

Passive flexion of neck

While the other symptoms would all indicate a worsening in the patient's status, they would not alone warrant an advancement in level of care.

Question #3:

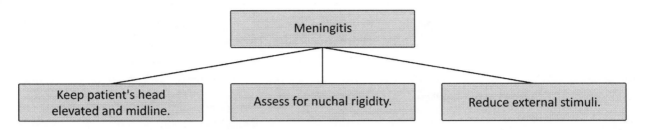

Considering the patient presented with vomiting, fever, a non-blanchable rash, and lethargy, the medical team should be on high alert for meningitis. While these symptoms can be consistent with HFMD, the key issue here is the non-blanchable rash. Rashes associated with HFMD will always blanch, similar to a sunburn. For the nursing assessments and interventions, keeping the patient's head elevated and midline and reducing external stimuli can help maintain ICP levels. Assessing for nuchal rigidity is also important to see if the meninges are inflamed. While a confirmative diagnosis can only be obtained from a spinal tap, the medical team will still need to assess for common symptomologies of meningitis.

Question #4: Taking the knowledge of a recent infection into account, the nurse should immediately focus on the potential diagnosis of bacterial meningitis. The signs of worsening bacterial meningitis to monitor for include stupor or increased lethargy, seizures, and paralysis. With the swelling of meninges, monitoring for signs of increased intracranial pressure (ICP) becomes a priority. Contracture/rigidity is more often seen with meningitis over atrophy; also, the patient typically becomes more lethargic (and can potentially progress into a coma/death) and does not experience acute hypervigilance as bacterial meningitis worsens. Lastly, worsening of this disease process will result in anorexia, not hyperphagia.

Question #5:

1. Assess for increased intracranial pressure (ICP)
2. Lumbar puncture for CSF collection (if not contraindicated)
3. Obtain blood cultures, CBC, CMP, and coag test
4. Initiate empiric antimicrobial therapy and dexamethasone (if not contraindicated)

The first thing to assess prior to diagnostics is ICP. If there is a suspicion of elevated ICP, a lumbar puncture could be contraindicated. The patient would then require a CT scan for diagnosis. If the patient is not suspected of having elevated ICP, a lumbar puncture with CSF collection should occur promptly, and blood cultures (and additional labs) should be obtained immediately after. Once these steps have been performed, empiric antimicrobial therapy should be administered. Time will be critical. If dexamethasone is not contraindicated, it can be administered to reduce any cerebral edema.

Question #6:

Statement	Understanding	No Understanding
"The best way to stop the spread of infection is hand hygiene."	☒	☐
"Antibiotics are the only cure for meningitis."	☐	☒
"Routine childhood vaccines can help prevent certain types of meningitis."	☒	☐
"Meningitis is not serious in the adult population due to developed immune function."	☐	☒
"She may have some temporary hearing issues from the swelling."	☐	☒

The best way to prevent the spread of infection is consistent and proper hand hygiene. Also, while there is no vaccine specifically for meningitis, routine childhood vaccinations can prevent certain types of infectious processes that lead to meningitis. This aids in the prevention of meningitis overall. While antibiotics are the only cure for bacterial meningitis, viral, fungal, and parasitic meningitis cannot be cured with antibiotics. While meningitis is more common in the infant stage and childhood/adolescent stage, it can still be a very serious condition for the adult population. Lastly, if the patient develops a hearing issue or hearing loss, it would be a permanent deficit as the result of neurological dysfunction from the severity of infection and inflammation.

Case Study #3

Question #1:

Past Medical History

Surgical History:

- Tonsillectomy est. 1982
- Wisdom tooth extraction est. 1990

Medical History:

- Diagnosed with HTN in 2013—prescribed amlodipine 10mg daily—patient reports taking medication inconsistently
- MVA leading to spinal cord injury resulting in paraplegia
- Diagnosed with T2DM in 2017—currently noncompliant with scheduled and sliding-scale insulin regimen

Admission Note:

Patient admitted for scheduled transmetatarsal amputation of the left foot following diabetic complications. Patient reports noncompliance with diabetes medications, also states that he doesn't check his blood sugar daily. He reports only checking his blood sugar once a week or when he "feels off." Patient is also noncompliant with dietary standards, stating he eats one to two small meals a day that consist mostly of refined carbs and/or fast food. BMI is 27. Patient reports short spurts of activity throughout the day, but he is able to resituate in bed/recliner. Patient also reports frequent stress incontinence, requiring him to wear incontinence underwear consistently.

Uncontrolled, prolonged HTN, uncontrolled diabetes, poor nutrition with low intake of protein, and frequent exposure to moisture from incontinence/friction with the incontinence underwear are all significant risk factors for skin breakdown. While a BMI of 27 is overweight, that is not a significant risk factor. Mobility-limiting obesity is a risk factor, but the patient is able to ambulate and make positional changes.

Question #2:

Patient Statement	Understanding	No Understanding
"I need to make sure I eat minimal protein."	☐	☒
"I need to make positional changes at least every two hours in the daytime."	☒	☐
"I need to report to the ED if I notice any signs of a sacral wound."	☐	☒
"I need to contact the home health agency if I notice a bad smell coming from my amputation site."	☒	☐
"If I don't follow my daily diabetic medication schedule, I need to at least follow my sliding-scale orders."	☐	☒

The patient needs to be educated on increasing his intake of protein to assist with the skin's firmness and elasticity. The patient will need to be educated on making positional changes at least every two hours in the day time when he is inactive. Blood flow can be compromised after two hours, which increases the risk of skin breakdown. If the patient were unable to make positional changes independently, the caregiver would need to be educated on positional changes every two hours. The patient would not understand discharge education if he stated that he would need to come to the ED if he noticed signs of a sacral wound. Considering the patient is being discharged onto a home health service, he would need to be educated on contacting the home health agency on the potential wound, as they would be an appropriate source for managing that level of care. The patient would be correct to contact the home health agency in the event of a foul odor coming from their amputation site unless otherwise instructed by the surgeon/medical provider. A localized infection can be promptly managed through home health, even if IV antibiotics are required. If the patient meets the sepsis protocol, the patient will need to report to the ED. Lastly, the patient stating that he can just follow his sliding scale insulin would not indicate understanding. Allowing blood sugar to get high in the first place is what causes most diabetic skin complications, resulting in small-vessel damage. The patient will need to be compliant with all prescribed diabetic medications.

Question #3: Early indicators of a pressure injury include erythema (redness/discoloration), induration (hardened/thickened skin), and shiny skin at the site. Keloids (excess scar tissue) are not an early indicator of a pressure injury. Warm skin, not clammy skin, would be an indicator of a pressure injury. Petechiae and pallor are also not indicators of pressure injuries.

Question #4:

Potential Medical Interventions	Indicated	Not Indicated
Clean site daily with hydrogen peroxide.	☐	☒
Remove pressure from the site at all times.	☒	☐
Wet-to-dry dressing changes BID	☐	☒
Apply skin barrier.	☒	☐
Assess for negative pressure wound therapy.	☐	☒
Pack the wound with iodoform.	☐	☒

The main goal with stage 1 pressure injuries is to keep it intact. By maintaining a clean, dry area with appropriate moisture in the form of dressings, lotions, and skin barriers, the medical team can assist in the prevention of the pressure injury progressing to stage 2. A stage 1 pressure injury will require a mild cleanser to keep the wound clean, such as mild soaps or normal saline. Hydrogen peroxide is damaging to the tissue, even when diluted. Wet-to-dry dressings are indicated for the removal of necrotic (dead) tissue, which is a far advancement from a stage 1 pressure injury. Similarly, assessing for negative pressure wound therapy and packing the wound with iodoform are also for advanced wounds. Negative pressure wound therapy is indicated for certain infections or heavily draining wound sites, while wound packing is meant for wounds with tunneling or undermining.

As previously stated, the goal is to keep skin intact. The medical interventions to be expected at this phase will include removing all pressure from the site at all times and applying an appropriate skin barrier (to be determined by facility protocol and/or medical provider orders).

Question #5:

10/24 @0821: Amputation site cleaned and dressed per MD order. Incision site maintains well approximated with no erythema, edema, drainage, or odor. Patient reported forgetting to take his pain medication, so Percocet 7.5 mg/325 mg administered upon arrival. Patient reported a verbal pain score of 6/10 during wound care, but reduced it to 2/10 prior to the end of the skilled nursing visit. Upon assessment of stage 1 sacral pressure injury, non-blanchable erythema and mild induration maintain with blistering present. Patient reports that the site occasionally itches. Warmness noted on injury. Wound measurements are: L 10.6 cm/W 7.2 cm/D <0.1 cm. Periwound blanchable erythema present with barrier cream in place.

Blistering, wound pruritus, warmness, and increased length/width of wound measurements are all indications of the wound worsening. Blistering is indicative of an increase in staging from stage 1 to stage 2. Stage 2 pressure injuries are no longer intact, as a blister is considered "open" because the protective barrier of the skin is compromised. Periwound having blanchable erythema is to be expected, and it can actually mean increased blood flow to the injury. In the event that area becomes non-blanchable, the wound would be expanding, and therefore worsening.

Question #6: The patient is at a higher risk for developing a localized wound infection if he has a stage 2 sacral pressure injury. Dehiscence occurs when previously approximated wound edges become partially or totally separated, leaving the wound bed open to air. Osteomyelitis can be seen in pressure injuries, but they typically

become more of a concern with stage 3 and especially stage 4 pressure injuries. Hematomas are typically seen with surgical incisions, not chronic pressure injuries. Tissue necrosis becomes a concern in the later stages and unstageable pressure injuries. Lastly, squamous cell carcinoma can be a complication of delayed wound healing, not a relatively new stage 2 pressure injury.

NCLEX PN Practice Tests #3 & #4

To keep the size of this book manageable, save paper, and provide a digital test-taking experience, the 3rd and 4th practice tests can be found online. Scan the QR code or go to this link to access it:

testprepbooks.com/bonus/nclexpn

The first time you access the tests, you will need to register as a "new user" and verify your email address.

If you have any issues, please email support@testprepbooks.com

Index

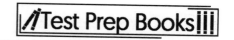

Dear NCLEX PN Test Taker,

Thank you for purchasing this study guide for your NCLEX PN exam. We hope that we exceeded your expectations.

Our goal in creating this study guide was to cover all of the topics that you will see on the test. We also strove to make our practice questions as similar as possible to what you will encounter on test day. With that being said, if you found something that you feel was not up to your standards, please send us an email and let us know.

We have study guides in a wide variety of fields. If you're interested in one, try searching for it on Amazon or send us an email.

Thanks Again and Happy Testing!
Product Development Team
info@studyguideteam.com

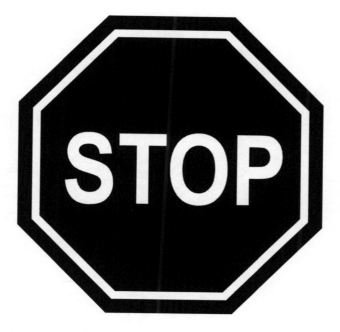

FREE Test Taking Tips Video/DVD Offer

To better serve you, we created videos covering test taking tips that we want to give you for FREE. **These videos cover world-class tips that will help you succeed on your test.**

We just ask that you send us feedback about this product. Please let us know what you thought about it—whether good, bad, or indifferent.

To get your **FREE videos**, you can use the QR code below or email freevideos@studyguideteam.com with "Free Videos" in the subject line and the following information in the body of the email:

     a. The title of your product

     b. Your product rating on a scale of 1-5, with 5 being the highest

     c. Your feedback about the product

If you have any questions or concerns, please don't hesitate to contact us at info@studyguideteam.com.

Thank you!

SCAN HERE